OUR HOLY FAITH

OUR HOLY FAITH

BOOK SEVEN

MESSIAH

TAN Books

Gastonia, North Carolina

Originally published in 1961 as *Our Holy Faith Book VII: Christ in Promise, in Person, and in His Church* by Bruce Publishing Company and reprinted in 1998 by The Neumann Press.

FOR UNIT ONE
Nihil Obstat:
> Peter G. Duncker, O.P., S.T.M., S.S.D.
> Censor Deputatus

Imprimatur:
> W Edward F. Hoban, S.T.D.
> Archbishop-Bishop of Cleveland
> November 23, 1960

FOR UNITS TWO AND THREE
Nihil Obstat:
> John F. Murphy, S.T.D.
> Censor Librorum

Imprimatur:
> W William E. Cousins
> Archbishop of Milwaukee
> April 6, 1961

This TAN Books edition has been re-typeset and enhanced with additional content and revisions, including modernized language and updates to the practices of the Catholic Church. Catechism questions and answers have been replaced with the TAN edition of *The Third Council of Baltimore: Baltimore Catechism 1–4*.

Scripture quotes are adapted from the Douay-Rheims 1899 American Edition.

Content revisions and updates by Elisa Torres
Interior design by Caroline Green
Cover design by www.davidferrisdesign.com

ISBN: 978-1-5051-1926-8
Published in the United States by
TAN Books
PO Box 269
Gastonia, NC 28053
www.TANBooks.com
Printed in the United States of America

Contents

Publisher's Note

The original editions of the *Our Holy Faith* series textbooks were published between 1959 and 1964. They were compiled by many different authors over the course of several years. Consequently, the texts varied in their organization from year to year, with similar sections appearing with different names throughout the series and often in varying sequences.

For greater ease of use and consistency, we have reorganized each book so that the Catechism lessons, tests, and other exercises are placed at the end of each relevant chapter or lesson. We have also included answer keys for your convenience in the back of each book.

While the teachings in the original editions remain relevant due to the enduring truths of our Faith, it was necessary to update other aspects in order to more accurately reflect the Church today. These new editions have been revised to incorporate some of the changes to the practices of the Catholic Church.

To the extent possible, we have adapted the text to reflect both the ordinary and extraordinary forms of the Mass and liturgical calendars. In addition to these updates, we have inserted, where relevant to the text, traditional prayers and quotes from the Bible, the Catechism, and the saints.

This new *Our Holy Faith* series is faithful to the work of the original authors. It honors the fundamental and unchanging truths of the Catholic Church and is heavily influenced by tradition. We believe it is the catechesis you can trust with your children's faith.

Introduction

Our work in religion this year will be devoted to a study of Bible History. Because our field is vast, we shall limit our study to important facts and to the broad outline and movement of events.

In the method we have chosen, it has been our hope to fulfill in some measure the desire of the late Pope Pius XII that emphasis be placed upon the meaning directly intended by the authors of Sacred Scripture without neglecting "the spiritual significance also intended and ordained by God."

Pope Pius XII pointed out in his encyclical on Sacred Scripture in 1943 that the supreme rule of biblical interpretation is to discover and define what the writer intended to express. Scripture scholars, therefore, must know the languages in which the books of the Bible were written. Most of the Old Testament was written in Hebrew, a language quite different from our modern language in its manner of expressing ideas. The New Testament and two books of the Old Testament were written in Greek. The Holy Father also warned us that the meaning intended by the inspired writers, or what Scripture scholars call the "literal sense" of Scripture, may not always be so easily grasped because the ancient writers used ways of saying things (literary forms) which are not the same as those which we employ today.

We believe that the original edition of this book relied too heavily on the historical critical method of biblical interpretation and often tried to explain away various aspects of the literal sense of Scripture. While a legitimate and useful method of biblical interpretation, it seems out of place and unnecessary in a seventh grade textbook introducing students to salvation history. Therefore, the editors at TAN Books have significantly revised portions of this textbook to present the biblical text as it is without delving too far, for example, into the different senses

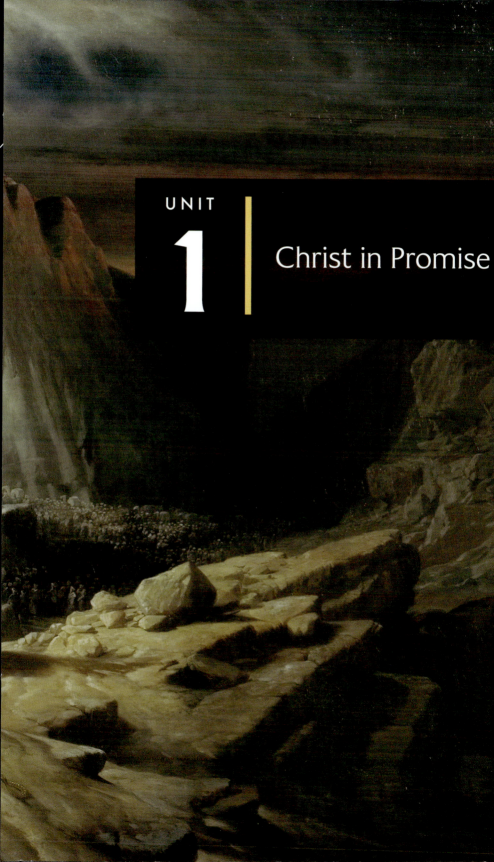

CHAPTER 1

A Preview of the Historical Account of God's Chosen People

Why We Study Bible History

It is natural for us to be interested in the history of our nation. We are eager to learn how and from whom we have derived the heritage which is ours. In order to gain such knowledge we study the history of our country. Before we begin the study of a history book, we find it useful to know something about the author, when he wrote, the sources of his information, and the purpose he had in writing. This will help us understand what he has written. As our study progresses, we study hard to discover the meaning of the statements he makes.

If we take care to learn the history of our national heritage, how much more care should we exert to learn the history of our spiritual heritage! This spiritual heritage has come to us through the Hebrews, God's Chosen People of the Old Testament. Its history is found in the Bible.

What the Bible Is

The Bible is a collection of sacred books written at various times, in various ways and in various places, by men whom God had selected for this purpose. Its earlier books were composed, at least in part, over a thousand years before the birth of Christ, whereas its final books were written during the years following the death and resurrection of our Lord. The Catholic Church assures us that the Bible contains the Word of God. This means that God inspired or enlightened certain men to write what He wanted written, so that we might know what God wishes us to know about Himself and our obligations to Him. Thus the Bible

is the Word of God and God is its principal Author, because the will to write came from Him and the truths found in the Bible are guaranteed by Him.

The Bible contains some truths that men could know only if God revealed them. If something is revealed directly by God, the ideas and sometimes even the words come directly from Him. But Moses and the other authors of the Bible knew some truths recorded in Scripture independently of revelation. They acquired these truths from their own study and

TERMS TO KNOW

- heritage
- ancestors
- Pentateuch
- "Literary form"
- tradition
- geology
- interpretation
- encyclical
- Genesis
- symbol

The Meaning of Messiah

We have just mentioned the Messiah, and we shall often use this word in the pages that follow. It comes from the Hebrew word which means "Anointed," just as Christ comes from the Greek word which means "Anointed." "Messiah" and "Christ," therefore, have the same meaning. In ancient times kings and priests were anointed in a solemn ceremony to signify their special consecration to God. Since our Savior is our Eternal King and our Supreme High Priest, He is known as *the* Anointed One, or Christ, or the Messiah.

reflection, from written accounts, or from the traditions and folk tales that were handed down among the Hebrew people by word of mouth. But no matter how the human authors of the Bible gained their knowledge of the truths related in Scripture, whether from divine revelation or by natural means, once they were inspired by God to set these truths in writing, their word is the word of God, although the various human authors wrote each in his own way, sometimes without even being aware that God was using them as His instruments.

The books of the Bible are divided into the Old and New Testaments. The Old Testament is a record of God's dealings with His Chosen People before the coming of Christ. This record tells the details of the covenant or agreement between God and man before the coming of the Messiah, when the Jews looked forward to the Promised Redeemer. It shows God's faithfulness to His promises. This account also tells of the history and hopes of the Chosen People, the prophecies which were made to them, their God-given Laws, and the advice which God thought they needed.

The New Testament is made up of those books which were written after the coming of Jesus Christ. These books tell of the fulfillment of God's promises, and the final covenant which God made with men through His Son, Jesus Christ. The first four books of the New Testament, the Gospels, were written by Matthew, Mark, Luke, and John, who were either Apostles or disciples of the Apostles. The New Testament also contains some books written to the first Christians by Christ's Apostles or their disciples. They are called the Acts of the Apostles, the Epistles, and the Apocalypse (Revelation). These books were written to tell the early Christians about Christ, about the nature and growth of His Kingdom the Church, and gave them instructions on how to live as members of Christ's Church.

Why the Bible Was Written

When an author writes a book he has a purpose or aim in mind. So too, God, the principal author of the Bible, had a definite purpose. His main purpose was to teach men religious truths so that they might acknowledge Him as the one true God, and live according to His will. The Bible tells of God, of man's relation to Him, of the rewards and punishments men might expect as a result of their use or abuse of God's graces and gifts. We may say, then, that Scripture was written with the purpose of making the one true God known, of proving His loving care in teaching us necessary religious truths, and of inspiring us to love Him in return.

The Bible, therefore, is not trying directly to teach science or history or any other branch of secular learning. If its human authors relate facts pertaining to these subjects, they present them as they were known and understood by the people of their own day. Many of their expressions may sound very odd to us today. We must remember, however, that the Bible is not in error when it reflects the viewpoint of past ages in secular fields of knowledge, because its purpose is to teach us religious truths. On the other hand we must likewise always keep in mind that these religious truths concern facts that really happened and are often conveyed to us by the narration of historical events.

Genesis and the Pentateuch

The first book of Sacred Scripture is Genesis—which means "beginning of things." It is the first part of the Pentateuch, as the opening five books of the Bible are called. The Pentateuch, after narrating the traditions known to the Hebrews about Abraham, Isaac, and Jacob, deals mainly with Moses as the leader and law-giver of God's people.

Recorded history in the Bible begins with the story of Abraham in the twelfth chapter of Genesis. As a prelude, the first eleven chapters of Genesis tell us about that long period of time which extends from Adam to the time of Abraham (19th or 18th century B.C.). In telling this part of the Bible story, Moses and the other authors of these first five books made use, in part, of existing folk stories and traditions which, under God's guidance, were adapted to the purpose of teaching the Hebrews certain basic religious truths and real happenings which God wished them to know.

God created all things, including man.

The Pentateuch

This word comes from two Greek words meaning "five books" or "five scrolls." They therefore comprise the first five books of the Bible, which, according to tradition, were written by Moses. They include:

- Genesis
- Exodus
- Leviticus
- Numbers
- Deuteronomy

Sometimes in the Old Testament we find two different accounts of the same event. Both convey fundamentally the same religious truth. The inspired authors preserved both accounts even though secondary details differed, because both were among the sacred traditions of the people. For instance, in Genesis the story of creation is told in two different ways: the first shows God commanding things to be created by a mere word: "Let there be light"; the second shows God working like a potter, molding a vessel from clay: "The Lord God formed man out of the dust of the ground." The variations show that the author is interested not so much in the details of how the world or man or woman was created as in the truth that God created all things, including man.

Basic Religious Truths in Genesis, Chapters 1–11

These eleven introductory chapters of Genesis narrate facts that really happened, although they are not presented as we now write history, and are intended to convey religious truths. Some of the great religious truths and facts which the first eleven chapters of Genesis teach by means of stories are:

- The creation of man and his original blessedness;
- Marriage instituted by God;
- Man's fall through original sin;
- God's promise of Redemption, and the means He used to carry out His plan;
- The Lord's Day is to be kept holy.

The stories of that age which were adapted by the authors of the Old Testament to convey these religious truths and real happenings are told in imaginative language. The story is not necessarily an eyewitness account of the facts included. Certainly there were, for example, no eyewitnesses

"In the beginning God created the heavens and the earth; the earth was waste and void; darkness covered the abyss, and the spirit of God was stirring above the waters" (Gn 1:1–2).

present when God created the universe. In fact, God did not reveal the exact manner in which He created the world, and so the authors could give an account of the "how" of the creation of the universe only in terms current in their day. But they did tell us the all-important truth and fact that *God created all things.*

Interpretation of the Bible

As the Bible presents it, God created the visible world as the work of six days. Our early ancestors accepted this. They had no reason to question a six-day creation. At that time, no scientific discoveries had been made to help determine the age of the world.

The science of geology, which has helped us learn how the earth was gradually formed over a period of millions of years, was unknown to our ancient ancestors. Until recently men did not know these scientific facts. They also had no knowledge of how early writers wrapped a truth in a well-known story. Because they did not know the "literary forms," or style of writing used in ancient days, they simply accepted everything in Genesis literally, that is, they concluded that the authors intended us to accept as facts many details which were intended to convey the truths they were teaching.

We now have a knowledge both of science and of early literary styles which was lacking to our ancestors. In a particular sense, this knowledge enables us to understand Genesis better than the Bible readers of past centuries. However, it should be noted that advancements in literary and historical analysis do not inevitably lead to a better understanding of Sacred Scripture.

Present-day interpretation of Genesis is based upon a declaration of Pope Pius XII, who wrote that historical investigation and archaeological discoveries have given us a better knowledge of the Bible.

The account of the fall in Genesis 3 uses figurative language, but affirms a primeval event, a deed that took place at the beginning of the history of man.[264] Revelation gives us the certainty of faith that the whole of human history is marked by the original fault freely committed by our first parents.

—*Catechism of the Catholic Church,* 390

The Meaning Intended by the Author

We have said that the biblical author of the stories in the beginning of Genesis was often inspired by God to adapt traditional stories to convey key religious truths and that these stories were sometimes imaginative. What the story meant or tried to say before the biblical author used it is not important; the meaning intended by the biblical author, that is, what he tried to tell us by using it, is important. The biblical account of the first sin committed by Adam and Eve will serve as an illustration to show what we mean.

The Bible story says that God had forbidden our first parents to eat of the fruit "of the tree of knowledge of good and evil." The story says that a particular fruit of a particular tree was chosen by God to be a test of obedience for our first parents. Part of what the story is trying to tell us is that God tested the obedience of Adam and Eve. We are obliged to believe that the devil tempted our first parents, and that Adam and Eve fell into sin. The fact that our first parents sinned by disobeying God was told in a story, using much figurative language (figurative meaning "symbolic"). The main religious truth in the story is the test of their obedience to God and its results. In other words, the fact that our first parents disobeyed God is told to us in the story under the symbol of eating a forbidden fruit. The wisdom of God is apparent in this. By the use of the story even the most primitive mind could easily and surely understand the religious truth that Adam and Eve disobeyed God when tested by Him.

FOR ME TO REVIEW

Questions and Exercises

(Answer these and all later tests on a separate sheet of paper.)

Part 1: Complete these statements

1. _____ is the name given to the first five books of the Bible.

2. _____ are those who came before us.

3. _____ tells the story of those who lived before Abraham.

4. _____ was the chief human author of the Pentateuch.

5. _____ is a style of writing.

6. _____ were God's Chosen People.

7. _____ is that which came down to us from our ancestors.

Part 2: Answer yes or no

1. We have received our spiritual heritage from the Hebrews.

2. Moses is the sole author of the Pentateuch.

3. Modern advances in our knowledge of history and science help us in the interpretation of Genesis.

4. Genesis 1 to 11 tells about the time before Abraham.

5. The stories in the first eleven chapters of Genesis lay the foundation for the history of the Hebrew people.

6. Because of biblical research we know more about the Bible than our ancestors did.

7. The work of Moses is based entirely upon tradition.

8. In Genesis the same story may be told in two different ways.

CHAPTER 2
The Goodness of God is Manifested in Creation

God Created the World

There was a time, millions and billions of years ago, when the world did not exist; but God existed. He is eternal. When we say that God is eternal we mean that He always existed and always will exist. The world, however, is not eternal; it did not always exist, and it would never have come into being if God had not made it. The creation of the world by God is the first great religious truth told in Genesis, the first book of the Bible. The first chapter of Genesis describes God as making the world out of nothing. The story of creation has many details. Let us examine the two accounts of creation which the Bible presents.

The First Story of Creation

"In the beginning God created the heavens and the earth; the earth was waste and void; darkness covered the abyss, and the spirit of God was stirring above the waters" (Gn 1:1–2).

These first two introductory verses tell us what the biblical story we are to study is about, and also gives us a hint as to how the story will be divided. As the account unfolds we shall see how God "shaped" and "adorned" the earth. God shaped the earth "which was waste and void" by bringing disorder into order. This is the work of the first three days which make up the first part of the account. Let us read the part of the biblical account which tells of the work of the first three days:

I. LIGHT

God said, "Let there be light," and there was light. God saw that the light was good. God separated the light from the darkness, calling the light Day and the darkness Night. And there was evening and morning, the first day (Gn 1:3–5).

II. FIRMAMENT

Then God said, "Let there be a firmament in the midst of the waters to divide the waters." And so it was. God made the firmament, dividing the waters that were below the firmament from those that were above it. God called the firmament Heaven. And there was evening and morning, the second day (Gn 1:6–8).

And God said, "Let there be lights in the firmament of the heavens to separate day from night; let them serve as signs and for the fixing of seasons, days and years; let them serve as lights in the firmament of the heavens to shed light upon the earth." So it was. God made the two great lights, the greater light to rule the day and the smaller one to rule the night, and he made the stars.

GENESIS 1:14–17

III. DRY LAND

Then God said, "Let the waters below the heavens be gathered into one place and let the dry land appear." And so it was. God called the dry land Earth and the assembled waters Seas. And God saw that it was good. Then God said: "Let the earth bring forth vegetation: seed-bearing plants and all kinds of fruit trees that bear fruit containing their seed." And so it was. The earth brought forth vegetation, every kind of seed-bearing plant and all kinds of trees that bear fruit containing their seed. God saw that it was good. And there was evening and morning, the third day (Gn 1:11–13).

God then adorned the universe by creating the beings who were to live in it. This was the work of the last three days which makes up the second part of the account. The biblical account of the fourth, fifth, and sixth days reads as follows:

IV. SUN, MOON, STARS

And God said, "Let there be lights in the firmament of the heavens to separate day from night; let them serve as signs and for the fixing of seasons, days and years; let them serve as lights in the firmament of the heavens to shed light upon the earth." So it was. God made the two great lights, the greater light to rule the day and the smaller one to rule the night, and he made the stars. God set them in the firmament of the heavens to shed light upon the earth, to rule the day and night, and to separate the light from the darkness. God saw that it was good. And there was evening and morning, the fourth day (Gn 1:14–19).

V. FISHES AND BIRDS

Then God said, "Let the waters abound with life, and above the earth let winged creatures fly below the firmament of the heavens." And so it was. God created the great sea monsters, all kinds of living, swimming creatures with which the waters abound, and all kinds of winged birds. God saw that it was good, and God blessed them saying, "Be fruitful, multiply, and fill the waters of the seas; and let the birds multiply on the earth." And there was evening and morning, the fifth day (Gn 1:20–23).

VI. LAND ANIMALS AND MAN

God said, "Let the earth bring forth all kinds of living creatures: cattle, crawling creatures and wild animals." And so it was. God made all kinds of wild beasts, every kind of cattle, and every kind of creature crawling on the ground. And God saw that it was good. God said, "Let us make mankind in our image and likeness; and let them have dominion over the fish of the sea, the birds of the air, the cattle, over all the wild animals and every creature that crawls on the earth."

God created man in his image.

In the image of God he created him.

Male and female he created them.

Then God blessed them and said to them, "Be fruitful and multiply; fill the earth and subdue it. Have dominion over the fish of the sea, the birds of the air, the cattle and all the animals that crawl on the earth." God also said, "See, I give you every seed-bearing plant on the earth and every tree which has seed-bearing fruit to be your food. To every wild animal of the earth, to every bird of the air and to every creature that crawls on the earth and has the breath of life, I give the green plants for food."

And so it was. God saw that all he had made was very good. And there was evening and morning, the sixth day (Gn 1:24–31).

After the six days of work, God rested. This fact is mentioned at the end of the biblical story of creation in the following words:

VII. SABBATH

Thus the heavens and the earth were finished and all their array. On the sixth day God finished the work he had been doing. And he rested on the seventh day from all the work he had done.

God blessed the seventh day and made it holy because on it he rested from all his work of creation (Gn 2:1–3).

The inspired author's plan for presenting the story of creation closely follows the nature of human labor. For six days the Hebrews worked during the daytime, stopped their work at night, and began it again in the morning. In the biblical account of creation the author, under divine inspiration, pictured God for a six day period as working during the day, stopping at night, and resuming His work again in the morning.

On the seventh day God rested. The Hebrews, following the example of God, were to set aside their work on the seventh day to honor Him.

The following chart of the inspired author's plan for telling the story of creation will show you how he divided the works of creation and how the first, second, and third days of each division are closely related to each other.

1st Division (God "shaped" the earth)		2nd Division (God "adorned" the earth)	
DAY	WORK OF CREATION	DAY	WORK OF CREATION
1	Light separated from darkness (day and night)	4	Sun for the day Moon and stars for the night
2	Firmament separated from water	5	Birds for the air and fish for the waters
3	a) Dry land separated from water b) Production of plant life	6	a) Land creatures b) Man
GOD RESTED			
Seventh Day			

NOTE THE FOLLOWING:

1. On the first day light is separated from darkness; on the fourth day the sun is created to light the day, and the moon and stars to light the night.

2. On the second day air and water are separated; on the fifth day birds of the air are created, and fish for the waters.

3. There are two works on the third day:

   a) dry land is separated from water;
   b) plant life is produced.

   There are also two works on the sixth day:

   a) land creatures are created;
   b) man is created.

   Both man and land creatures are to people the earth, and feed upon the plants.

   When we read the story of creation in Genesis, we must remember that it is not an eyewitness account because God alone saw the beginning of all things. The account is an artist's picture or an artistic presentation of how creation took place, sketched in words by the author of Genesis.

Our "Obligation"

As a Catholic, you will hear the word "obligation" in reference to our duty to attend Mass every Sunday and on holy days ("holy days of obligation"). We must never miss Mass unless we have a legitimate excuse, like an illness. In fact, it is a grave sin to miss Mass without a valid dispensation.

God Teaches Us to Keep Sunday Holy

Genesis speaks of the creation of the world in six days. It serves to teach us another important lesson. God "rested" not because He needed a rest, for God cannot ever become tired. When the Bible says that God rested on the seventh day it wishes to remind man to rest each week from his labors.

God had commanded the Hebrew people to work six days and to rest on the seventh. The last day of the week, Saturday, was the day of rest. This was changed to Sunday by the Apostles, because it was on this day that Jesus rose from the dead, and that the Holy Spirit descended upon the Apostles.

The Second Creation Story

In the second account of creation the story is told in a different way to teach other religious truths. The author of Genesis added this second story with an account of the temptation and fall of man. Both stories contain important religious truths which the author wanted to teach. The fact that he used both just as they were, without trying to make their details agree, further proves that he was interested only in teaching religious truths, and not in the historical exactness of the details of the story which he adapted to teach these religious truths. Let us now examine the second creation story.

When the Lord God made the earth and the heavens, there was not yet any field shrub on the earth nor had the plants of the field sprung up, for the Lord had sent no rain on the earth and there was no man to till the soil; but a mist rose from the earth and watered all the surface of the ground. Then the Lord formed man out of the dust of the ground and breathed into his nostrils the breath of life, and man became a living being (Gn 2:4–7).

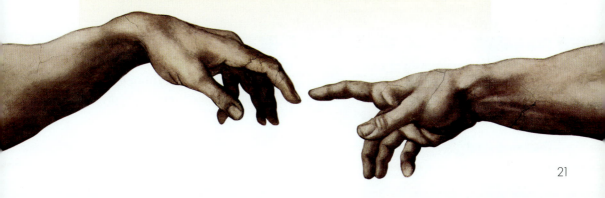

Here we are told that God formed the body of man and breathed into him a soul which made him intelligent and free.

Man's body is perishable; he is dust. The Bible story tells us this by saying that God took man's body from the dust of the earth. Here again, let us remember that these words are not to be taken in their literal sense. We know that God is a spirit, He has no hands. The Bible simply wants to tell us that, through God's power, man, in some special way, received an earthly body. The animals, of course, also have a body. Man, however, has something which makes him resemble God. The soul which God gives to each human being elevates man and distinguishes him from all animals.

The Bible calls the first man "Adam," which means "man" or "mankind." God created for Adam a helpmate like himself. She was called Eve, which sounds like the Hebrew word for "living," signifying that she was the mother of all the living.

In order to emphasize that woman is of the same nature as man, and that in marriage they are united by love, the inspired author pictures God taking a rib

The soul which God gives to each human being elevates man and distinguishes him from all animals.

22

from Adam, near his heart, and forming his wife from this rib. Just as the picture of God's forming Adam from the clay teaches that man is of himself mortal, so the picture of Eve's coming from the rib of Adam stresses her human nature and the union of husband and wife in marriage.

The Perfections of God Are Reflected in Men

MAN IN THE IMAGE OF GOD

God wanted men to be happy on earth. He created Adam and Eve in a state of happiness. He bestowed on them wonderful natural gifts, a body and an immortal soul, which made them different from and superior to animals. He gave them the natural gifts of an intellect that could know and learn and think and reason, a will free to choose what it wished to do, even whether to serve God or not, the physical gift of strength to master nature, and the use of the senses. Their most precious gift, however, was supernatural, sanctifying grace.

God also gave Adam and Eve certain other gifts higher than the natural gifts, but less than the supernatural gift of sanctifying grace. He gave them freedom from pain and sorrow, and immortality of the body or the possibility of entering Heaven without suffering or death. Their bodies and physical tendencies were under easy control of their wills.

In order to give us a good idea of this perfect happiness which our first parents enjoyed, the inspired writer of Genesis uses a story which tells us about an earthly paradise called the Garden of Eden. It was a wonderful garden, a rich and fertile place where trees of every kind grew.

To help us understand that God intended that Adam and Eve should live forever and never die, the sacred author, under the direction of God, tells us the story of a certain tree which grew in the Garden of Eden. It is called the "tree of life." The account of Genesis reads as follows:

The Lord God planted a garden in Eden to the east, and he put there the man he had formed. The Lord God made to grow out of the ground all kinds of trees pleasant to the sight and good for food, the tree of life also in the midst of the garden . . . (Gn 2:8–9).

Adam and Eve enjoyed a state of perfect happiness before the Fall.

God attached only one condition to the continuation of man's complete happiness: obedience to His commands. God put a prohibition upon our first parents. To let us know about it the sacred writer speaks of another tree in the garden, "the tree of the knowledge of good and evil," telling the following story which pictures God as saying to our first parents:

"From every tree of the garden you may eat; but from the tree of the knowledge of good and evil you must not eat; for the day you eat of it, you must die" (Gn 2:16–17). By this God told them that they must not disobey; they must not commit sin.

Since God had created Adam and Eve they owed Him

worship and gratitude; yet God had given them, as He has given every human being, a free will. He never forces anyone to love and serve Him. It follows that Adam and Eve were free to reject or accept His command. One would think that they should have been glad to obey God, as He had given them everything they could desire; nothing was lacking to make their happiness complete. How did it happen, then, that they in fact grievously offended God? They were tempted by the devil.

GOD CREATED INVISIBLE SPIRITS—ANGELS

Although Genesis tells only of the creation of the visible world, it is necessary to study the creation and fall of the angels to understand the part played by the evil spirit in the temptation and fall of our first parents. Besides man, God had created the

angels. Like God, they were pure spirits, that is, without bodies, whose beauty and strength we cannot describe. Like our first parents, these angels were tested to prove their loyalty to God, for they, too, had been created with free wills. Many of them rebelled against God and were cast into hell by the loyal angels under the leadership of St. Michael. It was one of these fallen angels, or devils, who persuaded Adam and Eve to rebel against God. These same devils try by every possible means to lead us into sin and away from God.

The Gifts of God Are Rejected by Man

ADAM AND EVE SIN

To help men understand the temptation of our first parents by the devil, the inspired author uses the story of the serpent tempting Eve. The Bible story tells us that the serpent approached Eve, telling her that she would not die if she and Adam ate the fruit of the tree of the knowledge of good and evil. He said that their eyes would be opened and that, like God, they would know good and evil. Eve took the fruit and ate it. Then she handed Adam the fruit, which he too ate. This story shows men that Adam as well as Eve disobeyed God. Through his act of disobedience to the command of God Adam, and with him all his posterity, fell from grace.

When Adam and Eve fell into sin, the whole human race fell with them. Just as children of parents who have lost all their money are born into the world poor, so we are all children of parents who have lost the treasure of sanctifying grace and thus are born without it. This is original sin; it means that we are born without sanctifying grace, although we are naturally destined for a reward that we can attain only if we possess sanctifying grace.

GOD CURSES SATAN

To help us understand this the Bible quotes God as saying: "I will put enmity between you and the woman, between your seed and her seed; he shall crush your head and you shall lie in wait for his heel" (Gn 3:15). This means that warfare between mankind and Satan would continue, but that God would send someone to conquer Satan and redeem mankind. From the New Testament we know that this Person is our Savior. This earliest prophecy is quite general; with each new prophecy, the picture of the Savior is to become clearer and more distinct.

The conqueror was to be the leader of all men, and carry the war against Satan to victory. Because Mary gave us Christ and is closely associated with Him in our redemption, one of the ancient translations ascribed the crushing of the serpent's head to her: ". . . she shall crush the serpent's head . . ." She was to co-operate in the victory over Satan.

GOD PUNISHES ADAM AND EVE

When we sin, our conscience warns us immediately that we have done wrong. The same thing happened to Adam and Eve. God at once spoke to them through their conscience. He scolded them for what they had done. He told them they would be punished. To their sorrow they realized only too well what a serious mistake they had made. Through their disobedience they had lost God's friendship.

When Adam and Eve were truly sorry for their sin, God forgave them. But God is just; one can never rebel against God without suffering punishment; Adam and Eve's rebellion consisted in a rejection of God and paradise, and their punishment for this accorded with their rebellion.

God told Eve that her children would cause her much trouble and suffering, and that she would be under the domination of her husband.

To Adam God said:

"Cursed be the ground because of you;

The Protoevangelium

This is the first hint that God will send a redeemer—a Messiah—to save humanity and crush the enemy. It refers, of course, to Jesus, and the "woman" from this passage refers to Mary. This biblical passage is called the "Protoevangelium." *Proto* means "first," and *evangelium* means "good news" or "gospel." Thus, this is referred to as the "first gospel," the first announcement of the coming of the Messiah.

in toil shall you eat of it all the
days of your life;
Thorns and thistles shall it bring forth to you,
and you shall eat the plants of the field.
In the sweat of your brow you shall eat bread,
till you return to the ground,
Since out of it you were taken;
for dust you are and unto dust
you shall return" (Gn 3:17–19).

Because of Adam's sin and the sins that followed, many things on the earth cause man suffering and inconvenience.

Sin upsets everything, and so it did with Adam and Eve. Up to this time their life had been happy and pleasant. Now they were to experience the hardships of labor, of suffering, of hunger and thirst, and of death. Worst of all, they learned that once they gave in to sin they would have to suffer other temptations. These temptations, from then on, would come not only from the devil but also from their own bodies (their own selves) and from the world around them.

God is not only just, He is also merciful. Hence He promised Adam and Eve that some day the evil of sin would be conquered. He did not tell them how, but He assured our first parents that Satan would be conquered. Adam and Eve thus knew that God forgave them.

CAIN AND ABEL

Our first parents, exiled from Paradise, that is, deprived of their state of happiness, soon experienced the meaning of God's words, "In the sweat of your brow you shall eat bread." They faced a world that rebelled against them just as they had rebelled against God. Work and hardship, suffering and death, were their lot.

Unfortunately this first sin was not the last. It was followed by many others, so that the descendants of Adam and Eve grew more and more wicked. This fact is illustrated by the story of the envious Cain who murdered his brother Abel.

Abel, the Bible story says, was pleasing to almighty God and to his parents. He offered his gifts with a just and unselfish spirit and proved his love by willingly sacrificing his best lamb as a victim. God accepted his gifts, as He later accepted His Son's sacrifice in the New Covenant.

At first, the story of Cain and Abel was told among the Hebrews apart from the story of Adam and Eve. Since it was, however, a sample of the wickedness of Adam's descendants, it was inserted immediately after the story of Adam and Eve with the result that Cain, a farmer, appears as the elder son of Adam and Eve. He offered the fruits of the field as a sacrifice to God. But his heart was not right before God. He envied Abel, his younger brother, so that God was not pleased with his offering. Cain's envy grew. Giving way to his passion, he murdered Abel and refused to repent. Finally he despaired of God's mercy, thus showing to what limits resistance to grace can lead.

God punished Cain by banishing him from the land of his father and making him a fugitive. He no longer had a part in carrying on the promise of a Redeemer.

God used Abel to prepare men's minds for another Son whose sacrifice was pleasing to His Father, and who would be slain by His envious brothers. God also intended to show that He would accept men's sacrifices only if their hearts were pleasing to God.

Very often in our study of the Old Testament we shall discover that certain persons, events, or things lead our minds to Christ or make us think of similar persons, events, or things in the New Testament, and the Church today. Some of these have been definitely intended by almighty God to serve as types. Others remind us of New Testament ideas and persons because of striking similarities. We shall refer to them as being prototypes, types, or figures of whatever persons, events, or things they prefigure.

Work and hard-
ship, suffering
and death,
are the lot of
fallen man.

Sin drove Cain from God and deprived him of happiness. This is a grave warning to us about playing with temptation to sin, especially against our fellow men.

In the New Testament our Savior summed up all the commandments into two: love of God and of neighbor. He further illustrated the importance of mercy and the brotherhood of men in the parable of the Good Samaritan.

In the death of Abel, Adam and Eve learned the meaning of an inclination toward evil and the malice of sin. Now they also became aware of what God meant by death.

The story ends by telling us that some time after the death of Abel, God gave Adam and Eve another son, the good and just Seth, through whom the worship of the one true God came down to later generations.

FOR ME TO REVIEW

Questions and Exercises

Part 1: Match column I with column II

Column I

1. Adam

2. Eve

3. Michael

4. Cain

5. Abel

6. Seth

Column II

A. the worship of the one true God came down to later generations through him

B. the leader of the loyal angels

C. left the land of his father and became a fugitive

D. prepared men's minds for another Son whose sacrifice was pleasing to His Father

E. means "man" or "mankind"

F. sounds like the Hebrew word for "living"

Part 2: Complete the following statements

1. The most precious gift bestowed on Adam and Eve by almighty God was _____

2. Besides man God created _____

3. The first book of the Bible is _____

4. The authors of Genesis were interested in teaching _____

5. An earthly paradise spoken of in Genesis is _____

Part 3: Answer yes or no

1. Eve was punished for the part she had in the sin.

2. God in His goodness created all things out of nothing.

3. None of the angels rebelled against God.

4. Abel showed his love for God by sacrificing his best lamb as a victim.

5. Cain, because of his jealousy, committed a great sin.

6. Genesis contains two accounts of creation.

7. Both angels and men were tested in order to prove their loyalty to God.

8. Angels are pure spirits without bodies.

9. Justice demanded that God punish Adam and Eve.

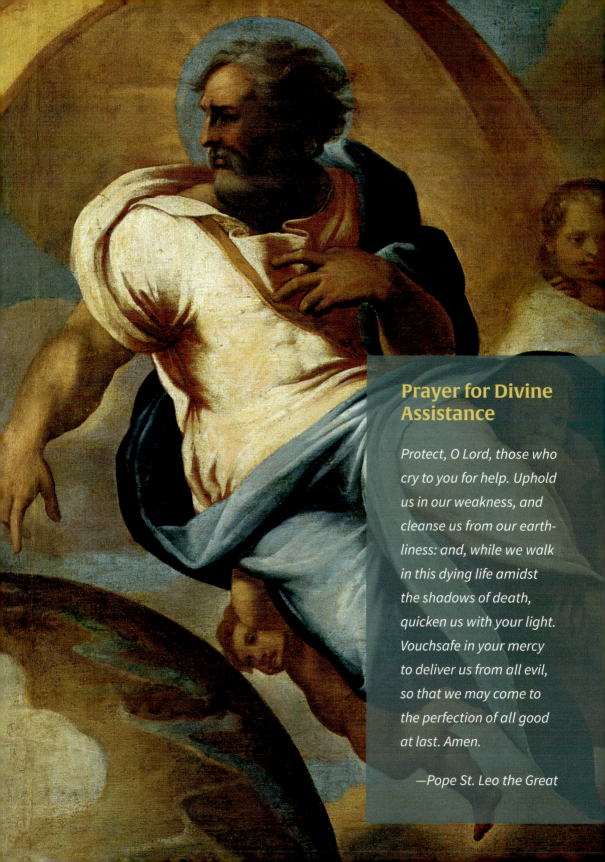

Prayer for Divine Assistance

Protect, O Lord, those who cry to you for help. Uphold us in our weakness, and cleanse us from our earthliness: and, while we walk in this dying life amidst the shadows of death, quicken us with your light. Vouchsafe in your mercy to deliver us from all evil, so that we may come to the perfection of all good at last. Amen.

—Pope St. Leo the Great

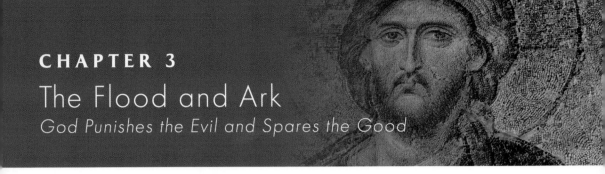

CHAPTER 3

The Flood and Ark
God Punishes the Evil and Spares the Good

Men Turn Away From God

We learned in the last chapter that, after the death of Abel, God sent Adam and Eve another child, Seth. He took the place of Abel in the eyes of his parents. Seth was the example of a life in which God's worship had the chief place. Once more, however, sin gained a hold on mankind. The Bible is not clear as to the exact details, but the inspired authors leave no doubt that mankind became so estranged from God that a radical purge was necessary.

Almighty God decided to show the sad state to which man had come and to indicate how His mercy would save them. How God did this, the biblical author tells us by using the story of a great flood.

The story of such a great flood is found not only in the Bible but also in the literatures of other peoples of the ancient East. Furthermore, archaeological discoveries in the Near East bear witness to a rather widespread flood. The inspired author has combined two separate accounts of the same story to tell of the flood. No doubt he used the two because each of them contained details that he needed to build up his complete account. Should you read the story of the flood from the Bible, you would discover that in certain details the two accounts differ. One account, for instance, says that the animals were taken into the ark two by two, and that the flood lasted forty days. The other account says that seven of each of the animals whose flesh could be used for food were taken into the ark, and that the waters receded at the end of 150 days. This seems to indicate that, under the guidance of almighty God, the sacred author was more interested in telling

the Hebrews that God punished men for their sins by a natural catastrophe than in telling them about any exact number of animals or other details of the story.

The story shows that God sometimes uses nature to carry out His justice. In this instance it was a flood which destroyed sinful people. This was not only a punishment for sin but also a warning to sinful men in the future. Let us now examine the story.

God Commands Noah to Build the Ark

In the midst of a wicked people, Noah, a descendant of Seth, pleased God by living a life of justice and holiness. Since God is good, He did not will to punish the innocent with the guilty. Because Noah and his sons Shem, Ham, and Japheth ('jaf-əth)[1] had no part in the general wickedness, He decided to spare them. He ordered His faithful servant Noah to build an ark or flat-bottomed boat of wood in which he and his family would find safety when the deluge came.

In God's wisdom the story had another purpose. The ark was intended to turn men's minds to the Ark of the New Covenant, the Catholic Church, which was to save men from the deluge of sin by the wood of Christ's cross.

When the ark was finished, heavy rains began to fall. Rivers overflowed their banks, and soon it looked as if the whole earth

TERMS TO KNOW

deluge
covenant
subside
catastrophe
patriarchs
Ark
Ararat
purge

---

[1] Pronunciations given in this book make use of the symbols given in Webster's Elementary Dictionary (Gold) (Springfield, Mass.: G. & C. Merriam Co., 1959).

The ark, coming to rest upon Ararat, was again a figure of the Church built upon Christ, who had promised that the gates of Hell shall not prevail against it.

The cleansing of the earth from the wickedness of sinners, who were destroyed in the flood while the good escaped by means of the ark, is a symbol of Baptism. In this sacrament the faithful pass over into a new life, but their sins, like enemies, are blotted out.

were covered with water. Everyone in that part of the country drowned; everyone, that is, except Noah and his family. They remained in the ark until the waters began to subside, and the ark came to rest upon the Mountains of Ararat ('ar-ə-rat), generally located in Armenia, between the Black and Caspian Seas.

Noah Teaches Us a Lesson in Gratitude

When the ground was dry enough, the story continues, Noah and his family left the ark. Their first thought was to thank God by offering Him a sacrifice. God was so pleased with this act of worship that He made a covenant, a solemn agreement, with Noah and through him with all mankind. He promised that He would not destroy the earth or mankind by another deluge. A beautiful rainbow appeared in the heavens to show Noah that God was pleased with the sacrifice and meant what He said. This sign should always remind men of His faithfulness and goodness.

Noah's Prophecy Concerning His Descendants

The story further relates that some time after the flood Ham proved to be an undutiful son by showing irreverence for his father. Because of this, Noah cursed him. Later, when the Chosen People settled in Palestine, the sacred writer describes the fulfillment of this curse in the enslavement of the Canaanites, who were thought to be the descendants of Ham. On this occasion Shem and Japheth showed reverence for their father, and because of this they were blessed by God.

The Chosen People, and above all our Savior, Jesus, were Semites, descendants from Shem. Japheth, Noah said, would share in the blessings of Shem.

The Ark and the Church

Noah's ark is a fascinating symbol for the Church. Just as Noah and his family and all the animals were saved from the flood by remaining inside the ark, so all of us who remain a part of the Church are saved as we travel across the rocky seas of life. Many churches are built to resemble the inside of a ship. The main part of the interior of a church is called the "nave," which is Latin for "ship." Additionally, the flying buttresses of many old cathedrals in Europe are said to resemble oars coming out the side of a ship.

The Great Ages of the Patriarchs

The Bible tells us that Noah lived 350 years after the flood, and that he was 950 years old when he died. Hence it might be well to speak here about the great ages given to the patriarchs of the Old Testament.

Sometimes, when speaking of a very old person, we say he is "as old as Mathusale" (mə-'thu-sə-lə). This expression is used because Genesis tells us that Mathusale lived to the ripe old age of nine hundred and sixty-nine years. By this assigning of great ages to the patriarchs the authors intended to show that men at the beginning of the world were much holier than they were in later times.

The Chosen People at this time had no clear revelation that rewards and punishments were to be expected in the next life as well as this. Accordingly they thought that goodness should be rewarded in this life, and wickedness punished. One reward for goodness that is stressed throughout the Old Testament is that of a long life. When the authors assign an ever-shorter life span, they indicate that men were being drawn away from God more and more by sin.

Let us remember this when a question arises in our minds as to whether or not some of the biblical characters we read about this year could have lived so long.

The Tower of Babel

We shall see soon that Abraham, from whom God was to raise up a people dedicated to His service, came from Ur, an ancient city in the Tigris-Euphrates ('tī-gris ü'frā-tēz) Valley. The biblical authors locate the next incident in the city of Babylon, the capital of several great Empires that arose in this valley.

People of different races lived in Babylon, since it was a great trading center, and also because the warlike people of Babylon had conquered not only their neighbors but also distant peoples. The Babylonians' desire for conquest disturbed the leaders of Israel, who knew that God alone was the supreme ruler of the world, and that proud human beings who tried to conquer the whole world were actually trying to take God's place. The Hebrew leaders knew, too, that God in His own good time could and would stop Babylon and bring her attempts at conquest to an end. The author tells how the people of Babylon learned their lesson in the story of the Tower of Babel ('bāb-l). Babel was the Hebrew word for Babylon. The story is inserted at this point to show that after the flood man continued to sin and that some even attempted to usurp God's dominion.

In Babylon there were a number of high brick buildings built like a staircase, whose towers seemed to reach to heaven. These were temples to their gods, the sun, moon, and stars. The Hebrews told of an attempt to build one of these towers. Men got together and decided that they would make themselves famous by building such a tower, but God put an end to their vain and foolish plan by simply making them all speak different languages.

We can and should learn an important lesson from this story for our own times. The story of the Tower of Babel is a striking symbol of ambition for world dominion. God wants no nation to conquer another; He wants all nations to be free. He has permitted different races and different languages to develop in order to safeguard our freedom. No nation can ever conquer the world, because those differences will sooner or later make men fight to throw off dominion by foreign nations. It has always happened this way in the past, and will always be in the future.

The story of the Tower of Babel also teaches us that pride displeases almighty God today even as it did in the far-distant past, and that man without God's help is doomed to failure. The lesson learned from this chapter should make us resolve to keep ourselves always in the presence of God, remembering that He is our kind and loving Father who is ever watching over us. If we live like this, no flood or disaster will ever separate us from His love. We shall be saved in His Ark of the New Covenant, the Catholic Church, as Noah was saved in the Ark of the Old Testament. God will be our tower of protection where no man-made tower could save us.

FOR ME TO REVIEW

Questions and Exercises

Part 1: Complete these statements:

1. _____ was a solemn agreement.

2. _____ was a symbol of Baptism.

3. _____ was a type of the Church.

4. _____ was a wicked city of ancient times.

5. _____ were the sons of Noah.

6. _____ proved himself an undutiful son.

7. _____ was blessed in a special manner.

8. _____ is the Hebrew word for Babylon.

9. _____ was the place where the Ark came to rest.

10. _____ was a sign of God's covenant with Noah.

Part 2: Questions to Check Your Reading

1. Why did God send the deluge?

2. Did Noah please almighty God by immediately offering sacrifice?

3. How is the ark a type of the Catholic Church?

4. What did Noah's descendants want to build?

5. Who were the sons of Noah?

6. What important lesson did God wish to teach men by the story of the Tower of Babel?

7. What covenant did God make with Noah?

8. Why is the flood considered a symbol of Baptism?

9. How did the flood serve as a warning to men in the future?

10. What did God wish to teach men by the story of Noah and the Deluge?

11. Can you name some ways in which we could please almighty God by showing Him gratitude?

☑ FOR ME TO DO

Each pupil need not do every one of the activities suggested at the end of this chapter or at any of the following chapters. These activities may be divided among groups or individuals, or the class may choose one or more.

1. Explain how God's justice is shown in His destruction of the human race by the flood.

2. Draw a picture of the Ark and the rainbow. Caption it— CHURCH; NEW COVENANT.

3. Select from the characters in our story some of their outstanding virtues. Give examples of these virtues in their lives, i.e., filial piety, brotherly love, fortitude, penance, gratitude, spirit of sacrifice, love of God.

4. Read the account of the Deluge from the Bible (Gn 6–9).

5. Outline the chapter. Then summarize or dramatize the story from the outline.

6. Look for a picture of a tower like the one the Babylonians wanted to build.

CHAPTER 4
Mankind Receives a Promise Through Abraham

The story of the first eleven chapters of Genesis has been told in chapters two and three in this book. These chapters summarized the beginnings of God's dealings with mankind.

The story of Abraham, which is told in this chapter, gives an account of the calling of God's Chosen People. With this story we are in a period of time which is well known to us from ancient written records and from the fascinating treasures archaeologists have uncovered in the Near East. These do not mention Abraham, but they give us a good idea of the customs of the time, customs that are often presupposed in the biblical accounts about Abraham.

In the story of the flood we learned that even before the death of Noah men forgot God and returned to their wicked ways. Only a few descendants of Sem remembered Him. Faithful to His promise to Noah, that He would never again destroy the world because of the sins of men, God chose a family to preserve the knowledge and worship of Himself. The promised Redeemer was to come from this family. The story of Genesis now becomes chiefly concerned with the names and activities of the ancestors of this one people. God chose Abraham to be the father and first leader of His Chosen People.

The Call of Abram

Abram, or, as he was later called, Abraham, first lived with his father, Thare, in a place in lower Chaldea (kalʹdē-ə) called Ur (today in Iraq). Later the clan of Thare moved north to Haran (today in Syria). Here God called Abram and told him to leave his country and become the founder of a great nation. This is the beginning of the Hebrew nation.

> "Leave your country, your kinsfolk and your father's house, for the land which I will show you; I will make a great nation of you. I will bless you and make your name great, so that you shall be a blessing" (Gn 12:1–2).

When the Bible says that God spoke to a person in the Old Testament, it does not always mean that He appeared visibly. Generally, we may suppose that God revealed His will invisibly.

Abram, showing great faith in God, took his wife Sarah, his servants and belongings, and with his nephew Lot departed for Canaan, which is today called Palestine, or the land of the Kingdom of Jordan and the Republic of Israel. Their flocks and herds increased so that there was no longer

TERMS TO KNOW

Messiah

Thare

Sodom

Canaan

Melchizedek

Gomorra

enough pasture land for both Abram and Lot. Because of this they decided to part. Abram said, "Let there be no strife between you and me, nor between my herdsmen and your herdsmen; for we are kinsmen . . ." (Gn 13:8). He permitted Lot to choose the parts of the land that he preferred.

Lot chose the region south of the Dead Sea and Abram kept the land north of the Dead Sea, which was later called Juda. He did not settle here, however, for Abram was a nomad shepherd, like the typical desert wanderer, the Bedouins of today. He wandered from place to place to find grazing for his flocks.

God Rewards the Peace-Loving Abram

God blessed Abram with great riches because of his unselfishness and love of peace. He repeated to Abram His promise that He would give him the lands he could see "to the north and the

Abram, a nomad shepherd, became the father of the Hebrew nation.

south and the east and the west." While at Hebron Abram built an altar to the Lord.

Lot settled in Sodom ('säd-əm), which was located in the fertile lands of the lower Jordan Valley. Eventually an invading army from the North and East attacked the kings of Sodom and the neighboring cities. Lot and his family were taken captives. On hearing of this, Abram gathered his servants and pursued the enemy. He finally overtook them by night, rescuing Lot and recovering all his possessions.

Melchizedek—Prefigures Christ

On the return journey from his victory over the enemy who captured Lot, Abram was met by Melchizedek (mel-'ki-se-dek), king and priest of Salem (Jerusalem), who offered bread and wine in sacrifice and blessed Abram. In gratitude for this blessing, Abram gave Melchizedek a tenth of everything he had. It was not an unusual practice in those days to donate one tenth of one's income for religious purposes.

Abram Destined To Be Father of God's Chosen People

God did not immediately fulfill His promise of making Abram the father of a multitude. In fact, it almost appeared as if He had forgotten His promise. Although

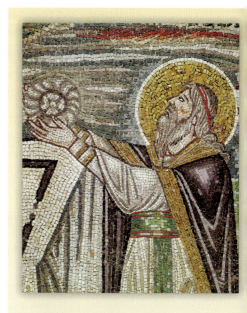

Melchizedek, who is mentioned in the Canon of the Mass, was a priest as well as a king. In those early days it was customary for the civil leader of a city to be also its religious chief. This same custom was also kept by the early Hebrews. Thus Abram also performed the priestly duties as head of his tribe.

Centuries later a Hebrew prophet wrote of the coming Messiah. He said, "You are a priest forever, according to the order of Melchizedek" (Ps 109:4). The prophet meant that just as Melchizedek had been both priest and king, so too, the Redeemer would be a king and a priest who would offer sacrifice with bread and wine.

Abram and Sarah were well advanced in years, their marriage was not blessed by children. God then appeared to Abram and told him that his wife Sarah would have a son from whom a great nation would arise. As a sign of this covenant with God, the sacred author mentions the change of Abram's name to Abraham. The two names were actually different forms of the same word. The longer form Abraham, however, when pronounced, suggested the Hebrew word meaning "father of a multitude." God said that Abraham was to be "the father of a multitude of nations." In God's plan Abraham was destined to be the father of all those who would share in the promises of the coming Redeemer.

God Renews the Promise of a Son

Time passed, but God had not yet sent Abraham a son. One day, as the aging Abraham sat before his tent, he saw three travelers coming toward him. He went out to meet them and offered them the hospitality for which the East is famous. He served the strangers, and, when they had eaten, one of them told Abraham that at the end of the year Sarah would have a son. Sarah laughed at the thought, which seemed impossible to her. The stranger said to Abraham, "Is anything too wonderful for the Lord?" (Gn 10:14.) Abraham then realized that it was the Lord with two angels to whom he had shown hospitality.

In this incident we see the generosity of Abraham. He is also shown to be a true friend of God. God, on the other hand, is very near to those whom He loves.

Abraham Intercedes for Sodom and Gomorra

The cities of Sodom and Gomorra (gə-ˈmōr-rə) were so wicked that the Lord told Abraham that He was going to destroy them. Abraham's nephew Lot lived in Sodom. Since he and his family had not acted as did their neighbors, they were to be spared.

Abraham pleaded with God to spare the cities if fifty good people could be found there. When he discovered that there were not even fifty, he reduced the number to forty, and eventually all the way down to ten. God would have heard his prayer, especially since it was so persevering, if he could have found only ten good people in Sodom and Gomorra.

Just before the destruction of the two cities, Lot, his wife, and family were warned to hurry away, else they too would be lost. They were even warned not to turn and look back. All obeyed except Lot's wife, who looked back at the city in disobedience to God and was turned into a pillar of salt. The two cities were completely destroyed.

 FOR ME TO REVIEW

Questions and Exercises

Part 1: Arrange this story of Abraham in sequence

1. Abraham rescues Lot.

2. God calls Abraham.

3. Melchizedek offers bread and wine.

4. Abraham moves into Canaan.

5. God makes promises to Abraham for the first time.

6. Abraham and Lot separate.

7. Abraham entertains three guests.

Part 2: How were the following related to Abraham?

1. Sarah

2. Lot

3. Thare

4. Melchizedek

Part 3: Complete these statements

1. Lot left Abraham and settled in _____

2. Abraham pleaded with God to spare the cities of _____ and _____

3. One of the three strangers who visited Abraham was _____

4. Canaan is now called _____

5. In the Old Testament, those persons who remind us of Christ are called _____

Part 4: Questions to Check Your Reading

1. Why did God set apart one nation as His own?

2. What promises did God make to Abraham?

3. How does the story of Abraham show that at times God rewards those who are faithful to Him with material blessings?

4. List the virtues which Abraham portrayed, and give incidents from the story which prove your answer.

5. How does Melchizedek prefigure Christ?

6. Which promise made to Abraham is the most important to us?

7. Which perfection of God is expressed in the Lord's words, "Is anything too wonderful for the Lord?"

8. Which incident proves that God is pleased when we pray for one another?

9. What should the story of Lot teach us? the story of his wife?

10. What does the story of Sodom and Gomorra teach us?

✓ FOR ME TO DO

1. Make a panel using symbols depicting the life of Abraham and the virtues practiced by him. You may use a cross to signify faith, an olive branch for peace, stars for his descendants, etc. Arrange them to form one symbolic picture of Abraham. Then write a short paragraph to explain the picture.

2. Read some stories of saints who were martyred for their faith.

3. In your notebook make an outline map of that part of Asia where Abraham lived. Show on it the city of Ur on the Euphrates River, where Abraham was born; the city of Haran, from which God called Abraham; and Canaan, the land promised to Abraham. Locate it on the globe. Then locate our country.

4. Choose and copy the prophecy which you like best.

5. In your missal or prayer book find the second prayer after the Consecration. Whose sacrifices do you find mentioned? Read and discuss the prayer.

CHAPTER 5

Abraham and the Sacrifice of Isaac

Remember how God promised Abraham that his children would be as numerous as the sands of the seashore and the stars in the sky, and that among his descendants were to be kings and princes. This was a very important promise, not only for Abraham but also for people of all times and all nations. A great nation would be descended from him. This nation God called His "Chosen People." From this family would come the Redeemer, who would restore to men the right to Heaven which Adam had lost by his disobedience.

We will continue to see how faithful God was to His promise. He showered many favors and blessings on these Chosen People, and kept alive in them the hope of the Messiah. In all their struggles He watched over them and guided them. He wanted them to remain faithful and devoted to Him, loving Him and serving Him until the day when the promised Redeemer would come.

The Promise of a Redeemer Is Repeated

Abraham was singled out from all the other men of the Old Testament to keep alive faith in the one true God and the promised Redeemer because he was a man of exceptional faith, who showed his great faith in deeds. When God told him he was to be the Father of countless descendants, he believed, although at an advanced age he was still childless. God rewarded him by the promise: "In you shall all the nations of the earth be blessed" (Gn 12:3).

Hagar and Ismael

In chapter 4 of St. Paul's letter to the Galatians, we are told that Abraham had two wives: one was a free woman, Sarah; the other was a slave girl, Hagar ('a-gär). Our Lord restored marriage to its primitive dignity of the union of one man and one woman. This was what God had originally intended. The book of Genesis mentions that Lamech ('la-mek) who is described

TERMS TO KNOW

- descended from him
- passing pleasure
- nations of the earth
- became heir
- only-begotten son
- Divine Providence
- were reconciled
- types or figures of Christ

as exceptionally cruel and vengeful, had two wives, perhaps to suggest that polygamy, as we call it, was one of the results of mankind's deterioration due to sin. In any case, God tolerated (without condoning) polygamy, even under the law of Moses. One of the customs among the Semitic (sə-ʹmi-tik) peoples at this time provided that a wife who was unable to have children might give one of her slave girls to her husband as a secondary wife. The children born of this second marriage would be considered, by a kind of adoption, as the children of the first wife. When Sarah realized that she could not have a child except by a miracle, because of her advanced age, she told herself that God willed her to have an adopted son, and so she arranged for Abraham to marry her slave girl, Hagar. A son was born, and Abraham named him Ishmael (ʹish-mä-l).

Later on, when there was constant quarreling between Sarah and Hagar, it was thought best that Hagar and Ishmael should leave the household of Abraham and provide for themselves. This decision was a terrible blow to Hagar, who would have despaired had not God assured her by a revelation that this was His will and that He would provide for her and her child. The Bible then mentions that Ishmael became the father of an important Arabian tribe of nomads.

Abraham—a Man of Faith

When Abraham and Sarah were very old, God sent them a son, Isaac. They watched over the boy with the greatest care. They knew that all the hopes and the fulfillment of God's promises were centered in him. The father's joy knew no bounds; it was through this child that a great nation was to be born, and eventually through a descendant of his, all nations would call themselves blessed.

God sent Isaac, the only son of Abraham by Sarah, that he might lead our minds to Christ, the only-begotten son of the

Father. Abraham's great love for Isaac suggests God the Father's greater love for His Son, and indeed for all His faithful children. God is showing us here how greatly He loves us, the members of His Church, the Chosen People of the New Testament.

Abraham's Sacrifice Foreshadows God's Sacrifice of His Son

The Bible relates this story of Abraham's sacrifice of Isaac in the following manner.

The Lord, in His infinite wisdom, commanded Abraham to sacrifice his son Issac. In holy obedience, Abraham took his son Isaac and, with some servants, started out for Moria (mə-ʹrī-ə), which later tradition identified as the mountain or hill upon which the temple

Isaac and Jesus

One aspect of this story that often gets overlooked is that Isaac went willingly to where he would nearly be sacrificed. We might be tempted to think he fought his father, but we read that he carried the wood for the sacrifice up the hill. This is yet another parallel between Isaac and Jesus, since Jesus, too, carried the wood that would be used in his own sacrifice up Calvary.

was built in Jerusalem. Abraham and Isaac had traveled three days when they saw the mountain in the distance. Abraham said to his servant, "Stay here with the donkey, while the boy and I go there to worship; then we shall come back to you" (Gn 22:5).

Isaac carried the wood for the sacrifice, and walked with his father to the place appointed for the offering. Abraham carried the fire and a sword. Upon reaching the spot, he built an altar, laid the wood upon it, bound Isaac and placed him on the altar. Then he took the knife, ready to sacrifice his son. At that moment an angel of the Lord called to him, "Abraham, Abraham!" "Here I am," Abraham answered. The angel said, "Do not lay a hand on the boy; do nothing to him. I know now that you fear God, since you have not withheld your only son from me" (Gn 22:11–12).

Just before Abraham sacrificed Issac, an angel of the Lord appeared and stayed his hand.

Abraham looked up and saw a ram caught by the horns in the bushes nearby. He offered this instead of his son as a sacrifice to God.

God was testing Abraham; and, after he had so successfully passed the test, God rewarded him with these words of promise: "I will indeed bless you, and will surely multiply your descendants as the stars of the heavens, as the sands on the seashore. . . . In your descendants all the nations of the earth shall be blessed, because you have obeyed me" (Gn 22:17–18).

Can you now see the deep meaning behind this story of Abraham and Isaac? Can you see how God in His love was trying to prepare men's minds for the great sacrifice of the Redeemer when He arrived? Whom does Abraham represent? Isaac? What does the sacrifice itself prefigure? Is God's great love for all men shown in this story? What other parallels do you find? Should we not love God who loves us so much?

God has showered us with divine goodness and given us many gifts. Perhaps some day He will test us to see whether we love the gifts more than we love Him. It often happens that boys are called to become priests or brothers, and girls are called to the convent, but they will not give up the pleasures of the world and obey God's will as Abraham did. Frequently He asks parents to sacrifice many comforts in order to bring up their children as good Catholics. Are you strong enough to prove that you love God enough to do all He asks of you? Name some ways that God may test your love for Him. Name some practices which will build the habit of quick and joyful obedience to God.

Jacob Continues the Blessing of Isaac

Before he died, Abraham saw how God would carry out His promise. He secured for his son Isaac a wife; her name was Rebecca. She was brought to Canaan, and was married to Isaac in the tent of his mother. In this, as in all other things, God was taking care of Abraham's family, and preparing for the future.

Many years passed before Isaac and Rebecca had children. Then twins were born to them, two sons, whom they named Esau and Jacob. Esau, who was born first, grew up to be a large man, rough and hairy. He was a hunter and farmer. Jacob, the younger son, was more like his mother, gentle and quiet; he was her favorite. She had been told by God that the younger son would be the greater, and that the older son would serve the younger.

Esau's Act of Selling the Birthright

The eldest son of every Hebrew family possessed what was known as the birthright. The birthright had certain material advantages; for example, the eldest son had the right to a double portion of the inheritance. But over and above this material advantage was something that was considered far more precious. The first-born son had the duty of carrying on the family name and of assuming the obligations of head of the household. Through the eldest son the promise given to Abraham was to descend. As first-born, Esau was entitled to a double share of his father's property and to the special blessing which the patriarchs bestowed on their oldest sons.

Esau did not value the rights and privileges he had as the first-born son, but Jacob longed for them. One day Esau came home from the hunt so very hungry that he foolishly sold his birthright to Jacob for something to eat. Esau thus lost his precious birthright, and then took an oath to show he knew what he was doing in the sight of God. By this he proved that he was unworthy to receive the promise of God. He preferred his temporary want, his appetite at the moment, to the gifts of God.

To give Jacob undisputed claim to the legal headship of the family one thing was still needed, his father's special blessing. To show us how Rebecca arranged that her favorite son, Jacob, should receive this blessing, the biblical author tells us the following story.

Isaac had grown old, and his eyes were so dim that he could scarcely see. He called Esau to him and said, "You see I have grown old; I do not know when I may die. . . . Prepare for me some savory food such as I like; bring it to me to eat, so that I may bless you before I die" (Gn 27:2–4). Esau did not tell his father that he had sold his birthright to Jacob. Isaac asked Esau to hunt some game and cook it for him. Esau agreed to do this.

Rebecca overheard the conversation. She called Jacob to her and said:

> "I heard your father tell Esau, 'Bring me some game; prepare some savory food for me to eat, and then I will bless you in the sight of the Lord before I die.' Now my son, do what I tell you. Go to the flock and bring me two choice kids that I may make of them savory food such as your father likes. Then bring it to him that he may bless you before he dies" (Gn 27:6–10).

Jacob answered her, "But Esau my brother is a hairy man, while I am smooth. If my father touches me, it will seem to him that I am mocking him. Thus I shall bring a curse on myself instead of a blessing."

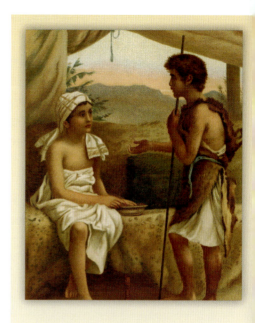

Esau's actions remind us of the sinner who foolishly sells his birthright to heaven for a short, sinful pleasure. How does this action of Esau symbolize the deeds of the Jewish people? How did they later forfeit their rights? In this way God permitted Jacob to become heir of the promise made to Abraham. God's favors and blessings would descend upon Jacob and his family. Upon them was placed the obligation of keeping before the minds of the people the hope of the Messiah.

"Let the curse fall on me, my son! Do but listen to me; go, get them for me," Rebecca replied (Gn 27:11–13).

Jacob went, selected the goats, and brought them to his mother, who prepared food such as his father liked. After this Rebecca took the best clothes of her elder son Esau, and put them on her younger son Jacob. She put skins of the kids on his hands and over the smooth part of his neck. Then taking the meat and some bread which she had baked, she gave it to Jacob to take to Isaac.

Jacob entered the room and said, "Father!"

Isaac answered, "Here I am. Who are you, my son?"

Jacob said, "I am Esau, your firstborn. I have done as you told me; sit up, please! Eat again of my game that you may bless me."

Isaac said, "Come close that I may touch you, my son, to know whether you are really my son Esau or not."

Jacob came near and his father touched him, for his eyesight was very poor. Then Isaac said, "The voice is the voice of Jacob, but the hands are the hands of Esau."

Isaac took the food which Jacob brought him and ate it. Then he turned toward Jacob and said "Come close and kiss me my son." Jacob came near and kissed him, and Isaac smelled the fragrant scent of his garments. And he blessed him and said:

"The fragrance of my son is like the fragrance of a field which the Lord has blessed! God give you dew from heaven, and fruitfulness of the earth, abundance of grain and wine. Let nations serve you, peoples bow down to you. Be master of your brothers; may your mother's sons bow down to you. Cursed be those who curse you, blessed be those who bless you."

Jacob had hardly left after receiving the blessing when Esau came into the room carrying the meat which he had prepared. He said, "Sit up, father, and eat of your son's game, that you may bless me."

Isaac said to him, "Who are you?"

He answered, "I am Esau, your firstborn son."

Isaac was amazed at these words. He said to Esau, "Who was it, then, that hunted game and brought it to me? Before you came I ate heartily and then blessed him; and he shall be blessed" (Gn 27:18–34).

When Esau heard this he became very angry, and planned to kill Jacob for having taken from him the blessing which he thought should be his. The ancient Hebrews, moreover, believed that a solemn blessing like this could never be withdrawn once it had been given, even if it had been obtained deceitfully. Esau, nevertheless, begged for another blessing for himself.

By permitting Jacob and his descendants to receive the birthright of Esau the firstborn, God was preparing men for that day when Christ's spiritual sons and daughters would take the place of the Chosen People of the Old Testament who did not appreciate their birthright and the privileges that went with it. Was He warning us also?

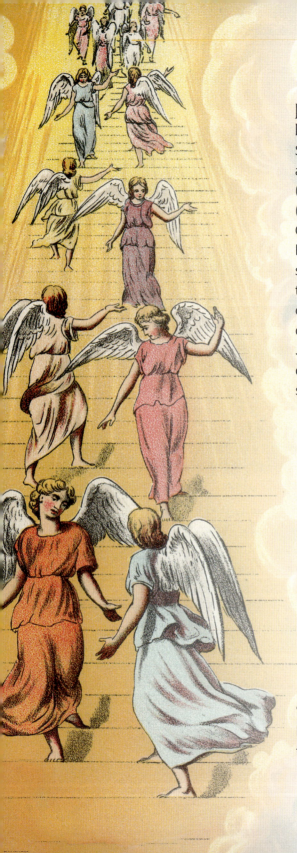

Jacob's Ladder—a Symbol of Divine Providence

Shortly after this, Jacob left Canaan and journeyed toward Haran ('ha-ran), both to visit his uncle Laban ('lā-bən) and to escape from Esau. One night while he was sleeping he had a vision in which he saw a ladder standing upon the earth, reaching to heaven. God was leaning on top of it. Angels were climbing up and down the ladder, presumably to take Jacob's prayers to God and to bring down to him God's blessings. God spoke these words to Jacob:

> "I am the Lord, the God of Abraham your father, and the God of Isaac. I will give you and your descendants the land on which you lie. They shall be as the dust of the earth. You shall spread abroad to the west, to the east, to the north, and to the south; and in you and in your descendants, all the nations of the earth shall be blessed" (Gn 28:13–14).

Jacob awoke and exclaimed: "Truly the Lord is in this place and I did not know it. How awesome is this place! This is none other than the house of God, and the Gate of heaven" (Gn 28:16–17). Jacob arose, took oil and poured it on the stone on which he had slept in order to consecrate it to God. He called the place Bethel ('beth-l), meaning "House of God."

In the New Testament, Jesus, the new Jacob, reminds us of Jacob's dream when He speaks of Himself joining heaven and earth, more wonderfully than angels moving constantly between Heaven and earth. He said: "Amen, amen, I say to you, you shall see the heavens opened, and the angels of God ascending and descending upon the Son of man" (Jn 1:51).

The Marriage of Jacob and Rachel

Jacob continued his journey until he met some shepherds. He asked them if they knew Laban. "We do," they answered. "Here comes his daughter Rachel with his flock" (Gn 29:6). Jacob went to her and greeted her, explaining that he was her cousin, the son of Rebecca. He helped her water the flocks, and then they went together to her father.

Laban was overjoyed when he heard that Jacob, his sister's son, had come to his home. He welcomed Jacob and asked what wages he wished for his services. Jacob answered, "I will serve you seven years for your younger daughter Rachel" (Gn 29:18). In ancient times the marriage contract included a "price" that the bridegroom was to pay for his bride. Since Jacob had as yet no possessions, he offered to work instead.

Laban answered, "It is better to give her to you than to another man; stay with me" (Gn 29:19). So Jacob served Laban for a number of years. But when he had earned enough to claim Rachel as his wife, Jacob found that the crafty Laban had changed his terms. First Jacob had to marry Rachel's elder sister, Leah, and only after working another period of years was he given Rachel. Meanwhile Jacob became wealthy and his family increased. After spending a number of years with Laban, he took his family and all his belongings and started on his return journey to Canaan.

Esau and Jacob Are Reconciled

On his way home Jacob sent messengers with gifts to Esau. They were directed to tell Esau that Jacob was returning from the household of Laban. The messengers returned saying, "We went to your brother Esau. He is coming to meet you with 400 men" (Gn 32:7).

Jacob was frightened and divided his people into two companies saying, "Should Esau come on one camp and attack it, the other will be saved" (Gn 32:9). He prayed very fervently for God's protection.

Jacob saw his brother coming in the distance, and running forward, ahead of his wives and children, he greeted him. Esau embraced Jacob and kissed him. He was no longer angry with him.

Esau was surprised and happy to meet the large family of his brother. Jacob said, "They are the children whom God has graciously given your servant" (Gn 33:5). After they had talked for a short time the brothers parted, each going his separate way. When he recalled God's promise, Jacob was filled with confidence that God would bring him back to the land of his fathers.

God Again Blesses Jacob

On Jacob's return to Canaan, the Bible relates how Jacob wrestled with Someone until daybreak. When the Stranger saw that he could not overcome Jacob, he said, "Let me go; it is dawn" (Gn 32:27).

Jacob answered, "I will not let you go till you bless me" (Gn 32:27).

Then the Stranger, who was God, blessed him and said, "You shall no longer be called Jacob, but Israel, because you have contended with God and men, and have triumphed" (Gn 32:29).

His name was changed when God renewed the promise He had given first to Abraham and then to Isaac. God chose Jacob, as He chose Abraham, to be the one through whom the nations of the earth would be blessed. The name Israel was understood by the people to mean "one who strives with God." This was to show that throughout his whole life Jacob and the people who descended from him would rely on God for the help which they would need. The Hebrews are often called Israelites, taking their name from Jacob (Israel) rather than from Abraham. Later they became known as Jews, that is, descendants of the tribe of Juda.

The Twelve Sons of Jacob (Israel)

Ruben, Simeon, Levi, Juda, Zabulon, Issachar, Dan, Gad, Aser, Nephthali, Joseph, and Benjamin

Jacob blessing
his twelve sons

Jacob's Twelve Sons

God blessed Jacob with twelve sons; and Jacob divided his titles and lands among them. They increased in power and their flocks were numerous. From Jacob and his twelve sons sprang the twelve tribes of the Chosen People of the Old Testament.

Jacob leads one's mind to Christ, and his twelve sons prefigure the Twelve Apostles who would be the spiritual fathers of the Chosen People of the New Testament. Thus mysteriously God was again signifying in advance what He would do to redeem the human race.

FOR ME TO REVIEW

Questions and Exercises

Part 1: Match column I with column II

Column I   **Column II**

A

1. Abraham	A. sons of Isaac
2. Sarah	B. God's Chosen People
3. Rebecca	C. House of God
4. Laban	D. father of many nations
5. Israel	E. father of Rachel
6. Esau and Jacob	F. one who strives with God
7. Bethel	G. Isaac's wife
8. Israelites	H. mother of Isaac

B

1. birthright	A. possessions
2. curse	B. a symbol of divine providence
3. titles and lands	C. to make friends again
4. reconcile	D. to wish evil to someone
5. an oath	E. inheritance of the eldest son
6. Jacob's ladder	F. calling on God to witness the truth of what we say

Part 2: Questions to Check Your Reading

1. Why is God's promise to Abraham important?
2. Who were the "Chosen People"?
3. In what ways did Abraham prove his great faith in God?
4. Describe the greatest test which God gave Abraham.
5. How is Isaac a type of Christ?
6. What did God promise Abraham for his obedience?
7. What were the names of Isaac's sons?
8. What were the privileges of the first-born son?
9. In what way is mortal sin like the selling of the birthright?
10. Describe Jacob's ladder.
11. What does Bethel mean?
12. Why do we call the Catholic Church the "Gate of Heaven"?
13. Explain how by these various persons and events God was preparing men's hearts and minds for Christ and His Church.

✓ FOR ME TO DO

1. Write a character sketch of Abraham: describe his faith, which made him a great leader of God's people.
2. Dramatize the scenes in which God made or repeated His Great Promise.
3. Play a question game, "How do I prefigure Christ or His Church?"
4. Imagine you are one of the faithful Jews longing for the coming of the Redeemer, and write a prayer begging God to send Him.

5. Cite incidents which show that Jacob practiced these virtues:

   a) gratitude to God

   b) brotherly love

   c) respect for parents

   d) obedience to God's commands

   e) confidence in prayer

   f) courage

   g) perseverance

6. Give some examples from the daily lives of boys and girls showing how they practice each of these virtues.

7. Discuss this statement: Everything in the Old Testament leads men's minds to Christ and His Church, proves God's love and care for us, and shows how we must love, obey, and serve God.

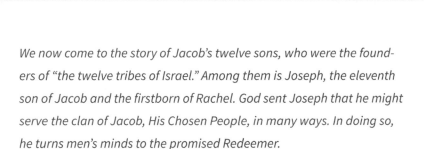

We now come to the story of Jacob's twelve sons, who were the founders of "the twelve tribes of Israel." Among them is Joseph, the eleventh son of Jacob and the firstborn of Rachel. God sent Joseph that he might serve the clan of Jacob, His Chosen People, in many ways. In doing so, he turns men's minds to the promised Redeemer.

Joseph was to hold an important position in Egypt, and thus direct the early history of Israel into an entirely new channel. The Egyptians bowed down before Joseph to acknowledge him as the official next in authority to the Pharaoh ('fer-ō), as the kings of ancient Egypt were called.

Joseph Is Sold by His Brothers

Joseph was Jacob's favorite son. He showed his preference for Joseph by giving him a beautiful long tunic or coat. This seemed to signify that Jacob regarded Joseph as a prince, which caused his brothers to be jealous of him. They also hated him because he reported their misdeeds to their father, and boasted of his dreams which foretold his future greatness.

One day Jacob sent Joseph to visit his brothers who were tending their flocks. He found them in Dothain ('dä-then) about twenty miles south of Nazareth. When they saw him coming, some of them wanted to kill him. But Ruben suggested instead that they should put him into a dry well to die of hunger and exposure. He secretly intended to rescue Joseph.

Ruben's suggestion was adopted. They stripped Joseph of his long coat and put him into the well. Later, when Ruben was away,

a caravan of Egyptian traders passed by. Juda, one of the brothers, proposed that they sell him as a slave to these merchants. They took Joseph from the well and traded him for "twenty pieces of silver."

Ruben was troubled when he returned and found the well empty. Jacob expected his oldest son to be responsible for the others. As a consequence, Ruben was afraid

TERMS TO KNOW

- Phutiphar
- Pharaoh
- Manasseh
- Ephraim
- Ruben
- Benjamin
- Egypt
- famine

to return home. When he told his brothers about his fear, they killed a kid and dipped Joseph's coat in its blood. Then they took the coat home and told their father that Joseph had been killed by wild beasts. Jacob recognized the coat and believed the story. He was filled with grief and could not be consoled. Meantime Joseph was taken to Egypt by the merchants and sold by them to Potiphar ('fu-ti-fər), a courtier of Pharaoh.

It was not long before Joseph won the confidence of his Egyptian master, becoming steward of his household. While Joseph was performing his duties of trust, Potiphar's wife became attracted to him, but he refused her attentions. This angered the sinful woman. She falsely accused Joseph to her husband, who had him put into prison.

The Imprisonment of Joseph

In prison Joseph gained the trust of the captain of the guard and was given charge of the other prisoners. Among these were the royal butler and the chief baker. Both of these officials had dreams which gave Joseph an opportunity to predict the future. The Egyptians took these dreams seriously and tried to make sense from them but without success. Joseph offered his services.

The butler told his dream to Joseph. He said, "In my dream there was a vine in front of me. Three branches were on the vine. It budded and blossomed, and its clusters ripened into grapes. Pharaoh's cup was in my hand and I took the grapes, squeezed them into his cup, and placed it in his hand" (Gn 40:10–11). Joseph explained that the three branches indicated three days at the end of which the king would restore his servant to his former office. Joseph requested that on his release the butler tell the king about his (Joseph's) own innocence so that he might also be released from prison.

After the baker heard Joseph explain the dream he said, "I, too, had a dream. I had three wicker baskets on my head. In the top basket was every kind of baked food for Pharaoh, but the birds were eating it out of the basket on my head" (Gn 40:16–17). Joseph explained that the three baskets also signified three days. After this Pharaoh would execute the baker and hang his body on a gibbet where the birds would eat his flesh.

Three days after Joseph had explained the dreams, Pharaoh held a great feast in honor of his birthday. He remembered the royal butler and gave him back his position. The chief baker, however, was hanged as Joseph had foretold. But the butler did not tell Pharaoh about Joseph.

Joseph Predicts the Future

About two years later, Pharaoh himself was disturbed by dreams. In one he saw seven fat cattle feeding on the banks of the Nile, while seven lean cattle came up from the river and devoured them. In another he saw a stalk of corn having seven full, ripe ears; then came seven thin, wasted ears which destroyed the good ones. The official interpreters of the court could make nothing of these dreams. Only then did the butler tell Pharaoh of Joseph and his interpretations of the dreams.

Joseph was brought to the king. At once he gave the meaning of these dreams to Pharaoh: there would be seven years of great abundance in Egypt, followed by seven years of severe famine. Joseph advised Pharaoh to provide for the coming famine by storing up the extra grain harvested during the seven abundant years so that it would be available during the seven years of scarcity.

Joseph as Governor

Pharaoh was pleased with Joseph. He saw that the young Hebrew had great wisdom. He appointed Joseph the chief officer in his kingdom, gave him the royal signet ring, a robe of pure silk and a gold chair as signs of his rank. He commanded the people to honor Joseph as governor of the country.

Egypt, over which he ruled, was located in the northeastern part of Africa, which included the valley of the Nile River. The people of Egypt depended then as now on the yearly overflow of the Nile to make the land productive. During a dry season they suffered so much that many died of starvation.

The Marriage of Joseph

Before the years of famine came, Joseph married the daughter of an Egyptian prince. Two sons were born of this marriage, the first was Manasseh (mə-ʹnas-se) and the second, Ephraim (ʹef-rä-ēm).

Joseph, Savior of His People During the Famine

During the fruitful years Joseph made preparations for the famine by storing the grain that was over and above what was needed. Then the lean years came. There was famine everywhere in the land. The people came to the king for food. Pharaoh told them simply, "Go to Joseph" (Gn 41:55). Joseph sold to the Egyptians the wheat which he had stored. Outsiders began to flock to Egypt to buy grain from Joseph, for the famine was felt elsewhere also.

Joseph was thirty years old when he was made ruler of Egypt. Pharaoh gave Joseph an Egyptian name. In ancient times a king might give a subject a new name to show that the subject belonged to him in a very special way.

Joseph Meets His Brothers

The famine was felt in Canaan, where Joseph's brothers heard that wheat could be obtained in Egypt. Accordingly, Jacob sent ten of his sons to Egypt to buy wheat. He kept only Benjamin, his youngest son, at home. The ten went to the governor of Egypt, but they did not recognize him as their brother whom they had sold into slavery twenty years earlier. On the other

God gives new names to His special servants throughout Scripture: Abram became Abraham, Saul became Paul, and Simon became Peter. Likewise, men and women are often given new names in the religious life. And even you might take on a "new name" in the sacrament of Confirmation.

hand, Joseph did recognize his brothers, but he acted as though he thought they were spies and he spoke harshly to them. The brothers protested their innocence. They were ten sons of twelve, they said, the youngest of whom was at home with his father and one was dead. Joseph had them put in prison for three days. Then he kept Simeon as a hostage in Egypt and sent the nine home. Simeon was to be released when the others returned with Benjamin. They were given the wheat they required and, without their knowledge, the money they paid for it was put back into their sacks with the wheat. They returned to Canaan and told their strange adventure to Jacob. He said that he would never allow Benjamin to go to Egypt.

Joseph Welcomes His Brother Benjamin

In time, however, famine and want forced Jacob to change his mind. He sent his sons to Egypt again. This time Benjamin went along, for they dared not go without him. When Joseph saw his brothers, he ordered a feast to be prepared and invited them to share it. This made them afraid and suspicious, especially since they had no explanation of the money which they had found in their sacks. Therefore, they went first to Joseph's steward and explained how they had found the money with the grain. He assured them and brought Simeon out of prison to join them. Next, they offered presents to Joseph. He accepted them and inquired about Jacob, their father. When he saw Benjamin, his full brother, he could not keep back his tears.

After the feast Joseph commanded the steward of the house to fill his brothers' sacks with grain and put the money of everyone back into his sack. In the top of the youngest boy's sack he ordered his own silver cup to be placed. This was done as Joseph commanded. The brothers arose in the morning and departed, not knowing what was in their sacks.

Joseph and Jesus

Does the story of Joseph remind you of the story of Jesus? Consider these parallels:

- Just as Joseph was the favored son of Jacob, Jesus was God's beloved son.
- Just as Joseph's brothers turned on him, Jesus was betrayed and abandoned by his closest friends; in fact, both were sold for a handful of silver.
- Joseph was stripped of his coat just as Jesus was stripped of his garments before the Crucifixion.
- Joseph was thrown into a pit in the earth, and Jesus was placed in a tomb after he died.
- Just as Joseph would one day save his people with the food he stored up during the famine, Jesus, too, saves us by offering us his body to eat.
- Joseph forgave his brother for their treachery, and Jesus forgave his tormenters from the cross, saying, "Father, forgive them, they know not what they do."

There are even more similarities between Joseph and Jesus than we have listed here. So in all of these ways and more, Joseph is a type, or foreshadowing, of Jesus.

The Finding of the Silver Cup

Joseph sent his servant and said, "Go, follow the men, and when you overtake them, say to them, 'Why have you returned evil for good? Why have you stolen the silver cup from me? It is the very one from which my master drinks. He will certainly guess where it is. This is an evil thing that you have done'" (Gn 44:4–5). The servant did as Joseph directed him. The brothers were so sure of their innocence that they put their sacks on the ground and opened them. The servant searched them and found the cup in Benjamin's sack.

The brothers returned to Joseph, and Juda spoke for the others, "We are indeed the slaves of my lord, both we and the one with whom the cup was found" (Gn 44:16).

Joseph answered, "Far be it from me to act thus. The one with whom the cup was found shall be my slave; as for the rest, go in peace to your father." Juda went nearer to Joseph and humbly pleaded to be taken in Benjamin's place. He told Joseph that the loss of Benjamin would surely cause his father's death.

Joseph Makes Himself Known

Joseph could no longer conceal his identity from his brothers. He commanded the Egyptians to go out of the room so that no stranger would be present. Then he said, "I am Joseph. Is my father still alive?" His brothers could scarcely believe him, and they were frightened. He spoke to them and said, "I am your brother, Joseph, whom you sold into Egypt. Do not be distressed nor angry with yourselves that you sold me here, for God sent me before you to save life. For two years now the famine has been in the land, and for five more years there will be neither plowing nor reaping. God sent me before you to preserve a remnant for you in the land, and to deliver you . . ." (Gn 45:3; 4–7). He told them to go and get their father and bring him to Egypt. Joseph gave them wagons and provisions and they started on their journey.

The Meeting of Father and Son

When Jacob heard from his sons that Joseph was alive, he was overcome with joy. He could scarcely believe that Joseph was governor of all Egypt. But when he saw the chariots and the gifts of the king, he said, "It is enough . . . my son Joseph is still alive; I will go and see him before I die" (Gn 45:28).

Jacob took his sons and their wives and their children and went to Egypt. Joseph hastened to meet his father. They embraced and wept for joy. Jacob said, "Now I can die, after seeing you still alive" (Gn 46:30).

Joseph took his father and brethren to Pharaoh, who welcomed them into the land and gave them property and possessions in Gesen ('ge-sin). Thus did the Israelites come to Egypt. They lived happily there for seventeen years. Then Jacob became ill, and he knew that he had not long to live. He sent for his sons that he might bless them before he died.

The Prophecies of Jacob

Jacob told each of his sons what share he would have in the promise of God.

Juda was to have the most important part in the carrying out of God's promise. "Juda, your brothers shall praise you; your hands shall be on the neck of your enemies; the sons of your father shall bow down to you. . . . The sceptre shall not depart from Juda, nor the staff from between his feet, until he comes to whom it belongs. To him shall be the obedience of nations" (Gn 49:8–10). This means that the scepter or the one who ruled would never depart from Juda. With Christ's coming it was made permanent.

Jacob also said to Joseph, "By the God of your father, may he help you; by the God, the Omnipotent, may he bless you, with the blessings of the skies above. . . . The blessings of your father surpass the blessings of my forebears to the limit of the timeless hills. May they rest on the head of Joseph, and on the brow of the prince among his brothers" (Gn 49:25–26).

The Death of Jacob and Joseph

Jacob thus blessed each one of his sons, and then he asked them to bury him in the land of Canaan. Joseph mourned the death of his father even more than the others did. He had Jacob's body mummified after the manner of the Egyptians. All of Egypt mourned for seventy days. Then Joseph and his brothers took their father's body back to Canaan and buried it there.

Joseph lived in Egypt for many years after this. When the time came for him to die, he called his brothers to him. He told them that they would some day return to the land of their father, asking them to take his body along when they left Egypt.

Thus God watched over his people and again renewed His promise of a Redeemer. From the Jews, that is, from the tribe of Juda, the Messiah was to be born.

Have you noticed that the Chosen People have been called by various names? Have you realized the distinction between these names? They are Semites, descendants of Shem; they are Hebrews, descendants of those who came out of Chaldea (Abraham); they are Israelites, descendants of Jacob (Israel); and finally, when practically the tribe of Juda alone remained, they are called Jews—members of the tribe of Juda.

God made known through Jacob that the Messiah was to be a king whose kingdom would include men of all nations. He was not only to be a victim, as Isaac was, but also a Savior of his people, as was Joseph.

Have you noticed the many ways in which God, in His great love for man, was preparing men's minds and hearts for the future Redeemer of the world by the events of the life of Joseph? In His infinite wisdom and knowledge He planned the events or permitted them to happen in such a way that they were a blessing not only to the people involved, but also to the future generations of the Old and of the New Testament.

Joseph, who was innocent, was hated by his brothers who sold him into slavery, even as Christ the innocent Lamb would be hated and given over to suffering and death by us, His sinful brethren. Joseph returned good for evil when he fed his brothers, and saved God's Chosen People of the Old Testament. Christ, too, would in the centuries to come deliver His Church of the New Testament from the slavery of sin and Satan, and would save His people with the gift of Himself in the Holy Eucharist.

Since the time of Christ other "Josephs" of the New Testament have given good example to their envious brothers; for example, the martyrs of the Church have been ill-treated, and have handed themselves over to their enemies to be persecuted; they prayed for and helped their persecutors. Do we not need great men and women today who will cast the shadow of Christ on the earth in the afternoon sun of the New Testament as Joseph cast the shadow in the morning sun of the Old Testament?

FOR ME TO REVIEW

Questions and Exercises

Part 1: Arrange these events in order

a) meets his brothers in Egypt

b) was sold into slavery

c) was hated by his brothers

d) interprets Pharaoh's dream

e) his father's grief

f) in the house of Potiphar

g) Benjamin and the silver cup

h) reveals himself to his brothers

i) his father settles in Gesen

j) saves the state from famine

k) governor of Egypt

l) in prison

m) interprets the dreams of the butler and the baker

Part 2: Matching

Match the following names given to the Chosen People with the person from whom they were derived, or with whom they are related. Then rearrange the columns so that the persons and names are in chronological order

Column I

1. Hebrew

2. Jew

3. Semite

4. Israelite

Column II

A. Juda

B. Abraham

C. Jacob or Israel

D. Shem

Part 3: Questions to Check Your Reading

1. Who were Joseph's father and mother?

2. Why were Joseph's brothers jealous of him?

3. Describe the conduct of Ruben.

4. What means did Joseph's brothers use to get rid of him?

5. How did they deceive their father?

6. Who was Potiphar?

7. Why was Joseph put into prison?

8. How did Joseph interpret the butler's and the baker's dream?

9. How did Joseph interpret Pharaoh's dream?

10. What was Pharaoh's conduct toward Joseph?

11. To whom was Joseph married?

12. How did Joseph prepare for the lean years?

13. How did Joseph return good for evil?

14. Relate the story of how Joseph met his brothers again.

15. To what part of Egypt did Joseph invite his father and family to come to live?

16. Was Pharaoh pleased with Joseph's invitation to his father?

17. In what way does Joseph, a prototype, lead men's minds to our divine Savior?

18. When Jacob was reunited with Joseph, he said, "Now I can die after seeing you still alive." Do you recall who it was who spoke similar words to those in the temple of Jerusalem many years after this?

19. Which of Jacob's sons was to have the most important part in the carrying out of God's promise?

 **FOR ME TO DO**

1. Draw a map and label the following: Dothain, Egypt, Canaan, Nile River.

2. Write a dramatization of the story of Joseph for a television performance. Use a double stage showing Christ and His Church fulfilling what Joseph foreshadowed.

3. Prepare for your notebook an explanation of the following:

   a) How the history of Joseph proves that God takes care of us.
   b) The prophecy which Jacob made on his deathbed.
   c) In what ways Joseph was a figure of our Savior.

4. Parallel the life and deeds of Joseph with the life and deeds of Christ.

5. Make a list of the sins of jealousy which boys and girls of your age commit. Discuss ways of avoiding these sins.

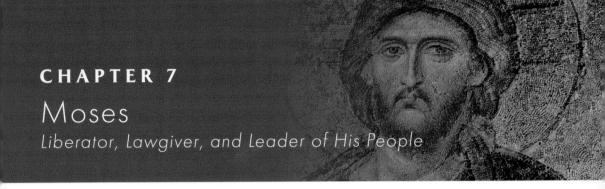

God Sends Moses to Free the Israelites

The Pharaoh in the time of Joseph belonged to the Hyksos ('hik-sos) or "Shepherd Kings." The Hyksos were people from Asia who had invaded and conquered Lower Egypt, that is, the part near the delta, in the eighteenth and seventeenth centuries B.C. Upper Egypt, that is, the part near the source of the Nile, was governed by Egyptian princes, who finally succeeded in driving out the "Shepherd Kings" and uniting Upper and Lower Egypt under the rule of the Egyptian kings. When the Hyksos were driven out by the native kings, the lot of the Hebrews in Egypt became sad and hard. They had lived peacefully in Lower Egypt under the Hyksos kings. Joseph, a foreigner in Egypt, had been given his position of power by a Hyksos Pharaoh, himself a foreigner.

By the time Joseph died, and for a while afterward, the number of Israelites had increased greatly. Then a new king, an Egyptian who had not known Joseph, ascended the throne. Fearing that the Israelites would become too powerful, he laid burdens on them in many ways, and finally reduced them to slave labor. They were no longer permitted to hold positions of trust and honor as they once had been under the Hyksos. If God had not watched over His people, their ruin would have been simply a question of time. Divine Providence, however, again manifested itself. God raised up a leader, Moses, out of the tribe of Levi. He was destined to free the Israelites from the slavery of Egypt, and to lead them to the Promised Land.

In the next few chapters we shall see how God guided and protected the Chosen People of the Old Testament, even as He

guides and protects His Chosen People of the New Testament if they remain faithful to Him. We shall learn how Moses led the Israelites for forty years. During this whole period his virtues were tested and exercised by many trials and hardships. As the story unfolds, we shall see how in many ways this journey is an image of our life "in this valley of tears," where God tests us by allowing us to be tempted while giving us help along our way.

Moses Is Saved From the Nile

Shortly before Moses was born the Pharaoh had ordered the drowning of every boy born to the Israelites. Moses' mother succeeded in hiding him for three months. When she found she could no longer keep his birth a secret, she placed the infant in a basket of bulrushes and put the basket into the water near the edge of the river Nile. She told the baby's sister Mariam to watch at a short distance so that she could see what happened to the child.

Soon after, Pharaoh's daughter came to bathe at the same spot. Seeing the

Moses was to be the deliverer of his people. In this he clearly resembles Christ, the Savior of His people. The Church discovered this, and so uses Moses as a figure of Christ. He was miraculously preserved from an edict of Pharaoh, as later, in the plan of God, Christ as a Child was to be saved from the edict of Herod during the slaughter of the innocents.

basket, she ordered one of her maids to bring it to her. On opening it and seeing the child she said, "It is one of the Hebrews' children" (Ex 2:6). She decided to rear it as her son. Mariam now approached the princess. She asked if she should call a Hebrew woman to take care of it. When told she could, she brought her own mother as nurse for her baby brother. Thus God saw to it that Moses was reared by his own mother. When he was old enough, he was brought to the princess, who treated him as her own son. She called him Moses, an Egyptian word meaning "son," which in Hebrew sounds like the word for "drawn from the water."

Moses Leaves Egypt

Even though Moses had been raised an Egyptian, he did not disregard the sufferings to which his own people were subjected. On one occasion, while visiting in Gesen, he saw an Egyptian beating one of the Hebrews. As no one was near, Moses struck the Egyptian and killed him. When he found out that Pharaoh had learned of his deed and sought his life, he determined to leave at once. He fled to Madian, a country in Arabia, south of Palestine.

Moses lived as a shepherd in Madian for a number of years. He married Sepphora ('zep-fō-rə), a daughter of Jethro ('jeth-rō), also called Raguel, the man whose flocks he tended.

During Moses' stay in Madian, the Pharaoh from whom he had fled died. The new king did nothing to relieve the sufferings of the Israelites. In their trouble the Israelites called upon God, who as always heard their prayers and remembered the covenant He had made with Abraham, Isaac, and Jacob.

The Burning Bush

One day Moses drove the flocks of his father-in-law to a place referred to in the Old Testament as Mt. Horeb ('hōr-eb) or Mt. Sinai ('sī-nī). God appeared to Moses under the appearance of a flame of fire in the midst of a bush. He said:

> "I am the God of your father, the God of Abraham, the God of Isaac, the God of Jacob. . . . I have witnessed the affliction of my people in Egypt and have heard their cry of complaint against their slave drivers, so I know well what they are suffering. Therefore I have come down to rescue them from the hands of the Egyptians and lead them out of that land into a good and spacious land, a land flowing with milk and honey. . . . I will send you to Pharaoh to lead my people, the Israelites, out of Egypt" (Ex 3:6–8).

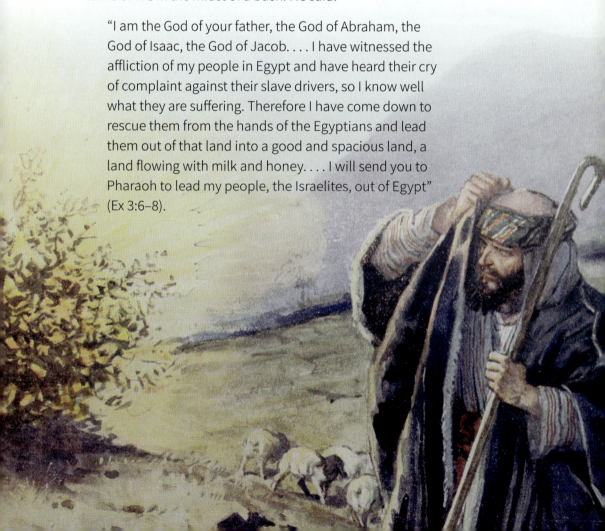

Understanding the Name "I AM"

When we read that God replied to Moses by saying His name was "I am who am," it can be a little confusing. What exactly does this mean? To understand this, just remember that God Himself is pure existence. You exist because God gave you existence, so you say, "I am (your name)". But God's existence does not depend on anything else, so He is just "I AM." Everything depends on Him for its existence, but He depends on no one for His own. If it's still a difficult thing to get your mind around, don't worry, because trying to understand the deep mysteries of God is difficult even for brilliant theologians!

"I will be with you . . . ," God assured Moses, when he tried to make objections. When Moses asked God to tell him who He was, God replied, "I am who am . . . say to the Israelites; the Lord (Yahweh), the God of your fathers, the God of Abraham, the God of Isaac, the God of Jacob, has sent me to you" (Ex 3:14–15). Thus God revealed Himself to Moses under the title of Yahweh, which in Hebrew sounds like the word for "He is," or "He causes to be." The Hebrews understood this name to mean that their God really exists. In this He showed Himself unlike the false gods of the heathens.

Later the Hebrews developed so great a fear of violating the Second Commandment that they used the title "Lord" (Adonai) (ä-dō-nä-ē) when they came across the name "Yahweh" in the sacred text. That is how "Lord" came into use as a name for God.

Moses Returns to Egypt

Moses began his great work of freeing the Israelites. He always carried in his hand "the rod of God" with which he was to work signs and wonders. Aaron, his brother and spokesman, went with him. The two gathered together the Israelites and made known to them the mission they had received from God. They proved this by working signs and wonders before all the people.

Then Moses and Aaron presented themselves before the Pharaoh and asked permission for the Hebrews to go into the desert to offer sacrifice. The king refused their request. At God's command, ten successive scourges, known as the Plagues, came upon Egypt. They are as follows:

The Ten Plagues of Egypt

First Plague—The waters of the Nile turned to blood.

Second Plague—Frogs came forth from the waters, covered the land, and even entered the houses.

Third Plague—Swarms of gnats bothered man and beast.

Fourth Plague—A pestilence of flies annoyed the people.

Fifth Plague—A cattle disease killed the beasts of the Egyptians but spared those of the Israelites.

Sixth Plague—Boils broke out on men and beasts.

Seventh Plague—A terrible hailstorm destroyed their crops.

Eighth Plague—Locusts devoured what the hailstorm had left.

Ninth Plague—A horrible darkness covered all Egypt except the land of Gesen, the dwelling place of the Israelites.

Tenth Plague—An angel killed the first born of man and beast.

During the first plague the Pharaoh begged Moses and Aaron to ask God to stop it. He agreed to let the Israelites go into the desert to offer sacrifices. However, no sooner had the plague ended than he went back on his word and was as cruel as before. In the same way after each of the next eight plagues Pharaoh agreed, went back on his word, and was punished by the succeeding plague. Finally God sent the terrible tenth plague.

The Paschal Lamb, a Figure of Christ, the Lamb of God

The tenth plague was the killing of the firstborn; it was the most terrible of all. Before sending this last proof of His justice, God commanded Moses and Aaron to assemble the Israelites and to order each family to prepare a lamb without blemish. These families were to sacrifice it on the fourteenth day of the month, sprinkle their doorposts with its blood, and then roast the lamb and eat it with unleavened bread and wild lettuce. They were to eat it standing, clothed for a journey.

This was not an unusual command, for as shepherds these people were accustomed to sacrifice a lamb each spring to obtain good flocks and to ward off evil spirits. Here, however, the usual practice of offering the lamb takes on a new meaning.

The Paschal Lamb is one of the best known figures of Christ, the Lamb of God, who was sacrificed to free God's Chosen People. In how many ways does the Paschal Lamb give us a better understanding of Christ, our Paschal Lamb?

Since no leavened bread was used during the week of the Pasch, our Savior used unleavened bread when He instituted the Eucharist at the Passover meal. That is why unleavened bread is used at Mass. It should remind us that the Eucharist is the fulfillment of the Paschal sacrifice which God instituted to prepare for this most wonderful of all sacraments.

By this sacrifice of the Paschal Lamb and by the delivery of the Israelites who offered and ate it, God prepared the way for the coming of that other Lamb who would be sacrificed to free His people from the slavery of sin and would lead them to the Promised Land.

The Death of the Firstborn

At midnight after the fourteenth day, the angel of death passed through the land of Egypt and killed the firstborn in every house, even in the palace of Pharaoh, because the doorposts were not sprinkled with the blood of the lamb.

The king was deeply shaken by the death of his eldest son, and was struck with fear by the punishment which God had dealt to every Egyptian family. He begged Moses and Aaron to see to it that the Israelites would depart immediately. This they gladly did.

The March to the Red Sea

The Chosen People set off for the Red Sea. On modern maps the Red Sea is a large body of water lying between Egypt and Arabia. It has two arms to the north, the one on the east today is called the Gulf of Akabah ('äk-ə-bä) and the one on the west the Gulf of Suez.

At the time when the Israelites left Egypt, the northern end of the western arm of the Red Sea (the Gulf of Suez) extended as far north as the Bitter Lakes. It is now commonly held that the crossing of the sea took place either north or south of the Bitter Lakes.

The Bible story tells us that the Lord went before His Chosen People by day in a Pillar of Cloud, and by night in a Pillar of Fire. He did this in order to show them the way through the dangerous lands.

In thus protecting the Israelites God wished to teach us that Christ and the Holy Spirit would lead the Christians through the shadow of sin to the light of grace. The Holy Spirit, in the person of the Church's leaders, continues to guide His flock safely through many dangers to the real Promised Land, our heavenly home.

Pharaoh Follows the Israelites

Pharaoh soon regretted that he had let his cheap labor supply go. Hearing, after three days, that they were still near the Red Sea, and thinking that they would be cut off from all escape, he gathered his army together and set out in pursuit of them. When the Israelites saw the Egyptians coming behind them, they were frightened and called upon the Lord for help. Moses calmed them saying, "Fear not! Stand your ground, and you will see the victory the Lord will win for you today. These Egyptians whom you see today you will never see again. The Lord himself will fight for you; you have only to keep still" (Ex 14:13–14).

The Red Sea Triumph

The angel of the Lord who had gone before the Israelites in the Pillar of Cloud now passed to the rear and kept the Egyptians from coming closer to them. To the Egyptians this Pillar was a dark cloud, but it illumined the night for the Israelites.

Almighty God then told Moses to lift up his rod, and stretch forth his hand over the sea and divide it, that the Israelites might cross it on dry ground. He obeyed and the waters opened. The Israelites passed over to the other side in safety.

The Egyptians followed them into what proved to be a fatal trap. God said to Moses, "Stretch out your hand over the sea, that the waters may flow back upon the Egyptians, upon their chariots and their charioteers" (Ex 14:26). He obeyed, and the waters swept back to their former place so quickly that the Egyptians were swallowed by the waves. In this way the Lord delivered Israel from the Egyptians, showing how He can and will always protect those who love and obey Him.

The Miracle at the Fountain of Mara

After their miraculous escape the Jews traveled from the Red Sea to Mount Sinai. During the journey they were to suffer many hardships. However, God did not forsake His Chosen People, and through Moses He worked several miracles to strengthen their faith and lessen their sufferings.

After crossing the Red Sea the Israelites marched for three days through the desert. They were unable to find any water. Finally, they came to a fountain; its waters, however, were so bitter that they could not be taken, and thus the Hebrews call it *Mara*, a Hebrew word for bitter. Then God told Moses to throw a piece of wood into the fountain and at once the bitter waters became sweet.

God Sends Quail and Manna

When the supplies which the Israelites had brought from Egypt began to fail, they started to complain against Moses for having led them to this desert place. In Egypt they had plenty; here they knew only hunger, thirst, blazing heat, numbing cold, danger, and hardship. Moses prayed, and God listened to his prayer. He sent quail to provide food for them. The people killed all they needed.

The next morning He continued to look out for their needs. A wonderful food fell from heaven. Everyone cried, "Manna," "what is it?" Thus we have the word *manna*. It was a miraculous food which fell during the night and in the early morning covered the ground around the Israelite camp. The manna was a small, white, crisp substance which tasted like wheaten bread mixed with honey. Though it could be eaten just as it fell from heaven, it could also be fixed in different ways to suit every taste. By telling the story of the quail and manna the author pointed out that God was watching over His Chosen People. His care provided sufficient food when it was accepted.

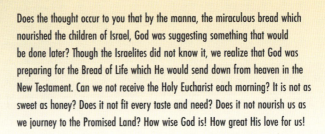

Does the thought occur to you that by the manna, the miraculous bread which nourished the children of Israel, God was suggesting something that would be done later? Though the Israelites did not know it, we realize that God was preparing for the Bread of Life which He would send down from heaven in the New Testament. Can we not receive the Holy Eucharist each morning? It is not as sweet as honey? Does it not fit every taste and need? Does it not nourish us as we journey to the Promised Land? How wise God is! How great His love for us!

The Waters of Horeb

The Israelites continued their journey through the desert until they arrived at a place called Raphidim ('räf-i-dēm). Here again they found no water, and again they complained against Moses. By God's orders, Moses struck the rock of Horeb with his rod, and immediately water gushed forth.

This rock from which the waters flowed when struck with the rod of Moses points to the Rock and Foundation Stone of the New Testament, Christ, who said, "He, however, who drinks of the water that I will give him shall never thirst; but the water that I will give him shall become in him a fountain of water springing up into life everlasting" (Jn 4:13–14). These waters are likened to divine grace. This grace flows to the children of God through the sacraments of Christ's Church.

Try to see the many ways in which the forty years spent in the desert by the Chosen People of the Old Testament, with water and food (manna) from God, lead our minds to our sojourn on earth. After being freed from the slavery of sin by passing through the waters of Baptism, we are fed by the Eucharist until we also reach the Promised Land (heaven).

The Battle With the Amalecites

At Raphidim the Israelites fought their first battle. It was against the Amalecites (ä-'mäl-ək-ītz), a people whom Hebrew tradition connected with the eldest son of Esau. Moses knew that the battle could not be won by the ordinary means of warfare alone. His people had been too long in slavery and had lost the courage and spirit necessary for success in battle.

Joshua was placed in command of a group of the most courageous Israelites. With his small band he marched against the enemy. Holding the rod of God in his hands, Moses climbed a nearby hill, accompanied by Aaron and another companion. From there he watched the course of the battle. Moses extended his hands and prayed for success in the battle. As long as his hands remained outstretched, Israel was successful. As soon as he let them down even a little, the Amalecites gained ground. When his hands grew weary, his two companions held them up. At sunset the Israelites returned to their camp victorious.

As Moses with outstretched arms prayed on the mount for the salvation of his people, he foreshadowed Christ who, at a later date, was to pray with outstretched arms on the cross for the salvation of all nations. Thus he reminds us that we by our prayers and good works should hold up the arms of Christ in His bishops and priests as they pray and work for the success of Christ's Kingdom.

Can you see how this incident gives us a fine example of prayer? Moses used every human means to insure success, but he added to his efforts the force of holy prayers.

This should impress upon our minds the all-important fact that we can do nothing of ourselves, but that we can do all things with the help of almighty God, especially if we persevere in prayer despite weariness and discouragement.

 ## FOR ME TO REVIEW

Questions and Exercises

Part 1: Complete these statements

1. _____ was to be sacrificed on the fourteenth day of the month.

2. _____ illumined the night for the Israelites.

3. _____ was God's title, which sounded like the Hebrew word for "He is," or "He causes to be."

4. _____ were scourges or misfortunes.

5. _____ was told to lead the Israelites out of Egypt.

6. _____ were defeated by the Israelites.

7. _____ was the spokesman for Moses.

8. _____ prefigured the Holy Eucharist.

9. _____ prefigured heaven.

10. _____ a Hebrew word for bitter.

Part 2: Questions to Check Your Reading

1. How was Moses saved from the edict of Pharaoh?

2. What mission did God give Moses?

3. Why did God send the plagues to Egypt?

4. How did Pharaoh oppress the Israelites?

5. How did God help the Israelites cross the Red Sea?

6. Name several great miracles worked by God for the Israelites on their journey from the Red Sea to Mount Sinai.

7. Why did God send manna from heaven?

FOR ME TO DO

1. Read from the Bible an account of one of the ten plagues and report on it to your class (Ex 7–12).

2. Explain the following Old Testament types in relationship to their fulfillment in the New Testament:
   a) the Paschal Lamb
   b) the passage through the Red Sea
   c) the manna
   d) the Israelites' forty years in the desert

3. Name some instances showing Moses' confidence in God.

4. Make a map to show the route of the Israelites from Egypt to the Promised Land. Retell the story for your classmates.

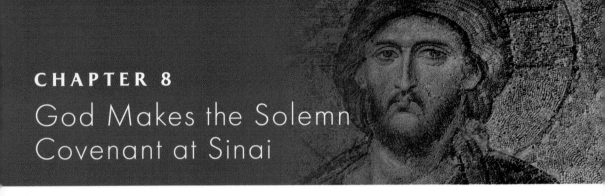

CHAPTER 8
God Makes the Solemn Covenant at Sinai

God Promises Protection to His Priestly Kingdom

Having journeyed for almost three months, the Israelites finally reached the wilderness in the southern end of the Sinai Peninsula. Near the foot of the highest peak of Sinai, they pitched their tents. Here God made a solemn covenant with the Israelites, confirming them as His Chosen People. He called Moses and said:

> "You have seen for yourselves how I treated the Egyptians and how I bore you up on eagle wings and brought you here to myself. Therefore, if you hearken to my voice and keep my covenant, you shall be my special possession, dearer to me than all other people, though all the earth is mine. You shall be to me a kingdom of priests, a holy nation" (Ex 19:4–6).

The people all answered, "Everything the Lord has said, we will do" (Ex 19:8).

God Makes Moses His Lawgiver

God continued to speak to Moses saying, "I am coming to you in a dense cloud, so that when the people hear me speaking with you, they may always have faith in you also . . ." (Ex 19:9). For two days the people prepared themselves. At dawn of the third day a solemn scene unfolded. From a thick cloud that covered the top of Mt. Sinai, lightning flashed, thunder pealed, and trumpets re-echoed so that all in the camp were filled with fear.

Then Moses was ordered to climb to the top of Mt. Sinai. There, out of the midst of a fire, the Lord spoke these words: "I, the Lord, am your God, who brought you out of the land of Egypt, that place of slavery. You shall not have other gods besides me" (Ex 20:2). God continued and gave the Ten Commandments to Moses. At the foot of the mountain the people stood trembling in fear. After Moses returned he told them that God wanted them to know that He was their God. They were to be bound to Him by a Solemn Covenant, and were to observe the Laws He would give them.

On this occasion God made Moses the Lawgiver of the Old Covenant. He thus foreshadowed the Lawgiver of the New Covenant, Christ, who summed up the Law into the two commandments of the love of God and love of neighbor.

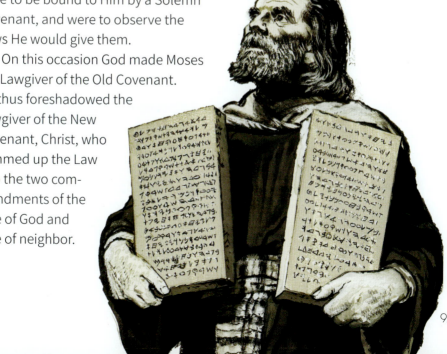

97

God Gives Laws Governing Sacrifices and Duties

The Bible gives the impression that God, in revealing the Ten Commandments, did so more directly to the people than with regard to the other instructions which He gave. In these latter, it is emphasized that He spoke through His go-between, Moses. After giving the Israelites the Ten Commandments, God spoke to them no more in His own person but in the person of Moses, His Law-giver, through whom He would make known His further precepts. While the people stood afar off, Moses was again called up to the mountain. God gave him other laws regarding divine worship and the civic or social duties of His people.

After he had received God's message, Moses went down and repeated it to the people. Hearing it they all cried out again, "We will do everything that the Lord has told us" (Ex 24:3). Moses then wrote the precepts in the Book of the Covenant. He also set up an altar, surrounded by twelve pillars representing the twelve tribes of Israel. The blood of the animals offered in sacrifice Moses poured on the altar—which symbolized God—on the Book, and on the people, calling solemnly: "This is the blood of the covenant which the Lord has made with you" (Ex 24:8). Thus the Hebrews became "blood relatives" of God. This pouring of the blood of the victim was a sign of their solemn agreement with God, just as the New Covenant was to be sealed with the Blood of Christ, our Victim, on the cross. This meaning would be made clear once Christ had died.

Moses led and preserved his people. In this he was like Christ, who established an Eternal Covenant with His Church through the twelve Apostles. When our Lord inaugurated this New Covenant at the Last Supper as He instituted the Eucharist and the Sacrifice of the Mass, He used almost the same words that Moses used in the ceremony at Mt. Sinai: "This is my blood of the New Covenant" (Mt 26:27). The Twelve Pillars would later on be applied to these same Apostles because they were to be set up as Pillars of His Church.

The Lord Gives the Ten Commandments

After this, Moses was again commanded by God to return to the mountain. This time he was accompanied by some of the elders of Israel. For six days they remained close to the Lord and worshiped Him. On the seventh day, after directing the others to go down and govern the people, Moses entered into the midst of the Cloud covering the mountain. He remained there forty days and forty nights, speaking with God. While in the Cloud, he received instructions concerning the rites to be observed in divine worship and the plans for constructing the Tabernacle. The Lord also gave Moses two stone tablets which contained the Ten Laws.

God Punishes the Israelites for False Worship

While Moses spoke with God upon the mountain, the impatient people forgot their solemn promise. They remembered that the Egyptians had images to worship. Doubting whether Moses would come down, the Israelites demanded that Aaron make images for them to worship in defiance of what God had commanded.

While Moses received the Ten Commandments, the Israelites became impatient and set up a golden calf to worship.

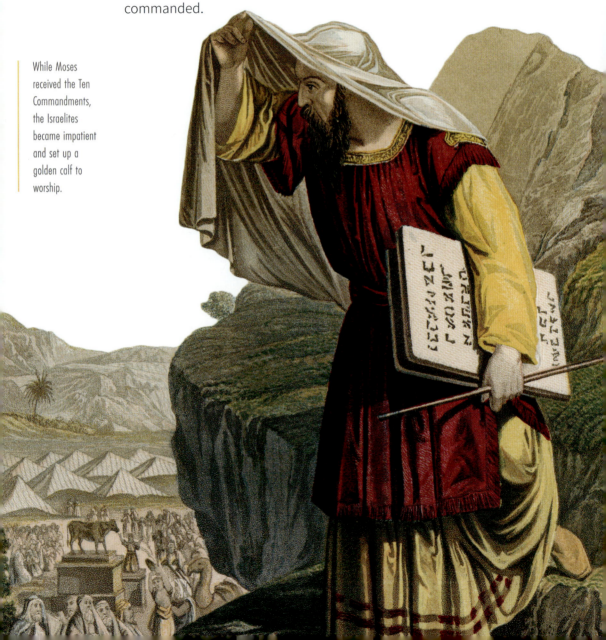

Aaron knew that it was wrong to make such a statue, but he gave in to their demands. He gathered the gold and fashioned a molten calf, probably a symbol of Yahweh's power, which the Israelites worshiped with burnt offerings. While they were dancing about the calf, Moses appeared, carrying the tablets of stone. Seeing what they were doing, he threw the tablets to the ground. After reproaching Aaron, Moses burned the golden calf and beat it to powder. Then he scattered it on the waters of a stream flowing down from Mt. Sinai, forcing the sinful Israelites to drink therefrom. This seems to have led to a rebellion against Moses.

Moses cried out with a loud voice, "Whoever is for the Lord, let him come to me!" (Ex 32:26.) The members of the tribe of Levi gathered around Moses. He ordered them to kill those who still desired unlawful worship of Yahweh. Many were killed while the rest repented and were forgiven. They obtained this forgiveness only through penance and the prayers of Moses.

The Idols of Today

Today, our idols may not be golden calves; they may be our phones and other technology, video games, sports, or some other hobby or object. An idol is anything that takes the place of God in our lives. For example, if we miss Mass one Sunday to play sports, that sport has become an idol. It may not seem like we are "worshipping" sports, but it is a form of worship if we choose it over our worship of God.

God Gives a Universal Law

The next day, at God's command, Moses cut two tablets of stone. These he took up to the mountain. God again had Moses write the Commandments upon them. Moses remained with the Lord another forty days and forty nights. During this whole time he neither ate nor drank. The Lord charged him to observe all the things which He would command concerning the conduct of the people and the manner in which the Israelites were to carry out divine worship.

Taking the two tablets of stone, Moses came down from Mount Sinai. His face was so radiant that the people could not look at him. When Aaron and the other Israelites saw this they were filled with fear. So Moses was forced to cover his face with a veil. He then told them all that he had heard from the Lord concerning the laws governing public worship, ceremonies, justice, and right conduct.

Moses Directs the Building of the Tabernacle

The inspired writer tells us that the Israelites repented their sins and renewed their loyalty to almighty God. Moses then directed the construction of the tent which was to serve as a place for divine worship and for God's abiding presence among His people. Because, at that time, they were a wandering nation, the Israelites built a tent temple. They could easily carry such a temple with them as they moved about from place to place. God's Chosen People would not build a permanent place to worship until they settled in towns. Much later we shall read about the temple which King Solomon built in Jerusalem. Since the traditions about the tent were meager, later writers based their description of it on their knowledge of Solomon's temple.

Sturdy wood frames supported the tent cloth. A curtain hung behind the columns at the entrance. The tent itself was divided by another curtain into two parts, the Sanctuary and the Holy of Holies. The Holy of Holies contained the Ark of the Covenant. This was a box made of precious wood, covered with purest gold. On top of the Ark were placed two images of angels with spreading wings, and within it two tablets of the Law and a measure of manna.

In the Sanctuary was a table holding the "loaves of proposition" or "showbreads," and either a seven-branched lamp-stand or seven lamps. The "loaves of proposition," twelve in number, were to be eaten only by the priests. This showbread, as it was also called, was a reminder for the Lord to bless His people, and for them to make offerings to Him.

Just outside the covered part of the tent temple was an Altar of Holocausts, on which were burnt the victims of the bloody sacrifices. Sometimes the entire victim was burned on the altar (holocaust); in other sacrifices part was burnt to signify that it was offered to God, whereas the rest was eaten by priests and people in a sacred banquet.

The priests washed their hands and feet in a bronze laver or huge basin before they went to offer the incense, or before they entered the Holy of Holies.

When the tent temple with its furnishings was finished and the vestments for the priests were completed, Moses consecrated them for divine worship.

God Institutes the Priesthood

Aaron and his sons were then brought to the entrance of the Tabernacle. First they washed with water from the bronze basin, then they were dressed in priestly robes and anointed with oil. Thus, at the beginning of the second year after the deliverance of the Israelites from Egypt, Aaron and his sons were consecrated priests and appointed to perform the sacred ministry to which God had called them. The priesthood was to remain in Aaron's family, which stemmed from the tribe of Levi.

The other descendants of Levi, called Levites, had shown their fidelity to God at the time when the unfaithful Israelites had worshiped the golden calf. For this reason they were chosen to assist the priests in the acts of public worship.

The Fiery Cloud Reveals God's Glory

In a special manner God showed Moses how pleased He was with the fulfillment of His commands. Sometimes by day a Cloud covered the tent temple and revealed the glory of the Lord. The tent was also called the Meeting Tent because it was appointed by God as the place where He would meet with Moses and the Israelites. By night a Fire remained over the tent and revealed to the Israelites the divine presence.

Feast Days and Sacrifices

Before the Covenant the Hebrews had celebrated certain feasts, especially feasts on which they begged God for favors and thanked Him for good flocks and crops. Gradually they changed the meaning of these feasts, using them to commemorate great events in their history.

Besides keeping the Sabbath or seventh day holy, the Israelites kept certain holydays. The "Pasch" or the Passover was celebrated in spring, on the fourteenth day of the first month of their year—that is the month that falls during part of March and part of April. This was to recall God's mercy toward them when the angel of death passed by their doors in Egypt. It was on this feast that the Jews sacrificed the Paschal Lamb.

Next came the great feast of Pentecost, fifty days after the Pasch or Passover, which celebrated the giving of the Law to Moses on Mount Sinai.

In fall, beginning on the fifteenth day of their seventh month, for seven days the Israelites celebrated the Feast of Tents. They thanked God for the harvest, reliving the days when they dwelt in tents during their journey through the desert.

Another great Jewish feast, the Day of Atonement or of public penance, was celebrated in the fall by the High Priest who entered into the Holy of Holies. He sprinkled the blood of a calf on the gold cover of the Ark, where God was especially close to

His People, in atonement for his own sins and those of the other priests. Other ceremonies also indicated the will of the people to put away sin.

There was also a daily offering of two lambs by the priest for all the people. This daily sacrifice is worthy of mention, because it would one day be used as a type of the Holy Sacrifice of the Mass. In the Mass the true Lamb of God is daily offered on our altars.

The March From Sinai

In the second month of the second year after the Israelites had fled from Egypt, God spoke to Moses in the Meeting Tent. He commanded him to gather the men into four camps and begin the march from Sinai. The "Cloud" or divine Presence, which had always been their beacon, rose once again from the tent and guided them through the wilderness. But soon the Israelites began once more to complain against Moses. They still longed for the pleasures of Egypt. Displeased at their conduct, God sent fire to destroy many of them. Although they repented, in a short time they forgot the punishment, and their constant murmuring caused Moses to cry out to God for help to govern his ungrateful people.

To relieve Moses, God commanded him to select seventy elders. These would share his burden, and with the aid of the Holy Spirit they would speak to the people concerning God's will.

God Supports the Authority of Moses

On one occasion Aaron and his sister Mariam challenged the authority of Moses. God rebuked them and praised the meekness and faith of Moses. As a punishment, Mariam was covered with a loathsome skin disease. Because of it she was forced to remain outside the camp until she had done penance for complaining against God's chosen leader.

Scouts View the Promised Land

The Israelites, guided by the Cloud, marched northward. They pitched their tents in the desert, on the border of the Land of Promise. Here God directed Moses to choose twelve of the chiefs to go as scouts to inspect the land of Canaan. These twelve were to bring back a description of the people, the cities, and some of the fruits of the land.

Joshua, the Savior of the Israelites

Among those chosen were Caleb of the tribe of Juda and Hoshea of the tribe of Ephraim. Moses changed Hoshea's name to Joshua ('jā-sü-ə). The Greek form of this name is Jesus.

The reason for this change is clear to us now. God intended Joshua to be a striking figure of our Blessed Savior. As Joshua, the Savior, would lead the Israelites into the Promised Land, so Christ, the Redeemer, would guide us to heaven.

God Commanded His People to Wander for Forty Years

The scouts returned, and some gave accounts of giants who dwelt in the land. They brought back some pomegranates, figs, and large clusters of grapes. The Israelites became excited and unmanageable; some were afraid of the tribes in and around Canaan, and wished to go back. Others were in favor of attacking Canaan at once.

The two scouts, Caleb and Joshua, tried, however, to reason with the people saying, ". . . do not rebel against the Lord! You need not be afraid of the people of that land; they are but food for us! Their defense has left them, but the Lord is with us. Therefore, do not be afraid of them" (Nm 14:9).

The Significance of the Number 40

We read that the Israelites wandered the desert for forty days. This isn't the only time in Scripture that we see the number forty having significance. Recall that Jesus fasted in the desert for forty days, and in the story of Noah, it rained for forty days and forty nights. In all cases, the number forty signifies a time of preparation. God was preparing the Israelites to enter the Promised Land; Christ was preparing for his public ministry; Noah was preparing to enter the new creation following the flood. As an interesting aside, babies live in the womb of their mothers for forty weeks before being born, another time of preparation, this time for a human life.

The Israelites, however, continued to cry out. They would have stoned Moses and Aaron had not the glory of the Lord appeared over the Tent. The Lord then told Moses that He would destroy the Chosen People. Again Moses pleaded for them.

God heard the prayer of Moses and spared the lives of the Israelites. Nevertheless He punished them for He is just. He said: "Of all your men of twenty years or more . . . who grumbled against me not one shall enter the land . . . except Caleb, son of Jephonne (jef-'ōn-ə) and Joshua, son of Nun" (Nm 14:29–30). The Lord then commanded Moses to move the camp into the wilderness. There the Israelites wandered for forty years.

God Continues to Guide His People

During the years that followed, the Israelites lived as a wandering people, as do the Bedouins in Arabia even today. Moses, assisted by Joshua and the seventy elders, governed them. The laws were explained to the people, so that they would remain faithful to God if they should become separated.

They continued on occasion to murmur and rebel against God. However, Moses always prayed to God not to punish them as they deserved. Nevertheless, of the thousands who crossed the Red Sea, only a few were permitted by God to enter the Promised Land.

Moses Is Resigned to God's Will

During their wanderings in the desert, the Israelites could find no water. They became dissatisfied and complained against Moses and Aaron. Moses and Aaron begged God to give them water to drink so that they would stop their complaining.

God told Moses to strike a rock with his rod, promising that water would come forth from the rock. In the presence of the people, Moses struck the rock twice, and water came forth from it.

It was on this occasion, the sacred writer says, that God told Moses he would not enter the Promised Land and that Moses accepted the sentence without complaint.

God Tries His People's Faith

The years passed slowly, while the Chosen People wandered through the desert among enemies, whom they often tried to conquer. The Hebrews had much to suffer before they reached the Promised Land. They were attacked by their Canaanite neighbors. God, however, always protected them. Whenever they murmured, Moses reminded them of the Solemn Covenant, teaching them to be content with whatever God sent them.

God Strengthens the Israelites' Courage

At one time, when they murmured about their food and the hardships of their journey, God punished them by sending "fiery" serpents with a poisonous bite that burned like fire. Many of the people died of the deadly bite. Others saw and realized that it was the result of their sins. They went to Moses for help. God told him to make a serpent of brass, and to set it up for the people to look upon with faith and be healed.

Our Lord recalled this incident when He spoke of His death on the cross:

> "And as Moses lifted up the serpent in the desert, even so must the Son of Man be lifted up, that those who believe in him may not perish, but may have life everlasting" (Jn 3:14–15).

By the bronze serpent raised on high and healing all who looked up at it, God foreshadowed the Redeemer who would appear in the form of sinful man, be raised on the cross, and by this means redeem man from eternal death.

As Moses cured the Israelites who looked upon the bronze serpent, so Christ would use the merits of His cross to heal men from the death of sin. The Church, the Mystical Christ, too, offers us a means of salvation through the sacrament of Penance, in which the priest uses the sign of the cross when absolving us.

The Deeds of Balaam

As the Chosen People proceeded to the south of Canaan and then north on the east side of the Jordan River, they encamped in the plains of Moab opposite Jericho ('je-ri-kō). The ruler of the Moabites feared that the Chosen People would overcome them. He, therefore, sent some messengers to Balaam ('ba-ləm), a famous fortuneteller of a tribe living on the Euphrates River. He wanted him to come and put a curse on these people. While the messengers were with Balaam, God warned him, "Do not go with them and do not curse this people, for they are blessed" (Nm 22:12).

Balaam said to the messengers, "Go back to your own country, for the Lord has refused to let me go with you" (Nm 22:13).

Soon after other messengers were sent to beg Balaam to come and curse the Israelites. He told them to stay with him that night because he wished to discover what the Lord wanted him to do. God came to Balaam in the night and said to him, "If these men have come to summon you, you may go with them; yet only on the condition that you do exactly as I tell you" (Nm 22:20). Balaam arose in the morning, saddled his donkey, and went with them.

An angel of the Lord stood in the way of Balaam as he rode along on the donkey. The beast, seeing the angel with sword drawn, turned out of the way and went into a field. Balaam beat it for leaving the path. Twice more the angel stood in their way. Each time the donkey refused to go forward and each time it was beaten by Balaam. The Lord then opened the mouth of the donkey, which said, "What have I done to you that you should beat me these three times?"

"You have acted so willfully against me," replied Balaam, "that if I but had a sword at hand, I would kill you here and now."

The animal answered. "Am I not your own beast, and have you not always ridden upon me until now? Have I been in the habit of treating you this way before?"

Balaam was forced to answer, "No" (Nm 22:28–30).

Balaam proceeded on his way. Instead of cursing the Israelites he gave them the following promise of a great blessing.

"I see him, though not now;
   I behold him, though not near;
A star shall advance from Jacob
   And a staff shall rise from Israel,
That shall smite the brows of Moab,
   and the skulls of all the Suthites"
(Nm 24:17).

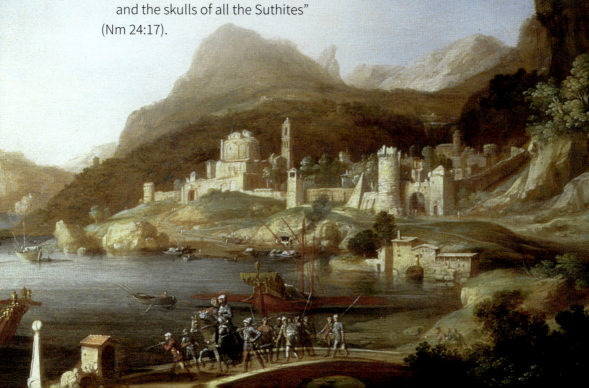

This prophecy was fulfilled first in a preliminary way, in King David who conquered the Moabites, but most perfectly in Christ, the supreme King, who conquered sin.

God Punishes Those Who Reject Him

Since the Israelites traveled through the lands of pagan peoples, they had to mingle with those who believed in idolatry and paganism. Some of the Israelites imitated these evil practices. God, being offended, punished by death many who committed these sins.

Moses Gives His Last Instructions to the Chosen People

At last the years of wandering drew to a close. The Israelites finally arrived opposite Canaan. After he appointed Joshua as his successor, Moses gathered the people together to give them the final directions and to urge them to remember God's goodness. He encouraged them to be holy and steadfast in their faith. He repeated God's laws to them, recalled the promised blessings if they remained faithful, and the punishments if they were untrue. Finally, he distributed the land among the twelve tribes, for in them the Covenant was to be preserved.

Moses, the Prophet, who led the people of the Old Testament from slavery to the Promised Land, prefigured Christ, who would lead the Chosen People of the New Testament from the bondage of sin to heaven, our Promised Land. He reminded all men that they may enter heaven if they keep the laws that God gave to Moses, and which He repeated and divided into love of God and love of neighbor. As a climax to his promise, Moses told the people that they would never be without a prophet, that is, one who would make known to them God's will.

FOR ME TO REVIEW

Questions and Exercises

Part 1: Match column I with column II

Column I

A

1. Aaron

2. Balaam

3. Mariam

4. Joshua

5. Caleb

Column II

A. was appointed the successor of Moses

B. was covered with a skin disease for questioning the authority of Moses

C. was sent as a scout to inspect Canaan

D. the priesthood was to remain in the family of

E. a famous fortuneteller

B

1. Tent Temple

2. Pentecost

3. Mt. Sinai

4. Daily offering of two lambs

5. Golden Calf

6. Holocaust

7. Tables of Law and Showbreads

8. the Pasch

A. a special kind of sacrifice in which the animal was consumed by fire

B. were kept in the Ark of the Covenant

C. recalling God's mercy toward them when the angel of death passed by their doors in Egypt

D. a Jewish feast commemorating the giving of the Law to Moses on Mt. Sinai

E. God gave the Ten Commandments to Moses on

F. foreshadowed the Holy Sacrifice of the Mass

G. the Israelites place of worship was called a

H. the Israelites persuaded Aaron to make for them a

Part 2: Complete these statements

1. The Tent Temple was divided into the sanctuary and the
   _____ .

2. The Tabernacle was another name for the _____ .

3. The Israelites were forbidden to worship _____ .

4. _____ is the day on which the Jews do public penance.

5. The title of God's Lawgiver was given to _____ .

6. God used the pagan fortuneteller Balaam to foretell that the
   King to come would be a child of _____ .

7. Moses assured the Israelites that they would never be without
   a _____ .

8. Christ's Kingdom on earth is _____ .

Part 3: Questions to Check Your Reading

1. Where did God give the Ten Commandments to Moses?

2. Why were the Israelites compelled to remain so many years in
   the desert?

3. What traits of character did the Israelites lack?

4. How do the struggles of the Israelites to enter the Promised
   Land correspond with our struggles to enter the eternal Promised Land?

5. Tell how God showed His power to the people at Mount Sinai.

6. Describe the tent built by the Israelites to serve as their
   Tabernacle.

✓ FOR ME TO DO

1. Write a character sketch of Moses.

2. Review the Ten Commandments—tell what each commands; what each forbids.

3. Recite from the Bible the last instructions of Moses to the Israelites.

4. Write a paragraph in which you illustrate which of the last instructions of Moses to the Israelites can be applied today.

CHAPTER 9

Joshua

The Savior of the Israelites, Leads His People

Moses had kept the worship of the one true God alive among the Israelites. He had led them safely through the desert to the land promised to Abraham and to his children. As his death approached, God told Moses to appoint Joshua as his successor.

God Assists in the Conquest of Canaan

It was no easy task to enter the Promised Land. The Jordan River had to be crossed, and the warlike, idol-worshiping inhabitants of Canaan had to be overcome. Joshua sent two spies to examine the land, particularly the city of Jericho. They sought shelter for the night in the home of a woman named Rahab ('rä-häb). When the king of Jericho heard that the two spies were staying in Rahab's home, he sent his soldiers to capture them. She hid the spies, later asking them to promise her that, when Jericho should fall into their hands, they would spare her and all that belonged to her because she had shown mercy to them and had not betrayed them.

Joshua knew that only with the help of God could the Promised Land be entered. Trusting God completely, he gave the signal for the march to begin. As they had done in the desert, so now the Israelites carried the Ark of the Covenant at the head of the procession. As soon as the priests with the Ark stepped into the river, the promise which God had made was fulfilled. He had said, ". . . when the soles of the feet of the priests carrying the Ark of the Lord, the Lord of the whole earth, touch the water of the Jordan, it will cease to flow; for the water flowing down from upstream will halt in a solid bank" (Jos 3:13).

Jericho Falls

The Israelites crossed the Jordan and entered the Promised Land. They pitched their tents near the city of Jericho and prepared for a siege. Jericho was like a gateway into Canaan and had to be captured first. When the Israelites saw this strongly fortified city, they became afraid.

After celebrating the feast of the Pasch, Joshua gave directions to capture the city as God had commanded. For six days the priests, followed by the army of Israel, marched around the city carrying the Ark. On the seventh day, after

TERMS TO KNOW

Rahab

inhabitants

Jericho

booty

Gabaonites

routed

Levi

conquest

Hai

Merom

circling the city for the last time, seven trumpets were sounded. At the same time the Israelites raised a mighty shout. The strong walls of the city collapsed. Jericho was captured and destroyed. Only the family of Rahab was spared, because she had protected the two spies whom Joshua had sent into Jericho. The Israelites entered and took possession of the city. They were warned, however, not to take anything from the city for themselves.

Hai Is Captured

The way into Canaan was now opened. God told Joshua to take the road leading to the North. This road was guarded by the city of Hai (hī). Confident of their strength, the Israelites sent only a select number of men to attack the city. They were not successful, and many Israelites were killed. Great fear came upon the people. Joshua prayed and learned from God the reason for their failure. Against God's will, some Israelites had taken things as booty from Jericho. After the guilty men were found and punished, the Israelites again attacked Hai, this time successfully.

Before continuing the conquest, Joshua offered a sacrifice to the Lord to thank Him for His help. Joshua also reminded the people of all the blessings that they would receive if they continued to worship the one true God.

Gabaon Is Subdued

The success of the Israelites frightened the remaining tribes of Canaan. They joined forces against them. Only the people of Gabaon ('ga-bə-ȯn) obtained peace, and that by deceiving Joshua. Two Gabaonites pretended to be from a distant country and told Joshua how they heard about and admired the God of Israel. Joshua promised not to injure their people. Later he discovered that they were from a nearby city. However, he kept the promise he had made to them. He did them no harm. Instead he made the people of Gabaon servants of Israel.

Next the Israelites surprised and routed five kings from the south, led by the King of Jerusalem. They had come as far north as Gabaon. The forces of the enemy were dispersed, and fled. God again helped His people because they relied on Him. They were about to deal their enemy a crushing blow when evening fell. Their leader, Joshua begged: "Stand still, O sun, at Gabaon, O moon in the valley of Aialon!" (Jos 10:12.)

From the way the story is told in the Bible we cannot be quite certain whether Joshua prayed for a miraculous lengthening of the day so that he could complete his victory, or for a sudden darkening of the sun, so that the enemy could not escape. In any case, his prayer was answered and his victory was complete. We need not be surprised to read that he words his prayer according to the picture of the world that people had at the time. Some ancient peoples believed that the sun was smaller than the earth and that it circled the earth daily from east to west.

God Fulfills a Promise

Once the tribes of the south were conquered, Joshua marched north and defeated the combined forces of the kings at the waters of Merom ('me-rom). One city after another was captured. God kept His promise, even though the Israelites had often doubted Him and rebelled against Him. He had brought His people "into a good and spacious land, a land flowing with milk and honey."

These wonderful things which God did in the Old Testament show us what He has in store for His Chosen People of the New Testament if we love, obey, and trust Him. He is always faithful to His promises. One promise which should make us very happy is that God will always be willing to help us if we sincerely ask Him. Another promise is that He will forgive any sinner, no matter how grievously he has sinned, if he truly repents. He blesses and punishes nations as well as individuals.

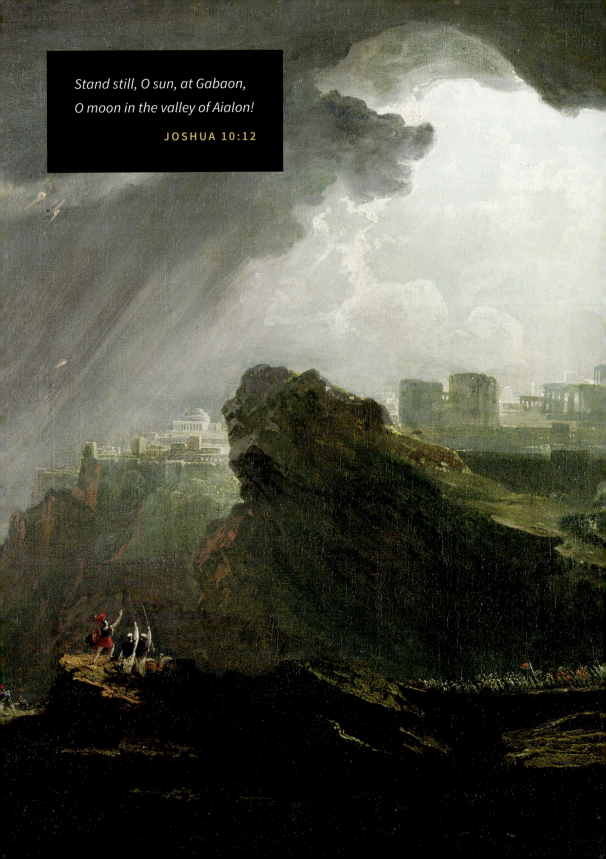

Stand still, O sun, at Gabaon,
O moon in the valley of Aialon!

JOSHUA 10:12

God's People Settle in the Promised Land

Joshua, as we have seen, was successful in conquering most of the land which God promised the Israelites. The complete conquest, however, took many years. Even a longer time elapsed before the land was divided and settled by the twelve tribes of Jacob. The descendants of Juda, from whose tribe the promised Redeemer was to be born, settled in the southern part of Canaan. Certain cities and pasture lands were given to the tribe of Levi, for the support of the priests and lesser ministers who were chosen by God to carry on the divine service. They would, however, be supported chiefly by the tribes whom they served. The tent temple, which was set up in Silo ('sī-lō), was the central place of worship as before. Joshua continued to be the leader of the Israelites. Otherwise, the tribes lived almost independently of one another.

Joshua Warns the Israelites

Joshua was dissatisfied because some of the idolatrous tribes still remained among the Israelites. After calling the leaders of the people together, Joshua reminded them that God's wish should be fulfilled. The inhabitants who worshiped false gods were to be driven out of Canaan, for they were a temptation and a source of sin to the children of Israel.

Joshua also reminded the Israelites of God's favors to them. He begged them to keep God's laws if they wished His blessing and protection. If they sinned, they were to expect nothing but punishment. Soon afterward Joshua died. He had been a most successful and a most religious warrior of God.

Joshua, a Figure of Christ, the Redeemer

Joshua kept the Israelites faithful to the worship of God throughout his long leadership. He prayed for his people and gained God's grace and pardon for them. He led them into the Promised Land. During his last days, he enjoyed the peaceful rest which he so well deserved for his constant obedience to Yahweh.

Christ our Savior overcame sin and death and opened to us Heaven, the true land of promise. So through history we know how well Joshua can be used as a type of Christ; he did for the Chosen People what Christ would do for the Church.

 ## FOR ME TO REVIEW

Questions and Exercises

Part 1: Complete these statements by choosing the correct ending from part B

A.

1. The inhabitants of Gabaon were made to work for the Chosen People because . . .

2. God allowed the Israelites to be oppressed by the pagan tribes because . . .

3. The tribes of Levi received no land in Canaan because . . .

4. The Israelites crossed the Jordan River safely because . . .

5. Rahab and her family were not harmed when Jericho was destroyed because . . .

B.

1. they were to be the priests among the people.

2. they trusted God.

3. they tricked Joshua into promising to spare them.

4. they protected the spies of Joshua.

5. they fell into idolatry.

Part 2: Complete these statements

1. The Ark of the Covenant was to be kept in the Temple in the city of _____ .

2. The Promised Land was divided among the tribes of _____ .

3. The first city to be captured by the Israelites was _____ .

4. Whenever Joshua was in doubt or needed help he _____ .

5. An important tribe of Israel that settled in the southern part of Canaan was _____ .

6. Joshua, by leading his people into the Promised Land, pre-figured _____ .

Part 3: Questions to Check Your Reading

1. What difficulties had to be overcome before the Israelites could occupy the land promised them?

2. How did Joshua show his trust in God?

3. Give an account of the siege of Jericho.

CHAPTER 10

God in His Divine Providence Rules Through His Judges

For many years after the Israelites settled in Canaan, God, from time to time, sent leaders called Judges to govern them. The Hebrew word which we translate by "judges" means that these men were leaders of God's people in times of trial and danger. In all there were fourteen Judges. Not everything recorded of these men can be imitated. God, however, can accomplish His aims despite the weakness and unworthiness of man. In this chapter we shall learn about three important Judges or defenders of Israel. They are Gideon ('ge-də-on), Samson, and Samuel. Each one had a definite work to perform for the Chosen People according to the plan of God. Each one adds to our knowledge of the Promised Redeemer.

God Calls Gideon to Guide the Israelites

GOD PERMITS INVASION

For some years after the death of Joshua, the Israelites were faithful to God. They had failed, however, to drive the pagan inhabitants out of Canaan. Instead they became friendly with them and even intermarried. Gradually they began to worship the false Canaanite gods and goddesses.

Bad companions are always dangerous to our faith. The Church discourages us from associating with evil people, even as God, through His leaders, had time and time again forbidden the Israelites to mingle with the pagans.

Idolatry is a serious offense against God. As a punishment for it, the Israelites often found themselves delivered into the hands of enemy tribes who treated them cruelly.

God permitted and sometimes caused this to happen in the Old Testament. By it He tries to teach us to see what will happen to us also in the New Testament. Our reward or punishment will depend on how we keep the commandments and the laws of Christ and His Body, the Church.

Once the people realized how great their sins were, they did penance and begged God to forgive them. He restored peace. Again and again He showed how much He loved them. He was patient with them and forgave them each time they showed their sorrow. He always gave them another chance when they asked, just as He gives us other chances to regain sanctifying grace every time we go to confession with sorrow for our sins.

THE ISRAELITES TURN TO GOD

When the people of Israel fell into the sin of idolatry, God permitted the Madianites ('ma-dē-ən-ītz) to invade part of their land. For many years the Madianites carried off the large harvests from the rich plains of Esdraelon (es-'dra-ə-lən), in what later was called Galilee. This misfortune led the people to remember God once more.

TERMS TO KNOW

Gideon

Judge

Manasseh

Madianites

repentant

Jerobbaal

Ephraim

Esdraelon

Baal

GIDEON IS CALLED BY GOD

Seeing that the Israelites were repentant, God forgave them and sent them a leader. He sent an angel to a young man by the name of Gideon of the tribe of Manasseh. The angel told him that God had chosen him to free the people of Israel from the Madianites. Gideon was surprised at this announcement, for he did not feel equal to this difficult task. He pleaded to be released from it. However, the angel promised him God's assistance. Gideon, nevertheless, asked for a sign to make sure that the message was from God. He prepared a sacrifice of a lamb and some loaves of bread. By this he wanted to beg God's help in overcoming his enemies. The angel touched Gideon's sacrifice with the tip of a rod, and set it on fire. Gideon was reassured by this sign. He believed that God would help him.

We, too, should be reassured by it. When God gives us a special call, He will also give us the help we need. We must, however, respond with courage and confidence. God still calls individuals to do great things for Him. He calls rich and poor, bright and dull, young and old. All are alike to Him. If they generously accept God's call as Gideon did, they can, with God's help, accomplish great things.

GOD REAFFIRMS GIDEON'S CALLING

Before the actual attack on the Madianites, Gideon asked for still another sign. Placing some fleece—that is, lamb's wool—on the ground, he prayed that the dew might fall on the fleece but not on the ground. The next morning the fleece was so wet that the water wrung from it filled a jar. The following night he asked that the dew might fall on the ground but not on the wool. Again God did as Gideon asked.

GIDEON GUIDES THE ISRAELITES

Gideon no longer hesitated. Relying on the promise of God, he courageously attacked the Madianites, who were much stronger than the Israelites.

Gideon overthrew the altar of Baal ('bo-l), which had been erected in his own village. Then he summoned the men from three other tribes and led them against the Madianites. Many thousands joined his forces. However, it was not by means of these numerous troops that God wished to secure victory for the Israelites. They were to place their confidence in God rather than in their own strength. Twice Gideon was instructed by God to reduce the size of the army.

What was a "Judge" in Ancient Israel

Nowadays, when we hear the word "judge," we think of a courtroom. A Judge is the man or woman who presides over a legal hearing. In ancient Israel, a Judge may have also helped settle legal disputes, but his or her duties went far beyond that. Judges were also political and military leaders. While some Judges are better known than others (like Samson and his long hair and Herculean strength!), the Bible, in the book of Judges, mentions eleven leaders who were said to "judge" Israel. They were:

- Othniel
- Shamgar
- Deborah
- Gideon
- Tola
- Jair
- Jephthah
- Ibzan
- Elon
- Abdon
- Samson

GIDEON DEFEATS THE MADIANITES

When the time for the attack came, Gideon divided his small force into three groups. He then armed them with trumpets and with torches hidden in pitchers. At midnight they stole into the camp of the enemy and surrounded them. Suddenly, at a signal from Gideon, the Israelites blew the trumpets and knocked the pitchers together until they broke. Surprised and panic-stricken by the noise and the flashing lights, the Madianites in their confusion killed one another. The remnants of the army retreated west across the Jordan River. There the Madianites were met and defeated by the Israelites of the tribe of Ephraim.

GIDEON, THE ENEMY OF THE FALSE GODS

Grateful for the deliverance from their enemy, the Israelites wished to make Gideon king. He refused, however, saying that God alone should rule over them. As long as Gideon lived as Judge of Israel, the people remained true to God.

His efforts to destroy the idolatrous worship of false gods were thought to have earned for him a second name by which he was known, Jerobbaal (je-'rōb-bə-l), which in Hebrew sounds like "enemy of Baal" (that is, false god). After his death, however, the Israelites soon forgot the Lord who loved them and had delivered them from their enemies.

FOR ME TO REVIEW

Questions and Exercises

Part 1: Choose the correct answer

1. Gideon ruled over Israel as a
   (1) king (2) prophet (3) judge

2. At the time of Gideon, Israel was troubled by the
   (1) Philistines (2) Moabites (3) Madianites

3. Gideon was from the tribe of
   (1) Manasseh (2) Ephraim (3) Juda

4. A sin into which the Israelites repeatedly fell was
   (1) blasphemy (2) idolatry (3) perjury

5. The Israelite army conquered the enemy because the Israelites had faith in
   (1) Gideon (2) God (3) Baal

Part 2: Complete these statements

1. The rich plains of Canaan which were overrun by enemy tribes were called _____ .

2. A name which means "enemy of false gods" _____ .

3. Before Gideon accepted the angel's message he asked for

   _____ .

4. Gideon offered a sacrifice of bread and _____ .

5. Gideon, attacking the powerful enemy by God's command without any weapon, showed he had the virtues of

   _____ .

Part 3: Questions to Check Your Reading

1. How were the inhabitants of Canaan a source of evil to the Israelites?

2. Why were the Israelites often oppressed and troubled by hostile tribes?

3. How did God show the repentant Israelites that He forgave the evil they did?

4. What signs did Gideon receive to assure him that it was God who wished to make him a leader?

5. In the campaign against the Madianites, how did God prove that the strength of Israel lay completely in God?

6. By what means did Gideon overcome the enemy?

7. Give two incidents from the story that prove Gideon was a humble man.

8. What lesson can we learn from this story of Gideon as to how God will act toward us, the Chosen People of the New Testament?

✓ FOR ME TO DO

1. Compose riddles about the Old Testament characters. Use them in a game.

2. Review your knowledge about the temptations and near occasions of sin.

3. Read *Lives of the Saints* and find to what special work some of them were called. Be sure to include your patron saint.

4. Visit the neighboring churches to see what characters from the Old Testament were used in the decorations or stained glass windows of the church.

5. Discuss Gideon's sense of unworthiness and lack of ability to fulfill the mission to which God called him. Discuss God's call to the priesthood or the religious life.

6. Locate modern photographs of places in Palestine mentioned in this chapter, for example, the Plains of Esdraelon.

Samson Portrays the Strength of the Son of God and the Weakness of Man

During the period of the Judges a new tribe, the Philistines ('fil-is-tēns), a people related to the Greeks, invaded Canaan and founded cities on the coast of the Mediterranean. It is from the Philistines that Canaan came to be known as Palestine. The Philistines began to crowd out the Israelites from the most fertile land. Seeing His people humbled and sorry for their sins, God took pity on them. He raised Samson from the tribe of Dan to defend the people of Israel from this new enemy.

SAMSON'S BIRTH IS FORETOLD BY AN ANGEL

Before Samson was born, an angel appeared to his mother and announced that she would have a son who would save his country from the Philistines. The angel appeared again. This time Samson's mother called her husband, Manoe (ma-'nō-ə). The angel repeated the prophecy of the birth of a son. He stressed the fact that this child was to be a Nazirite, that is, a person especially consecrated to the Lord. He would be obliged not to use wine or strong drink, and to refrain from cutting his hair as a mark of holiness.

SAMSON—THE STRONG ONE

The son born to Manoe and his wife was named Samson. From his very youth he showed great strength. He became the strongest man in Palestine. Once, when Samson was on a journey, a young lion attacked him. The spirit of the Lord came upon Samson. He seized the lion and tore it apart with his bare hands. Later Samson found that bees had built a honeycomb in the dead lion's mouth. He gave some of the honey to his father and mother.

SAMSON BECOMES AN ENEMY OF THE PHILISTINES

Some time later Samson disobeyed God's wishes and married a Philistine woman. At the wedding feast, he proposed a riddle about the honeycomb in the lion's mouth, telling them, "Out of the eater came forth food, and out of the strong came forth sweetness" (Jgs 14:14). If the Philistines guessed the riddle within seven days, he promised to give them thirty robes and as many cloaks. On the other hand, if they failed to give the correct answer, they would give him an equal number of robes and cloaks. Unable to guess the riddle, they threatened his wife. She became frightened, and during the seven days of the feast she kept begging Samson to tell her the answer to the riddle. On the seventh day, he yielded.

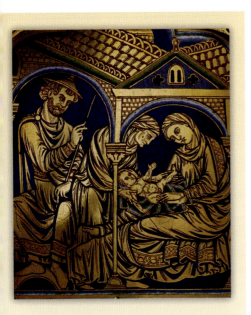

Barren Women in the Bible

Samson's birth was miraculous because his mother was thought to be barren, meaning she was unable to conceive and bear a child. This is a common theme in Scripture. Other women thought to be barren were Sarah, Rebekah, Rachel, Hannah, and Elizabeth, among others. All of these women's children grew up to be amazing and very special people who carried out God's plan of salvation for humanity, including John the Baptist (son of Elizabeth) and Samuel (the son of Hannah). Of course, the most miraculous birth of all is Jesus to the Virgin Mary. God puts his majesty on display through these miraculous births and shows us that, with Him, anything is possible.

Samson knew he had been betrayed when the Philistines gave the answer, "What is sweeter than honey, and what is stronger than a lion?" (Jgs 14:18). In his anger he killed thirty men. He took their garments and gave them to the wedding guests as he had promised. Then he returned to his father's house. From then on there was no peace between Samson and the Philistines.

Some time later Samson returned to the Philistines only to find that his wife had married someone else. Enraged, he caught three hundred foxes, tied them tail to tail in pairs and fastened burning torches between the tails. He then let them run into the harvest fields of the Philistines. All the crops were destroyed, including the vineyards.

A large group of men from the tribe of Juda fell upon Samson and bound him with heavy cord. Then they delivered him to his enemies, the Philistines. They did this to escape punishment themselves. Samson easily broke the cords, and with the jawbone of a donkey killed a thousand men. In fact, unassisted he raided several cities of the Philistines, and escaped each time because of his strength.

Samson's strength has caused the Church to use him as a figure of Christ, the Strong One of God. We Christians, too, when we are faithful, are like Samsons, strong ones of God. When we no longer obey His laws we lose our strength.

133

SAMSON'S DEPARTURE FROM GOD BRINGS MISFORTUNE

In time Samson became friendly with another Philistine woman, named Dalila (də-'lī-lə). She, too, was bribed by the leader of the Philistines, who wanted to learn the secret of Samson's strength. Several times Samson gave her false answers. Finally, worn out by her pleadings, Samson revealed that his strength was in his uncut hair. That is, his strength depended on his consecration to God. If he cut his hair, he would break his vow as a Nazirite and lose his strength. Dalila gave this information to the Philistines. When the opportunity came, she had Samson's hair cut while he slept. He awoke to find himself in the hands of the Philistines, his strength gone. The Philistines then put out Samson's eyes and shut him up in prison. There they made him grind grain.

SAMSON AGAIN BECOMES A STRONG ONE OF GOD

Samson had done many things that were displeasing to God. God's gift, however, was withdrawn only when Samson proved that he had no intention of observing his Nazirite vow. During his imprisonment, Samson had time to think over his sinful life and repent. He let his hair grow, and thus showed God that he wished to be consecrated again to Him.

SAMSON'S DEATH

One day the Philistines held a great feast in honor of their gods. Wishing to amuse themselves, the people had Samson, a blind, helpless man, brought before them. Samson asked permission to lean against the pillars that supported the house. Then he prayed, "O Lord God, remember me! Strengthen me, O God, this last time" (Jgs 16:28). Almighty God heard his prayer. His strength returned. Laying hold of both the pillars upon which the house rested, he shook them. The entire building fell, killing Samson and many Philistines. By his own death, however, he killed more of God's enemies than he had during life.

FOR ME TO REVIEW

Questions and Exercises

Part 1: Answer yes or no

1. The Judges whom God selected were perfect men.

2. Samson was a Nazirite from his birth.

3. Samson, leading a large army, checked the advance of the enemy.

4. Samson in his strength is a type of Christ.

5. Samson's birth and special mission were foretold to his parents.

6. Samson fought against the Moabites.

7. Samson prepared men's minds to recognize the coming Redeemer.

8. Samson did many things that were not pleasing to God.

9. Samson was from the tribe of Juda.

10. Samson was Judge over Israel for many years.

Part 2: Questions to Check Your Reading

1. When did Canaan become known as Palestine?

2. What news did the angel announce to Manoe and his wife?

3. Relate incidents from the life of Samson which show his strength.

4. What mistakes led to Samson's defeat?

5. In what way did Samson fulfill the work God assigned to him?

6. How did Samson prepare men's minds to recognize the coming Redeemer?

FOR ME TO DO

1. List five means which you can use to gain spiritual strength to overcome sin.

2. Compare the character of Samson with that of Gideon.

God Speaks to Samuel

We have seen how God's goodness, patience, and wisdom were continually being manifested in the history of the Chosen People. On the other hand, the forgetfulness and ingratitude of the Israelites are also plainly evident. Although the Israelites had no special leaders after their entrance into the Promised Land, God gave them Judges, to guide them to victory over the enemy each time they repented. Samuel was the last of the Judges of Israel, and also a prophet.

ANNA'S PRAYER IS ANSWERED
A faithful couple, Elcana (el-ˈkan-ə) and his wife Anna, lived in Canaan when Eli (ˈhē-lī) the high priest was Judge of all Israel. Anna's heart was sad because God had not blessed her with a child. She made a vow that if God blessed her with a son she would "give him to the Lord all the days of his life" (1 Sm 1:11). God finally heard her prayers and sent her a son whom she named Samuel, which means "asked of God."

SAMUEL IS CONSECRATED TO GOD
Anna remembered her promise to God. When Samuel was three years of age, his mother took him to the sanctuary at Silo. There he lived with the high priest. Samuel performed his duties in the sanctuary faithfully, growing in favor with God and man.

ELI SHARES IN THE GUILT OF HIS SONS

The high priest Eli had two wicked sons. They had often scandalized the Israelites by their wrongdoing in the temple. Eli knew of his sons' sinful actions, but he did not punish them. Although God warned him to put an end to the evil ways of his sons, Eli did nothing. The time was drawing near when God would punish both the wickedness of the two sons and the negligence of the father.

GOD SPEAKS TO SAMUEL

The boy Samuel was sleeping one night quite close to the tent temple when he heard a voice calling him. Thinking it was Eli, he went to him. Eli, however, said he had not called him. The call was repeated a second and a third time. Finally Eli realized that Samuel was hearing the voice of the Lord. He told Samuel to go back to bed and if he heard the voice again he should say, "Speak, Lord, for your servant is listening" (1 Sm 3:9). Samuel did as he was directed. God told Samuel that Eli would be punished because he had failed to correct his evil sons. The following morning Samuel told Eli what God had said. Eli humbly answered, "It is the Lord: let him do what is good in his sight" (1 Sm 3:18).

What can you do to be more attentive to the will of God in your life?

137

In Eli's death we can see that God expects parents to teach and guide their children. Would you say that all those in authority have a similar responsibility toward those under their care?

GOD WITHHOLDS HIS HELP FROM ISRAEL

During the rule of Eli the Philistines again fought against Israel, inflicting great losses upon them. Would that lead you to think that the Israelites were keeping the law of God? To inspire the Israelite army to fight more bravely and to gain help from God, the Ark of the Covenant was brought to the camp. Despite its presence, God did not protect the Israelites, because they had sinned. The Philistines made another and more damaging attack. Thousands of Israelites were killed, among them the two sons of Eli. What was far worse, the enemy carried off with them the Ark of the Covenant. News of this terrible disaster soon reached Eli. On hearing of the capture of the Ark, Eli fell from his chair, broke his neck, and died. He was punished as God said he would be.

THE ARK, A BLESSING TO THOSE ONLY WHO FEAR GOD

The capture of the Ark of the Covenant brought nothing but misfortune to the Philistines. At the end of seven months, they were only too happy to restore it to Israel, along with presents of gold.

When the Ark of the Covenant was returned, the sons of Jeconiah (jə-kə-ˈnī-ə) refused to share the joy of the people. They were struck dead. God did this to show that He expected reverence to be shown for the Ark, for in it He dwelt with Israel in a special manner.

SAMUEL BECOMES A PROPHET JUDGE OF ISRAEL

After the death of Eli, Samuel assumed the leadership of Israel. The people considered him not only a Judge but also a Prophet of the Lord, for what God said through Samuel came true.

Samuel spoke to the people of Israel. He said, "If you turn to the Lord with all your hearts and put away the strange gods from among you, the Lord will deliver you out of the hands of the Philistines" (1 Sm 7:8). The people believed and obeyed. They fasted, prayed, and solemnly pledged to worship only Yahweh, the one true God of Israel.

SAMUEL'S PRAYER CONQUERS THE ENEMY

The Philistines, meanwhile, gathered their forces against Israel. The Israelites grew frightened. They did not lose confidence, however, because they knew Samuel's power with God. As the Philistines began the attack, Samuel offered a sacrifice to God, who rewarded him with a victory. By prayer, combined with sacrifice, he triumphed.

During the many years that Samuel ruled Israel, he lived in Rama ('rä-mə), north of Jerusalem, where he built an altar to Yahweh. Faithful to the service of the true God, Samuel considered it his duty to encourage and demand faithfulness to Him from all the tribes of Israel.

 FOR ME TO REVIEW

Questions and Exercises

Questions to Check Your Reading

1. Why did Samuel's parents send him to live with the high priest?

2. Why did Eli share in the guilt of his wicked sons?

3. How did God give Samuel the message for Eli?

4. Why was Samuel called a Prophet?

5. Why was the Ark of the Covenant brought to the battlefield?

6. What were the results of the battle with the Philistines?

7. What incident occurred to show an accent in the Old Testament on fear?

8. How did Samuel say the Israelites could conquer the Philistines?

9. Why did God help the Israelites in the last attack of the Philistines?

10. What responsibility did Samuel consider was his as Judge of Israel?

Ruth

RUTH ACCEPTS THE GOD OF ISRAEL

Let us now turn to an incident in the story of God's love quite different from the stories of battle we have been studying. During the rule of the Judges, a woman named Naomi (nō-'ā-mē) lived with her family in the land of Moab (mō-ab), on the eastern side of the Jordan. She had left her home in Bethlehem to escape a famine. Now that her husband and two sons had died, she prepared to return to her home town. Her daughters-in-law, Orpha ('ar-fə) and Ruth, accompanied Naomi. They were not Israelites. On the way Naomi tried to persuade them to remain with their own people, the Moabites. Orpha returned, but Ruth would not leave her mother-in-law. She spoke these beautiful words, "Wherever you go, I will go, wherever you lodge, I will lodge; your people shall be my people, and your God my God" (Ru 1:16).

Naomi and Ruth reached Bethlehem in the land of Juda at harvest time. Since they were poor, Ruth went out into the field to gather grain which the reapers had left. She was not ashamed of her poverty, nor did she avoid work.

The field where Ruth gathered grain belonged to a wealthy, charitable man by the name of Boaz ('bō-ōz). He was a distant relative of Naomi's husband. Seeing Ruth there, he instructed the reapers to drop grain purposely so that Ruth could gather more. Later he was convinced of the virtues of Ruth. He saw her modesty. He appreciated her willingness to work. He was touched by her care and affection for Naomi. So Boaz married her. He provided, then, both for Ruth and Naomi.

Ruth was thus greatly rewarded, for she not only was relieved of poverty but became the mother of Obed ('ō-bid), the grandfather of David, of whose family many years later Christ the Redeemer was to be born. Ruth was, therefore, a member of the family from which Christ descended. In thus choosing to descend from Ruth, who was a Moabite and a stranger to the Israelites, Christ wished to show men that He was the Savior not only of the Israelites but of all mankind.

 FOR ME TO REVIEW

Questions and Exercises

Part 1: Complete these statements

1. _____ was a high priest.

2. _____ were leaders of God's people in times of danger.

3. _____ captured the Ark of the Covenant.

4. _____ was the name given to the descendants of Jacob.

5. _____ was the city where Samuel built an altar to God.

6. _____ was a law with some accent on fear.

7. _____ was the last judge of Israel.

8. _____ was married to Ruth.

9. _____ was a law with great accent on love.

10. _____ was the place where Samuel's mother took him to the sanctuary.

Part 2: Who said?

1. "Speak, Lord, for your servant is listening."

2. "I will give him to the Lord all the days of his life."

3. "It is the Lord, let him do what he thinks best."

4. "If you turn to the Lord with all your hearts . . . the Lord will deliver you out of the hands of the Philistines."

5. "Wherever you go, I will go, wherever you lodge I will lodge; your people shall be my people, and your God my God."

✓ FOR ME TO DO

1. Act with great respect in the presence of the Blessed Sacrament.

2. Say a "Hail Mary" daily to know your vocation.

3. Rely upon the judgment of your parents. Obey them even if you do not understand the reason for their command. Pray for them.

4. Read the 1st Samuel to find out the evil actions of the sons of Eli.

5. Discuss the obligation of parents to train and discipline their children in good habits of virtuous living.

CHAPTER 11
God Allows Kings to Rule

*In this chapter we will learn more about God's goodness and fidelity
to His promises. Working through Judges, God saved His people from
destruction, and so kept the true religion alive among them. During
the time of Samuel the Israelites were not contented. They wished to
be governed by an earthly king who, they hoped, would lead them and
bring them victories in their battles. These worldly people thought a
king would conquer lands and make of them a mighty nation.*

The Israelites Under King Saul

GOD DIRECTS SAMUEL TO ANOINT SAUL KING

God answered their prayers and sent Samuel to anoint Saul King
of Israel. In God's plan the kingship in Israel was a preparation for
the coming of the Redeemer. Often the prophets promised, when
the Israelite kings disappointed the hopes of the people, that one
day God would send them the perfect King who would fulfill all
their hopes.

The Lord made known to Samuel the day that he was to
anoint Saul. When Saul came to the city he met Samuel and
asked his help in finding some animals that had strayed. Then
the Lord said to Samuel, "Behold the man of whom I spoke to
you. This man shall reign over my people" (1 Sm 9:17).

The following day Samuel took oil and poured it upon Saul's
head, saying, "The Lord has anointed you to be prince over his
land, and you shall deliver his people out of the hands of the
enemies that surround them. And this shall be a sign to you, that
God has anointed you to be prince" (1 Sm 10:1).

When Saul went home he told his father that he had seen Samuel, but did not mention that he had been anointed king. Later, Samuel called together representatives of the tribes of Israel and told them that God had selected a king from among them. They were, however, to appoint him by lot. They cast lots. The choice fell on the tribe of Benjamin,

TERMS TO KNOW

- rejected
- Jonathan
- Goliath
- anointed
- harpist
- embittered
- cast lots
- armor-bearer

then upon the clan of Metri ('me-trē) and finally upon Saul. They looked for him in the crowd, but could not find him. They searched for him and found him in his own home. Quickly they brought him to the place of election. As the people made way for him they were amazed at his height, for he was taller than any man in Israel. Samuel said, "Surely you see that there is none among all the people equal to him whom the Lord has chosen." With one accord the crowd shouted, "God save the king!" (1 Sm 10:24.)

SAUL LEADS HIS PEOPLE TO VICTORY

The city of Jabes ('jä-bis) had been taken from the Israelites and was in possession of the Ammonites ('am-mən-īts). Saul saw an opportunity to unite the Israelites under his rule by a victory over the Ammonites. He butchered the oxen with which he had been plowing and sent a piece to every tribe, commanding them to unite with him in battle or suffer the fate of those same oxen. The fear of the Lord fell upon the people, and they went out to battle as one man. The Ammonites were driven out, and all the people were happy to approve the choice of Saul as their king.

SAUL IS PUNISHED BY DEFEAT

Since Saul's chief task was to defend his people against the Philistines, he began the work of driving them out of the land. But soon Saul no longer depended upon the guidance of God, especially as it was given to him through Samuel. He began to act as if it were by his own power and strength that he won the victories.

On one occasion the Philistines marched into the land of the Israelites with large armies. The men of Israel were frightened, and some of them fled. Saul waited for Samuel seven days. Seeing that his soldiers continued to desert, he became impatient. He was anxious to start the battle. Samuel, however, commanded him to wait until he, as God's representative, would offer the sacrifice to God. Saul finally disobeyed Samuel's command

and offered the sacrifice himself. Later Samuel came and asked, "What have you done?" Saul told Samuel that he was forced to do it.

Samuel answered, "Because you have not kept the commandments of the Lord, your dynasty shall not continue" (1 Sm 13:13).

God continued to watch over his people. Despite Saul's sin He allowed the Israelites to gain many victories, and made them a strong and powerful nation.

When the Israelites went to war against the Amalecites, God, through Samuel, commanded Saul to kill the king and his people and to destroy all their possessions. Saul won the battle and conquered the Amalecites, but he again disobeyed God. He chose for himself the best of their flocks, of their ornaments, and of all that was beautiful. He also spared their king despite the command of God.

GOD ASKS OBEDIENCE OF THE KING

Samuel, God's prophet, questioned Saul about his actions. Saul explained that he simply meant to offer a sacrifice of the things taken from the defeated people. God, however, had not asked for that; He had asked for the great and difficult sacrifice of obedience.

Samuel asked Saul, "Does the Lord desire holocausts and victims, in preference to obedience to his voice? For obedience is better than sacrifice

> Samuel told Saul, "Obedience is better than sacrifice." Can you see that obedience is sacrifice —sacrifice of the will? Through obedience God is offered man's highest and most prized possession—his own free will. This makes it clear that obedience to God's will is better even than sacrifice. Christ has told us this also both in word and in deed. Can you cite a few examples?

and to obey means more than to offer the fat of rams." Samuel continued: "Therefore, as you have rejected the word of the Lord, so the Lord has also rejected you and taken the kingship from you" (1 Sm 15:23). Saul, however, was recognized as king as long as he lived.

Throughout the Bible, as with David, God often raises up the lowly to do great things.

DAVID IS ANOINTED KING

After Saul's disobedience, Samuel went to Bethlehem at God's direction to offer sacrifice and to anoint the man who was to succeed Saul. God directed Samuel to the home of Jesse ('ī-sa). There he worshiped God by offering Him sacrifice. When Samuel asked Jesse if all his sons were present, he was told that the youngest, David, was in the fields tending the sheep. At Samuel's request the boy was brought in.

When Samuel saw the strong and handsome David, he heard the Lord say, "Arise and anoint him, for this is he" (1 Sm 16:12). Samuel took a horn of oil and, pouring it on him, anointed David in the presence of his family.

Saul did not know that David had already been anointed to replace him, yet he was greatly depressed and embittered at being cast off by God. He asked his servants, to bring him a man who would play some music to comfort him, for he was feeling very lonely. The harpist they brought to Saul was David, whose music pleased Saul so much that he made him his armor-bearer.

THE FRIENDSHIP OF DAVID AND JONATHAN

Saul's son, Jonathan, met David and soon they developed a wonderful friendship. They lived together in the palace and enjoyed each other's company. One day they made a promise that they would always be loyal to each other. Jonathan gave David his coat, together with the rest of his royal garments, as a sign of his loyalty. God blessed their friendship because it was good and unselfish.

DAVID SLAYS THE WARRIOR

The Bible contains another tradition about the way David first met Saul. The Philistines sent a great giant to challenge anyone of the Israelites to fight him. No one dared, except David, who happened to be visiting his brothers in camp. He went to the king and offered to fight the giant. Saul in desperation accepted David's offer and presented him with his own armor. David said, "I cannot go dressed this way, for I am not used to it" (1 Sm 17:39). Instead, taking a sling and five smooth stones, as well as his shepherd's staff, he went to meet the warrior, who was called Goliath (gə-'lī-əth).

In this victory of David over Goliath, God was actually preparing His People for the approaching Messiah. Through David He would make known later how great would be Christ's victory over the devil. David, a shepherd, armed with only a staff, a sling, and five smooth stones killed the warrior. Our Lord, the Divine Shepherd, would one day conquer the devil with His cross and five wounds.

Goliath taunted him. David gathered five stones for his slingshot. He fearlessly shot a stone from his sling and hit the giant in the forehead. Goliath was stunned and fell to the ground. David ran to the fallen giant and cut off his head. The rest of the Philistines fled in terror, pursued by Saul's army. When the Israelites returned, Saul grew jealous, for he heard what the people were singing in praise of David. They said, "Saul slew his thousands, and David his ten

thousands" (1 Sm 18:7). David was truly greater, not in height or in strength, but because of his obedience. He had relied entirely on the Lord.

David had learned how strong he could be with God's help. Once before he had saved his flock of sheep by slaying a lion and a bear. Now he hoped to bring unity to his people by leading them to show love and obedience to God, just as Abraham, Joseph, and Moses had guided the people and kept them from straying.

SAUL PERSECUTES DAVID

Saul was not grateful to David for winning the victory; rather, he was filled with envy and hatred toward him. Saul even tried to kill David by throwing a spear at him. When this failed, he sent David into a fierce battle with the Philistines, hoping that he might be killed. David depended on the help of God and was again victorious. He decided, however, not to return to Saul; instead he went to Rama to seek the protection of Samuel.

Saul was still determined to kill David. Sometimes he even followed him to where he was camping. Once David and his men found Saul asleep in a cave. David's soldiers wished to slay Saul but David stopped them. Instead he cut off the hem of Saul's robe. Later he showed it to him as a proof that he could have killed him. David would not harm Saul because he knew he was the anointed of the Lord.

THE PHILISTINES FIGHT AGAINST ISRAEL

The Philistines had moved into the land of Canaan again. They began to gather their forces for another war against the Israelites. Soon they had a huge army and felt certain of victory.

When Saul saw the army of the Philistines he was afraid. He knew that he no longer had God's help, and Samuel was dead. While Samuel lived, the Philistines had been held in check. Now Saul knew that he stood alone against the enemy.

THE DEATH OF SAUL

In the battle many Israelites were slain. The rest fled from the field. The Philistines killed Jonathan and two other sons of Saul. Knowing that he had no chance to escape, Saul took his sword and fell upon it.

God had chosen Saul to rule over his people. He also gave him wisdom and strength to overcome his enemies. Saul proved himself ungrateful by taking to himself the glory and honor of the victories he won. What capital sin prompted him to try to take the life of David and to seek his own honor?

FOR ME TO REVIEW

Questions and Exercises

Part 1: Complete these statements

1. _____ anointed Saul King of Israel.

2. Saul won victories for his people over _____ and _____ .

3. Saul's greatest work was in defending his people against the _____ .

4. As long as he obeyed God Saul was _____ .

5. Because of his disobedience, God took from Saul _____ .

6. Saul belonged to the tribe of _____ .

7. _____ , the son of Saul, and David became close friends.

8. David overcame the giant _____ .

9. Samuel told Saul, "_____ is better than sacrifice."

10. The last of the Judges was _____ .

Part 2: Questions to Check Your Reading

1. Give three reasons why the Israelites wanted a king.

2. How did Samuel know that Saul was to be king of Israel?

3. What did Samuel prophesy when he anointed Saul as king?

4. Describe Saul at the time of his anointing.

5. Saul was anointed by Samuel in God's name. When are we anointed by God's priests? In which sacraments?

6. How did Saul give renewed courage to the Israelites?

7. How was Saul punished for offering sacrifice in Samuel's place?

8. In what way did Saul disobey God in the war with the Amalecites?

9. Why did Saul make David his armor-bearer?

10. How did David escape from Saul's wicked plans?

⊘ FOR ME TO DO

1. Write an imaginary message from one Israelite to another, telling of the anointing of Saul.

2. Describe Saul's life and character after his sins of disobedience.

3. Explain this sentence, "Obedience is better than sacrifice."

4. Recall incidents from the story which illustrate these vices: pride, greed, jealousy.

The Israelites Under King David (C. 1010–970 B.C.)

Saul sinned, and the kingship was taken away from him and given to David and his descendants. David, who became one of the greatest leaders of the Chosen People, was both a great soldier and a just ruler. From his family the Messiah was to be born. In the prophecies of Jacob God had promised that the tribe of Juda would bear the scepter, the sign of kingship. Saul, the first king, had belonged to the tribe of Benjamin. When David became king, the kingship of Israel passed to the tribe of Juda, and thus the prophecy of Jacob was fulfilled in part.

DAVID, KING OF ALL ISRAEL

After Saul's death, God commanded David to go to Hebron ('he-brŏn), where the tribe of Juda made him king. While David was ruling over Juda, Isboseth ('is-bō-seth) one of Saul's sons, had been made king of the other tribes by Abner, general of Saul's army. Thus two kings ruled over the tribes of Israel at the same time. Only the tribe of Juda followed David and recognized him as their king. David's soldiers, with Joab ('jō-əb) at their head, set out to fight the followers of Isboseth. They were victorious.

Many other battles were fought before the people could be made to realize that David had been appointed by God to be their king. Finally they agreed to accept him. Representatives from all the tribes gathered at Hebron, where they set up a throne and made David king of all Israel. At this time, Jerusalem was held by a Canaanite tribe, the Jebusites ('jeb-ə-sīts). David waged war against them, took the city, and made it his capital. Since it had belonged to none of the tribes and was a natural fortification, it helped to unite the tribes of Juda and Israel. Thus Jerusalem became the "City of David."

THE DEFEAT OF THE PHILISTINES

When the Philistines heard that David had captured Jerusalem, they renewed their attacks against Israel. David, however, defeated them and forced them to retire to the seacoast. From that time on they ceased to be a serious threat. In this way David showed that he was a great general. With God's help he was the defender of his people.

THE ARK OF THE COVENANT IS BROUGHT INTO JERUSALEM

Grateful to God for His great goodness, David promised to serve Him faithfully. During the time of peace he decided to bring the Ark of the Covenant to Jerusalem. He selected seven choirs to sing before the Ark. He also formed the priests and people into a great procession, which he personally led into the city.

Before entering the city, however, the procession was stopped, and David offered sacrifice to God. He then humbly put aside his royal cloak and danced before the Ark. When David's wife Michol ('mi-kōl) saw him dancing in this way, she became angry. She did not want him to act so common. But he said to her, "I will both play and make myself even more common than I have done, and I will be little in my own eyes" (2 Sm 6:22).

On this occasion David taught us how to show our love of God publicly. Even though people should ridicule us for the love and the respect which we show Christ in the Blessed Sacrament, we should imitate David's courage. He was a noble king who, despite the opinion of others, humbled himself before a mightier Lord.

David's wife, Michol, was punished for her pride by remaining childless all her life. No greater affliction could have befallen a Hebrew wife.

When the Ark was brought into Jerusalem it was placed within the tent that David had set up. Many holocausts and communion sacrifices were offered before it.

Even after all these ceremonies David was not satisfied. He said to Nathan the prophet, "Do you see that I live in a house of cedar wood and the Ark of God is in a tent?" (2 Sm 7:2). He wanted to build a temple for the Ark. At first Nathan agreed, but later God revealed to Nathan that David should leave this project to his son. God, however, was pleased with his desire and promised to bless him in many ways.

A holocaust was a sacrifice in which the victim was consumed by fire, and thus given to God, as it were, completely. A peace offering or communion sacrifice, however, was burned in part and the rest was eaten by the priest and the family of the one who offered it: a sacred banquet in which God was thought to take part invisibly.

GOD'S PROMISE TO DAVID

Through Nathan God made known to David that the kingship over the Chosen People would remain forever with his family. This promise was fulfilled in a way far more wonderful than even David realized, since Jesus Christ, the Son of God, the Eternal King, descended through Mary from King David.

The prophets often expressed their revelation in poetic form, and used figures of speech such as we find in poetry. In Nathan's prophecy there is a play on the word *house*, which in Hebrew as in English can mean a place to live in or also a dynasty, as for example when we speak of the house of Windsor or the house of Savoy. Through Nathan God recalled that David had the good intentions of building a *house* for Him. This God said was not necessary. As a reward for his good intention, however, God promised "to make David great, and *to build a house for him.*" Nathan speaking for God, explained:

> When your days are over, and you sleep with your ancestors,
>> I will make your posterity continue after you,
>> I will make firm your royal throne forever . . .
> I will be a Father to him,
>> he shall be a son to me . . .
> Your house and your kingship shall endure always in my presence, your throne shall be firm forever (2 Sam 7:12–14, 16).

David then went to the Lord, that is, he took his place before the Ark of the Covenant, and thanked God very humbly for all that he had received in this great promise, especially that the Messiah would descend from his family. He talked to God in the tent and praised Him, just as we do when we pay Him a visit in church.

David showed his kindness to the people in many ways. For instance, he sent messengers to find out if any one of the house of Saul was still living. David wished to help them because of his friendship for Jonathan. He found only Jonathan's son who had been lame since his father's death. David, a truly greathearted man, sent for him and gave him a place in his own palace. He said to him, "I will restore to you the lands of Saul, your father, and you shall eat bread of my table always" (2 Sm 9:7).

DAVID SINS, BUT THEN REPENTS

David committed the very serious sin of adultery with Bathsheba, the wife of one of his soldiers. As a result, she conceived a child. To conceal his adultery from the young woman's husband, David sent a letter to his general Joab. He commanded him to put Uria (ü-′rī-ə), the husband of Bathsheba, in the front lines so that he would be killed in battle. Uria was killed as David had planned. Shortly afterward David married Bathsheba.

God sent Nathan the prophet to David. The prophet told him a parable about two men in a certain city, the one rich and the other poor. The poor man had nothing at all except one little lamb which he loved very much. The rich man, who had a great many sheep and oxen, once had a visitor, for whom he wished to prepare a meal. Instead of taking one of his many sheep, the rich man took and butchered the only lamb of the poor man (2 Sm 12:1–4).

This story made David very angry. He said, "The man that did this is a child of death. He shall restore the lamb fourfold, because he did this thing" (2 Sm 12:5–6).

"You are that man!" Nathan told David. By taking the wife of his soldier, he explained, David had committed a very serious sin. David acknowledged his sin and was sincerely sorry.

THE REVOLT OF ABSALOM

The greatest sorrow in David's life was the revolt of his son Absalom ('ab-sä-ləm) against him. An ambitious man, Absalom wanted at all costs to rule in David's place. He stirred up the people to revolt against his father.

Absalom made the people think that they would be better off if he were king. He sent word to all the tribes of Israel that when the trumpet was blown they would know that Absalom was king. He made many promises, and as a consequence won some to his side.

Shortly afterward, Absalom went to Hebron. There he gathered together a great number of men. Even some friends of David were deceived and joined this party. A messenger was sent to David to tell him that all Israel had gone over to his son Absalom.

David received the news with sadness, and prepared to leave Jerusalem in order to save his people. He knew that when Absalom came into the city to take it, much blood would be shed.

THE VICTORY OF DAVID

As soon as Absalom learned that David had left Jerusalem he took a large number of soldiers and went in pursuit of him. He pursued his father beyond the Jordan.

David divided his soldiers into three companies, with Joab and two other generals as leaders. He intended to lead one company himself. The people, however, persuaded him not to go into the fray. As the armies prepared to do battle David begged them, "Save the boy Absalom" (2 Sm 18:5).

The armies met and there was a fierce battle. The army of Absalom was defeated. Absalom realized that he would be slain if he were captured. He immediately left the field, hoping to escape. As he was riding away his head struck a branch of a tree and he hung there unconscious. Joab saw him and thrust three lances into him. After making sure that he was dead, Joab's soldiers took his body and buried it in a pit in the forest.

News of the victory was brought to David. But he was not overjoyed; instead he asked, "Is the young man Absalom safe?" When he learned of his son's death, his grief knew no bounds.

DAVID'S GRATITUDE TO GOD

When David returned to Jerusalem, many people went out to meet him and to offer him homage. David found that peace had come to the kingdom. He could now give more time to the services at the tabernacle, where the Ark of the Covenant was kept. He laid down rules for divine services, and arranged to have groups of singers and musicians for all religious ceremonies. He selected groups of Levites and appointed them to care for the Ark. He also assigned men to guard the treasure in the temple.

THE PSALMS OF DAVID

David was not only a great warrior and ruler; he is also remembered in tradition as the sweet singer of Israel. A number of the sacred hymns which are preserved in our book of Psalms were composed by David. Although the one hundred fifty Psalms were written at various times and by various psalmists, the book is often called David's Psalter because he was the best known of the Psalmists, and because his influence pervades a large portion of the Psalter.

TERMS TO KNOW

- Psalms
- revolt
- Levites
- Absalom
- ridicule
- Hebron
- Messiah
- Prophet
- Nathan
- ambitious

David ruled his people wisely for forty years. He did much to promote the honor and glory of God. When he was about to die he sent for his son Solomon and said to him:

"My son, it was my desire to build a house to the name of the Lord. But the word of God came to me saying, 'You have shed much blood, and fought many battles; you are not the man to build a house to my name. The son that shall be born of you, shall be a peaceful man; for I will give him rest from the enemies that surround him. Therefore he shall be called Peaceable [Solomon]. He shall build a house to my name'" (1 Chr 22:7–9).

To build this house of the Lord, David gathered great quantities of gold, silver, brass, iron, copper and wood, and many precious stones. He told Solomon to begin work on the temple for the Ark as soon as possible. In addition to the materials for the temple, David gave his son very exact and detailed directions about the building and the furnishings. Before he died, David gave this parting advice, "Know the God of your father and serve him with a perfect heart and a willing mind" (1 Kg 2:3). David kept the important part of his message to the last. Solomon was to build an earthly temple, but the essential task of his life was to know God and try to please Him in all his actions. Only in this way could Solomon fulfill the purpose for which he was made.

FOR ME TO REVIEW

Questions and Exercises

Part 1

1. Make a list of five words that describe David.
2. Why is the book of Psalms sometimes called David's Psalter?
3. David was a king who had a strong faith in God and wonderful courage. Give two examples from his life which prove this.

Part 2: Match the words in column I with the words in column II

Column I   Column II

SET 1

1. Jonathan   A. first king of the Israelites
2. David   B. captain of David's army
3. Nathan   C. anointed David King of Israel
4. Juda   D. Philistine warrior overcome by David
5. Joab   E. the Shepherd King
6. Goliath   F. Saul's son who was a friend of David
7. Samuel   G. David's son whom he loved and forgave
8. Bathsheba   H. prophet who guided David
9. Saul   I. tribe to which David belonged
10. Absalom   J. the married woman with whom David sinned

SET 2

1. Psalms   A. chief city of David
2. Abner   B. were subdued by David
3. Scepter   C. captain of Saul's army
4. Solomon   D. tribe to which Saul belonged
5. Jerusalem   E. were written mostly by David
6. Benjamin   F. was assigned to build the temple
7. Philistines   G. staff borne by a ruler as a sign of authority

Part 3: Questions to Check Your Reading

1. Why was the taking of Jerusalem by king David an important victory?

2. How did David show respect for the Ark of the Covenant?

3. Why was David so successful in war?

4. How was David's wife Michol punished?

5. Did David build a temple for the Ark?

6. What three important things did God promise David through the prophet Nathan?

7. Was David grateful to God for His blessings?

8. How did David show kindness to Saul's family?

9. What did David do when Nathan pointed out the seriousness of his sin?

10. How did Absalom bring sorrow to David?

11. How did Absalom meet his death?

12. Was David sorry about the victory?

13. What message did David give his son Solomon?

14. How does David in his life foreshadow what Christ would be and do?

FOR ME TO DO

1. Find quotations from the Old Testament that foretell that the Redeemer would come from the family of David. Read Psalm 109.

2. Compare the characters of Saul and David.

3. Tell one of the incidents in David's life, and show how it proves God's love for us.

4. Prepare a video in which David makes a speech to the people of his time. Bring in some of the prophecies about the Redeemer.

5. Show how David practiced these virtues:

   a) reverence for God
   b) reverence for God's Anointed One,
   c) sympathy
   d) Saul
   e) sincere love of friends
   f) gratitude to God
   g) sorrow for sin
   h) humility

6. Read Psalm 121, which commemorated David's arrival in the Holy City. In it he named Jerusalem, his capital city, the seat of government. Prepare this psalm for choral speaking. Recite it as if you were a pilgrim in that triumphant procession that entered the Holy City.

7. Psalm 129 is the sixth of the Penitential Psalms. It is used in the liturgy of the Church as a prayer for the faithful departed. Unite with the Church in reciting this prayer for the souls in purgatory.

The Reign of Solomon

*Solomon, one of David's younger sons, was not yet twenty years old
when he became king. He began his reign by carefully following the
advice that David had given him.*

THE WISDOM OF SOLOMON

When we read the many beautiful descriptions of wisdom in
the Bible, we must remember that the inspired writers think of
it always as not merely natural knowledge, but the knowledge,
or even the "knowhow" that brings us closer to God. God is
described as having wisdom, and according to this boundless
wisdom He created all things, and also revealed Himself to His
people. In the New Testament our Savior is spoken of as God's

wisdom because He is the perfect revelation of God to mankind. In some of the Masses of our Lady, what is said of divine wisdom in the Old Testament is applied to her, because in her God's wisdom shines forth so beautifully.

At the beginning of his reign, Solomon was visited by God and asked what gift he desired to have. Solomon begged for wisdom because he wished to rule his people justly. His request pleased God, who rewarded Solomon by granting him not only what he asked but also riches and honors. He promised Solomon a long life if he would keep His commandments.

During his reign Solomon gave many proofs of his great wisdom. People from distant countries heard about his wise decisions. Among these people was a queen who ruled the country Saba ('sa-bə) in Arabia. Since she could not believe all that she had heard about Solomon, she set out for Jerusalem to find out for herself. She took with her gifts of gold and precious stones. When she arrived in Jerusalem, the queen asked Solomon many questions, all of which he was able to answer. She then gave him the gifts she had brought, and returned to her own country convinced that the reports about Solomon were true.

Solomon wrote many proverbs. These contain short rules of life, warning his people to avoid evil and encouraging them to do good. These proverbs warn, for instance, against pride, associating with the wicked, and against the sins of the tongue. They recommend mildness, charity, and forgiveness. You might look up some of them and discuss their meaning.

THE CONSTRUCTION OF THE TEMPLE
Solomon remembered that David had asked him to finish building the temple.

The Israelites, however, were not skilled at building with wood. Their houses were generally made of stone, as there were very few trees in their land. Solomon asked Hiram, the King of Tyre (tīr), to give him trees from the Lebanon Mountains. The king sent him cedars and fir trees, both of which were durable. The stone for the temple was quarried in the mountains of Juda and in Jerusalem itself. The outer walls were limestone, while the inner walls were covered with planks of cedar wood. On this wood Solomon had figures of palm trees and blossoming flowers carved so skillfully that they seemed to grow from the wall. The carvings were overlaid with gold.

Solomon's Temple was not a place for "congregational worship" such as our churches are today. In fact, only a very few were permitted inside the temple proper. The worshipers, both priests and laymen, stood in the courtyard.

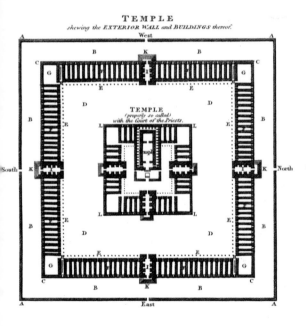

TEMPLE
shewing the EXTERIOR WALL and BUILDINGS thereof.

TEMPLE
(properly so called) with the
COURT of the PRIESTS on an ENLARGED SCALE.

REFERENCE

A Outer Wall
B Court of the Gentiles
C Outer Wall of the Court of the Children of Israel
D Court of the Children of Israel
E Galleries round the Court of Israel, supported by rows of Pillars

F Chambers round the Court of Israel
G Rooms at the corners of the Court, for the use of the Priests
H Stairs leading to the upper Chambers
I Porches of the principal Gates
K Steps of the principal Gates
L Outer Wall of the Court of the Priests

REFERENCE

A Outer Wall of the Court of the Priests
B Court of the Priests
C Chambers for the Singers, Guards, and various offices for the Priests
D Marble Tables on which the Beasts were killed
E Chambers where the Meat was prepared for the Offerings
F Porches of the principal Gates
G Steps of the principal Gates
H North Gate and Porch, here the Beast were killed on D
I Pillars supporting the Galleries round the Court of the Priests

K Stairs leading to the upper Chambers of the Priests
L Small Apartments round the Temple, where the necessaries were kept for its use
M Holy of Holies
N Holy Place
O The Porch
P Steps at the Porch of the Temple
Q Altar for Burnt offerings
R Steps of the Altar
S Wall of separation round the Altar
T Stairs to the upper Apartments
V Wall of the Temple properly so called

The porch or vestibule of the temple was at the east end of the temple grounds. Beyond the porch was the Holy Place, which was similar to our sanctuary. The walls and even the floor of this room were covered with plates of fine gold, fastened together with nails of the same metal. In this Holy Place stood the Altar of Incense, the Table containing the Loaves of Showbread, and the Seven-branched Candlestick. These sacred objects in the sanctuary could be seen by those who stood in the courtyard.

At the western end of the Holy Place was another room in the shape of a cube of thirty feet. Before the entrance hung a veil of violet, purple, and scarlet, embroidered with Cherubim. The veil entirely concealed the interior room, called the Holy of Holies, which contained the Ark of the Covenant. It was almost as sacred to the Israelites as our tabernacle is to us.

The temple was begun in the fourth year of Solomon's reign and was finished in the eleventh year. During its erection, no noise of hammer, or of ax, or of any tool was heard, because all the parts of wood were fitted together beforehand. These parts were probably made outside the temple area, were brought to it, and put in place quietly. Only in such a way can we explain why the temple was built without the sound of hammer or other tools. Although the Temple followed the plans of the tent or Tabernacle, it far surpassed it both in size and grandeur. Solomon built it in Jerusalem on Mount Moria, at the spot where Abraham is believed to have prepared to sacrifice his son Isaac and where David had erected an altar to the Lord.

THE DEDICATION OF THE TEMPLE

When the temple was completed, the priests and Levites brought the Ark of the Covenant to the Holy of Holies on the Feast of Tabernacles. All the people gathered together for this great event and many sacrifices were offered. The day was one of great joy for all the tribes of Israel. They had built and now offered to God a beautiful Temple, one of the world's most famous buildings.

By building this magnificent temple, Solomon rallied his people to the worship of the one true God, thus pointing to a time when our Lord would change the world, an immense temple of idols, into a temple of the one true God. In what way did Christ accomplish this? Is this work completed? In return for Solomon's faithfulness God promised to protect him and his people, provided they obeyed His commands and lived honest and upright lives.

In it and through it the Israelites would be united in their worship of God. The Temple would serve as a bond of union among the tribes of Israel, as the Church of Christ unites people of all nations and races to the end of time. But above all it would be the place of God's abiding presence among His Chosen People.

At the dedication of the Temple, the Israelites promised to serve God faithfully.

SOLOMON'S WEALTH INCREASES

Solomon built several cities, carried on trade with other countries, and increased his wealth greatly. Then Solomon built a palace of untold richness. In it was an assembly hall with furniture of gold. The vessels he used in his dining hall were also of gold. He built one wing of his palace for a pagan wife, whom he married against the command of God.

SOLOMON DISOBEYS THE LAW OF GOD

Anxious to make friends with the Pharaoh of Egypt, Solomon married his daughter and brought her to Jerusalem. He married other pagan women, too, in order to have their countries allied with him. This intermarriage with pagans was displeasing to God. But Solomon had become proud and forgot that he needed God. He surely knew that marrying pagan women would bring him into bad company and draw him away from God. He had been given greater wisdom than most men have, but he misused this wonderful gift.

SOLOMON'S KINGDOM DECLINES

David had collected the money for the building of the Temple, but Solomon spent lavishly. He not only taxed the people heavily for the support of the palace but also forced them to work almost like slaves on his various projects. Naturally they became very dissatisfied.

As Solomon grew older he became very fond of pleasure, abusing his wonderful gift of wisdom. He seriously offended God by building temples for the false gods of his pagan wives. Worse still, he worshiped these gods himself, thereby giving scandalous example to his people. Thus, unjust taxes and idolatry led to the destruction of the unity for which David had worked so hard.

GOD PUNISHES SOLOMON

God was very displeased with Solomon. He said to him, "Because you have done all this, I will divide and rend your kingdom, and will give it to your servants. Nevertheless, in your lifetime I will not do this, for David your father's sake; but I will tear it out of the hand of your son" (1 Kg 11:11–12).

God gave the northern part of the kingdom to Jeroboam (je-'rō-bō-əm) one of Solomon's captains. The prophet Ahia (ə-'hī-ə) told this captain that after Solomon's death he should rule the ten tribes who lived in the north. When Solomon heard this, he tried to kill Jeroboam, but the latter fled to Egypt and lived there until the death of Solomon.

Solomon reigned about forty years as king of Israel. When he died he was buried with his father in Jerusalem, the city of David.

 FOR ME TO REVIEW

Questions and Exercises

Part 1: Match the Old Testament types or figures listed in column I with the statements made in column II

Column I	Column II
1. David's staff of wood	A. Christ's triumph over Satan
2. Saul anointed by the High Priest	B. Christ abandoned by His Apostles
3. David abandoned by his friends	C. Christ's cross
4. Solomon built the Temple	D. Christ established the Church
5. David's five stones	E. Christ the King, the anointed Messiah
6. David's victory over Goliath	F. the Redeemer's five wounds
7. Solomon gifted with wisdom	G. Jesus Christ persecuted by the Jews
8. David persecuted by Saul	H. Christ, the Eternal Wisdom

Part 2: Complete each sentence by giving the necessary word or words

1. _____ succeeded his father David.

2. _____ anointed Saul King of Israel.

3. _____ built a Temple in Jerusalem.

4. _____ was the son of Saul who was a friend to David.

5. _____ was the room in the Temple in which was placed the Ark of the Covenant.

6. _____ was the gift Solomon asked of God.

7. _____ are short sayings full of wisdom.

8. _____ are poems or sacred songs.

9. _____ was the name of the giant whom David overcame.

10. _____ was the prophet who guided David in difficulty.

Part 3: Questions to Check Your Reading

1. How did Solomon use his wisdom to rule his people?

2. How did God show His pleasure at Solomon's prayer for wisdom?

3. Why did the Queen of Saba (Sheba) visit Solomon?

4. What was Solomon's purpose in marrying wives from other nations?

5. Where did Solomon get the wood he needed for the Temple?

6. Name the main parts of the Temple.

7. Why do you think Solomon made the Temple so beautiful?

8. Describe the Holy of Holies.

9. How did Solomon dedicate the Temple?

10. Did Solomon remain true to God and keep His laws?

11. What were the consequences of his sin?

Part 4: Match each word with its meaning

reputation	idolatry	Pharaoh	unity
dedication	convinced	scandal	proverbs
magnificent	parallel	wisdom	prosperity

1. time of success

2. persuaded

3. oneness

4. richly ornamented

5. King of Egypt

6. estimation in which one is held

7. short sayings full of wisdom

8. habit of judging rightly in all things

9. anything equal to or resembling another in essential particulars

10. divine worship given to images

11. word or action which is the occasion of sin to another

12. setting apart for sacred purposes

 **FOR ME TO DO**

1. Imagine you are conducting people through the Temple of Jerusalem, and point out interesting things about it. Then imagine you are showing people through a Catholic church and explain the more important features.

2. Write a composition on the pride of Solomon and its consequences.

3. Explain one of the proverbs that Solomon wrote.

   a) A wise son makes the father glad, but a foolish son is a grief to his mother (Prv 10:1).

   b) The slack hand impoverishes: but the rich hand of the diligent enriches (Prv 10:4).

   c) The memory of the just will be blessed: but the name of the wicked shall rot (Prv 10:7).

   d) It is the lips of the liar that conceal hostility; but he who spreads accusations is a fool (Prv 10:18).

   e) Anger is relentless, and wrath overwhelming—but before jealousy who can stand? (Prv 27:4.)

4. Write a short descriptive paragraph for a Guessing Game. Include David, Samuel, Saul, Solomon, Absalom, Joab, Jonathan, Nathan, and any others that you wish to use.

5. Write a news article on one of the following:

   a) The Parts of the Temple and Their Use

   b) The First Feast Celebrated in the Temple

   c) Solomon's Palace

   d) The Dedication of the Temple

6. Discuss how a marriage where the same religious beliefs are not shared by husband and wife endangers and sometimes leads to loss of faith, especially of the children.

God Guides His Chosen People Through Prophets

After Solomon's death, the kingdom was divided as God had warned.
The Israelites had disobeyed God by their numerous sins. God punished
them by dividing His Chosen People into two kingdoms: Israel, with
ten tribes on the north; Juda, with two tribes to the south. The Lord,
however, sent holy men to both kingdoms to speak to the people in His
name, primarily about existing conditions, but also about the future.
These men were called prophets. They spoke for God.

The Division of the Kingdom

REHOBOAM'S EVIL ADVISERS

When Rehoboam ('rō-bō-əm) succeeded Solomon, his father, representatives of all Israel came to him and pleaded, "Your father laid a painful yoke upon us. You must take off a little of this most heavy burden, and we will be faithful subjects."

Rehoboam said to them, "Come again after three days." He then took counsel with the old men that had advised his dead father.

They said, "If you yield to the people today, they will be your servants always." However, he rejected the good counsel of the old men. Instead he followed the bad counsel of the younger men who had been educated with him. They urged him to show no weakness.

And so Rehoboam answered the people, "I will add to your yoke. My father beat you with whips; but I will beat you with scorpions" (2 Chr 10:4–11).

The ten tribes to the north, refusing to submit to the new hardships imposed upon them by Rehoboam, rebelled. They set up a separate kingdom and called it the Kingdom of Israel. They chose Jeroboam, one of Solomon's captains, as their king. The tribes of Juda and Benjamin lying to the south, under Rehoboam, became the kingdom of Juda. Thus, the kingdom of the Chosen People was divided as God had warned.

JEROBOAM'S SANCTUARIES

Jeroboam set up two golden calves, one in Bethel near the border of Juda, to the south, the other in Dan in the northern part of his kingdom. These represented Yahweh's footstool. He said to the people, "Go no more up to Jerusalem. Behold this is your God who brought you out of the land of Egypt" (1 Kgs 12:28). He also built temples and hired priests who were not of the tribe of Levi. Thus he led the people into forbidden forms of worship and gradually into idolatry.

Then through the prophet Ahia the Lord said to him, "Because you have rejected me, I will destroy your dynasty."

TERMS TO KNOW

- Rehoboam
- Jeroboam
- Israel
- Benjamin
- Juda
- Bethel
- Dan
- Solomon
- Ahia

"Because you have rejected me, I will destroy your dynasty."

REHOBOAM DISPLEASES GOD

Although Rehoboam, King of Juda, saw with his own eyes the harm which his cruel actions produced, he did nothing to change his way of life or to improve the lot of his people. The worship of the true God was permitted only in the temple at Jerusalem. Rehoboam allowed the people to erect altars in other places where superstition and at times even idolatry were practiced. For these offenses God permitted the king of Egypt to overcome Rehoboam in battle. As a result there was no peace in Juda. War also was carried on frequently between the two kingdoms of Juda and Israel. Eventually, like the ten tribes of the kingdom of Israel, the two tribes of the kingdom of Juda would be destroyed.

GOD GUIDES HIS CHOSEN PEOPLE THROUGH PROPHETS

✓ FOR ME TO REVIEW

Questions and Exercises

Part 1: Complete the following statements

1. After the death of Solomon, his son _____ became the king of the Chosen People.
2. The ten northern tribes separated and accepted _____ for their king.
3. _____ introduced unlawful worship of Yahweh in the kingdom of Israel.
4. The tribes of Benjamin and Juda remained under the rule of _____ .
5. This southern kingdom was called _____ .

Part 2: Questions to Check Your Reading

1. Who succeeded Solomon?
2. What caused the division of the Twelve Tribes?
3. By whom was each of the kingdoms ruled?
4. How were many people in Israel led away from the worship of the true God?
5. In what way did the people of Juda offend God?
6. How did God show that He was displeased with Rehoboam and his people?
7. What fate awaited both kingdoms?

✓ FOR ME TO DO

1. Write a paragraph in which you tell why it would have been wiser for Rehoboam to follow the advice given to him by the older men.

Elijah Preserves the True Faith in Israel

The people of the ten tribes which formed the northern kingdom of Israel were led further and further astray from the worship of the one true God. Taking a great part in promoting this evil worship were their own evil kings. The all-merciful and patient God, however, sent Elijah the prophet to perform great miracles in Israel and to be His instrument in preserving the true religion. The kings and to some extent the people misunderstood the works of Elijah and did not return fully to God as might have been expected.

KING AHAB BRINGS PUNISHMENT UPON ISRAEL

In Sacred Scripture Ahab is pictured as one of the worst kings of Israel. He committed many crimes and did not prevent his wicked wife, Jezabel ('Je-zä-bel), a princess of Phoenicia (fə-'nē-si-ə), from promoting the worship of her false gods.

Ahab wished to enlarge his royal gardens. To do so he needed an adjoining vineyard which belonged to Naboth ('na-bōth). The owner refused to sell. The wicked Jezabel quickly overcame this difficulty. She persuaded her friends to accuse Naboth of blasphemy and treason. On the word of these false witnesses, Naboth was stoned to death and his property confiscated.

On his way to take possession of the vineyard, Ahab met Elijah. The prophet had come to announce God's message.

In his message to Ahab, Elijah foretold that the king would be killed on the very spot where Naboth had been stoned. This would be a punishment for his greed in seizing the vineyard and in taking the life of Naboth. Elijah also predicted that a like fate awaited the rest of his wicked family.

AHAB DOES PENANCE

The king believed Elijah and became afraid. He humbly begged God's forgiveness. This was not the first time that Ahab had offended God. In his victories over the Syrians, he had also disobeyed Him. On another occasion Elijah told Ahab that some of the punishment would not come upon the country until after his death. Later Ahab forgot his promises to God and again refused to obey the prophets.

To please Jezabel, Ahab even built a temple to her favorite god Melkart. She killed the true priests of God who protested and chose hundreds of wicked priests and false prophets to carry on services at this temple.

TERMS TO KNOW

- Ahab
- Beelzebub
- blasphemy
- Elisha
- Jezabel
- Melkart
- Naboth
- reproved
- Sarepta
- Ezekiel

All this profoundly offended God, who sent the prophet Elijah to foretell to Ahab the punishment which his sins would bring upon the country. No rain would fall in Israel for three years, and as a result the crops would fail. All this took place just as Elijah had predicted. The people naturally suffered much during the terrible famine that followed.

ELIJAH IS FED MIRACULOUSLY

Ahab was angry with the prophet and blamed him for the drought. Elijah was forced to flee for his life. God directed him to a lonely valley of the Jordan where a raven brought him bread twice a day.

Later, when even the streams dried up from the drought, God told Elijah to go farther north to Sarephta (sä-'ref-tä), a city of the Sidonians (sī-'dō-ni-əns). There, hungry and thirsty, he begged for food and drink from a poor widow who was in need of food herself. What little she had was not sufficient for even one meal for herself and her son. At the command of Elijah, however, she shared it with him. God rewarded her charity. From then on

the widow would never again experience hunger, because the meal in her bowl and the oil in her pitcher would never be exhausted. God worked this miracle for her. Some time later, the widow's son became ill and died. She immediately sought out Elijah, who came and brought the boy back to life.

ELIJAH PROVES THE POWER OF GOD

Once again, God sent Elijah to King Ahab. The country was now suffering from lack of rain for the third year. Elijah summoned the king with all his false prophets to meet with him on Mount Carmel. Afraid to disobey, Ahab set out. When all were assembled, Elijah spoke to them, "If the Lord (Yahweh) is God, you should obey him" (1 Kgs 18:21). Elijah then proposed a test by which he would prove whether his God or the god of the false prophets was the true one.

Two altars were set up with a sacrifice upon each. First the hundreds of false prophets were to call upon the gods of Jezabel to ignite their sacrifice. For a half day they shouted, danced, and called upon their gods with no results. Exhausted and bleeding from self-inflicted cuts, they finally gave up, defeated.

Elijah then dug a trench around the altar upon which his sacrifice rested. Over the victim itself Elijah poured so much water that it ran off into the trench around the altar and filled it. At the time appointed

The Prophets: More than Seers of the Future

There is a common misconception that the prophets were simply men who predicted future events. There was indeed an element of their ministry that dealt with what might happen in the future, but there was so much more to their mission. Their mission was to call the people back to God when they had wandered and sinned. They spoke of God's goodness, power, and majesty, and chastised those who fell into the practice of worshipping pagan gods. The future calamities they spoke of were more warnings of what could happen in the future if the people did not turn back to God, rather than a prediction of a future event that was assured to happen. That being said, the people often ignored the prophets warnings, and those warnings would then come to pass.

for the sacrifice, Elijah prayed fervently to the Lord. Immediately fire descended from heaven and burned not only the sacrifice but also the altar. The heat of the fire even dried up the water in the trench. Astounded by the miracle, the people accepted the God of Elijah and fell on their knees to adore Him. This wonder clearly proved the power of prayer and of faith.

On still another occasion Elijah was forced to flee to escape the revenge of the scheming Ahab and his wife Jezabel. Elijah made his way to the desert of Sinai and, saddened at the thought of the idolatrous Israelites, hoped that he might die. With these thoughts in mind he fell asleep. An angel of the Lord awakened him and said, "Arise, eat, for you have yet a long way to go" (1 Kgs 19:7). Elijah looked around and saw beside him some food. This food kept him from dying of hunger, and strengthened him for his forty-day journey to Mount Sinai.

The night he arrived the Lord appeared to him and said, "What are you doing here, Elijah?" (1 Kgs 19:9.) Elijah told the Lord how he grieved over the Chosen People, who had turned away from the true faith, destroyed God's altars, and killed His prophets. "Go out and stand on the mountain before the Lord" (1 Kgs 19:11), he was told. When he had done so, a mighty storm was unleashed which rent the rocks. An earthquake and lightning followed, so that the upheavals which accompanied the giving of the Commandments to Moses were repeated. But the Lord was not in the storm, or the earthquake, or the lightning. A gentle breeze followed, which signified the spiritual nature of God and the intimacy with which He spoke to His prophets. God told Elijah to return to Israel: he had important work still to do. For one, he must appoint Elisha as his successor. Gently the voice of God told Elijah to return and anoint Elisha to be prophet in his place.

Elijah obeyed the command of God and, returning, found Elisha plowing with oxen. Elijah put his mantle upon him. Elisha bade farewell to his parents and home, and followed Elijah.

THE DEATH OF AHAB

When the Syrians again crossed the Jordan, Ahab sought help from the Kingdom of Juda. A prophet, Micah, warned Ahab that he would be killed in battle, but he did not heed the warning. During the battle Ahab was seriously wounded and died at the very place where Naboth had been stoned.

THE ATTEMPT TO ARREST ELIJAH

One of the sons of Ahab, evil like his father, succeeded as king of Israel. Severely injured in an accident, he sent servants to learn of Beelzebub (bē-'el-zə-bŭb), a false god, if he would regain his health. On the way to the pagan temple, his servants met Elijah, who reproved them for consulting a false god. He also sent sad news to the king. He foretold that he would die of the injury. Angered, the king immediately sent out a company of fifty soldiers to arrest Elijah. As they were about to seize him, a fire from heaven destroyed them.

The king grew even angrier and sent another group of fifty men to search for Elijah. These soldiers were also burned to death. When a third company of fifty men laid hands on Elijah, God directed him to go with them and repeat his previous message to the king. Elijah did, and the king died as the prophet foretold. Several years later the evil Jezabel also died in a horrible manner.

ELIJAH IS TAKEN BY GOD

The day arrived when Elijah was to leave this world. The prophet Elisha was with him. Wishing to be alone as the time for his departure drew near, Elijah said to Elisha,

It has often been said that Elijah must return before the end of the world and preach penance, then die like other men. But Our Lord said that St. John the Baptist had carried out the mission of Elijah. Probably, then, Elijah is already in heaven and will not have to return to this earth.

"Stay here because the Lord has sent me to Jericho" (2 Kgs 2:4). But Elisha would not leave him, for he also knew that soon Elijah would depart.

When they reached the Jordan River, Elijah struck the water with his mantle. A dry path appeared. Over this they safely crossed. Elijah then inquired what gift he should ask for Elisha. His spiritual son answered that he wished to have the special portion given to the first-born son, that is, he wished to continue the work of Elijah as perfectly as possible.

Suddenly a fiery chariot with fiery horses appeared between them. In it Elijah was taken away alive by God. Elisha was left behind holding the mantle of Elijah.

Elisha the Prophet

ELISHA SUCCEEDS ELIJAH

Elisha continued the work of Elijah. He never tired of teaching the people and of urging them to remain faithful to God. Like Elijah, he also had the gift of performing miracles. Once, by means of a pinch of salt and a blessing, he purified the waters of a spring near Jericho which was unfit for drinking.

This miracle, although performed centuries ago, reminds us of the blessing of water by the Church. Indeed, in the blessing of water the miracle of Elisha is mentioned. Why does the Church use salt in the blessing of water?

THE END OF THE KINGDOM OF ISRAEL (721 B.C.)

In the eighth century before Christ, after many years of patience, God finally allowed the destruction of the sinful people of the ten tribes of the kingdom of Israel. The King of Assyria came with a great army, took the capital city, Samaria (sə-'ma-ri-ə), after a long siege and led most of the people into captivity to Assyria. The kingdom of Israel had at last come to an end. Those who remained mingled with new settlers who were sent in, and later with those who returned from exile. Out of this mixture arose the Samaritans.

THE PROPHETS OF GOD

Many prophets are mentioned in the history of the Chosen People. Through these prophets God spoke to His Chosen People, the Israelites, and told them what He wished them to do. The prophets also taught and explained the Law. Often they performed miracles to prove their divine mission. They led the people back to God after they had strayed away from Him. Gradually the prophets acquainted the Chosen People with the coming Messiah. In doing this, they prepared the way for the new kingdom which the Redeemer would establish on earth.

Many of the prophecies of the prophets Isaiah (ī-'sā-ə), Jeremiah (je-re-'mī-ə), and Ezekiel (ē-'zē-ki-l), are recorded in the Bible at great length. These prophets, along with Daniel, are called the Major Prophets. The book of Daniel, however, is somewhat different from the books of Isaiah, Jeremiah, and Ezekiel. In its present form it was written in the second century B.C. and speaks mysteriously of the persecution of the Jews at that

Major and Minor Prophets

The distinction between Major and Minor Prophets is not how important they are but how long their book of the Bible is. The major prophets' books are longer, while the minors' are shorter.

Five Major Prophets
- Isaiah
- Jeremiah
- Ezekiel
- Daniel

Twelve Minor Prophets
- Hosea
- Joel
- Amos
- Obadiah
- Jonah
- Micah
- Nahum
- Habakkuk
- Zephaniah
- Haggai
- Zechariah
- Malachi

time and of the Kingdom of Christ. Other prophets, like Amos, Micah, Hoshea, and Malachi, are known as the Minor Prophets, because their books are smaller than those of the Major Prophets.

The prophets were not always able to carry out God's commands, as we have seen in the story of Elijah. Often they were persecuted, and their lives were endangered. Nevertheless, they trusted in God. He protected them, aiding them in marvelous ways to carry out their mission for Him.

God sent prophets at different times from the days of Moses until the time of the Machabees ('mak-ə-bēs). From the days of the Machabees until our Lord, God's message could be learned as read in the inspired books of the Old Testament or as explained by the scribes. Furthermore, all the prophecies concerning the Messiah and His Kingdom would soon be fulfilled because the Redeemer Himself was about to come.

FOR ME TO REVIEW

Questions and Exercises

Part 1: Match the following sentences with the correct ending

1. God sent Elijah to the people of Israel _____.

2. God was displeased with the people of Israel because _____.

3. The poor widow always had enough to eat because _____.

4. The gods of Jezabel could not light the sacrifice because _____.

5. Naboth was put to death because _____.

6. Ahab built temples for false gods because _____.

7. God protected Elijah because _____.

8. God forgave Ahab some of his temporal punishment because _____.

A. he wished to please his wicked wife.

B. he served God faithfully.

C. to try to make them obedient to God's Law.

D. they worshiped false gods.

E. they were not true gods.

F. Ahab desired to possess his vineyard.

G. God rewarded her charity.

H. he was sorry for his sins.

Part 2: Questions to Check Your Reading

1. How did King Ahab offend God?

2. What were some ways in which God punished Ahab and the people of Israel?

3. What event in the story of Elijah showed the power of prayer?

4. In what ways did Elijah foreshadow Christ?

5. Give examples of God's Divine Providence toward Elijah.

6. To what sin did Ahab's unlawful desires of the vineyard lead?

7. What incident proved that God forgives a repentant sinner?

8. What were some of the miracles Elijah performed?

9. Which miracle of Elisha reminds us of the blessing of water?

10. For what purpose did God send prophets to His Chosen People?

11. How did the end of Israel, the northern kingdom, take place?

✓ FOR ME TO DO

1. Give a floor talk on the courage of Elijah.

2. Dramatize a scene from the story of Elijah.

3. Imagine you are Elijah. Reprove King Ahab for his many sins.

4. Sometimes people do forbidden things to get what they desire. List some of these things, and after each one tell how a commandment may be broken in trying to get this forbidden thing. Discuss with the class.

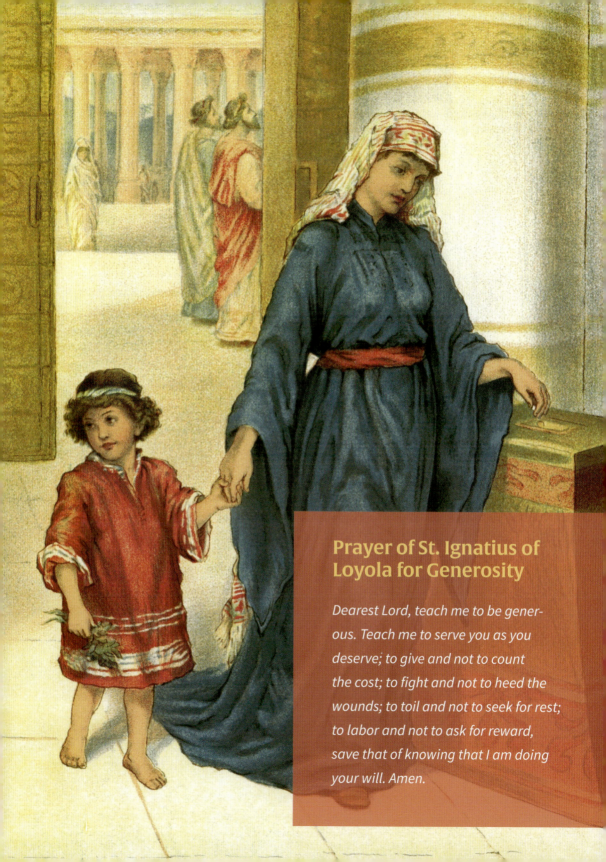

Prayer of St. Ignatius of Loyola for Generosity

Dearest Lord, teach me to be generous. Teach me to serve you as you deserve; to give and not to count the cost; to fight and not to heed the wounds; to toil and not to seek for rest; to labor and not to ask for reward, save that of knowing that I am doing your will. Amen.

CHAPTER 13

The Prophets Isaiah, Jeremiah, and Ezekiel

From the account of the Chosen People thus far we can learn that nations decline and lose their freedom when they turn away from God. The downfall of the Ten Tribes of Israel in the northern kingdom was brought about by their own infidelity. It was a just punishment for sin. Of what sin in particular were the Israelites guilty?

The two southern tribes were also led into captivity a century and a half later because their kings, the kings of Juda, permitted pagan enemies to enter their territory. The prophets had warned the people of Juda against entering into alliance with other nations, and against pagan influences. The Jews did not heed the warning. As a consequence they were punished by exile and by war. Yahweh sent His prophets to the people in exile to bring them back to His worship. These prophets were needed to keep God's laws before the minds of the faithful.

The Prophet Isaiah

THE EVANGELIST OF THE OLD TESTAMENT

God sent a number of prophets to the people of the northern kingdom of Israel. When they refused to listen to these prophets they were punished by being taken captive. God also sent prophets to Juda. One of the greatest of these was Isaiah. You will see how Isaiah by his prayers, warnings, and his holy life saved the people of Juda for a time from the ruin which their sins deserved. He preached to the Jews concerning the Messiah. He predicted the Messiahnic reign so clearly that the Fathers of the

Church have called him the prince of the prophets, and the Evangelist of the Old Testament.

THE CALL OF ISAIAH

Do you recall how surprised Moses, David, and Gideon felt when God chose them to lead His people to victory? Isaiah was also amazed to learn that the Lord had called him. While praying in the temple one day he beheld a wonderful vision of the Lord, seated upon a throne and surrounded by angels. In awe, these angels covered their faces with their wings and sang these words, "Holy, holy, holy, the Lord God of Hosts: all the earth is full of his glory" (Is 6:3).

Isaiah was unable to look at this heavenly vision; ancient Hebrews thought that a vision of God was the signal for death. He could only bow low and cry, "Woe is me, I am doomed! because I am a man of unclean lips; and I dwell in the midst of people that have unclean lips" (Is 6:5).

At these words one of the angels touched his lips with a live coal, saying,

TERMS TO KNOW

- Isaiah
- captivity
- Assyrians
- Sennacherib
- Joatham
- Babylon
- Hezekiah
- Jerusalem
- Nineveh
- Emmanuel
- Babylonians
- prophecies
- Ahaz

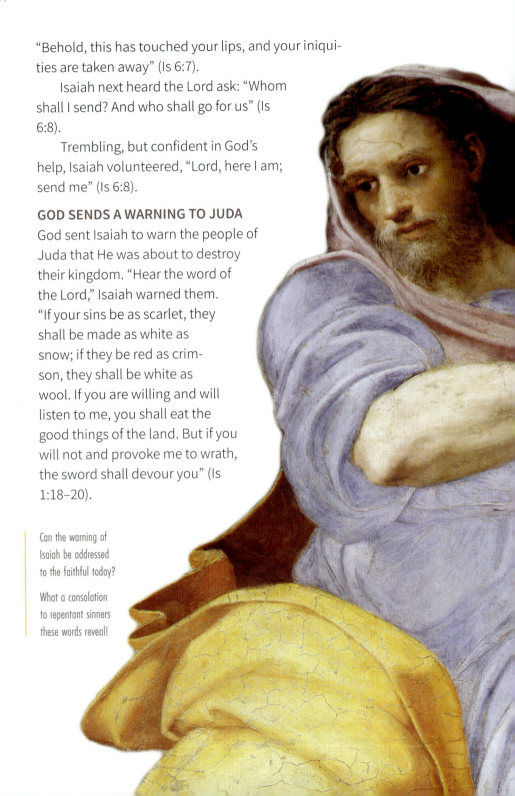

"Behold, this has touched your lips, and your iniquities are taken away" (Is 6:7).

Isaiah next heard the Lord ask: "Whom shall I send? And who shall go for us" (Is 6:8).

Trembling, but confident in God's help, Isaiah volunteered, "Lord, here I am; send me" (Is 6:8).

GOD SENDS A WARNING TO JUDA

God sent Isaiah to warn the people of Juda that He was about to destroy their kingdom. "Hear the word of the Lord," Isaiah warned them. "If your sins be as scarlet, they shall be made as white as snow; if they be red as crimson, they shall be white as wool. If you are willing and will listen to me, you shall eat the good things of the land. But if you will not and provoke me to wrath, the sword shall devour you" (Is 1:18–20).

Can the warning of Isaiah be addressed to the faithful today?

What a consolation to repentant sinners these words reveal!

AHAZ, A WICKED KING OF JUDA

Joatham ('jō-ə-thəm), who reigned for only two years, was followed by his son Ahaz ('ak-əz) as King of Juda. Ahaz was a wicked king, who favored the practices of the pagan Canaanites. Moreover, to please the Assyrians, he introduced features of their religion into Juda. For these sins God punished him by allowing his enemies to invade his kingdom. Instead of heeding this warning and the pleas of the prophet Isaiah, Ahaz only did greater evil.

EMMANUEL PROMISED

The kings of Syria (Aram) and Israel decided to unite all the small states of Palestine and Syria to wage war on Assyria, which had begun a policy of aggression with the purpose of bringing the entire Near East into one mighty empire. When King Ahaz refused to join the alliance, these kings invaded Juda, intending to dethrone Ahaz and install a king who would join their efforts against Assyria. When word was brought to Ahaz that the armies of Syria had already reached Israel and were ready to proceed to Juda, he and all the people trembled with fear. He decided to appeal for help to Assyria, the very aggressor that was threatening the whole then-known world.

195

Only one man in Juda was not disturbed by the threat of invasion, the prophet Isaiah. He was told by God to meet Ahaz, who was inspecting an aqueduct, and order the king of Juda not to appeal to Assyria. The kings of Aram and Israel would not succeed: they were like two smoking torches already burned out that could do no harm. Isaiah warned the king that only trust in Yahweh could save him: "Unless your faith is firm," he said, "you shall not be firm" (Is 7:9).

The king said nothing, but he was not convinced. When Isaiah heard that he was collecting the temple treasures to send them to Assyria as payment for help, he went boldly to the palace to make a final plea. So convinced was he of God's mission that he offered to work any kind of miracle to prove to King Ahaz that he was God's messenger. "Ask of Yahweh your God a sign for yourself, wherever you wish—in the depths of the netherworld or high in the heavens." But the king, who had gone too far in his project, hypocritically answered: "I will not put Yahweh to the test" (Is 7:11–12).

After this unworthy excuse of the King, Isaiah indignantly replied and solemnly proclaimed: "Listen, O house of David! Is it not enough for you to weary men, must you also weary my God? Therefore the Lord himself will give you this sign: the virgin shall be with child, and bear a son, and shall name him Emmanuel. He shall be living on curds and honey by the time he learns to reject the bad and choose the good. For before the child learns to reject the bad and choose the good, the land of those two kings whom you dread shall be deserted" (Is 7:13–16).

This prophecy is one of the most important and at the same time one of the most mysterious of the Old Testament.

MAJOR PROPHETS

Isaiah, Jeremiah, Ezekiel, Daniel

Even today experts do not agree on the interpretation of everything it contains. One thing, however, is certain: Isaiah surely wanted to insist that the projects of the kings of Israel and Aram to overrun the land of Juda and even to do away with the Judean dynasty would fail because Yahweh, by His prophet Nathan, had already solemnly promised David that his kingdom would last forever. The Messiah had to be the final and everlasting king of David's dynasty. Hence when some seven centuries later the angel announced to St. Joseph that his wife, Mary the virgin, was to be the mother of Christ, St. Matthew notes that thus was to be fulfilled the prophecy of Isaiah.

BETHLEHEM THE BIRTHPLACE OF THE MESSIAH

Another prophet who lived at the same time as Isaiah, Micah, also referred to our Lady in his prediction of the Savior's birth; it seems that he has Isaiah's prophecy in mind, and for that reason it is quoted here. You will notice that when Herod consulted the scribes in order to answer the Magi's inquiry about the birthplace of the Messiah, they quoted this text:

ISAIAH

JEREMIAH

EZEKIEL

DANIEL

But you, Bethlehem-Ephratha
    too small to be among
    the clans of Juda,
From you shall come forth for me
    one who is to be ruler in Israel;
Whose origin is from of old,
    from ancient times.
(Therefore the Lord will give them up, until the time
    when she who is to give birth has borne,
And the rest of his brethren shall return
    to the children of Israel.)
He shall stand firm and shepherd his flock
    by the strength of the Lord,
    in the majestic name of the Lord, his God;
And they shall remain, for now his greatness
    shall reach to the ends of the earth;
    he shall be peace (Mi 5:2–4).

Did you Know?

Bethlehem, the town were Jesus would be born, means "house of bread." This is rich with meaning since Jesus is the Bread of Life.

EMMANUEL KING OF PEACE

To console the people of Israel and Juda during the Assyrian threat, Isaiah on several occasions reminded them of the coming Messiah, who would be the light of the world and would bring about universal peace and justice:

> The people who walked in darkness
>   have seen a great light;
> Upon those who dwelt in the land of gloom
>   A light has shone (Is 9:2).
> For a child is born to us, a son is given us;
>   upon his shoulder dominion rests.
> They name him Wonder-Counselor, God-Hero,
>   Father-Forever, Prince of Peace.
> His dominion is vast
>   and forever peaceful,
> From David's throne, and over his kingdom,
>   which he confirms and sustains
> By judgment and justice,
>   both now and forever.
> The zeal of the Lord of hosts will do this! (Is 9:6–7.)

EMMANUEL AND THE GIFTS OF THE HOLY SPIRIT

Isaiah also foretold that the Messiah would be a new David (whose father was Jesse) and would be endowed with the gifts of the Holy Spirit.

> A shoot shall sprout from the stump of Jesse,
>   and from his roots a bud shall blossom.
> The spirit of the Lord shall rest upon him:
>   a spirit of wisdom and of understanding,
> A spirit of counsel and of strength,
>   a spirit of knowledge and of fear of the Lord,
>   and his delight shall be the fear of the Lord.
> Not by appearance shall he judge,

nor by hearsay shall he decide,
But he shall judge the poor with justice,
and decide aright for the land's afflicted.
He shall strike the ruthless with the rod of his mouth,
and with the breath of his lips he shall slay the
wicked.
Justice shall be the band around his waist,
and faithfulness a belt upon his hips (Is 11:1–5).

HEZEKIAH, KING OF JUDA

Ahaz was succeeded by his son, Hezekiah, who became as renowned for his piety as his father had been for his wickedness.

Hezekiah, like David, was a man according to God's own heart. He destroyed the altars on which idols had been worshiped and broke the images. At his command the priests and Levites cleansed the Temple and removed the pagan altar which Ahaz had built. Hezekiah restored the divine services as they had been performed in the time of David. In atonement he ordered all the people to observe the great feast of the Passover. To this celebration he invited the Chosen People from the north who had not been deported in 721 B.C.

GOD REWARDS HEZEKIAH

God rewarded Hezekiah by giving peace and security to his kingdom. However, on one occasion he was allured by worldly advisers against the advice of Isaiah, who preached that Juda's only alliance must be with Yahweh. He attacked the Philistines and refused to pay tribute to Assyria. Sennacherib (se-'nak-ə-rib), the king of the Assyrians, promptly came into Juda with a great army and took many of the Judean cities.

Hezekiah now took the gold of the temple and sent it to the Assyrians. He submitted to their rule. Sennacherib, however, was not satisfied with this. He sent messengers to Jerusalem demanding the surrender of the city. These messengers offended God grievously because they said that the Assyrians were stronger than God.

Hezekiah, like David, was a man according to God's own heart.

ISAIAH ADVISES HEZEKIAH

Hezekiah now sent word to Isaiah. He told them what the messengers had demanded. Isaiah answered, "Thus says the Lord: Be not afraid of the words which you have heard, with which the servants of the king of the Assyrians have blasphemed me. Behold, I will send a spirit upon him, and he shall bear a message and shall return to his own country; and I will cause him to fall by the sword in his own country" (Is 37:6–7). Isaiah advised King

Hezekiah to place his trust in God. By so doing he would protect his kingdom successfully against the Assyrians.

When Hezekiah learned that the Assyrians were marching against Jerusalem, he repaired the walls of the city and built a tunnel to conduct water from Jerusalem's main water supply into the city. He gathered as large an army as he could and begged the men to be brave against the enemy. When the Assyrians attacked the city, God proved to Hezekiah that his people should trust more in His help than in their own power. The strength of the Chosen People was neither in their walled cities nor in their armies but in the greatness of God.

Some time later the messengers of Sennacherib returned to Hezekiah and repeated their demands. The king went to the temple and prayed to God for help. Isaiah sent word to him that the Lord had heard his prayer and would drive away the Assyrians. He told Hezekiah that he need have no fear. God would protect Jerusalem and carry out the promises He had made to David. Isaiah said that Sennacherib would return to his own country and would never again appear in Juda.

That night, the Bible tells us, a messenger of the Lord was sent to Sennacherib's army, which was camped south of Jerusalem, and killed a large number of the Assyrian soldiers. When Sennacherib saw all the dead, he departed for his own city, Nineveh. Shortly after this Sennacherib was slain by his two sons as he was worshiping in the temple.

God, through Isaiah, saved His people from the Assyrians. He later foretold that they would be carried into captivity by the Babylonians. A Persian king, Cyrus ('sī-rəs), would set them free.

FOR ME TO REVIEW

Questions and Exercises

Part 1: Complete the following statements

1. _____ a Persian king, would later free God's Chosen People from captivity.

2. _____ was a king who tried to bring the Chosen People back to the faithful service of Yahweh.

3. _____ was the song Isaiah heard the angels singing.

4. _____ was the nation that Isaiah said would one day take the Jewish people captive and make them serve them.

5. _____ was the kingdom that God was about to destroy because of their sins.

6. _____ spoke more about the Messiah than any other prophet.

7. _____ was king of the Assyrians at the time God saved His people from that nation.

Part 2: Questions to Check Your Reading

1. How was Isaiah called by God?

2. What was the warning God gave Isaiah for the people of Juda?

3. How was King Ahaz unfaithful to God?

4. What did King Hezekiah do to save Juda from being destroyed?

5. How did God reward Hezekiah?

6. Why did Isaiah tell Hezekiah that the day would come when the Babylonians would take all his treasures, and his people would be taken as captives?

7. Why was the country of Juda happy under Hezekiah?

8. What were some of the prophecies of Isaiah?

FOR ME TO DO

1. Print some of the prophecies of Isaiah on posters, which may be used for a bulletin board display.

2. God never disappoints those who trust in him. How does the story of Hezekiah prove this statement?

3. How did God reward the confidence which Hezekiah placed in Him?

4. Write a prayer in which you ask God to help you be faithful to Him and His commandments, especially in times of trial or disappointment.

Jeremiah, a Tender Prophet

After the death of King Hezekiah and the prophet Isaiah, the Kingdom of Juda fell away from God. They were given many opportunities to repent before their kingdom also was destroyed. For forty years, as we shall see, the great prophet Jeremiah (je-re-'mī-ə) lived among them, warning them of the misery that would befall them. But they did not listen.

THE RULERS BEFORE THE BABYLONIAN CAPTIVITY

Manasseh (mən-'as-sə) succeeded his father Hezekiah on the throne of Juda. A weak ruler, he killed many prophets and priests and rebuilt the altars to the false gods which his father had destroyed. Because of his bad example the people became more sinful than the pagans. After the second attack of the Assyrians, the city of Jerusalem was captured and Manasseh was taken prisoner.

His son Amon (a-mən) succeeded as king. He continued his father's evil ways. The sinful lives of ruler and people brought the kingdom of Juda nearer to destruction.

Next Amon's son Josiah (jə-'sī-ə) became king of Juda. He tried to root out idolatry and to restore the true religion to his kingdom. But the faithless people brought down upon themselves the anger of God. Josiah reigned for thirty-one years and was killed in battle against the Egyptians. He was succeeded by Jehoahaz ('jō-ə-kaz), who reigned for only three months and was then taken captive to Egypt. Jehoiakim ('jō-ə-kim), another son of Josiah, was put on the throne. But once more he led the people away from God and into captivity.

THE CALL OF JEREMIAH

God raised up a great prophet at this time to warn the people that they were in danger of being destroyed by their enemies. This great teacher and prophet was Jeremiah. He came from a priestly family which resided at Anatoth ('an-ə-toth), a few miles north of Jerusalem. In calling him, God said: "I have made you a prophet to the nations" (Jer 1:5).

Jeremiah was afraid and answered, "O Lord, I cannot speak, I am too young" (Jer 1:6).

But God replied, "You shall go to all those to whom I shall send you. . . . Have no fear . . . for I will be with you to deliver you" (Jer 1:7–8).

The Lord then touched the mouth of Jeremiah and said, "Behold, I have put

TERMS TO KNOW

- Manasseh
- Jehoiakim
- Yahweh
- Amon
- Baruch
- Lamentations
- Josiah
- Nebuchadnezzar
- Zedekiah
- Jeremiah
- destruction
- Jehoahaz
- idolatries
- Babylonian Captivity

my words into your mouth" (Jer 1:9). He indicated, by this, that when a prophet speaks in God's name, he is really imparting the word of God. At the same time Jeremiah had a vision in which he saw vividly the tragic warnings he was to speak.

JEREMIAH WARNS THE PEOPLE

Jeremiah showed the people how ungratefully they had spurned God's love. God would punish them severely if they did not repent.

During the reign of Jehoiakim, the Chosen People, still indifferent to God, fell again into idolatry. Jeremiah let them know that if they continued in their evil ways, their country would be destroyed and they, like the people of the northern kingdom, would be taken into captivity.

JEREMIAH'S PROPHECY FULFILLED—THE BABYLO-NIAN CAPTIVITY

The warnings of Jeremiah soon came true. Nebuchad-nezzar (nä-bu-kō-'dȯn-ə-sōr), king of Babylon, besieged Jerusalem and captured the city. King Jehoiakim died during the siege, but his son Jeconiah or Joakin was taken prisoner to Babylon, along with many of the nobles and skilled artisans of Juda. Zedekiah (se-de-'kī-ə), another son of King Josiah, was given the throne, but as a subject of Babylon.

ZEDEKIAH ALSO REBELS (587 B.C.)

Zedekiah began well, listening to Jeremiah and asking for his counsel and prayers. One party in Juda, however, was constantly agitating for rebellion against Babylon. Jeremiah knew that rebellion would be fatal. It was God's will that for the present Juda should remain subject to Babylon. To illustrate this, Jeremiah wandered through the streets of the city with a yoke upon his neck to show the people the fate that would be theirs if they

In filling his mission of warning, strengthening, and praying for the Jews, Jeremiah was doing what Christ later would do. In the New Testament Christ was to pray over Jerusalem, foretell its destruction and promote salvation for those who would follow Him.

continued their wickedness. They were not to rely on an alliance with Egypt but were to place their trust in God. He wrote messages to those already taken captive and urged them to settle down in Babylon and raise families because it would be many years before they could return to Palestine.

But Zedekiah was weak and finally yielded to the agitation. Nebuchadnezzar laid siege to Jerusalem for the second time when Zedekiah joined the Egyptians against the Babylonians.

After a siege of eighteen months, a break was made in the walls and the city was taken (587 B.C.). Zedekiah fled, but the pursuing enemy captured him. He was brought to Nebuchadnezzar, and his children were put to death in his presence. Then Zedekiah was blinded and taken to Babylon.

THE DESTRUCTION OF JERUSALEM (587 B.C.)

After Jerusalem fell all valuable furnishings were taken from the houses of the city. Important buildings were destroyed. The walls of the city were leveled to the ground. According to a Jewish tradition, Jeremiah and certain Levites secretly removed the Ark of the Covenant and the Altar of Incense before the Babylonians could reach the Temple. They carried them across the Jordan and hid them in a secret cave in Mount Nebo ('nē-bō). The Ark and the Altar have never been discovered.

The ruins of Jerusalem, and of Solomon's Temple in particular, inspired Jeremiah or a similar prophet to write the *Lamentations*. In these he describes the destruction of Jerusalem and the great suffering of the

The Church in the Divine Office prays the Lamentations during Holy Week to recall the sufferings of our Redeemer.

people. These hymns recall the goodness and mercy of God over the centuries. They also make clear that He will find another way to bring about the coming of the Promised Redeemer.

Jerusalem was completely destroyed, as Jeremiah had foretold. Thus the Kingdom of Juda came to an end. God had made this kingdom great and glorious under David. He would have made it still more glorious, because through it He had wanted to draw all nations to know and serve Him. Evil kings and sinful people in Israel prevented this. They forgot the true God, who then permitted their kingdom to be destroyed and the people themselves to be carried away as captives.

The few who remained in Juda were misled by a fanatic who assassinated the governor appointed by the King of Babylon. Fearing punishment, they went to Jeremiah to ask for advice. Jeremiah told them that, if they remained in Juda, God would protect them. But they did not believe Jeremiah, and fled to Egypt, forcing Jeremiah to go with them.

THE LAST YEARS OF JEREMIAH

In Egypt, Jeremiah found the Chosen People worshiping the idols of the Egyptians. He tried to bring them back to the service of Yahweh, the true God, by telling them how their countrymen had suffered for a similar sin. He predicted that the Babylonians would take Egypt, and as a consequence they would suffer. Even here they paid no attention to him. Despite the hardness of the sinful Jews, Jeremiah exercised great trust in Divine Providence by continuing to preach and prophesy.

After serving God as His faithful prophet for many years, Jeremiah died in Egypt. He had dictated to Baruch (bə-'ruk), his secretary, a summary of the messages to the Chosen People that God had sent through him. These messages are sad prophecies because they tell what God in His goodness had done to help His people remain faithful. They show how the Israelites, who had been protected by God for seven hundred years, were finally destroyed by their own wickedness. But these messages are encouraging as well, since they show how faithful God always is to His promises. Although the Chosen People had not obeyed God, He would preserve among them unharmed a faithful family from whom the Redeemer of mankind would come.

Jeremiah prophesied the destruction of the Babylonian empire in the following words, ". . . it shall be no more inhabited forever." He foretold that the Jews would be in captivity in Babylon for seventy years. He also predicted their return to the land of their fathers. And most beautifully of all, he foretold that God would make a new covenant with His people, to replace the Old Covenant that had been broken. This New Covenant would be everlasting. Our Lord established this Covenant at the Last Supper when He said: "This is my blood of the New Covenant" (Mt 26:28).

 FOR ME TO REVIEW

Questions and Exercises

Part 1: For each of the following give the name of the person, people, country, or conditions described

1. Jeremiah spent his last years in _____ .

2. The King of Babylon at the time Jerusalem was destroyed and the Chosen People of the Kingdom of Juda were taken into captivity was _____ .

3. _____ helped Jeremiah write the messages which God had sent to the Chosen People.

4. The prophet _____ foretold the destruction of Jerusalem.

5. The last King of Juda before it fell was _____ .

6. The nation that destroyed Jerusalem and took the people of Juda into captivity was _____ .

7. The king by whom Jerusalem was destroyed was _____.

8. _____ was a holy, pious King of Juda.

Part 2: Questions to Check Your Reading

1. What kind of rulers did the Kingdom of Juda have?

2. What can you say about the reign of Josiah?

3. Who foretold the destruction of Jerusalem?

4. Describe how Jeremiah was called to be a prophet.

5. Who destroyed Jerusalem and carried the people of Juda into captivity?

6. What caused the downfall of Jerusalem?

7. Were the Lamentations preserved in the Bible?

8. When does the Church read the Lamentations?

9. What did Jeremiah prophesy about Egypt and the Jews who lived there?

10. Describe the last days of Jeremiah.

11. Do you recall the Ark of the Covenant? What was in it? Where was it kept in the Temple?

12. Did God intend the fate of the Chosen People of the Old Testament to serve as a warning to the Chosen People of the New Testament if they do not remain faithful to God?

FOR ME TO DO

1. Make a visit to the Blessed Sacrament to make an act of contrition for your own sins and to pray for poor sinners who do not listen to God's warning to repent.

2. Read some of the prophecies of Jeremiah and then write a composition as to how you think Jeremiah instructed the Chosen People.

3. Write a letter about the Babylonian Captivity.

4. Write a letter to King Josiah praising him for the good deeds he had done for his people.

5. Write the name Jeremiah, one letter under the other. After each letter write a sentence describing this prophet. Have the sentence begin with letters in Jeremiah's name. Write an acrostic using Jeremiah's name and his virtues.

6. Compare:

    a) Jeremiah singing the Lamentations among the ruins of the Temple while his people were in Babylon in captivity, and

    b) The Church lamenting the spiritual ruin of her children made captive by their sins.

7. Jeremiah relied on Divine Providence. Name other leaders who have manifested a similar reliance on the goodness of God. How can we in our daily lives show that we have complete trust in Divine Providence?

The Prophet Ezekiel

THE MISSION OF THE PROPHET EZEKIEL

In Babylon, the people of the Kingdom of Juda lived among pagans, who practiced idolatry, and this was a serious threat to the national patriotism and especially to the religion of the Jews. To preserve the national as well as the religious future of Israel, and the religious future of the world, God called another prophet, Ezekiel, to guide His people.

Even before the destruction of Jerusalem, Ezekiel had spoken of the trouble and the punishment that was to come. After the city's fall, Ezekiel consoled the exiles for whom this news had been a terrible blow. His preaching was similar to that of Jeremiah. The Chosen People saw clearly that the prophecies of Jeremiah and Ezekiel had been fulfilled. They knew that they had failed to heed the warnings of the prophets. They grew discouraged and wondered if God would ever again show them mercy. Ezekiel urged them not to give up hope in the divine promises. He reminded them that God would take care of Israel and defend His people against hostile nations. He also taught the people that each one of them would be rewarded or punished according to his works.

Ezekiel often repeated to them the promise that they would return from exile. In fact, he is sometimes called the prophet of the restoration and the father of Judaism, as the religion of the period after the exile in Babylon

The Babylonian Captivity of the Papacy

The captivity of the Jewish people in Babylon was such a major event in salvation history that it has come to be used as a symbol for other events throughout history. For example, the Church speaks of a "Babylonian Captivity" for the papacy, when it was moved from Rome to Avignon, France from 1309 to 1376. Today, we cannot picture the pope living anywhere other than Rome, but for nearly a century, he lived in France (this is also called the "Avignon Papacy"). There were many factors that lead to this unprecedented situation, but chief among them was the pressure the papacy was under from the French crown, who wanted to wield its influence on the Church. Thankfully, the papacy was eventually moved back to Rome, where the pope has resided to this day.

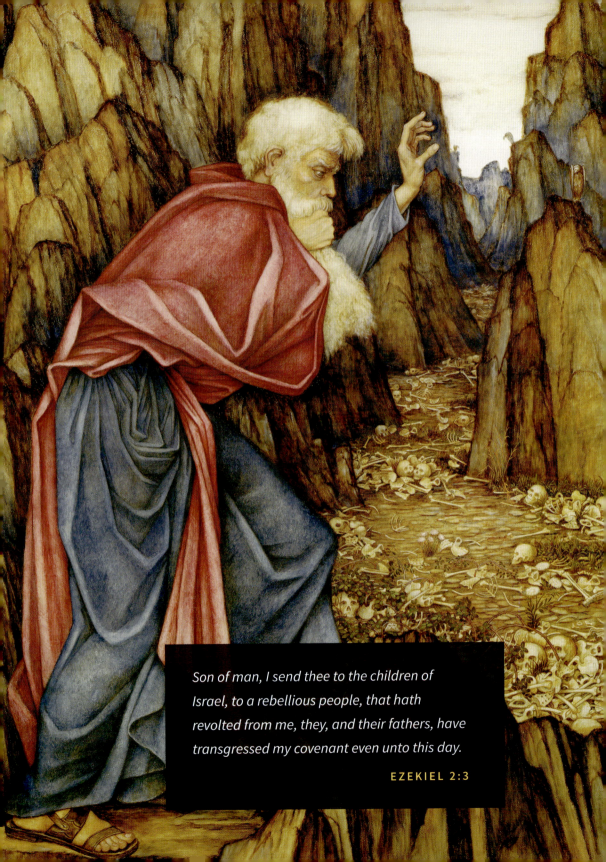

Son of man, I send thee to the children of Israel, to a rebellious people, that hath revolted from me, they, and their fathers, have transgressed my covenant even unto this day.

EZEKIEL 2:3

reminds us also of the resurrection of the dead. In this vision he was shown a huge valley, over which the bones of thousands of slain were scattered. These bones symbolized the Hebrews in exile: they were dead as a nation and with no human hope of rising again. Now Ezekiel was commanded by God to prophesy, that is, to speak in God's name. He obeyed and commanded the bones to come to life. We can almost hear the rattling as each bone finds its right place in the thousands of skeletons that result. They are clothed anew with flesh, and finally, as Ezekiel continues to utter God's word, they once more receive the breath of life! In this vivid way, the prophet comforted the Jews and assured them that they would return to Palestine and once again be God's Chosen People. He did not live to see the restoration, but he did help to prepare the way for it by his preaching.

Isaiah's restoration prophecy begins with the words: "Be comforted, be comforted, my people, says your God. . . . Your slavery is at an end, your sins have been expiated" (Is 40:1–2). He assured them that soon Yahweh would lead them back to Palestine in a new Exodus that would surpass the first Exodus from Egypt. Often he pictured this return against the background of the coming of Christ. And four of his most famous poems give us the most beautiful picture we have in the Old Testament of the work of the Messiah to come. He describes the Messiah as a gentle and kind teacher who will bring salvation not only to Jews, but to the Gentiles as well. This Messiah will eventually be cruelly persecuted and put to death by His people. His sufferings, however, were not for His own sins, as was commonly thought in the Old Testament, but for the sins of all mankind. The prophet sees that the Messiah, although put to death, will nevertheless triumph and be acclaimed as the Savior of mankind. Again and again, these wonderful prophecies of the Second Isaiah, as he is often called, are quoted in the New Testament.

FOR ME TO REVIEW

Questions and Exercises

Part 1: Answer yes or no

1. Ezekiel helped to preserve the national and religious future of Israel.

2. The Chosen People did not become discouraged after the destruction of Jerusalem.

3. Ezekiel is called the prophet of the restoration because he often spoke of the return from exile.

4. Ezekiel lived to see the restoration of the Chosen People.

5. The teaching of Ezekiel was much like that of Jeremiah.

6. The Chosen People were not exposed to temptation during their exile in Babylon.

7. An unknown prophet described the Messiah as a kind teacher who would bring salvation to Jews and Gentiles alike.

Part 2: Questions to Check Your Reading

1. Why was the national patriotism of the Chosen People threatened in Babylon?

2. Who was sent by God to guide His Chosen People at this time?

3. Of what did Ezekiel speak before the destruction of Jerusalem?

4. How did Ezekiel console God's People during the exile?

5. Why is Ezekiel sometimes called the prophet of the restoration?

6. Did Ezekiel live to see the restoration of the Chosen People?

And I will give them one heart, and will put a new spirit in their bowels: and I will take away the stony heart out of their flesh, and will give them a heart of flesh: That they may walk in my commandments, and keep my judgments, and do them: and that they may be my people, and I may be their God.

—Ezekiel 11:19-20

CHAPTER 14

God Directs the Rebuilding of Jerusalem

The years of captivity foretold by Jeremiah had now ended. The exiles anxiously awaited the day of their promised liberation. Cyrus, King of Persia, conquered Babylon (539 B.C.) and shortly thereafter (538 B.C.) issued a decree which granted full freedom to the Jews and also permitted them to take with them the sacred vessels of Solomon's Temple, which Nebuchadnezzar had carried into Babylon.

Because God wanted the people to remain faithful to Him, He continued to send messages to them through the prophets. The following story of Haggai and Zechariah shows how God did this.

Haggai and Zechariah

THE ISRAELITES RETURN TO THE PROMISED LAND

The first Jews to be deported as captives to Babylon left Juda in 598 B.C. During the years of the captivity an even larger number went into exile. The Babylonians had ruled over the land of Juda through a governor whom they appointed from a neighboring province.

When the captivity ended, only fifty thousand pilgrims returned to their own country. The majority of these were men of strong faith, but some were indifferent, and others were looking for adventure. Most of the Jews had, however, done well for themselves in Babylon and remained behind. They may have thought they could better help with the rebuilding of their fatherland by staying where they were.

The leader of the returning exiles was Zorobabel (zə-ˈrō-bə-bəl), who belonged to the family of the kings of Juda and was designated as the representative of the Persian King, Cyrus, to govern the province. The spiritual leader of the returning exiles was Joshua, the high priest.

God is equally anxious about His Chosen People in the New Testament. He wishes them also to be led to the Promised Land of Eternity. To achieve this purpose, Christ has provided that the pope, His Vicar on earth, should guide the members of His Church to the kingdom of heaven.

The Jews who returned needed God's help. He gave it to them chiefly through inspired leaders such as Zorobabel and Joshua. Moreover, He sent them two prophets, Haggai and Zechariah. These fearless men brought God's messages to encourage and guide the people in their actions.

As soon as the Jews had settled in the city, they built an altar for the morning and evening sacrifice, and the sacrifices on the principal feast days.

TERMS TO KNOW

Haggai
Joshua
Zorobabel
accompanied
Israelites
Cyrus
scribes
Persians
difficulties
glorious
Darius
Zechariah
sacrifice
magnificence

219

RECONSTRUCTION OF THE TEMPLE

King Cyrus ordered the rebuilding of the Temple in Jerusalem. Preparations for this were made in the second year after the return to Jerusalem. Laying the foundation stone was a solemn occasion. The priests, vested in their robes, offered sacrifices; the trumpets sounded, and the people sang songs of joy.

The Samaritans who lived in the territory of the former Kingdom of Israel went to Zorobabel and Joshua, saying that they also adored the God of Israel. The Jews would not, however, permit them to help rebuild the Temple to the true God. This made the Samaritans angry.

THE DIFFICULTIES OF THE CHOSEN PEOPLE

The Samaritans sent word to King Cyrus that the Jews were building the Temple as a fortress to resist him. Cyrus believed this report and ordered his representative, the governor of Samaria, to prevent the completion of the Temple.

Besides this, the Jews had many other difficulties to face. Because of a poor harvest and a long dry season which came upon the country, the people were often without food. In addition, their unfriendly and selfish neighbors also caused them trouble.

The prophets Haggai and Zechariah were told by God that these troubles had come upon His people because they had neglected Him. They had rebuilt their own homes first and had allowed the Temple of God to remain in ruins. Zorobabel and Joshua were disturbed by this message. Again they called upon the people to continue the rebuilding of the Temple. They also urged them to have regular services to honor God. Haggai and Zechariah, under divine inspiration, foretold the great glory that would grow out of their zeal for the Temple.

THE NEW KING, DARIUS, AIDS IN THE REBUILDING

Darius (də-ʹrī-ùs), the second successor of Cyrus, permitted the Jews to continue the building. He even gave them large sums of money and herds of cattle to promote their worship. For four and a half years they labored on the construction of the new Temple, the foundation of which had been laid twenty years before. When it was completed, the people dedicated the Temple by offering many sacrifices. Haggai, in God's name, promised that eventually the temple would surpass in glory even Solomon's: "I will move all nations and the treasures of all nations shall come, and I will fill this house with glory . . . and greater shall be the glory of this last house than of the first" (Hag. 2:8–9).

Though the prophet did not clearly foresee this, the prediction was fulfilled with the coming of Christ, who established a universal Church in which He is invisibly present.

Zechariah also was God's spokesman in these times of discouragement. In a series of mysterious visions, which he described to the people, he assured them of God's continued protection and of the eventual coming of the Messiah.

A later prophet, whose writings we find in the last chapters of the book of Zechariah, predicted the coming of Christ as a humble, kindly king like David, who would enter Jerusalem triumphantly. Christ fulfilled this prediction on Palm Sunday. He also prophesied how the Divine Shepherd would be struck, His flock scattered, and how the Messiah would eventually be slain by His people.

THE JEWS ARE WARNED BY THE PROPHETS

Haggai and Zechariah reminded the Israelites that the city and its temple had been destroyed because their fathers had not obeyed God's Law. If the people wished to remain faithful to God and if they wanted the Savior to come, they were to study and keep the law with all their hearts. The men who explained the law to them were known as scribes.

Never after their return from exile did the Jews worship idols. Instead, they showed a deep interest in God's Law and manifested a desire to obey it. The prophets told them that fasting alone would not please God, but the good conscience with which they did it. They were also urged to help the widows and orphans, to be kind to strangers, and to love one another.

FOR ME TO REVIEW

Questions and Exercises

Part 1: Answer yes or no

1. Did Haggai and Zechariah have much to do with the rebuilding of the temple?

2. Did God permit the children of Israel to return to Jerusalem to prepare for the coming of the Messiah?

3. Did the Jews fall into idolatry upon their return to Jerusalem?

4. Did the prophets tell the Jews that the Messiah would come in a short time?

5. Did all the children return to Jerusalem?

6. Did Zorobabel and Joshua rebuild the temple?

7. Was the new Jerusalem under a Persian governor?

8. Did Haggai and Zechariah bring the people messages from God?

9. Did the Jews begin the work of rebuilding by first offering sacrifice?

Part 2: Match column I with column II

Column I

1. Zorobabel

2. Darius

3. Haggai and Zechariah

4. Cyrus

5. Samaritans

Column II

A. the leader of the returning exiles

B. lived north of Jerusalem

C. permitted the children of Israel to go back to Jerusalem and to build again the temple of God

D. son of Cyrus

E. two prophets who carried the message from God to the people

Part 3: Questions to Check Your Reading

1. Who permitted the Jews to return to Juda?

2. Who were Zorobabel and Joshua?

3. How did Haggai and Zechariah guide the Chosen People?

4. Why did God permit the Chosen People to suffer many difficulties after they returned to Jerusalem?

5. What did the prophets tell the people they must do to please God?

6. How did Darius, the King, aid the people?

7. What promise did Haggai make regarding the temple?

8. How many of the things which Zechariah foretold about the Messiah and His Kingdom can you remember?

☑ FOR ME TO DO

1. Make a map of the Persian Empire and Egypt on a sheet of paper. Use colored pencil to show each country.

2. Prepare a report that the governor of Jerusalem might have sent to the King of Persia, giving the story of the rebuilding of the temple.

3. God punished the Chosen People for leaving their temple in ruins. Make two columns on a chart:. Title one column, "How Boys and Girls Can Help the Church." Title the other column "How Adults Can Help the Church." In each column list as many items as you can.

Ezra and Nehemiah

GOD ORDERS EZRA TO LEAD THE JEWS TO JERUSALEM

Many Jews who had remained in Babylon were now ready to return to Jerusalem under the leadership of Ezra, a priest and a scribe. He was commanded by God to purify the religion in the Holy City. On arriving in Jerusalem, Ezra found that many Jews had married pagan wives. These he rebuked, reminding them of the evils which would result from their mixed marriages.

GOD DIRECTS NEHEMIAH TO REBUILD THE WALLS OF JERUSALEM

During the time Ezra worked untiringly among the wayward Jews, there lived in Persia Nehemiah (ne-he-'mī-ə), a Jew of noble birth who was an official at the Persian court. When he heard that Jerusalem had reached such a sad state, he begged the king to allow him to go to Jerusalem to help rebuild its walls. The Persian king consented and sent Nehemiah to Jerusalem, where as governor, he went about his task with zeal.

Under Nehemiah's direction half of the people were armed to protect the city. The others worked with such energy that in fifty-two days the walls enclosing the city were completed. Nehemiah then appointed a governor to take his place and named Jerusalem as the permanent capital. He chose by lot one tenth of the people to live there, permitting the rest to dwell in whatever town of Juda they wished.

EZRA HELPS TO REFORM THE JEWS

Nehemiah then called the people together so that Ezra might read to them the Law of Moses. When Ezra had finished, they celebrated the Feast of Tabernacles together. Then the people publicly acknowledged that God had punished them justly for their sins. They resolved to reform their conduct, and to live according to the Law.

NEHEMIAH ENFORCES THE SABBATH OBSERVANCE

After spending twelve years in Jerusalem, Nehemiah was recalled to the Persian Court. He soon returned to Jerusalem, however, where he found that many abuses had crept in during his absence. For example, the law of the Sabbath was not observed. As Nehemiah told the people: "In those days, I saw some treading the wine presses on the Sabbath, and carrying all manner of burdens and bringing them into Jerusalem. Some merchants of Tyre who dwelt there, brought fish and wares to sell to the children of Juda" (Neh 13:15–16). Nehemiah worked tirelessly to correct these abuses.

Malachi

MALACHI IS SENT BY GOD TO ENCOURAGE THE JEWS

Ezra and Nehemiah struggled to keep the Jews faithful to God, who next sent Malachi the prophet to assist His people. He was one of the last prophets sent to the Jews before St. John the Baptist, the "angel" or messenger, came to prepare the way for the Messiah. Whenever the Jews complained about their unfair treatment, or their poor crops, Malachi reminded them that such things happened because of their sins.

Malachi is remembered for his vigorous sermons against mixed marriages and divorce, but most of all for his prediction that a perfect, universal sacrifice would one day take the place of the sacrifices of the Old Law: "I have no pleasure in you, says the Lord of hosts; I will not accept offerings from your hands. From east to west my name is great among the nations, in every place incense is burnt, a pure offering is presented to my name" (Mal 1:10–11).

FOR ME TO REVIEW

Questions and Exercises

Complete the following:

1. Ezra returned with many Jews to Jerusalem from the exile in _____ .

2. The rebuilding of the walls of Jerusalem was encouraged and directed by _____ .

3. Nehemiah tried to correct the abuse of the _____ .

4. Malachi was one of the last prophets before _____ .

5. Malachi predicted that a perfect, universal sacrifice would one day take the place of the sacrifices of the _____ .

The Rule of Antiochus (175–163 B.C.)

INTRODUCTION

From the time of the restoration of Jerusalem, the Jews were governed successively by Persia, Egypt, Syria, and Rome. Under the rule of Persia and Egypt, the Jews were allowed to observe their own religious laws and customs, as long as they paid taxes and adhered to the foreign policy of the overlord. Under Antiochus IV (an-ˈti-ō-kəs), a Syrian king, thousands of loyal Jews suffered death rather than submit to his attempts to paganize the Jewish state. Among these martyrs were a brave mother and her seven sons.

This mother and her boys were ordered to eat pork to test their obedience to the king. As this was seriously forbidden by the religion of the Jews, they said that they would rather die than offend God. For refusing to do as they were told they were put to death, after the most terrible torments. Antiochus ordered the tongue of one to be cut out. His feet and hands were torn off. Then, in the presence of his mother and brothers, he was burnt to

A Foreshadowing of the Martyrs

The story of this mother and her seven sons, who chose torture and death over the possibility of offending God, were Jewish martyrs. They would serve as a sign of courage to those who lived in the New Testament, letting them know that they must also resist the sinful demands of evil rules. Many of Jesus's early followers were martyred, and of course we have seen many martyrs for the Church throughout history. This Old Testament story was a foreshadowing of the deaths so many of the faithful would have to experience.

death over a slow fire. They prayed with him for courage to accept his sufferings. He died bravely, declaring that he would obey God rather than the king.

One by one his brothers were put to death while enduring horrible torments. At last only the youngest boy was left. The king promised him great riches and honors if he would renounce the Jewish religion. His mother begged him to die courageously. He promised his mother that he was going to be brave as his brothers had been. He was. After seeing her last son suffer martyrdom, the mother herself was put to death.

Eleazar (el-ʹā-ə-zär) was another famous martyr. He was an old man, greatly revered by the people. He had been a scribe for many years. His friends urged him to pretend to eat the forbidden food so as to escape death, but Eleazar refused. He pointed out that the bad example he would give would encourage others to apostatize. Instead, he went joyfully to his death.

THE WORK OF JUDAS MACHABEUS

God did not forget His people in this great national and religious crisis. He raised Mathathia (math-ə-ʹthī-ə) and his five brave sons—John, Simon, Judas, Eleazar, and Jonathan—to fight for faith and freedom.

Mathathia and his sons fled to the hill country of Juda, where they were joined by many other zealous Jews. They gathered an army, attacked many towns, and drove out the forces of the king. Wherever they found Jews who had disobeyed God, they punished them. When Mathathia died, his son, Judas Machabeus (mak-ə-'bā-əs), became commander. He defeated the forces of Antiochus in four battles. Judas finally succeeded in occupying the mountain upon which the Temple was located. He did this because Antiochus had set up an idol in the temple. So great a sacrilege was this that it was called "the abomination of desolation."

When Antiochus heard of the success of Judas Machabeus he became very angry, and led a huge army against Jerusalem. But a revolt and other troubles forced the king to return to Syria, where he was assassinated. The war continued, however. Eventually Judas Machabeus fell bravely in battle.

After his death, his brother Jonathan and later his brother Simon became leaders of the people. Under the leadership of these Machabees more victories were won and peace was finally established.

Their successors, known as Hasmonean (has-'mō-ne-ən) princes, however, did not follow in their footsteps, and gradually the irreligious policies and intrigues of the Hasmoneans led to the downfall of the independent Jewish state.

The Romans were called in to settle their quarrels. They seized the government, and Herod, an Idumaean (ī-dù-'mē-ən), was appointed king of the Jews (37–4 B.C.). The fullness of time had now come for the birth of the Savior, the Son of David who would be King of the Jews. He of whom the prophets had spoken, whose life and sufferings had been so often foreshadowed by the saints and figures and predicted by the prophets of the Old Testament, was now at hand. The Old Testament was drawing rapidly to a close.

THE BOOK OF DANIEL

The Prophet Daniel

According to the story as it is recorded in the book of Daniel, the exiled Hebrews and the Prophet Daniel were destined to spread the knowledge of the one true God among the Babylonians. Among the captives from the Kingdom of Juda were four noble youths. The Babylonian King chose them to be especially trained to serve as pages in his court. In this position the dangers to their faith were great. One of the youths, named Daniel, managed to get permission for them to eat only such food as was allowed to the Israelites. God was pleased with their self-denial, made them healthy and strong, and gave them great knowledge and wisdom.

Daniel Prophesies That the Kingdom of God Will Last Forever

Nebuchadnezzar, the King of Babylon, so the story continues, had a disturbing dream. His wise men were unable to interpret it. Daniel, inspired by God, explained the dream to him. It prophesied the rise and fall of great nations. It also indicated that the Kingdom of God upon earth, the Church, would never be destroyed, and would take unto herself all the kingdoms of the world.

The King Is Forced to Admit the Power of God

Nebuchadnezzar had set up a huge golden image. All were commanded to worship it under penalty of death. Daniel's three companions refused to do this. In consequence they were thrown into a furnace heated seven times hotter than usual. The fire in it erupted and consumed the men who had cast them in, but the youths inside were preserved from harm by an angel of God. The King, amazed at the miracle, acknowledged the power of the God of Israel.

Daniel Foretells God's Judgment on Babylon

Another Babylonian king desecrated the sacred vessels which had been carried away from the temple in Jerusalem. Once, while he was using them profanely, there appeared a hand which wrote mysterious words on the wall. Daniel alone was able to interpret the writing, which foretold the disaster which would strike the country and the king. That very night the King was slain and the Babylonian empire was taken by the Persians.

Daniel in the Lion's Den

Daniel again rose in importance under Darius the Mede. Envious leaders demanded that Daniel be punished because he prayed to the God of Israel. Against his will, the King was persuaded to cast God's prophet into a den of lions. The next morning the King was overjoyed to find Daniel unharmed. Daniel was saved from death to prove that the God of the Israelites was the true God. The miracle caused the King to issue a decree that, "All men shall fear the God of Daniel. For he is the living and eternal God forever; and his Kingdom shall not be destroyed" (Dn 6:26).

God Reveals Himself to the Pagans

Another story is told of the Persian King Cyrus who befriended Daniel. One day Daniel proved to the king that the Babylonian gods had no power and that their priests were frauds. He also succeeded in killing a monster which the Babylonians worshiped as a god. The angry populace again demanded his death. Thrown into a den with seven lions, Daniel was again preserved by a miracle. For six days Daniel remained unharmed in the den. He was fed

by a prophet whom the angel carried there. On the seventh day, when the king found Daniel alive and uninjured, he exclaimed, "Great are you, O Lord, the God of Daniel" (Dn 14:40). Once more Daniel was placed in a position of honor and trust.

Susanna

Another story added later to the book of Daniel tells of a young wife, Susanna, who was both beautiful and virtuous. One day she was tempted to commit a serious sin with two elders, who were respected by the people, since they did not know how wicked these men were. Susanna refused to sin, even though she knew that the elders would try to harm her. They did, in fact, publicly accuse her of a serious crime, for which the people were about to stone her to death, when suddenly Daniel appeared and demanded a new trial for the innocent Susanna. He separated the elders and questioned each one by himself. It was soon seen that they were telling lies and had falsely accused the good young woman. They, then, were condemned to death for their perjury and attempt to destroy Susanna. This story was told to show the Jews how God does not desert those who are faithful to Him, even if the whole world goes against them.

The Vision of the Son of Man

Besides stories, the book of Daniel also contains a number of prophetical visions about the Kingdom of God to come. The most famous of them is the one in which the prophet sees the kingdoms of this world as four beasts, which try to destroy the Kingdom of God. But God had judged these kingdoms and condemned them to destruction. The Messiah appears; God the Father gives Him the everlasting Kingship which supplants all human king-ships. In this vision the Messiah, who is identified with His Chosen People just as Christ is identified with His Church, is called "One like a son of man." But He is seen coming from Heaven, and so He is not merely a human being. Our Lord often called Himself Son of Man to make known that He was the Messiah described in the vision of Daniel.

Jews Who Remembered Their Covenant With God

Shortly after the time of the Machabees, a group of pious Jews, disgusted with the sad condition in Judea, fled to the desert and lived a life of prayer and study, thus to prepare the way for the Lord. Since 1947 many manuscripts which they copied have been discovered hidden in caves near the Dead Sea. These are the oldest copies of the Hebrew Old Testament that we now possess.

Other Jews who lived during this troublesome period longed to have their unhappy lot bettered in a material way. Not all of the Jews though were lacking in virtue and courage. Many of the Chosen People had borne their hardships courageously. They had kept constantly in mind their covenant relationship with God.

Those who lived in this manner had gradually developed into a truly spiritual Israel. Among this faithful, chosen band were Joachim and Anna, the parents of Mary; and Zechariah and Elizabeth, the parents of John the Baptist; the shepherds, who were the first to visit the Christ Child; Anna and Simeon, who were in the temple at the time of our Lord's Presentation; Joseph, the spouse of Mary; and above all Mary, who was to become the Mother of Jesus. In the next unit we shall study in detail the important part which each of these holy souls played in the life of the Savior who was about to come.

 FOR ME TO REVIEW

Questions and Exercises

Part 1: Match column I with column II

Column I	Column II
1. Eleazar	A. a group of pious Jews
2. Herod	B. was unable to interpret the mysterious writing on the wall
3. Daniel	C. caused the downfall of the Jewish state
4. Jonathan and Simon	D. a scribe who was martyred for his faith
5. Machabees	E. an Idumaean who was appointed king of the Jews
6. Hasmoneon princes	F. parents of John the Baptist
7. Antiochus IV	G. a prophet who represented the Chosen People
8. Mathathia	H. a Syrian King who tried to paganize the Jews
9. Babylonian King	I. brothers of Judas Machabeus who ruled wisely
10. Zechariah and Elizabeth	J. the father of Judas Machabeus

Part 2: Questions to Check Your Reading

1. Name the two conditions under which the Jews were allowed to observe their religious laws and customs.

2. What lesson should the faithful of the New Testament learn from the sufferings of the brave mother and her seven sons?

3. Why were Mathathia and his sons national heroes? Religious heroes?

4. Who cleansed the Temple?

5. Explain two of Daniel's prophecies.

6. Why was Daniel saved from death in the den of lions?

7. Name several people mentioned in the chapter who were to be closely connected with the Savior.

CHAPTER 15

God Protects Those Who Trust in Him

The Story of Job

A holy man named Job lived in Arabia. He had seven sons, three daughters, and many servants.

So as to test Job's righteousness, God allows Satan to tempt his servant. Satan believes that Job is holy only because he has been given many blessings and material benefits. If Satan were to take these away, would Job remain faithful? Satan begins his malicious work: In a short time, Job lost everything. Bands of robbers killed his servants and stole his flocks. During a violent storm his house was destroyed, and all of his children were killed. Job accepted these afflictions with resignation to God's holy will.

God also permitted Job to be stricken with a disease which covered his body with ugly sores. Yet Job did not cease to love God, but adored Him saying, "The Lord gave, and the Lord has taken away. Blessed be the name of the Lord" (Jb 1:21).

Job's loyalty to God was further tried when his former friends told him that God must be punishing him for his sins. Job, however, protests that he is innocent. Part of Job's suffering was his inability to explain the cause of these great evils. While Job accepted his suffering, and his trust in God remained firm, he also questioned God and expressed great frustration at the misfortune he had experienced. God's response to Job challenges the notion that all suffering is simply a punishment for sin. Suffering is a great mystery, and to attempt to solve this mystery—like Job's friends—is to place oneself in the position of God, who

alone knows all things. God asks Job, "Have you commanded the morning since your days began, and caused the dawn to know its place? . . . Can you draw out Leviathan with a fish-hook, or press down his tongue with a cord?" (Jb. 38:12, 41:1). In response to these questions which forth God's greatness, Job remains silent in his humility. In our suffering God does not ask us to provide an explanation—we may question, we may express frustration, but as Job shows us, ultimately, we must trust in God's great plan for our lives.

The patience of Job so pleased God that He blessed him more abundantly than before his trials. God gave him more sons and daughters and increased his wealth to twice its former size. He regained his health completely and lived many happy years.

A Lesson in Suffering

The story of Job teaches us a great lesson about human suffering. Many have received comfort and strength in reading it as they experience heavy burdens and troubled times. Job bore his many hardships with patience and humility. We must continue to have faith during trying times, knowing that God uses all things for the furthering of our salvation, including those times when we suffer.

FOR ME TO REVIEW

Questions to Check Your Reading

1. What was Job's outstanding virtue? How did he prove it?

2. How did God reward Job for his patience in suffering?

3. Name some ways in which everybody can practice patient suffering.

4. What lessons does the story of Job teach us?

The Story of Jonah

In the story of the prophet Jonah we see how God wished to prepare not only the Chosen People but also the Gentiles for the reception of the Redeemer.

The story of Jonah was not intended to be taken as history. The author, whose name has not come down to us, wished to show how ridiculous certain Jews of his time were who would have nothing to do with the Gentiles, that is, with all who were not Jews; they practically excluded the Gentiles from God's plan of salvation. To defend their position, these Jews did what segregationists sometimes do, they quoted Scripture, or rather, they misquoted Scripture. It is quite true that, in the writings of the prophets before the Babylonian exile, we find repeated warnings to the Hebrew people not to make agreements and alliances with foreign countries. The Chosen People were to rely on God alone. But these prophets also predicted that some day the Gentiles would recognize the one true God. The Jews who disliked the Gentiles paid no attention to these prophecies; they quoted only the statements that would seem to give them reason for their hatred.

The author of the book of Jonah had a good sense of humor, which God's inspiration did not suppress. He also had an inspired insight into God's plan for the Gentiles and he knew that the segregationists were wrong. He was one of a small group of Jews who protested against the teaching that God cared only for the Jews. Such teaching was foolish, and so God inspired the writer to picture this attitude in such a way that people would laugh at it. Since the Jews who rejected the Gentiles quoted the prophets to justify their actions, the author made his hero a prophet. He gave him the name Jonah, the name of a prophet who had lived several centuries earlier, of whom we know little more than his name.

According to the account, Jonah was commanded by God to preach to the people of Nineveh, the capital of ancient Assyria, and to threaten them with destruction, unless they repented of their sins. Do not forget that no nation had caused Israel more trouble than Assyria. Assyria stood for the worst of the Gentiles. Of course, Assyria had long since disappeared, and the location of Nineveh was not even known. The author knew only the names and the wickedness which they stood for from the stories he had heard about them.

Since Jonah, in the story, stood for the segregationist Jews, he is pictured as resisting God's command. He refused to be the means of converting the hated Assyrians and thus make them escape punishment. He tried to avoid God's call by booking passage on a ship which was sailing to Tarshish. Here again the author wishes to make Jonah look ridiculous because every Jew at that time knew how impossible it would be to try to escape from God, who ruled the entire universe which He had created.

Shortly after the vessel got under way, a raging storm tossed the boat fiercely and threatened to capsize it. By casting lots the sailors learned that Jonah was the cause of the storm. In order to save the ship the captain threw Jonah into the sea, but only after the prophet himself urged the captain to do so. However, Jonah was miraculously rescued. God sent a huge fish which swallowed Jonah and in three days vomited him unharmed upon the shore. Jonah was right back where he started!

When God again commanded Jonah to preach repentance to the heathen in Nineveh, he no longer refused. He went among the people and warned them that within forty days God would destroy them, unless they turned away from their evil ways. The king and all his pagan subjects believed Jonah at once. They fasted and did other acts of penance, outwardly showing that they were sincerely sorry for the evil they had done. The infinitely merciful God accepted their penance and spared them, just as He had so often spared the Chosen People.

Jonah should have been happy. No other prophet had ever had such success, even with the Israelites! But Jonah was by no means happy. Hence, when he saw how repentant the Ninevites were, he pouted like a spoiled child and complained, "Ah, Lord, isn't this just what I told you when I was still in my own country? I know that you are a God of kindness and mercy, slow to anger, rich in love, and ready to cancel punishment. I should like to die; that would be better than living under these circumstances!" The story ends with the Lord asking him why He should not be patient with Nineveh, whose people are, after all, as ignorant in religious matters as children, since they had not received revelation from Him as the Israelites had.

We also learn from this story that we cannot flee from God. His omnipotence and justice can and often does reach to the farthest ends of the earth. We should think of this, especially when we are tempted to sin.

Another clear lesson which the story teaches is that there is no segregation in God's eyes. If we fail to love and associate with people because of their nationality or color, we are not true children of God who loves all and commands us to love all.

Do you remember how our Lord applied some of the texts of this story about Jonah to Himself?

Three Days in Darkness

One thing people don't know about this story is that Jonah's experience in the belly of the whale foreshadows Jesus. Recall that Jesus was in the tomb for three days after he was crucified, just as Jonah spent three days in the darkness of the whale's belly.

FOR ME TO REVIEW

Questions to Check Your Reading

1. What lessons does the story of Jonah teach?

2. Can a sinful nation or people still obtain mercy from God by showing repentance?

3. Compare God's command to Jonah with the vocation of the missionary today. Do boys and girls of today sometimes try to avoid God's call to serve Him?

4. How can school children help the missions?

5. Are the Chosen People of the New Testament the only ones Christ came to save?

Tobit

To remind the Israelites of God's goodness toward those who are loyal to Him, the Bible tells the story of Tobit. Tobit was a member of one of the tribes of Israel taken into captivity in 722 B.C. He had always been a just and pious man. The story of his faithfulness to God and of its reward gives us an idea of the religious and civil status of the Israelites who were carried captive into Assyria.

TOBIT PRACTICES THE LOVE OF NEIGHBOR

After the Kingdom of Israel fell, Tobit with his family was taken to the Assyrian city of Nineveh. The wicked life of the Assyrians and the mistreatment he often suffered at the hands of the captors did not change him. Tobit remained pious and charitable. At times the Assyrian kings would favor Tobit and give him much freedom: Tobit would use the opportunity to comfort his fellow captives and to relieve their miseries as much as he could. At other times he was in disfavor, but that did not prevent Tobit from continuing his acts of charity.

TOBIT OBEYS GOD RATHER THAN MAN

The king, Sennacherib, treated the Israelites with great cruelty. In his anger he killed a large number of captives and ordered their bodies to be left unburied on the highways. In ancient times people believed that the soul could not rest in peace if the body was not properly buried. At the risk of his own life, Tobit buried them. At times the wife of Tobit disapproved of his daring but courageous charity. Nevertheless, Tobit would not stop.

GOD TRIES TOBIT

Once, when Tobit was exhausted from performing his works of mercy, he lay outside the house to sleep. Hot droppings from a bird flying overhead fell into his eyes, blinding him. This misfortune was followed by others, but never once did Tobit complain. He even thanked God, since it was the will of God that he should be blind. Finally, poverty overtook him and his family was in need.

TOBIT ADVISES HIS SON

The troubles of Tobit multiplied so greatly that he thought he would soon die. Concerned about the salvation of his son's soul, Tobit decided to give him some good advice. He called the young Tobit and among other things he said, "All the days of your life have God in your mind, and take heed you never consent to sin nor transgress the commandments of the Lord our God" (Tb 4:6). By word and example Tobit tried to rear his son in piety and in the practice of virtue.

AN ANGEL ACCOMPANIES YOUNG TOBIT

Tobit decided to send his son to a distant city to collect a debt. At the wish of his father, the young Tobit looked for a guide. He soon met a young man who knew the way and was willing to accompany him. Tobit did not realize at the time that his companion on the journey was the Archangel Raphael. He introduced the stranger to his father, who blessed them saying, "God be with you on your way and his angel accompany you" (Tb 5:21).

YOUNG TOBIT FOLLOWS THE ADVICE OF THE ANGEL

At the end of the first day, the travelers reached the Tigris River, where they rested and bathed. Here a huge fish attacked Tobit. At the angel's command, Tobit seized it and drew it out of the water. The angel directed Tobit to save its heart, gall, and liver, which could be used as medicine.

In the course of the journey, they came to a city in which a relative of Tobit lived. The angel advised Tobit to stop there and ask for the daughter, Sarah, in marriage. Tobit did so. When the girl's father learned who young Tobit was, he was pleased and gave him his daughter together with a rich dowry.

The marriage feast prolonged the journey, and Tobit knew his parents would be worried. He showed his devotion for them in the words, "Let me depart, for I know that my father and mother are troubled on my account" (Tb 10:9).

During the wedding celebration, the angel continued the journey and collected the debt for Tobit. Without further delay, they returned to Nineveh. When he reached home, young Tobit anointed his father's eyes with the gall of the fish and his sight was restored.

Tobit and his father wished to reward the faithful companion. They offered him half of their riches, but he refused to accept their offer. He then revealed that he was the Archangel Raphael. He told Tobit that his prayers and works of mercy had been pleasing to God, but that it had been necessary to try him by temptation.

A LESSON ON TRUST IN GOD'S PROVIDENCE

In this story of Tobit our duties toward the dead and the lesson of giving alms are given an important place. The story also teaches us to respect family life and have regard for the sacredness of marriage. It is, however, the daily trust in the Providence of God, our nearness to a kind and loving God that our heavenly Father especially wishes to impress upon us in the book of Tobit.

 FOR ME TO REVIEW

Questions to Check Your Reading

1. What works of charity did Tobit perform?

2. How did Tobit prove his loyalty to God?

3. How was the young Tobit protected on his journey?

4. Tell parts from the story which prove that young Tobit loved his parents.

5. Why does God sometimes allow the faithful to be visited by misfortune?

6. What is God trying to teach us by the book of Tobit?

Esther

The story of Esther is told in the book of that name. At the time of the Captivity her family had been taken from Jerusalem to Babylon. At the death of her parents she was adopted by her father's brother, Mordecai, who lived in the capital of Persia.

When the king granted permission to the Jews to return to Jerusalem, many of them, like Esther, preferred to stay in the Persian Kingdom. They had been there for fifty years or more and most of them must have been born in exile. They were accustomed to the land and did not wish to leave although they were free to return to their own country. The Persian kings were kind to them because they found that the Jews were helpful in governing the kingdom.

ESTHER IS CHOSEN QUEEN

The king, as the story goes, sent messengers to all parts of his empire to bring to his palace the most beautiful women of his realm. Esther was among those brought to the king. She came with her uncle, Mordecai, who was anxious about the safety of his adopted daughter. The moment the king saw her, he chose her for his queen, not knowing that she was a Jew.

The king's chief adviser, Haman, and some soldiers planned to kill the king and to rule in his place. Mordecai discovered the plot and told Esther. She immediately reported it to the king in Mordecai's name. The soldiers were put to death, but Haman was not suspected.

Haman planned revenge against Mordecai because he hated him for foiling the plot. To do this he accused the Jews of having special laws which set them apart from other people. He persuaded the king to publish an edict, ordering all Jews to be put to death on a certain day, and directing the confiscation of their wealth.

Esther: A Type of Mary

Esther serves as a type of Mary. Just as she was made queen, so Mary is the Queen of Heaven, and just as she interceded for her people by going to the king, so the Virgin Mother intercedes for us before the true King in heaven.

ESTHER INTERCEDES FOR HER PEOPLE

When Mordecai heard of the plot, he asked Esther to plead for her people. In Persia there was a law which forbade anyone to approach the king without being summoned, but Esther was willing to risk her life for the lives of her people. First of all she asked the Jews to fast for three days. She fasted and prayed with them. Finally she was ready to go to the king and to expose herself to the danger of death.

Dressed in her royal robes, Esther went to the king uninvited. When she saw him seated upon his throne she became frightened. She almost fainted at the sight of his angry look. Soon the king's expression changed. He stepped from his throne and raised her up until she recovered.

He said to her, "What is the matter, Esther? Fear not, you shall not die; this law was not made for you, but for all others. Come near then and touch the scepter" (Est 5:12–13). When Esther was able to speak to the king, she invited him to a banquet that she had prepared. At the banquet Esther asked the king and Haman to come to another banquet on the following day. According to oriental customs, important decisions were not to be made hastily.

Haman boasted to his friends that he had been invited to a royal banquet. He said his happiness would be complete if Mordecai were hanged. He built a gibbet, a wooden framework for hanging people, intending to ask the king to hang Mordecai on it.

That night the king could not sleep. He called in the historians and asked them to read the history of his reign. He learned how Mordecai had discovered a plot against him. He decided that Mordecai must be rewarded for saving his life. The next morning the king sent for Haman and asked him how a king's friend should be honored. Haman, thinking it was he that was meant, said that he should be dressed in the royal robes and led through the streets on the king's horse. A servant should go before him and cry out that this was the honor the king wished to give to his special friend. The king ordered Haman to honor Mordecai in this way.

The following day the king and Haman came to the second banquet which Esther had prepared. The king turned to Esther and said: "What is your petition, Esther, that it may be granted you? Although you ask the half of my kingdom you shall have it!"

This gave Esther courage and she said, "If I have found favor in your sight, O King, and it please you, give me my life, and the life of my people, for we are given up to be destroyed. We have an enemy whose cruelty influences the king."

The king was surprised to hear this and asked her what enemy had power to do such things. Esther answered: "Haman is our wicked enemy" (Est 7:2–6).

The king had Haman, his chief adviser, hanged on the very gibbet which he had prepared for Mordecai. The Jews were saved from death and Mordecai was given Haman's high position in the kingdom. In this way Esther defeated the evil plans of the enemy of her people.

GOD WATCHES OVER HIS CHOSEN PEOPLE

The story of Esther shows the hate of which the Jews were the object in the ancient world because of the peculiarity of their life which seemed to pit them against the authority of the rulers. The sufferings of the Jews as depicted in this story are similar to those they endured under Antiochus.

The main idea behind the account of Esther is a religious one. The elevation of Mordecai and Esther, and the deliverance which resulted, reminds us also of the history of Joseph which is told in Genesis. We recall that he was persecuted, then exalted for the salvation of his people. In the story of Joseph, God did not outwardly show His power, but He directed the events.

In the Hebrew book of Esther, which does not mention God, His Providence also guides the action throughout. The characters in the story know it, and put all their confidence in God, who will see to it that His plan of salvation is carried out.

This interesting story points out how surely God disposes all things. In most marvelous and unforeseen ways does He bring about His designs either for the punishment of the wicked, or for the protection of the good.

FOR ME TO REVIEW

Questions to Check Your Reading

1. Why did Haman hate Mordecai?

2. What did Esther do to save her people?

3. How did the king receive the petition of Esther?

4. How does the story of Esther resemble that of Joseph?

5. Why did God so carefully protect the children of Israel?

6. What does God teach us by the story of Esther?

Judith

We now come to another story of how God preserves the good from evil. It tells of another valiant woman, Judith. We see again how God presents Himself as making use of a good woman to do great things for Him. Like Esther, Judith, too, saved her people, the Jews.

The story tells us that Holofernes (hȯ-lō-ʹfer-nəs), an Assyrian general, marched against Palestine after the Jews had returned to Jerusalem. He threatened the city of Bethulia (beth-ʹul-ē-ə) by digging a trench around the city and cutting off its water supply. As the people were dying of thirst, they decided to surrender if no help came within five days.

JUDITH—"THE GLORY OF JERUSALEM"

There lived in Bethulia a beautiful and virtuous widow, Judith, who loved her people very much. She was disappointed in them because she felt that they were wrong in setting a time limit to the power of God. She prayed earnestly and then called the leaders together and scolded them for their lack of trust in God. She informed them of a plan by which she hoped she could deliver the city from the siege. She asked them to pray and fast together with her so that God might strengthen her in this undertaking.

In a few days Judith with some of her maids went to the camp of the enemy. They were brought before Holofernes. She told him that she had run away from the city to escape the cruelty of his soldiers when the city should fall. Holofernes was pleased with her.

Believing that she would betray her people into his hands, he promised her his protection and gave her a tent for her use. There Judith spent her time praying that God would direct her in her dangerous undertaking.

On the fourth day after her arrival at the enemy's camp Holofernes gave a feast for his officers. He invited Judith and her maids to come to this banquet. At the feast, Holofernes drank a great deal of wine and was overcome with sleep. While he slept, Judith cut off his head and carried it to Bethulia. After she had assembled the leaders and the people, she showed them the head of Holofernes. She asked them to praise God who protected her and who by her hands had killed the enemy.

Judith saved the people of Judea from the Assyrian general Holofernes.

At daybreak the soldiers of Bethulia attacked the Assyrians. Without a leader, the Assyrians were easily defeated and many of them were slain.

Judith was praised, not only by her townsfolk but by all Judea. She was called the "Glory of Jerusalem."

GOD AGAIN SAVES HIS PEOPLE

The author of the book wished to point out the religious idea behind the events in the story. Holofernes, the servant of Nebuchadnezzar, represents

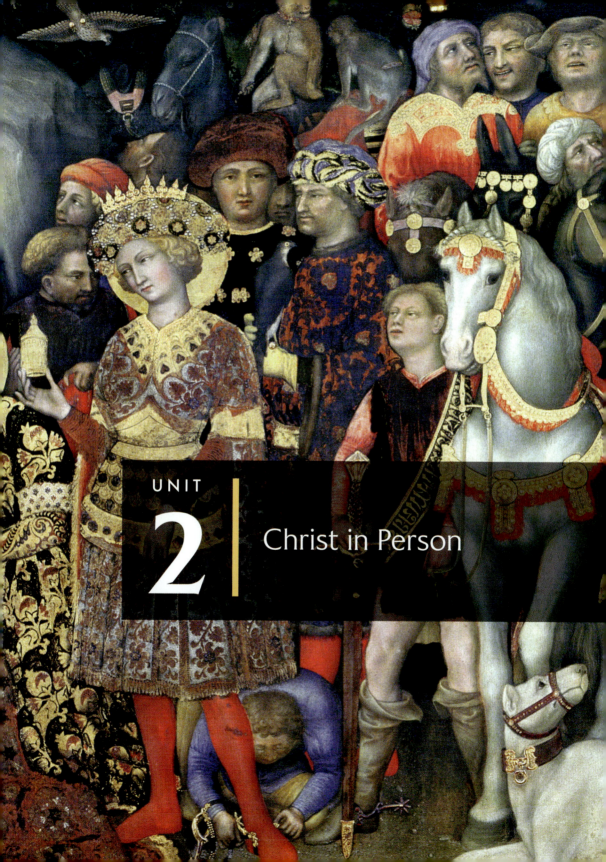

CHAPTER 16
God Sends John the Baptist

To prepare the Jews for the Redeemer's arrival upon earth, God chose a man of whom the prophet Malachi, in God's name, had said, "Behold I send my messenger, and he shall prepare the way before my face" (Mal 3:1). It was John the Baptist who fulfilled this prophecy. Recall the striking events that surrounded his birth, for by them God wished to emphasize the importance of John's mission.

Zechariah and Elizabeth

Among the hills of Judea in the little town of Ain-Karim, not far from Jerusalem, lived the priest Zechariah and his wife Elizabeth. Both faithfully observed the law of God. Zechariah and Elizabeth were good not only before men, they were also "just before God."

For many years Zechariah and Elizabeth had prayed for a son. It was their one great sorrow that God withheld this blessing from them. They were now quite old and no longer expected any children. Nevertheless, as you have so often seen in the history of the Chosen People, nothing is impossible to God. He was about to bless them with a son who would become a great saint and the precursor, and the forerunner, of the coming Savior.

The Birth of St. John Is Announced

When it was Zechariah's turn to serve in the temple, he left his home and came to Jerusalem. One day he was selected for the important duty of burning incense on the golden altar in the Holy Place. As he put incense on the coals, an angel appeared to him. Zechariah was afraid. But the angel said, "Do not be afraid, Zechariah, for thy petition has been heard, and thy wife Elizabeth shall

bear thee a son and thou shalt call his name John" (Lk 1:13). The angel also revealed that his son would prepare the way for the Redeemer.

Zechariah's Doubt

To Zechariah the promise of a son was too good to be true. He doubted the angel's words, asking, "How shall I know this?" (Lk 1:18.)

The angel answered, "I am Gabriel, who stands in the presence of God; and I have been sent to speak to thee and to bring thee this good news. And behold, thou shalt be dumb and unable to speak until the day when these things come to pass, because thou hast not believed my words, which will be fulfilled in their proper time" (Lk 1:19–20).

Out in the court, the priests and the people were impatiently waiting for Zechariah. According to custom the priest who offered incense was to give them a solemn blessing. On his return the people noticed that Zechariah lifted his arms in benediction, but could not speak. They understood that he had seen a vision.

Zechariah returned to his home when his week of priestly service at the temple was over. By means of writing or signs he shared the wonderful news with his wife Elizabeth. She also rejoiced that God had so generously answered their prayers.

The Birth of St. John

The time came, as the angel had foretold, and a son was born to Elizabeth. The neighbors and relatives wished to call the child

TERMS TO KNOW

- Ain-Karim
- Benedictus
- precursor
- Zechariah
- benediction

John the Baptist in Art

John is often depicted according to how he is described in the New Testament, wearing garments made of camel hair. He is also often depicted pointing. This is symbolic of how he was the last major prophet who pointed to the coming of the Messiah. John "prepared the way" for the coming of Christ, so in a sense, he points us to the one who followed him.

by his father's name. Elizabeth disagreed, saying, ". . . he shall be called John." The relatives protested and appealed to the father. Unable to speak, Zechariah wrote, "John is his name" (Lk 1:60–63). Instantly Zechariah regained his speech. This miracle amazed the people and made them wonder about the greatness of the child.

The Benedictus

Zechariah was overjoyed and grateful for the wonderful ways of the Lord. Filled with the Holy Spirit, he began to praise God with a wonderful prayer which we call the *Benedictus*.

"Blessed be the Lord, the God of Israel, because
he has wrought redemption for his people,
And has raised up a horn of salvation for us, in
the house of David his servant,
As he promised through the mouth of his holy
ones, the prophets from of old;
Salvation from our enemies, and from the hand of
all who hate us,
To show mercy to our forefathers and to be mind-
ful of his holy covenant,
Of the oath that he swore to Abraham our father,
that he would grant us,
That, delivered from the hand of our enemies, we
would serve him without fear,
In holiness and justice before him all our days.
And thou, child, shalt be called the prophet of the
Most High, for thou shalt go before the face
of the Lord to prepare his ways,

To give his people knowledge of salvation through forgiveness of their sins,

Because of the loving-kindness of our Lord, wherewith the Orient from on high has visited us,

To shine on those who sit in darkness and in the shadow of death, to guide our feet into the ways of peace" (Lk 1:68–79).

The Precursor

Zechariah thanked God for giving him a son who would be a great prophet and who would have the privilege of making the Redeemer known to the Israelites. He also expressed his gratitude for the salvation which God prepared for the whole world.

From his early years, John was inspired by God to lead a life of penance. He left home and went into the desert of Judea where through prayer and fasting he prepared for the work foretold before his birth.

FOR ME TO REVIEW

Questions and Exercises

Part 1: Complete the following statements. Use a separate sheet of paper.

1. For a long time God withheld from Zechariah and Elizabeth the blessing of a _____.

2. The mission of John the Baptist was foretold by the prophet _____.

3. The part of the temple where the angel appeared to Zechariah was called _____.

4. _____ chose the name of John for the son of Zechariah.

5. Because Zechariah doubted the angel he became _____ .

6. The name of the prayer Zechariah said when he regained his speech is _____ .

7. The name of John did not satisfy the _____ .

8. The mission of St. John the Baptist was to _____ .

9. John prepared for his future work by _____ .

Part 2: Questions to Check Your Reading

1. How did God test the perseverance in prayer of Zechariah and Elizabeth?

2. List the things the angel revealed to Zechariah.

3. What connection did the birth of John the Baptist have with the coming Redeemer?

4. Why did Zechariah and Elizabeth insist on the name of John for their son?

5. What lessons can we apply to ourselves from the story of Zechariah and Elizabeth?

6. How was the fact that the child John was destined for great things brought to the attention of the neighbors?

7. For what favors in particular is Zechariah grateful for in his prayers?

8. How did John the Baptist prepare for his mission?

☑ FOR ME TO DO

1. Make a list of Bible characters whose names were chosen for them by God Himself.

2. Find some of the texts referring to John the Baptist in the Masses for Advent.

3. Read Luke 1:16–17 to find the name of the great prophet with whom the angel compared St. John the Baptist.

4. Say at least a short prayer daily to the saint whose name you were given in Baptism in order that the saint may intercede for you with God.

5. Try to pray with more confidence and perseverance when you ask God for favors.

CHAPTER 17
God the Son Becomes Man to Be Our Redeemer

Mary Receives the Angel's Message

In a little town of Galilee called Nazareth lived a virgin named Mary. She was promised in marriage to a man named Joseph. Both were from the tribe of Juda and the family of David. Mary was the cousin of Elizabeth, the wife of Zechariah. One day, about six months after the angel had visited Zechariah, Mary was working and praying in her home. She might have been thinking of the Redeemer and longing for His coming. Suddenly her room was filled with heavenly light. The angel Gabriel appeared before her. "Hail, full of grace," he greeted Mary, "The Lord is with thee. Blessed art thou among women." This greeting puzzled Mary. She wondered why the angel should praise her so highly. The angel explained that she would become the Mother of the Savior, and he continued,

> "Thou shalt call his name Jesus. He shall be great, and shall be called the Son of the Most High; and the Lord God will give him the throne of David his father, and he shall be king over the house of Jacob forever; and of his Kingdom there shall be no end" (Lk 1:28–33).

The feast of the Annunciation commemorates the angel's visit to Mary.

Our Redemption Begins

Mary did not doubt but sought more understanding from Gabriel. "And Mary said to the angel, 'How can this be, since I have no husband?'" (Lk 1:34). The angel answered, "The Holy Spirit shall come upon thee and the power of the Most High shall

overshadow thee; and therefore the Holy One to be born shall be called the Son of God" (Lk 1:35). The angel also revealed to Mary that her cousin Elizabeth would have a son.

Mary consented to be the Mother of the Savior, saying humbly, "Behold the handmaid of the Lord; be it done to me according to thy word" (Lk 1:38). At these words the Incarnation took place; our redemption began. The prophecy of Isaiah came to pass in its fullest and deepest meaning: "Behold a maiden shall conceive, and bear a son, and his name shall be called Emmanuel" (Is 7:14). God the Son took on human flesh in the womb of the most holy Virgin Mary. God the Son became man.

Can you see why we honor the Blessed Virgin Mary as the "Cause of our joy"? Mary co-operated in our salvation. Through Mary our Redeemer was given to us. Do you recall the words in which God referred to Mary's Son after the sin of Adam and Eve, "He shall crush your head . . ."? (Gn 3:15.) Mary was never touched by original sin. She is the Immaculate Conception and through her Son she crushed the power of Satan.

TERMS TO KNOW

- Galilee
- Caesar Augustus
- decree
- Nazareth
- Magnificat
- originated
- Micah
- independent

Mary's Fiat

You may sometimes hear the Annunciation described as "Mary's fiat." Fiat is a Latin word that means "let it be done." By saying yes to God in becoming the mother of his Son, she was aligning herself to God's will, saying, "let it be done according to thy Word." We echo Mary's fiat each time we say the words "thy will be done" in the Our Father.

"Mary showed complete trust in God by agreeing to be used as an instrument in his plan of salvation. She trusted him in spite of her nothingness because she knew he who is mighty could do great things in her and through her. Once she said 'yes' to him, she never doubted. She was just a young woman, but she belonged to God and nothing nor anyone could separate her from him."

—ST. TERESA OF CALCUTTA

Mary, the First Christian Missionary

A Christian missionary is one who brings the Word of God to those in other regions. We see Mary as an exemplar of what it means to be a missionary in the story of her visit to Elizabeth. As soon as she receives the Word into her womb, she goes "with haste" to visit her cousin, Elizabeth. She brought the Word to someone in need and performed an act of charity by tending to her elder cousin during her pregnancy.

Mary Visits Elizabeth

Mary rejoiced to hear the good news about her cousin Elizabeth. She made the long journey to Judea to help Elizabeth and to celebrate with her cousin over the favors and blessings God had sent them.

When Mary entered the home of her cousin, Elizabeth in her joy cried out, "Blessed art thou among women . . ." (Lk 1:42). Then, realizing what a great honor it was to have Mary visit her, she added, "And how have I deserved that the mother of my Lord should come to me?" (Lk 1:43.)

The Magnificat

The Blessed Virgin Mary answered with these inspiring words:

"My soul magnifies the Lord, and my spirit
rejoices in God my Savior;
Because he has regarded the lowliness of
his handmaid; for behold, henceforth all
generations shall call me blessed;
Because he who is mighty has done great
things for me, and holy is his name;
And his mercy is from generation to generation
to those who fear him.
He has shown might with his arm, he has
scattered the proud in the conceit of their
heart.
He has put down the mighty from their
thrones, and has exalted the lowly.

He has filled the hungry with good things, and the rich he has sent away
empty.
He has given help to Israel, his servant, mindful of his mercy—
Even as he spoke to our fathers—to Abraham and his posterity forever"
(Lk 1:46–55).

We call this prayer the *Magnificat*. It is a prayer of praise. In it, Mary expresses her feelings of gratitude for God's benefits to her, praising Him for His justice toward all, and for His mercy toward the people of Israel.

After remaining with Elizabeth for three months, Mary returned to her home in Nazareth.

Joseph Learns of Mary's Privilege

Joseph did not know that Mary was to be the Mother of the divine Savior. However, an angel appeared to him before their marriage and said, "Do not be afraid, Joseph, son of David, to take to thee Mary thy wife, for that which is begotten in her is of the Holy Spirit. And she shall bring forth a son, and thou shalt call his name Jesus; for he shall save his people from their sins" (Mt 1:20–21). Joseph believed the angel who revealed to him the mystery of the Incarnation, and accepted the responsibility of caring for the divine Redeemer and His Blessed Mother.

The Emperor's Decree Aids God's Plan

Palestine was no longer an independent country. Rome ruled it through Herod, an Idumaean. Since Caesar Augustus , the Roman Emperor, wished to have all his subjects counted, he issued a command for a census. For this purpose, each person had to enroll in the town where his family originated. Since Mary and Joseph were of the royal family of David, they had to enroll in the city of David, that is, Bethlehem. Can you see how this decree of the emperor helped to fulfill God's designs? The prophet Micah had long ago foretold that the Savior would come from

Bethlehem. The emperor's decree took Mary and Joseph from their home in Nazareth to Bethlehem where the prophecy would be fulfilled.

FOR ME TO REVIEW

Questions and Exercises

Part 1: Choose the Correct Answer

1. Mary lived in the section of Palestine known as
   a) Judea
   b) Samaria
   c) Galilee

2. Elizabeth was Mary's
   a) sister
   b) cousin
   c) aunt

3. The angel who carried God's message to Mary was
   a) Raphael
   b) Gabriel
   c) Michael

4. The prophecy stated that the Messiah was to be born in
   a) Bethlehem
   b) Nazareth
   c) Jerusalem

5. Mary descended from the family of
   a) Joseph
   b) Zechariah
   c) David

6. The prophecies stated that the Mother of the Savior would be
   a) rich
   b) famous
   c) a virgin

7. Mary answered Elizabeth's greeting with a prayer of
   a) sorrow
   b) joy and thanksgiving
   c) petition

8. Mary's prayer is called the
   a) Magnificat
   b) Benedictus
   c) Nunc Dimittis

9. The feast which commemorates the angel's visit to Mary is called the
   a) Incarnation
   b) Immaculate Conception
   c) Annunciation

10. The prayer which recalls the conversation between Mary and the angel is the
    a) Angelus
    b) Hail Holy Queen
    c) Memorare

11. Mary learned that Elizabeth was to have a son from
    a) Zechariah
    b) an angel
    c) Joseph

12. Joseph learned that Mary was to be the Mother of God from
    a) Mary
    b) an angel
    c) Holy Spirit

13. The city where Joseph and Mary had to enroll was
    a) Bethlehem
    b) Rome
    c) Nazareth

14. At this time Palestine was subject to
    a) Egypt
    b) Rome
    c) Syria

Part 2: Questions to Check Your Reading

1. Who was Mary?
2. For what purpose did God send the angel Gabriel to Nazareth?
3. Why did the angel's greeting puzzle Mary?
4. What things did the angel reveal to Mary?
5. What prophecies did Mary fulfill?
6. How does Mary share in the work of the redemption?
7. Why did Mary visit Elizabeth?
8. What part of the *Hail Mary* is composed of Elizabeth's words?
9. Of what did Mary speak in the *Magnificat*?
10. How did Joseph learn that Mary was to be the mother of God?
11. Why did Mary and Joseph make the trip to Bethlehem?
12. How did the Emperor's decree help to fulfill God's plan?
13. What practices from the life of Mary and Joseph can we apply to our own?

✓ FOR ME TO DO

1. Plan a project about the Blessed Virgin Mary which includes the following:
   a) Stories which prove Mary's love for mankind, including her appearances at Lourdes, Fatima, or Guadalupe.
   b) Pictures which portray the Blessed Virgin under various titles, such as the Immaculate Conception, Star of the Sea, Our Lady of Sorrows, and the like.
   c) Make a list of the more prominent feasts of our Lady with brief comments on each.

2. Study "*The Annunciation*", a painting by Fra Angelico (above).

3. Read the explanation given in your catechism for the following words:
   Immaculate Conception, Annunciation, Incarnation

4. Try to find out which countries have adopted the Blessed Virgin Mary as their patroness.

5. Review the catechism lesson on the Incarnation.

6. Recite the *Angelus* with great attention and reverence.

7. Say the *Magnificat* as a prayer of thanksgiving for all the graces God has given you.

8. Attend the services in honor of the Blessed Virgin Mary at your parish church.

CHAPTER 18
Christ Is the Fulfillment of the Promise

At length the promise of a Redeemer was fulfilled. God had sent to earth His only Son who would be the new Adam. By His humility and obedience, He would repair the spiritual disaster brought about by the pride and disobedience of the first Adam. In this chapter we shall read the story of the birth of the Messiah and learn how He revealed His presence on earth to the Jews and to the Gentiles.

Mary and Joseph in Bethlehem

After a difficult journey of four or five days on foot, Mary and Joseph reached Bethlehem in the hills of Judea. The city was crowded with others who had come to enroll for the census. Private lodging was difficult to find. In fact, Mary and Joseph found none and were forced to seek shelter in a stable.

The stable was a part of a cave outside the town, and in it was a manger for the fodder which was given to the animals. Here Joseph and Mary prepared to remain for the night. They saw in this discomfort the will of God and accepted it.

The Birth of the Redeemer

"And it came to pass," the Scripture records, "while they were there that . . . she brought forth her firstborn son, and wrapped him in swaddling clothes, and laid him in a manger . . ." (Lk 2:6–7). It was at night when the town was asleep that the Son of God chose to come quietly upon earth to fulfill the promise made by His Father. No one suspected that the Messiah, whom the Chosen People had awaited for so many centuries, had come. Only Mary and Joseph were there to welcome Him.

The Redeemer Reveals Himself to the Shepherds

On that first Christmas night shepherds were tending their sheep near Bethlehem. These poor men were the first to receive the wonderful news of the newborn Savior. A brilliant light suddenly changed the dark into the brightest day. Then an angel's voice told the frightened shepherds not to fear, for he had a joyful message for them, "for today in the town of David a Savior has been born to you, who is Christ the Lord. And this shall be a sign to you: you will find an infant wrapped in swaddling clothes and lying in a manger" (Lk 2:11–13). Instantly a choir of angels appeared and sang: "Glory to God in the highest, and on earth peace among men of good will" (Lk 2:14).

The shepherds were filled with joy. They hastened to Bethlehem and "they found Mary and Joseph, and the babe lying in the manger" (Lk 2:16). After they paid homage to Christ, they returned to their flocks, praising the God of Israel and spreading the glad news.

TERMS TO KNOW

- Magi
- Circumcision
- frankincense
- Presentation
- Simeon
- myrrh
- Nunc Dimittis
- manger
- swaddling
- Epiphany

Jesus, the Divine Savior

At a ceremony prescribed by the Jewish Law, which took place eight days after His birth, the Divine Infant was given the name Jesus. This holy name means "savior." In an earlier Church tradition, this event was once celebrated on the Octave of the Nativity (on New Year's Day).

The Presentation in the Temple

Another law of the Jews obliged the parents to bring their first-born to the temple to offer him to the Lord. This was to remind the Israelites that their child belonged to God because the angel of God had spared their firstborn when Moses led the Israelites out of Egypt. Then, as a sign that they were buying the child back, the parents would offer a sacrifice to God.

Simeon's Hope Is Realized

At this time there lived in Jerusalem a pious old man named Simeon. The Holy Spirit had revealed to him that he would not die until he had seen the Promised Redeemer.

As Mary and Joseph with Jesus entered the temple, Simeon, under the inspiration of God, recognized the Savior. He took the child in his arms and uttered a prayer of thanksgiving and prophecy, the beautiful *Nunc Dimittis* (also known as *The Song of Simeon*).

> *"Now, Master, you let your servant go in peace. You have fulfilled your promise.*
> *My own eyes have seen your salvation,*
> *which you have prepared in the sight of all peoples.*
> *A light to bring the Gentiles from darkness; the glory of your people Israel." (Lk 2:29–32).*

Simeon blessed them and said to Mary: "This child is destined for the fall and for the rise of many in Israel, and for a sign that shall be contradicted." He added: "Thy own soul a sword shall pierce" (Lk 2:34–35).

Anna Recognizes the Messiah

The prophetess Anna came to the temple at the time of the Presentation. She, too, was given the grace to recognize the Promised Redeemer. Giving thanks for this great favor, she spread the news of the Messiah to the people of Jerusalem.

The Redeemer Reveals Himself to the Gentiles

We have already mentioned that the Gentiles also awaited a Redeemer. They had heard of Him from the Jews in exile and from other Jews who had settled in many places outside of Palestine.

The Magi had noticed an unusual star or heavenly phenomenon which they interpreted as a sign that the expected king had been born. Knowing that the Jewish people were looking for a king to be born, they went to Jerusalem, the capital, and asked, "Where is the newborn king of the Jews? For we have seen his star in the East and have come to worship him" (Mt 2:2).

The Gifts of the Magi

The Magi offered the Holy Infant gifts of gold, frankincense, and myrrh. The early fathers of the Church saw deep meaning in these gifts: the gold signified that Christ is a King; frankincense, that He is God, and would establish His royal priesthood; and myrrh, that He is also man, and would suffer death (myrrh was used to anoint the bodies of the dead to help with the odor).

The Magi stopped at the palace of Herod and made the same inquiry. Their question made Herod uneasy. He became anxious about his throne. Gathering the Chief Priests and Scribes, he inquired about the prophecies concerning the birth of the Messiah. They told him that Christ was to be born "in Bethlehem of Judea." Pretending that he wished to worship the newborn king, Herod instructed the Magi to visit him again on their return journey and bring him information about Christ. Herod's real intention was to murder the Holy Child.

The Magi had hardly continued their journey a short way until the star, which had disappeared for a while, reappeared and brought them to the Divine Infant. The Wise Men recognized in the Holy Child not only the King of the Jews, but the Son of God, the Redeemer of the world. They fell on their knees before Him. Thus another prophecy of Isaiah was accomplished, "And the Gentiles shall walk in the light, and Kings in the brightness of thy rising" (Is 60:3). We celebrate this event as the Feast of Epiphany on January 6. It is also called "Little Christmas" and the "Christmas of the Gentiles."

The Return of the Magi

The Magi did not visit Herod on their way home. An angel warned them in their sleep that Herod wished to harm the Child. They, therefore, left Judea secretly by another road. When they arrived home, they spread the news of the newborn Savior among their people, the Gentiles.

The Holy Innocents

When he realized that the Magi would not return, Herod became furious. He gave orders that, in the vicinity of Bethlehem, all the male children up to two years of age were to be killed. Herod felt that by this means the Christ Child would not escape death. The soldiers of Herod carried out this order and put to death the innocent baby boys.

The Holy Family Escapes Into Egypt

But Herod did not accomplish his purpose, for the Divine Child was saved. During the night an angel appeared to Joseph and told him to flee to Egypt at once with the Holy Child and the Blessed Virgin. They were to remain there until God would tell them to return. Joseph neither delayed nor asked questions, but arose and, taking Mary and the Child Jesus, departed for Egypt.

The Return From Egypt

After some years, Herod died. The angel came to Joseph with the news that he was to return to Palestine. Joseph left his work and home behind and set out again for the Holy Land. On hearing that Judea was ruled by a son of Herod who was equally as cruel as his father, Joseph feared for the safety of Jesus. He decided to return to Galilee, the northern part of Palestine, to the little town of Nazareth.

FOR ME TO REVIEW

Questions and Exercises

Part 1: Match column I with column II

Column I
Column II

A

1. Joseph	A. taught us the way a Christian father loves his family
2. shepherds	B. Wise Men from the East
3. Mary	C. spread the news of a Savior
4. angels	D. patron of the Catholic Church
5. Simeon	E. planned to take the life of Jesus
6. Magi	F. said the Nunc Dimittis
7. Anna	G. announced the birth of the Messiah to the shepherds
8. Jesus	H. mother of the Savior
9. Herod	I. means "Savior"
10. Holy Family	J. heard the news of the birth of Christ first

B

1. Nazareth	A. city of David
2. Bethlehem	B. Jesus spent His hidden life there
3. Jerusalem	C. where Mary and Joseph found Jesus
	D. Mary lived there before the birth of Christ
	E. where Christ was born
	F. where the Magi inquired for the "King of the Jews"
	G. where the shepherds heard the angels sing
	H. where Mary offered the Christ Child in the temple

C
_____

1. Circumcision	A. Feast of the Magi
2. Presentation	B. Son of God became Man
3. Annunciation	C. birth of the Redeemer
4. Incarnation	D. Mary offered Jesus in the temple
5. Nativity	E. Gabriel came with a message to Mary
6. Epiphany	F. Christ received the name of Jesus

Part 2: Question to Check Your Reading

1. Why did Mary and Joseph seek shelter in a stable?
2. What great event took place that night in Bethlehem?
3. Tell how the shepherds learned of the birth of the Savior.
4. When was the name Jesus given to the Infant?
5. What Law did Mary and Joseph obey forty days after the birth of Christ?
6. Of what did Simeon speak in his prayer as he held the Christ Child?
7. How did the people in Jerusalem hear of the birth of the Messiah?
8. Why did the Magi who were Gentiles come to adore the "King of the Jews"?
9. Why was Herod's plan to destroy the Christ Child unsuccessful?
10. What lessons can we derive for ourselves from the flight of the Holy Family?
11. Why do we call the years Christ spent in Nazareth with His parents Christ's hidden life?
12. What is the one incident that the Gospels record during this period of Our Lord's life?
13. Why was the Holy Family so exceedingly happy together?
14. What important prophecies were fulfilled in the birth and early life of the Savior?

FOR ME TO DO

1. Read that part of the life of St. Francis of Assisi which relates how the custom of the Christmas crib originated.

2. It is said that the Christmas tree represents Jesus Christ who is the Tree of Life in the New Testament; the lights on the tree indicate that Christ is the Light of the world, and the decorations symbolize the blessings and graces which Christ brought us when He was born upon this earth. Write an explanation of the above ideas in your own words.

3. Find out why the Blessed Virgin and St. Joseph are often pictured with a lily.

4. These are some of the virtues practiced by St. Joseph: firm faith, resignation, humility, great confidence in God, obedience, chastity, and industry. Can you give incidents from the life of St. Joseph to illustrate each of these virtues?

5. Make a list of the feast days that are centered around the Christmas season.

6. Study the picture of the "Virgin in Adoration" by Correggio.

7. Find the part of the Mass that contains the Song of the Angels (Lk 2:14).

8. Read *The Other Wise Man*, by Van Dyke.

9. Say the names of Jesus, Mary, Joseph with reverence and think upon their lives every day.

10. Do your best to bring love and unity into your home.

11. Pray to St. Joseph daily for the grace of a happy death.

12. Try to do only what will please the Christ Child.

Alma Redemptóris Mater

Loving Mother of the Redeemer,
who remains the accessible Gateway of
Heaven, and Star of the Sea,
Give aid to a falling people
that strives to rise;
O Thou who begot thy holy Creator,
while all nature marvelled,
Virgin before and after
receiving that "Ave" from the mouth of
Gabriel, have mercy on sinners.

CHAPTER 19

John the Baptist Begins His MIssion

Before John the Baptist was born, an angel announced the work for which he was destined. John's vocation was not an easy one, he met much opposition, but he never faltered. In preparing the way for the Redeemer, he showed us how we must be prepared to follow the vocation which God gives us.

John Prepared the Jews for the Redeemer

Before Christ began His public life, John left the desert to prepare the minds and hearts of the Jews to receive the Messiah. He urged the people to change their sinful lives, preaching the need for repentance.

John baptized the people in the Jordan River. This baptism was not the sacrament, but a symbol of repentance. John told them about the Messiah and what they must do to be worthy of Him and to belong to His Kingdom. Who belongs to Christ's Kingdom today?

In the early days of the Church when persecutions of the Christians were widespread, a person who wished to be baptized had to be ready to face martyrdom. Does Baptism put any obligation upon us members of Christ's Church today? Does our reception of the sacrament of Baptism signify that we are ready to repent of our sins?

The Sanhedrin

The Roman rulers allowed the Jewish people much freedom in their government and religious practices. The Sanhedrin (an assembly of judges) was the highest authority over the Jewish people, although it had to obtain the permission of the Roman procurator (an administrator) to sentence anyone to death. The Sanhedrin was composed of seventy-two members chosen from among the Chief Priests, the Scribes, and the elders with the High Priest at the head.

John attracted the attention of the Sanhedrin. His sermons drew large numbers of people and thereby disturbed the Sanhedrin, for it claimed authority to grant permission for anyone to preach. Its members thus kept close watch on all that John did.

The Scribes

Certain men who specialized in the study of the Law of Moses were known as Scribes. It was their duty to explain the Law to the people, and frequently they

TERMS TO KNOW

- Sanhedrin
- Herod Antipater
- procurator
- Pharisees
- Herodias
- faltered
- Sadducees
- Salome

disputed with Jesus about certain points of the Law. During this time, almost all Scribes were known as the "Pharisees."

The Pharisees

The Pharisees were a group of Jews who made special efforts to observe the Law faithfully and to follow the traditions that had been handed down by the Scribes. They gave much time to prayer, and they practiced good works like fasting and almsgiving. In matters of faith, they were more enlightened and progressive than the Sadducees, but many of them became proud and intolerant, often concerned more with the outward observance of the Law than with true love of God and neighbor. They refused to have anything to do with Gentiles (non-Jews) or with those who associated with Gentiles. Because the people looked upon them as holy men, the Pharisees exerted great influence.

The Sadducees

The Sadducees were a separate sect of Jews, and to them belonged many of the nobility, wealthy people, and priests. Unlike the Pharisees, they were very narrow-minded with regard to matters of doctrine. The Sadducees believed mainly in the world of material things, and consequently, they denied spiritual truths like the immortality of the soul, the resurrection of the body, and the existence of angels.

The Sadducees and the Pharisees differed so much in their doctrines that they were not ordinarily on friendly terms. They joined forces, however, in opposing John the Baptist and Christ.

John Is Severe With the Leaders of the People

Members of the Sanhedrin were often among the multitude that gathered about John. Since he knew that at heart many of them were evil with no intention of improving, John spoke to them severely. He warned them that their salvation was not insured merely because they were the Chosen People of God. They would

have to change their wicked lives, repent of their sins, practice charity, and fulfill the duties of their state in life. As leaders among their people, they had the special obligation of directing the Jews according to the laws of God.

John's Humility

The leaders of the Jews sent representatives to learn all about John. In answer to their direct questions, John humbly admitted that he was not a prophet, nor Elijah, nor the Messiah, only "the voice of one crying in the desert, 'make straight the way of the Lord'" (Jn 1:23).

John always spoke most humbly of himself. At one time he stated that he was not even worthy to untie the cord on Christ's sandal. When his disciples complained of the miracles Christ was working, John told them, "He must increase, but I must decrease" (Jn 3:30).

John Is Imprisoned

John's life of prayer and penance had made him a strong character. He even had sufficient courage to approach the ruler of Galilee, Herod Antipater (son of Herod the Great), and openly rebuke him for unlawfully living with Herodias, the wife of his half-brother Philip. Urged by the wicked Herodias, Herod was persuaded to cast John into prison.

In prison, John could not teach, but that was no longer necessary, as the Messiah Himself was teaching the people. John had completed his work. The disciples of John brought him news of the increasing wonders which Jesus was performing. John was glad that the Messiah had begun His work of redemption. At times he sent his disciples to question and observe Jesus. This gave them a better opportunity to recognize in Jesus the promised Redeemer. Christ, on the other hand, spoke of John and praised him highly before the people, saying, "There is not a greater prophet than John the Baptist" (Lk 7:28).

The Death of John

In the meantime, Herodias was scheming to take John's life. Her chance came during a feast at which her daughter Salome danced. Herod, pleased with the dance, publicly promised to give her anything she asked. Prompted by her mother, the girl demanded the head of John the Baptist. The king was reluctant, for he feared the people who loved John, but dreading the laughter and sarcasm of the guests, he ordered the execution. John's head was brought on a dish and given to the girl.

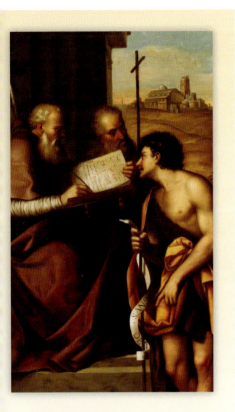

A Tale of Two St. John's

The story of St. John the Baptist's defense of the sacrament of marriage before a corrupt ruler would be echoed approximately fifteen centuries later through the story of St. John Fisher, a bishop of the Church who stood up to King Henry VIII of England when he sought a divorce from his wife to remarry his mistress. Both men were beheaded for their defense of marriage.

FOR ME TO REVIEW

Questions and Exercises

Part 1: Match column I with column II

Column I

1. Sanhedrin
2. Scribes
3. Pharisees
4. Sadducees

Column II

A. denied the existence of angels

B. composed of seventy-two members

C. would have nothing to do with the Gentiles

D. studied and interpreted the Law

E. held supreme power over the people

F. considered themselves better and holier than others

G. belonged to the wealthy class of people

H. denied the immortality of the soul

I. were strict in outward observances of religion but neglected charity

Part 2: Complete the following

1. St. John stressed the need of doing _____ .

2. John urged the people to _____ their _____ lives.

3. John baptized the people as a symbol of their _____ .

4. John spoke most severely to the _____ .

5. To attain heaven we must practice _____ and fulfill the _____ .

6. Great responsibilities are imposed upon the _____ of the people.

7. John taught along the shores of the _____ .

8. John was straightforward and courageous in condemn-
   ing _____ for his sins.

9. John encouraged his disciples to question and follow

   _____ .

10. Christ said, "There is not a greater prophet than _____"

Part 3: Question to Check Your Reading

1. How did John the Baptist prepare the people for receiving
   the Redeemer?

2. In what way was the mission of John similar to that of priests
   of today?

3. Why did John baptize? Was John's baptism a sacrament?

4. What obligations does the sacrament of Baptism put upon
   us?

5. Why did the Sanhedrin take such keen interest in John?

6. Of whom was the Sanhedrin composed? What were its
   powers?

7. How did the Pharisees differ from the Sadducees?

8. Who were the Scribes?

9. Why did John speak more severely to the leaders than to the
   common people?

10. Give incidents from the life of St. John that portray his virtues
    of humility, fortitude, faithfulness to duty, and his spirit of
    mortification.

11. Why was John put to death?

12. What example did John set for the Apostles, for early Chris-
    tians, and for us?

FOR ME TO DO

1. Write a character sketch of John the Baptist. Read two or three of the best sketches to the class.

2. Find the two parts of the Mass in which we mention the name of St. John.

3. Faithfully try to do your duties as a loyal member of the Church.

4. Often say a prayer to the Holy Spirit to know your vocation and for the grace to follow it.

CHAPTER 20

Christ Begins His Public Life

Christ was not satisfied merely to open heaven for us; He wanted to do everything possible to help us get there. In His public life He taught all men by word and example how they were to live and act.

Jesus Is Baptized

Before Christ actually began to teach, He went to the Jordan River where John had been baptizing those who wished to lead more holy lives. Christ showed His humility by asking to be baptized with the sinners. Inspired by the Holy Spirit, John recognized Jesus, the Son of God. He did not consider himself worthy to baptize his sinless and holy Master. Nevertheless, when Jesus insisted, John obeyed and baptized Him. During the baptism the Holy Spirit appeared in the form of a dove above Jesus and a voice from heaven was heard saying, "You are my Son, the Beloved; with you I am well pleased" (Lk 3:22).

Jesus Retires to the Desert

To show us how we ought to prepare for the important undertakings and duties in our life, our Lord then withdrew into the desert where He prayed and fasted for forty days. Here, to teach us an important lesson, Christ allowed the devil to tempt Him.

Christ knew that all men must undergo temptations. By His example He wanted to show us how to overcome them. Christ, therefore, permitted Himself to undergo temptation by Satan.

The Devil Tempts Christ

The devil knew that Jesus was a very holy man, because not once had the devil succeeded in tempting Him to sin. At the baptism he heard the voice from heaven addressing Jesus as "beloved Son." But just as today we call all those who are in the state of grace children of God and brothers and sisters of Christ, so in the Old Testament the chosen people are called, as a nation, God's "son" and sometimes very holy individuals are referred to as "sons of God." That Jesus was very holy and pleasing to God, the devil already knew. Now he began to suspect strongly that Jesus was the long-promised Messiah. And if this was true, then Satan knew that his reign over men was doomed, because the Messiah was to overcome sin and bring about the reign of God, the reign of holiness.

TERMS TO KNOW

Bethsaida

indignant

self-conceited

Nathaniel

Cana

beverage

Capernaum

Lake Gennesaret

Passover

The devil knew that some of the Old Testament prophecies had foretold that the Messiah would overcome sin by suffering and dying for mankind. He knew, too, that many of the Jews wished to have a glorious Messiah who would work many striking miracles, who would bring about such earthly prosperity that they would no longer have to work, and above all, a Messiah who would conquer the world and punish the enemies of the Jews. The devil decided that if he could persuade Jesus to be this kind of Messiah instead of a suffering Redeemer, he might still keep his hold on mankind.

He first suggested that Jesus work a miracle to satisfy His hunger, a miracle for His own personal benefit. Needless to say, it would not have been wrong for our Lord to partake of food after His long fast. But He was to give us always an example of complete trust in God; His Father would send Him food when and in the way He decided. Jesus was completely submissive to His Father and never took things in His own hands. Hence, He refused the devil's suggestion by quoting from the Old Testament book of Deuteronomy (8:3), from a sermon in which Moses reminded the people that God had tested them by letting them hunger so that He would give them the manna from heaven; this would teach them that God has His own way of taking care of our needs and is not limited by what we know or can do: "Not by bread alone does man live, but by every word that comes forth from the mouth of God."

The devil next suggested that Jesus show Himself to the people and announce Himself to be the Messiah with a spectacular miracle. Like a "superman" He should throw Himself from the highest part of the temple, and prove that God would send His angels to protect Him. But this suggestion Jesus also repelled. We dare not demand miracles of God: that is putting Him to a test that we have no right to demand. For a second time, Jesus quoted Scripture, the Old Testament (Dt 6:16) warning that we may not thus tempt God: "Thou shalt not tempt the Lord thy God."

Finally, almost in desperation, Satan suggested that he and Jesus make a compromise. If He is the Messiah, He is to conquer the world. Why do this by suffering and bloodshed? Since men have given themselves into Satan's power by sin, he is already master of the world; hence, if Jesus submit to him, he will make him king without further ado: "All these things will I give thee," Satan promised, as he showed to Christ's imagination the kingdoms of the world, "if thou wilt fall down and worship me." Indignantly Jesus replied: "Away with you, Satan! for it is written, 'Worship the Lord your God, and serve only him.'"(Mt. 4:4–10).God the Father showed at once that Jesus' confidence was justified by sending angels to minister to Him. He did this again when Jesus had a similar painful struggle in the Garden of Gethsemane.

A year and a half after this, Jesus told His Apostles plainly that some day He would have to suffer and die. St. Peter was shocked, criticizing our Lord for thinking such things. Our Lord then severely rebuked St. Peter, and used the same words that He had used to the devil: "Begone Satan . . ." The Hebrew word "*Satan*" means adversary. Since St. Peter was opposing God's plan, he was an adversary. He was suggesting something similar to what Satan suggested in the desert: that our Lord should not

Christ Works His First Miracle

During the feast, the Blessed Virgin Mary noticed a shortage of wine. This was the customary drink of the people and scarcity of it would have caused great embarrassment to the wedding party. Immediately, Mary went to Jesus and said, "They have no wine" (Jn 2:3).

Jesus answered her, "My hour has not yet come" (Jn 2:4). The answer sounded like a refusal, but Mary knew that Jesus would refuse her nothing.

She, therefore, told the servants, "Do whatever he tells you" (Jn 2:5). What does this teach us of the power of the Blessed Virgin Mary?

Christ directed the servants to fill six jars with water and to take some to the chief steward who was responsible for the wine. He tasted it and found it was no longer water but the most excellent wine. Greatly surprised, the steward wondered at the fine quality of the wine. As he did not know what Christ had done, he asked the groom why this best wine was saved for the end of the feast. He learned the truth about the miracle from the servants.

Christ worked this first public miracle to please His Mother and to strengthen the faith of His disciples.

Jesus then left Cana and went to Capernaum on the shores of Lake Gennesaret where He spent a few days. Because the feast of the Passover was approaching Jesus then departed for Jerusalem.

Cleansing of the Temple

The Jewish services at the temple, as will be recalled, required the sacrifice of an animal. At first the buying and selling of the animals was done outside the temple. Gradually, however, the marketing was carried on within the Court of the Gentiles, the outermost enclosure of the Temple. The money-changers also did a thriving business there because coins with pagan images had to be exchanged for temple money. Everywhere there was noise, disorder, and irreverence.

It was such a scene of confusion that Jesus witnessed as He entered the temple on His arrival in Jerusalem. Angered by this irreverence, Jesus took a few cords and knit them into a whip. Then, in His just anger, He drove out the shouting merchants, the bargaining pilgrims, and the panic-stricken animals from the temple. With holy indignation He overthrew the tables of the money-changers,

The Symbolic Significance of Cana

The story of Christ's first miracle at Cana, changing the water into wine, is significant on several levels. One of the most important aspects of the story of the wedding feast at Cana is how it points to Mary's intercessory role. Mary took note of the couple's embarrassing situation and went to her Son to ask for help. Similarly, she can take note of what we need and go to her Son to ask that we receive it. It's not that Jesus needs Mary to work miracles, but rather that he loves her so much he takes great joy in fulfilling her requests, and she constantly makes requests of him on behalf of her spiritual children. This miracle is also significant because in turning the water to wine, Jesus was foreshadowing his passion, when his blood would be spilled and we would one day drink it to bring life back into our souls. As Archbishop Fulton Sheen once wrote, "He turned the water to wine so that one day he could turn the wine to blood."

spilling the coins over the ground. No one dared stop Him. They knew that they had sinned. To the surprised disciples this was another hint that Jesus might be the Messiah.

The Enemies of Christ

This incident left the leaders of the Jews in a rage. The priests were in control of all affairs in the temple and were indignant at what they considered the boldness of Jesus; their pride was hurt. Angrily they approached Christ, but dared not touch Him. Instead, they asked what authority He had to do such a thing, but the conceited priests did not understand His answer: "Destroy this temple," He replied, "and in three days I will raise it up" (Jn 2:19). Christ's answer only made the Pharisees angrier. Scarcely had Christ begun the work of redemption when He fell into disfavor with the Jewish authorities. Throughout His life the majority of these self-important people were His bitter enemies.

 FOR ME TO REVIEW

Questions and Exercises

Part 1: Who spoke these words? To whom were they spoken?

1. "You are my Son, the Beloved; with you I am well pleased."

2. "Worship the Lord your God, and serve only him."

3. "Behold the Lamb of God."

4. "Can anything good come out of Nazareth?"

5. "They have no wine."

6. "Follow me."

7. "Destroy this temple and in three days I will raise it up."

8. "My hour is not yet come."

9. "Man does not live by bread alone."

10. "Do whatever he tells you."

Part 2: Arrange in sequence

1. Jesus performs His first public miracle.

2. Jesus is tempted in the desert.

3. Jesus calls His first disciples.

4. Jesus is baptized by St. John the Baptist.

5. Jesus attends the marriage feast of Cana.

6. Jesus cleanses the temple in Jerusalem.

Part 3: Identify the disciples

1. Brought his friend to Jesus.

2. His name was changed to one which means "rock."

3. Did not believe that the Messiah could come from Nazareth.

4. Was a brother to Peter.

5. Followed Jesus together with Andrew.

Part 4: Questions to Check Your Reading

1. Name the two outstanding acts of our Lord before He began His public teaching.

2. How was the mystery of the Holy Trinity revealed to John the Baptist?

3. What reasons did Christ have for allowing the devil to tempt Him?

4. In what three ways did the devil tempt Christ?

5. What are the answers with which Christ conquered the devil?

6. How did John point out Christ to his disciples?

7. Who were the first disciples of Christ?

8. How was each one called?

9. Can you give two reasons why Christ attended the marriage feast at Cana?

10. What occurred at the wedding which proved that through Mary we can receive many favors from Christ?

11. How did the miracle at Cana affect the disciples?

12. What took place in the court of the temple which angered Christ?

13. How did Christ show His authority?

14. Why did the cleansing of the temple anger the priests and Pharisees?

15. What did Christ mean when He said, "Destroy this temple and in three days I will raise it up"?

FOR ME TO DO

1. Prepare a presentation on temptations. Refer to the catechism. Cover these four main ideas:

    a) What are temptations?

    b) What are the sources of temptations?

    c) When do temptations become a sin?

    d) How can we overcome temptations?

2. Divide an outline map of Palestine into its three main sections: Galilee, Samaria, and Judea. Put in the following places connected with the life of Christ, and give at least one incident that happened in each place: Bethlehem, Bethsaida, Capernaum, Cana, Jerusalem, Nazareth, Lake Gennesaret, Jordan River.

3. Name the virtues which Jesus showed in this part of His public life.

4. Look through the Old Testament for references which symbolize our Lord's forty-day fast. The forty-day fast of Moses on Mt. Sinai before he published the Law is one example.

5. Let these questions help you to make a resolution for today.

   - Do you frequently perform some little act of mortification to make you strong in time of temptation?

   - Do you remember to pray when temptations come?

   - Do you pray the rosary daily to gain Mary's intercession?

   - Do you behave in church as in the house of God?

CHAPTER 21

Christ Prepares for His Kingdom by Preaching and by Miracles

Jesus Teaches in Galilee

After the feast of the Passover Jesus and His disciples returned to Galilee. Many Galileans had seen or heard of the miracles which He had performed at the feast in Jerusalem, and were prepared to receive the message He was about to give them. The Galileans were more friendly than the Judeans and far more willing to listen to the teachings of Jesus.

Jesus was warmly received in Galilee. For a year and a half, He went through Galilee stopping at the various villages, spending most of His time, however, in Capernaum. He explained that the Kingdom of God referred to God's dominion over all creatures, that His Chosen People were in a way the Kingdom of God, and that the Messianic Kingdom would be universal, embracing all nations. It would also be perpetual and indestructible, and would bring peace and holiness. The Messiah would show the way to heaven by His example and instructions.

The Jealousy of the Scribes and Pharisees

In the days when our Lord lived on earth, the Jews went to the synagogue on the Sabbath (then, on Saturday) to pray and to be instructed in their religion. This was the most important service, although there were services also during the week. After the opening prayers lessons were read from the books of Moses (the Pentateuch) and from the Prophets. Then someone would be called upon to explain it to them. Jesus was often called upon to give the explanation. He would use the Old Testament reading to teach the people about the Messiah and the Kingdom He was to establish. Taking them back to the time of the patriarchs and prophets, He would show them how the promise of a Redeemer encouraged the fallen race. Then by means of His teachings He would lead them to the understanding that Christ would repair the losses caused by Adam; to the Church He would be a true Noah, the founder of a new people; more than Abraham, He would be the Head of the people whom God had chosen; in a better sense than Jacob, He would be the favorite and blessed One of God; more than Joseph would He return good for evil; and more effectively than Moses would He free His people from the bondage of sin and nourish them with the True Bread come down from heaven.

It was not always easy to teach the people. Often Jesus would explain the lesson by telling parables or stories which they could more readily understand. The people listened attentively to Him. Jesus would frequently strengthen their faith by performing miracles.

Many of the Scribes and Pharisees became jealous of our Lord's influence on the people. Jesus was the target of their injustice and persecution especially when He spoke of establishing a New Kingdom from which they were excluding themselves by refusing to accept Him. Though Christ explained the prophecies to them, they refused to believe Him.

Jesus Cures the Officer's Son

On His missionary journeys our Lord preached repentance and the coming of the Kingdom of God. As He passed through the various villages, people came out to welcome Him. When He approached Cana, where He had worked His first miracle, a certain official of Herod's court came to Him and asked Him to cure his son who was dying at Capernaum. Jesus worked this miracle without leaving Cana. He simply said to the father, "Go; your son will live." (Jn 4:50). The official believed Him and went home. When his servants told him the hour at which the child grew better, he knew that it had happened at the very moment when our Lord had spoken the word. The official and his entire household were converted to faith in Christ.

The Miraculous Draught of Fishes

One day, as our Lord stood by the Lake of Gennesaret, a large crowd gathered. In order to address so large a multitude, He decided to speak to them from the lake itself.

He saw, near the shore, two fishing boats. The owners were washing their nets. One of the boats belonged to Simon Peter. Jesus entered this boat. When it had been drawn out a little from the shore, He sat down, and from the boat taught the assembled crowd.

After Jesus had finished His discourse He said to Peter, "Put out into the deep, and lower your nets for a catch" (Lk 5:4). St. Augustine interprets these words of our Lord as spoken of distant nations to whom the Gospel was afterward to be preached.

Peter said to our Lord, "Master, the whole night through we toiled and have taken nothing; but at thy word I will lower the net" (Lk 5:5). As soon as they had done this they took in such a catch of fishes that their nets began to break. The other boat had to come to their aid. Both ships were filled. On seeing this, Peter fell at the feet of Jesus and said, "Depart from me, for I am a sinful man, O Lord" (Lk 5:8).

His Church is here figured by the boat of Peter, and our Lord's entering Peter's boat clearly foreshadowed Peter's primacy, that is headship, in the Catholic Church from which our Lord continues to speak to mankind.

Jesus said, "Do not be afraid; from now on you will be catching people" (Lk 5:10). What did Jesus mean by these words?

When Peter and the other three were told that they were to be fishers of men their minds were enlightened by the Holy Spirit to recognize that Jesus was greater than a prophet. They understood that the miraculous catch signified their new apostolate. They left their nets and followed Christ.

When Jesus calls us to come after Him let us imitate the prompt obedience of the Apostles who, if they had hesitated, might have lost the opportunity of establishing Christ's Church.

The Cure of the Paralytic

Soon after this, Jesus was teaching in Capernaum. Some Scribes and Pharisees had come to spy on Him, to find out about His works and His doctrines. While He was speaking, a man suffering from paralysis was brought to the door. Because of the great crowd of people, it was impossible to get near Jesus. Those who brought the sick man climbed to the flat roof of the house, and after removing some tiles let the sick man down into the room where Jesus was teaching.

Seeing such faith Jesus said, "Friend, your sins are forgiven you" (Lk 5:20). On hearing these words, the enemies of Jesus said, "Who is this man who speaks blasphemies. Who can forgive sins, but God only?" (Lk 5:21.)

Jesus, knowing their thoughts, asked if it were easier to cure the man than to forgive his sins. "But," He continued, "that you may know that the Son of Man has power on earth to forgive sins," He said to the paralytic, "I say to you, stand up and take your bed and go to your home" (Lk 5:24). The sick man did as Jesus said, praising and glorifying God, as did all the others, except the Scribes and Pharisees.

FOR ME TO REVIEW

Questions and Exercises

Match column I with column II

Column I	Column II
1. Cana	A. Caused Jesus much trouble
2. Judea	B. "...from now on, you will be catching men" was said by
3. Galilee	C. When in Galilee Jesus spent most of His time in
4. Simon Peter	D. Was no longer safe for Jesus to preach in
5. Pharisees	E. Was converted to faith in Christ
6. Jesus	F. "Man, thy sins are forgiven thee," was said to the
7. Jews	G. Went to the synagogue to be instructed in their religion
8. Capernaum	H. Jesus cured the ruler's son without leaving
9. Paralytic	I. Christ began His teaching concerning the eternal Kingdom in
10. Certain Ruler	J. "Depart from me, for I am a sinful man, O Lord," was said by

CHAPTER 22

Christ Establishes His Kingdom

The son of God came to establish a Kingdom in order, among other things, to give back to man the grace that had been lost through Adam. By means of this Kingdom, His Church, Christ would unite men with His Father into one family. But before He started His Church, Christ carefully prepared the people for it. He taught them by telling them stories or parables and He strengthened their belief in Him by working miracles. People were attracted by His kind words and gentle ways and many followed Him. From these He selected twelve Apostles. He gave these Apostles great power because they and their successors were to spread His Kingdom to the whole world until the end of time. By reading the lessons our Lord taught, we understand better how we should live, because we are members of this Kingdom.

Selection of the Apostles

One day James, the son of Zebedee, was with his father in a boat. They were mending nets when our Lord passed by. Jesus stopped and spoke to James. After that, James left his father and became a disciple of Christ. Matthew, who was a publican (a tax collector) was the next one called to be a disciple of Christ.

Soon after this Jesus went up to the top of a mountain alone to pray. He spent the night in prayer, and in the morning He came down to His disciples who were waiting for Him. He now definitely associated twelve of these disciples with Himself in a more intimate and permanent manner. He finished His work of

selecting the twelve Apostles. The names of the twelve were: Simon, to whom He gave the name Peter; James and John, the sons of Zebedee, whom He once called the Sons of Thunder; Bartholomew, sometimes called Nathaniel; Andrew; Philip; Matthew; Thomas; James, the son of Alpheus; Thaddeus, also called Jude; Simon the Canaanite, also called Simon the Zealot, and Judas Iscariot .

These twelve men were instructed by Christ and later sent forth to tell the people about His Kingdom. For this reason, they are called "*Apostles*," a word meaning "*sent*" in Greek. Jesus told them to preach the Kingdom after His own example, by actions more than by words, by doing good more than by preaching. For this He would give them power to heal the sick, to drive out devils, and to restore the dead to life. By these miracles they were to prove the truth of their doctrine and the divinity of Jesus Christ. Later, when our Lord ascended into heaven, they would be in charge of His Church. They were to unite men with God and with one another and carry on Christ's work of Redemption by bringing His grace and truth to all men. Because the Apostles spread the Kingdom of God, the Church, throughout the world, and because the pope and bishops today are the successors of the Apostles, it is called the "*Apostolic Church*." By what other marks is the Church of Christ known?

Jesus Instructs the People

Despite Jesus knowing that they were imperfect and world-ly-minded, He still loved the Apostles. He knew that they would disappoint Him, but He also understood their love for Him. He appreciated the sacrifices they made for Him. The Apostles were happy at having found the Messiah and they gladly accepted our Lord's invitation to become His disciples. On one occasion they went with Jesus to the side of a mountain where a group of peo-ple was waiting for Him. Here Christ gave a long, important talk which is called the *Sermon on the Mount*.

This Sermon outlines Jesus' program and especially high-lights the difference between His standards and those of the world. Christ instructed the people and gave them rules to follow that would bring true happiness into their lives. These eight rules are called The Beatitudes. Each one begins with a blessing and ends with a reward.

> *Blessed are the poor in spirit, for theirs is the kingdom of heaven.*
> *Blessed are the meek, for they shall possess the earth.*
> *Blessed are they who mourn, for they shall be comforted.*
> *Blessed are they who hunger and thirst for justice, for they shall be satisfied.*
> *Blessed are the merciful, for they shall obtain mercy.*
> *Blessed are the clean of heart, for they shall see God.*
> *Blessed are the peacemakers, for they shall be called the children of God.*
> *Blessed are they who suffer persecution for justice' sake, for theirs is the kingdom of heaven (Mt 5:3–10).*

It was a teaching that was new to the people. Blessed are the meek, the poor, the peacemakers! The people wondered, for they had never heard anyone talk the way Jesus spoke that day. They compared the Beatitudes with their own rule of life which had been "an eye for an eye, a tooth for a tooth." They realized that the law of Christ was more noble. Jesus had won their admiration with His lesson about this law of love which would bring them happiness.

Christ Instructs His Disciples

Jesus told His disciples that they must be the "salt of the earth." Salt flavors and adds to the taste of food; it also keeps food from spoiling. Christ's disciples, and this includes us, are to be like salt, making sinful men good and pleasing to God.

Our Lord also called His disciples the "light of the world." This means that Christ's followers are to lead men to the truth by their good example, thereby driving out the darkness of ignorance and wrong ideas from the minds of men and showing them the way to heaven.

After our Savior had explained to the disciples their mission and work, He described the relation of the New Law to the Old Law. "Do not think that I have come to destroy the Law or the Prophets. I have not come to destroy, but to fulfill" (Mt 5:17). Jesus is explaining that to fulfill is to make perfect and also to make real what was foretold by types and figures in the Old Law.

Then Christ continued to explain that the New Law demands more than external acts and ceremonies. "For I tell you, unless your righteousness exceeds that of the Scribes and Pharisees, you will never enter the kingdom of heaven" (Mt 5:20).

The Scribes and Pharisees kept the law in its outward appearance, but that is not enough. Christ expects our interior thoughts and motives to come from love of God and love of our neighbor. The new law of love commands us to love even our enemies. While the Old Law forbids killing, the New Law forbids angry thoughts and words and evil deeds.

Christ reminded the people, "You have heard that it was said, 'You shall love your neighbor and hate your enemy.' But I say to you, Love your enemies and pray for those who persecute you, so that you may be children of your Father in heaven; for he makes his sun rise on the evil and on the good, and sends rain on the righteous and on the unrighteous" (Mt 5:43–45). Then Jesus gave His Golden Rule: "In everything do to others as you would have them do to you; for this is the law and the prophets" (Mt 7:12).

Christ ended the Sermon on the Mount with the following parable:

"Everyone therefore who hears these my words and acts upon them, shall be likened to a wise man who built his house on rock. And the rain fell, and the floods came, and winds blew and beat against that house, but it did not fall, because it was founded on rock" (Mt 7:24–25).

Christ compares the person who listens to His words and obeys them to a "wise man." The temptations and sufferings of this life will not change a man who rests upon the solid foundation of Faith. He who believes firmly in Jesus Christ and lives according to the truths He taught will be able to resist temptation and false teachings and will save his soul from destruction.

Jesus taught in Parables

Do you know what a parable is? You probably know it's a story, but it's more than that—it's a story that aims to teach a moral or spiritual lesson. Jesus taught in parables because he knew we learned best this way. By listening to a story, our imaginations are captured and we place ourselves in the shoes of the characters, allowing us to better sympathize with them. This way of teaching was more effective than simply telling us what to do and how to live; instead, he showed us how to live.

 FOR ME TO REVIEW

Questions and Exercises

Part 1: Complete these statements

1. A story which contains a hidden truth is called a _____.

2. Jesus changed _____'s name to Peter.

3. _____ and _____ are called the Sons of Thunder.

4. Bartholomew is sometimes known by the name _____.

5. Christ did not come to destroy the Old Law but to _____ it.

6. The _____ are rules for happiness; they begin with _____ and end with _____.

7. The _____ and _____ kept the law in its outward appearance only.

8. The Old Law forbids killing but the New Law is based on _____.

9. _____ was a tax collector who became one of the Twelve.

10. Christ compared the person who listens to His words and keeps them to a _____.

Part 2: Questions to Check Your Reading

1. What was the Savior's great mission on earth?

2. Name the sons of Zebedee who became Apostles.

3. What did our Lord do before He chose His Apostles?

4. Who was the publican who became a disciple of Jesus?

5. In what manner were the Apostles instructed to preach the Gospel?

6. What does the word "Apostle" mean?

7. What are the eight rules for happiness called?

8. In what way did the New Law differ from the Old?

9. Why did Christ call His disciples "light of the world"?

10. Explain the relation of the Old Law to the New Law.

11. How can you prove that you have built your "house" (your life) upon a rock?

12. Can you give an example of a foolish person who built his house upon sand?

⊘ FOR ME TO DO

1. Search the New Testament for information about one of the Apostles. Describe one of his character traits that should be admired and imitated.

2. Recite the Beatitudes.

3. Recall some incidents in the lives of the Old Testament characters which illustrate the meaning of one of the Beatitudes. For example, Abraham, Job, Judith, Moses, Tobit, Joseph, or King David.

4. Pretend you are a news reporter who was in the crowd when Jesus taught the Beatitudes. Write a story about it. Describe the place, what and how Christ taught, and the people's reaction to the Sermon.

CHAPTER 23

Christ's Parables Describe the New Kingdom

By means of parables Christ described the new kingdom of God, that is, the new Chosen People and the new Church He would establish. Here another prophecy is fulfilled: "I will open my mouth in parables, I will utter things hidden from the foundation of the world" (Ps 77:2).

In these stories Christ conveyed spiritual ideas by means of comparisons based on happenings of the everyday life of the people. He did this in order to make it easier for men to understand His doctrines. They enjoyed listening to the parables and searching for the supernatural truths hidden in them. But in some cases, the parables seemed to have the very opposite effect. Listeners who were hostile to our Lord only went away more hostile.

After our Lord's Ascension, the Apostles noticed the same unhappy result when they retold the parables or repeated other teachings of our Lord. Those who were well disposed seemed to understand and appreciate what they said or, at least, asked for further understanding, while those who came to listen for wrong motives usually left confirmed in their evil disposition. As the Apostles reflected on this mystery, they recalled sayings which our Lord repeated on different occasions:

> "To you it is given to know the mystery of the kingdom of God;
> but to those outside, all things are treated in parables, that
> 'Seeing they may see, but not perceive;
> and hearing they may hear, but not understand'" (Mk 4:11–12).

Let us first see how Christ describes His new kingdom.

Parables of the Kingdom

THE SOWER

One of the parables is about the man who sowed seed in his field. As he spread the seed some fell on ground that was not deep; consequently, when the blades sprang up, they withered in the heat of the sun. Some fell among thorns, and the thorns choked them. Finally, some fell on good ground and brought forth fruit (Mt 13:3–8).

Do you know the meaning of this parable? What does the seed represent? What is one reason for the "seeds" failure to produce good in our hearts? What should we learn from this parable?

THE GOOD SEED AND THE WEEDS

Perhaps you remember the parable of the man who sowed good seed and then an enemy came and sowed worthless weeds over the good seed. Both were allowed to grow until the harvest. The wheat was separated from the weeds (or "chaff"), which was thrown into the fire to burn, while the wheat was gathered into barns (Mt 13:24–30). Who sows the good seed? The weeds? What is meant by the harvest? To what are the faithful compared? The wicked? What lesson does the parable teach?

THE MUSTARD SEED

Jesus foretold the miraculous growth of His Church in the parable of the mustard seed. The mustard seed is very small, yet grows into a bush so big that the birds of the sky dwell on its branches (Mt 13:31–32). What does the fact that the Church is spread over the whole world prove? Why did Christ choose the mustard seed for this parable?

THE LEAVEN

To show us how the kingdom of Christ changes the hearts of men Jesus told the story of the leaven or yeast. When yeast is put into flour or dough, it soon passes through every bit of it, changes it and makes it pleasing to the taste (Mt 13:33). Of what is the "leaven" a figure? How does it explain the spread of Christ's Church? Of what is the "dough" a figure? What is the meaning of this parable? Why did Jesus found His Church?

THE TREASURE

In another parable our Savior said, "The kingdom of heaven is like a treasure hidden in a field; he who finds it hides it, and in his joy goes and sells all that he has and buys that field" (Mt 13:44). Again, our Lord compared His kingdom to a "pearl of great price," giving us to understand its incomparable value (Mt 13:45).

THE NET

In another parable, Christ foretold the separation of the good from the wicked in the Day of Judgment. He compared His Church to a net which fishermen cast into the sea and draw out filled with fish of every kind. Very carefully the good fish are picked out and saved and the bad ones are cast away. At the Judgment the good will be separated from the wicked and each individual will be rewarded or punished according to his deeds (Mt 13:47–50). Here Christ warns us to avoid being Catholic in name only. Some Jews made this mistake by believing that they would be saved merely because they were Jews (according to their blood lineage). The large fish net holds many fish. When it is drawn to the shore the selection begins.

Parables on Membership in the Kingdom

In the previous parables we have seen Christ describing His kingdom. In the parables that follow, Jesus points out the virtues that are necessary for those who desire to become members of His kingdom.

THE GOOD SAMARITAN

It was autumn and near the time for the celebration of the Feast of the Tabernacles. This feast was held every year to give thanks for the harvest and to commemorate the successful ending of the long journey of the Chosen People through the wilderness. On His way to Jerusalem Jesus met a scribe who tried to engage Him in argument. The scribe, who had studied the religious law of Israel, asked Jesus what he must do to gain eternal life. Jesus replied to his question by asking him to answer his own questions. "What is written in the law? What do you read there?" The lawyer was forced to give the familiar answer in the words of the law, which was also part of the daily prayer of the Jews:

"Thou shalt love the Lord thy God
with thy whole heart,
and with thy whole soul,
and with thy whole strength,
and with thy whole mind;
And thy neighbor as thyself" (Lk 10:26–27).

Jesus, in a kindly manner, told the scribe that he was correct, by saying, "Thou hast answered rightly; do this and thou shalt live" (Lk 10:28).

The scribe quickly asked, "And who is my neighbor?" (Lk 10:29.)

Christ then told the parable of the Good Samaritan to teach the lesson of mercy and the brotherhood of all men. The Jews refused to accept the Samaritans and the Gentiles as brothers, holding them in disdain and contempt. Here are the inspired words of the evangelist, St. Luke:

"A man was going down from Jerusalem to Jericho, and fell into the hands of robbers, who stripped him, beat him, and went away, leaving him half dead. Now by chance a priest was going down that road; and when he saw him, he passed by on the other side. So likewise a Levite, when he came to the place and saw him, passed by on the other side. But a Samaritan while traveling came near him; and when he saw him, he was moved with pity. He went to him and bandaged his wounds, having poured oil and wine on them. Then he put him on his own animal, brought him to an inn, and took care of him. The next day he took out two denarii, gave them to the innkeeper, and said, 'Take care of him; and when I come back, I will repay you whatever more you spend.' Which of these three, do you think, was a neighbor to

the man who fell into the hands of the robbers?" He said, "The one who showed him mercy." Jesus said to him, "Go and do likewise." (Lk 10:30–37).

Some of the doctors of the Church point out that Christ, besides teaching us the lesson of the mercy we should have for those in trouble, is also explaining to us that He is the Good Samaritan. Through His priests He binds the wounds caused by sin and takes us to the "Inn", His Church, where He cares for us until His second coming at the end of the world.

THE RICH MAN AND LAZARUS

Christ spoke another parable about the dangers and the responsibilities of those who possess wealth. There was a certain rich man who wore fine clothes and feasted lavishly every day. There was also a hungry beggar called Lazarus who lay at the rich man's gates. Lazarus, who was covered with sores, which the dogs came and licked, asked only for the crumbs that fell from the table of the rich man, but not even these were given to him.

In a few years the beggar died and was taken to heaven. The rich man also died and went to hell. In the midst of the flames the rich man, lifting up his eyes, saw Abraham and Lazarus, and he cried out, "Father Abraham, have pity on me, and send Lazarus to dip the tip of his finger in water to cool my tongue, for I am tormented in this flame" (Lk 16:24).

Abraham answered, "Son, remember that thou in thy lifetime hast received good things, and Lazarus in like manner evil things; but now here he is comforted whereas thou art tormented. And besides all that, between us and you a great gulf is fixed, so that they who wish to pass from this side to you cannot, and they cannot cross from your side to us" (Lk 16:25–26).

The rich man begged Abraham to send Lazarus to warn his relatives not to do as he had done, for then they too would come to this place of torment. Abraham answered, "They have Moses and the Prophets, let them hearken to them" (Lk 16:29). But the rich man continued to protest, saying that if someone from the dead appeared to them they would surely believe. Abraham answered, "If they do not hearken to Moses and the Prophets, they will not believe even if someone rises from the dead" (Lk 16:31).

In this parable the rich man represents those who are hardened because of their selfish use of wealth, while Lazarus, like Job, is a figure of the patient sufferer. God, in His justice, makes all things right, if not in this world, then in eternity.

THE RICH FOOL

While Jesus was in the house of one of the Pharisees, He told this parable. By it He wished to warn His followers against greed.

> "The land of a rich man produced abundantly. And he thought to himself, 'What should I do, for I have no place to store my crops?' Then he said, 'I will do this: I will pull down my barns and build larger ones, and there I will store all my grain and my goods. And I will say to my soul, Soul, you have ample goods laid up for many years; relax, eat, drink, be merry.' But God said to him, 'You fool! This very night your life is being demanded of you. And the things you have prepared, whose will they be?' So it is with those who store up treasures for themselves but are not rich toward God" (Lk 12:16–21).

THE PRODIGAL SON

Since the Pharisees were criticizing our Lord for His kindness to sinners, He directed the following parable to them: A certain man had two sons. The younger of them said to his father, "Father, give me the share of the property that falls to me" (Lk 15:12). The father then divided his wealth between his sons. After receiving his share the younger son went to a distant country. Here he made friends quickly and spent all his money in sinful entertainment. He had no thought of home while he was leading this life of pleasure. But his so-called friends deserted him when his money was gone. At this same time a famine came upon the country and he found himself in want. In order to get food he asked one of the farmers of the place if he might tend the swine. One day while taking care of the animals he thought of his father and how the servants at home had plenty to eat and were well clothed. Filled with sorrow for his past life, the son decided to return to his father and ask his forgiveness.

His aged father, sorrowing over the loss of his son, was accustomed to watch each day to see if his boy would return. One day he saw his son in the distance. The father ran to meet him and, throwing his arms about him, kissed him. The young man, overcome with sorrow, fell on his knees and sobbed, "Father, I have sinned against heaven and before thee. I am no longer worthy to be called thy son" (Lk 15:21).

The father called to his servants, "Fetch quickly the best robe and put it on him and give me a ring for his finger and sandals for his feet; and bring out the fatted calf and kill it, and let us eat and make merry; because my son was dead, and has come to life again; he was lost and is found" (Lk 15:22–24).

When the older brother, who was working in the fields, came home and heard the music and dancing, he asked one of the servants the meaning of the celebration. When he learned it was because of his brother's return he was angry and would not go into the house. When the father heard that his elder son would not join in the rejoicing he went out and urged him to come in. The older son argued with his father that he had always done as the father wished and had worked steadily all these years without asking anything for himself. Then the father answered him kindly, "Son, thou art always with me, and all that is mine is thine; but we were bound to make merry and rejoice, for this thy brother was dead, and has come to life; he was lost and is found" (Lk 15:31–32).

The Scribes and Pharisees were angered by this parable. They knew that our Lord directed it to them.

Who are you?

Who are you in this parable? Are you more like the son who squandered his riches, or are you more like the older brother who was proud and bitter and jealous? Perhaps you have something in common with the father or the servants, or even all the characters in the parable!

The Jewish people, represented by the elder son, had
been the chosen servants of God, while the Gentiles were
a figure of the younger son who obtained forgiveness. To
all mankind Christ gives the lesson of His Father's eager-
ness to forgive a repentant sinner and restore to him his
former rights and the dignity of sonship. God alone can
love like this; and our minds find it hard to
grasp the lesson. If we are in the state
of grace, we must be thankful for
God's infinite mercy in preserving us
in His love and grace and at the same
time we should rejoice with God and His
angels over the conversion of sinners.

THE LOST SHEEP

While Christ was preaching to the people, the Pharisees and the scribes frequently came to listen to Him. When they saw the crowd they complained to each other that Christ welcomed sinners and ate with them. Jesus, who knew their thoughts, told the following story:

> "What man of you having a hundred sheep, and losing one of them, does not leave the ninety-nine in the desert, and go after that which is lost, until he finds it? And when he has found it, he lays it upon his shoulders rejoicing. And on coming home he calls together his friends and neighbors, saying to them, 'Rejoice with me, because I have found my sheep that was lost.' I say to you that, even so, there will be joy in Heaven over one sinner who repents, more than over ninety-nine just who have no need of repentance" (Lk 15:4–7).

In this parable Jesus teaches the value of every person in God's eyes. When a man strays away from God through sin, He seeks to draw him back by means of grace, by sermons, by books, and by the good example of other people. Just as the shepherd carefully carried home the lost sheep, so does God show mercy and compassion to the sinner. How often, too, do our priests go about their flocks searching for the lost sheep! The prophet Ezekiel, speaking for Christ, says, "I will seek that which is lost." Do you remember an Old Testament character who foreshadowed that Christ would be a Shepherd and a King?

THE LOST COIN

Christ, knowing the stubbornness of the scribes and the Pharisees, tried to reach their hearts by bringing to them more forcibly the lesson of God's mercy. He spoke another parable to them. "What woman," He said, "having ten drachmas [a Greek coin equal to a day's wage], if she loses one drachma, does not light a lamp and sweep the house and search carefully until she finds it?" (Lk 15:8.) Jesus described the joy of the woman when she found the coin and how she told her neighbors about her good fortune. Jesus added: "Even so, I say to you, there will be joy among the angels of God over one sinner who repents" (Lk 15:10).

THE TWO SONS

One day when Jesus had begun to preach to a little group that had gathered about Him, the chief priests and elders questioned His right to address the crowd. Our Lord answered them by telling the following parable:

> "A man had two sons; and he came to the first and said, 'Son, go and work today in my vineyard.' But he answered and said, 'I will not'; but afterwards he regretted it and went. And he came to the other and spoke in the same manner. And this one answered, 'I go, sir'; but he did not go. Which of the two did the father's will?" (Mt. 21:28–30.)

St. Jerome explains this parable by saying that the first son is an example of the repentant sinner, who acknowledges that he had made a mistake. The second son represents those who pretend to obey God's Laws but actually reject them.

THE MARRIAGE FEAST

Another parable which Jesus told contained a very special lesson for the Jewish leaders, because they felt that they would be saved because they were of the "seed of Abraham." The fact that they must be converted in their hearts and deeds was a teaching they did not sufficiently emphasize.

> "The kingdom of heaven is like a king who made a marriage feast for his son. And he sent his servants to call in those invited to the marriage feast, but they would

not come. Again he sent out other servants, saying, 'Tell those who are invited, Behold, I have prepared my dinner; my oxen and fatlings are killed, and everything is ready; come to the marriage feast.' But they made light of it, and went off, one to his farm, and another to his business; and the rest laid hold of his servants, treated them shamefully, and killed them" (Mt. 22:2–6).

When the king heard of it, he was angry; and he sent his armies, destroyed the murderers, and burnt their city. He told his servants to go into the streets and invite all that they could find there. The servants did as they were commanded and gathered in both the good and the bad and the wedding room was filled with guests.

After all had been seated the king came in to see the guests, and he saw there a man who was not wearing a wedding garment. The king accordingly said to the man, "Friend, how didst thou come in here without a wedding garment?" The man kept silent. The king said to the waiters, "Bind his hands and feet and cast him forth into the darkness outside, where there will be the weeping and the gnashing of teeth" (Mt 22:12, 13).

Those who were invited and would not come to the feast represent all who refuse Christ's invitation to belong to His kingdom; the man without the wedding garment represents those who will not be able to enter heaven because they do not have on the garment of grace. St. Jerome tells us that in the marriage and in the supper the chief thing is the end and not the beginning. Christ says, "For many are called (the beginning), but few are chosen" (the end). This saying is a Hebrew way of stating emphatically that not all who are first called will finally be chosen. All are called to partake in the heavenly banquet, but only those who make the necessary preparations by receiving graces will share in the feast.

THE WICKED VINE-DRESSERS

Another parable that Jesus told to the leaders of the Jews was the story of a man who planted a vineyard and let it out to vine-dressers, then went abroad for a long time. When the harvest was gathered, the owner sent his servant to collect the profits. The vine-dressers mistreated the man and sent him away. The master sent another servant but he, too, was treated in the same manner. Then the owner decided to send his son, because he thought the vine-dressers would have more respect for one of his family. When these wicked men saw the son they plotted to kill him. After this evil deed they thought that the vineyard would be theirs. But Jesus ended the parable by saying that the owner of the vineyard "will come and destroy those vine-dressers, and will give the vineyard to others" (Lk 20:16).

God sent many prophets and even His own Son as messengers to the Jews, but the Jews would not listen to them. In the fullness of time God took the vineyard, His Church, from the Jews, and gave it to the Gentiles. Is God's treatment of His Chosen People of the Old Testament a warning to us His Chosen People of the New Testament? Explain.

THE TALENTS

Jesus wished to teach His disciples the necessity of making the most of their time and ability. He compared Himself to a man who was about to take a long journey. He called his servants and put his property and possessions in their care. To one he gave five talents (a coin). To another, he gave two talents, and to the third, he gave one talent; to everyone according to his ability. The master then went away.

The one who received the five talents went into the market place and traded, gaining five more. The one who received two talents also traded and gained two other talents. However, the servant who had received one talent dug a hole in the ground and buried it.

Time passed and the master returned. He called his servants together that they might give an account to him. The one who had five talents brought five more. The master was pleased and said to him, "Well done, good and faithful servant; because thou hast been faithful over a few things, I will set thee over many; enter into the joy of thy master" (Mt 25:21). In the same manner the master spoke to the servant who had two talents and who returned to him four. But the servant with the one talent returned it to the owner, saying that since he knew the master was a stern man and that he was afraid of losing it he buried the talent in the ground. The master asked him why he did not put the money in the bank; then at least he would have gained interest on the money. The servant was unable to give a satisfactory answer to the Lord, who said to those about him, "Take away therefore the talent from him, and give it to him who has ten talents" (Mt 25:28). The master ordered the unprofitable servant to be cast forth into the darkness.

This parable suggests that everyone is given enough grace to receive salvation. Man, because he has a free will, may reject this grace and therefore lose eternal life, or by making good use of it, increase grace and thus obtain salvation.

THE TEN VIRGINS

Jesus warned His followers that they must be prepared at all times for the final call into eternity. He told them that they must be like the prudent virgins who were waiting the arrival of the bridegroom. Five of these ten virgins in the parable were wise and took a supply of oil with them for their lamps. The other five were thoughtless and had with them only the oil that was in their lamps. It happened that the wedding party was late and the ten virgins lay down to rest. At midnight there was an announcement that the party had come. The five wise virgins trimmed their lamps which burned brightly because of the good supply of oil. The foolish virgins likewise trimmed their lamps but the flames flickered and went out, for the oil was used. The foolish virgins asked the wise ones for part of their oil but, fearing that there would not be enough, the latter advised the foolish virgins to go to those who sold oil and buy a supply. While these went to make the purchase the bridegroom came and those who were ready went in with him to the marriage and the door was shut. The other virgins came, and seeing the door closed, called out, "Sir, sir, open the door for us!" He answering said: "Amen, I say to you, I do not know you." Our Lord's final words were: "Watch, therefore, for you know not the day nor the hour" (Mt 25:1–13).

 FOR ME TO REVIEW

Questions and Exercises

Part 1: From the parables of Christ listed below certain truths are clear concerning the kingdom of God. Write the name of the parable beside the truth.

- The Treasure Hidden in the Field
- The Wheat and the Chaff
- The Net
- The Pearl of Great Price
- The Sower
- The Mustard Seed
- The Leaven

1. The Church from a small beginning soon spread over the whole world.

2. God's grace gradually works its way into men's hearts until it completely changes them.

3. The good and the bad will be together in the Church of Christ on earth.

4. God gives His grace to all men but it fails to produce good in many hearts.

5. Our Faith is precious, above everything else on earth.

6. Some men receive God's grace and perform good works but they sin after a while and forfeit the good they received.

7. Not every person who is baptized and received into the Catholic Church will get into heaven.

8. The kingdom of God is worth giving up everything else in the world.

9. The grace of God does not even take root in some hearts.

10. At the end of the world there will be a separation of the good from the evil.

Part 2: Questions to Check Your Reading

1. What parable did Jesus use to foretell the growth of His Church?

2. How did Christ point out that the good and the bad would always be together in His Church on earth?

3. What lesson did our Lord teach in the parable of the leaven?

4. Which of the parables of the kingdom of God do you like best? Why?

5. To what did our Lord compare Faith?

6. How can rich people be "poor in spirit"?

FOR ME TO DO

1. Dramatize a scene from the life of a saint and show how he gave all he had to purchase the pearl of great price, the kingdom of God. For example, Maria Goretti, Isaac Jogues, St. Stephen, etc.

2. Give a three-minute talk on:

   a) The parable you like best and why.

   b) Foreign missions help the growth of God's kingdom.

3. Have a discussion on the virtues of Christ which are revealed by the parables: His prudence, His deep knowledge of human nature and the hearts of men; His love, kindness, and consideration even for His enemies; His courage and perseverance, His moderation, etc.

4. Jesus made use of everyday things in His parables. If He were here now what are some of the images He would probably use? Take one of the parables and substitute our modern objects or ideas, but be careful to keep the true meaning of our Lord's parable.

5. Select a parable that appeals to you and have a group dramatize it.

6. Retell the parable of the Prodigal Son changing "certain man" to read "God" and the "son" to read "a sinner."

7. In the story of the "Talents" give the servants names and put them in a situation in modern times. Be sure in each case to bring out the lesson Christ wished to teach.

CHAPTER 24

Jesus Works Some Miracles to Strengthen the Faith of His Followers

The prophets foretold that the Messianic age would be a time of miracles, of striking interventions by almighty God. For example, in the book of Isaiah we read: "Then shall the eyes of the blind be opened, the ears of the deaf shall be unstopped. Then shall the lame man leap as a hart, and the tongue of the dumb shall be free" (Is 35:5–6).

Under the Jewish Law, the saints and prophets worked miracles, but they did so in the name of God, from whom they had their authority. Jesus, however, distinguished Himself from those who went before and from those who came after Him, because He worked all His miracles in His own name, generally by a simple word of command.

Some men accepted these miracles as proof of Christ's divinity. The miracles increased their faith in Christ, filled them with confidence, and deepened the love of God in their hearts. Others, like some Pharisees, blinded by pride and worldly ideas of a Messiah, would not believe and became resentful and envious of Christ.

Let us now see the wonderful power of Christ as shown in His miracles.

Jesus Cures a Sick Man at the Pool of Bethsaida

The Pharisees were severe about enforcing the law of the Sabbath, making so many regulations about keeping it holy that people became confused. Christ tried to correct this by telling the people that the Sabbath was made for man and not man for the Sabbath. God wanted men to rest on that day and raise their

minds and hearts to Him; He did not want them to worry scrupulously about minute regulations.

One Sabbath day in Jerusalem, Jesus came to a pool called Bethsaida. Near the pool was a kind of hospital where sick people stayed and waited for the stirring of the waters, for they believed that the first person to go into the pool after it was stirred would be healed. Jesus found a man there who had been paralyzed for thirty-eight years. When our Lord asked the man if he wished to be cured, he replied, "I have no one to put me into the pool when the water is stirred; for while I am coming, another steps down before me" (Jn 5:7).

Jesus said to him, "Rise, take up thy pallet and walk" (Jn 5:8). Immediately the man was cured. He arose, took up his bed, and went away.

When the Pharisees saw the man carrying his bed they accused him of violating the Sabbath. He answered them, "He who made me well said to me, 'take up thy pallet and walk'" (Jn 5:11). The Pharisees, who later learned that it was Jesus who had told the man to carry his bed, were angered at our Lord. They believed that He was setting Himself up as equal to God and were henceforward searching for ways to accuse Him of sin.

Jesus Cures the Man With the Withered Hand

On another occasion Jesus, as was His custom, went into the synagogue on the Sabbath. There were many people present, among them a man with a withered hand, and the Pharisees were sitting in the place of honor. They were watching to see whether He would cure on the Sabbath, so that they might have some charge to bring against Him.

Jesus knew their thoughts. He then looked on the sick man who stood in the midst of the people. His right arm was stiff and thin, but there was a hopeful expression in his eyes. Jesus spoke to him kindly, "Arise and stand forth in the midst" (Lk 6:8). Then Jesus faced His scheming enemies and, still trying to soften their hearts, said, "I ask you, is it lawful on the Sabbath to do good, or to do evil? To save a life, or to destroy it?" (Lk 6:9.)

Jesus then said to the man, "Stretch forth thy hand" (Lk 6:10). He stretched it forth and it was restored.

The Pharisees, filled with fury, tried to think of ways to harm Jesus.

The Cure of the Centurion's Servant

At Capernaum, one time, Jesus was met by a group of Jewish elders, who had been asked by a Roman centurion to beg Jesus to heal his favorite servant who was at the point of death. The Jews explained to Jesus that the Roman officer did not consider himself worthy to come. They assured our Lord that he was a good man whose petition should be granted. They told Jesus that he had built a synagogue for the Jews and that he was good to them (Lk 7:5).

Jesus went with them to the home of the centurion. When He came near, the centurion met Him saying, "Lord, I am not worthy to have you come under my roof; but only speak the word, and my servant will be healed. For I also am a man under authority, with soldiers under me; and I say to one, 'Go,' and he goes, and to another, 'Come,' and he comes, and to my slave, 'Do this,' and the slave does it" (Mt 8:8–9).

Jesus was pleased with the centurion and praised him for his great faith. This Roman officer proved his faith in Christ by declaring before all the people that Christ could heal the sick man merely by power of His will, without even entering his house. To the centurion and to those who were with him, Jesus said, "Amen I say to you, I have not found such great faith in Israel. And I tell you that many will come from the east and from the west, and will feast with Abraham and Isaac and Jacob in the kingdom of heaven, but the children of the kingdom will be put forth into the darkness outside; there will be the weeping and the gnashing of teeth." Then Jesus said to the centurion, "Go thy way; as thou hast believed, so be it done to thee." And the servant was healed in that hour (Mt 8:10–13).

Christ here prophesied that pagans and Gentiles, because of their faith, would taste the joys of Heaven. The children of the kingdom, the Jews, to whom the Redeemer came, would be last because of their unbelief. Has this prophecy of Our Lord been fulfilled?

By this miracle Jesus testified to His divinity. He healed the centurion's servant and thereby proved that He is truly God. Here Jesus shows that His love extends to all men, including sinners, lepers, beggars, and even a pagan Roman officer. It is God's will that all men belong to His kingdom.

The centurion had firm faith and great humility. We practice these virtues when we consider ourselves worthless servants before God and say at Mass, "Lord, I am not worthy that you should enter under my roof, but only say the word and my soul shall be healed."

The Son of the Widow of Nain

The following day Jesus went to the village of Nain, near Mount Tabor. As Christ and His Apostles came near the city, they met a funeral procession on its way to the burial grounds. Four men were carrying a stretcher on which lay the body of a young man. He was the only son of his widowed mother. Jesus pitied the grief-stricken mother. He went to her and consoled her, saying,

"Do not weep" (Lk 7:13). Then He walked close to the stretcher and touched it. Those who carried it stood still. Jesus looked down on the lifeless figure and spoke, "Young man, I say to thee, arise" (Lk 7:14).

The young man moved, opened his eyes, and sat up. Jesus took him and gave him to his weeping mother. For a moment, she looked in surprise and then threw her arms around her son and held him close to her. The crowd of people who were watching began to glorify God saying, "A great prophet has risen among us," and "God has visited his people" (Lk 7:16).

This miracle is symbolic of the future resurrection, when God will raise up all men from the grave. Even now it has its fulfillment in the sacrament of Penance, where Jesus Christ, through His priest, raises up the sinner from the death of sin.

Jesus Calms the Sea

Another miracle showed Christ's power over the forces of nature. One evening after Jesus had finished speaking to a crowd, He and His disciples decided to cross the Lake of Gennesaret to its eastern shore. During the trip a violent storm arose. Since the lake is below sea level, enclosed by hills, it is subject to sudden, severe squalls. The waves were nearly engulfing the ship. Meanwhile, Jesus was sleeping in the stern of the boat. His frightened disciples awakened Him calling, "Master, we are perishing" (Lk 8:24).

Jesus rebuked them, "Where is your faith?" (Lk 8:25.) Then rising up, He commanded the wind and the sea saying, "Peace, be still" (Mk 4:39). At once, the wind ceased and there came a great calm.

The bewildered disciples questioned one another, "Who, then, is this, that even the wind and sea obey him?" (Mk 4:40.)

By this miracle Christ was trying to make men appreciate God's care and concern for His future Church. The boat is symbolic of the Church, the lake of the world, and the violent storm is the opposition to which the Church is subjected. Christ wished by this miracle to teach an important fact which we should always bear in mind, namely that He is ever present with His Church though He seems for a time to neglect her. He is keeping a continual vigil over His Church, and never fails to calm the disturbance which it is undergoing. He said, "I am with you all days." Just as He was with His Chosen People leading them in the form of a cloud by day and a pillar of fire by night, so is He with us today.

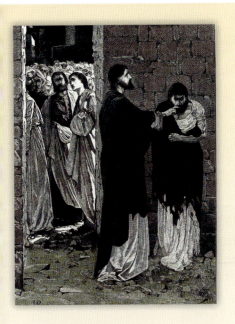

The Healing of Spiritual Maladies

Jesus healed many people who were blind, deaf, or mute. In this, we see a symbol of what he yearns to do for us spiritually. While we may not be blind or deaf, we can be "blind" to spiritual things, not seeing the harmful effects of our sins, for example, or we may be "deaf" to hearing the call of God in our lives, refusing to listen to his will. Just as Jesus cured these physical maladies during his public ministry, so he wants to heal our spiritual maladies now through the sacraments.

The Daughter of Jairus

Jesus came again to Capernaum where many people were waiting to see Him. Among them was an official named Jairus, who asked Him to come to his house, for his only daughter was dying. Jesus did not go at once but ministered to those who had gathered around Him. Meanwhile messengers came from the home of Jairus to tell Jesus that He need not bother coming because the girl was already dead. Jesus said, "Do not be afraid, only have faith" (Mk 5:36).

When He came to the house He permitted only Peter, James, and John and the parents of the girl to enter with Him. Taking the girl by the hand He said, "Girl, I say to thee arise!" (Mk 5:41.) She rose and walked. Before leaving the house Jesus gave strict orders that no one should be told of this occurrence. But the fame of the miracle was spread throughout the country.

The Cure of the Deaf and Dumb Man

At Decapolis, a region of ten independent cities on the east side of the Jordan, the crowd brought a deaf and dumb man to Jesus, and asked Him to lay His hand upon him. Jesus, leading the man aside from the crowd, put His fingers into his ears, and with a little saliva touched his tongue. Then with His eyes raised heavenward, He said, "Eph-pheta Ephphatha!" (which means, "Be opened") (Mk 7:34). At once the man could hear and speak, and news of this miracle also spread far and wide.

The Demon-Possessed Child

By means of another miracle Jesus taught His Apostles the necessity of faith. An anxious father had asked the Apostles to drive an evil spirit out of his possessed child but they had been unable to do so. When Jesus arrived the father begged Him to rid his son of the evil spirit. Jesus commanded the evil one to depart and restored the boy to his father.

The Apostles asked Jesus in secret how it was that they had been unable to cast out the evil spirit. He explained to them that their failure was due to their want of faith. Their faith had probably failed them because of the difficulties of the cure. He told them that if they had faith as a large as a grain of mustard seed, they might move mountains (Mt 17:14–19). By perfect faith even the greatest obstacle could be overcome. What lessons can we learn from this miracle? How strong is our faith in Christ?

The Cure of the Man Born Blind

On another Sabbath, as Jesus was leaving the temple in Jerusalem, He saw a man who had been blind from birth. His disciples asked Him, "Rabbi, who has sinned, this man or his parents, that he should be born blind?" (Jn 9:2.)

Jesus answered, "Neither has this man sinned, nor his parents, but the works of God were to be made manifest in him. I must do the works of him who sent me while it is day; night is coming, when no one can work. As long as I am in the world I am the light of the world" (Jn 9:3–5). After saying this, He spat on the ground, and made clay of spittle. Spreading the clay upon the blind man's eyes, Jesus said to him, "Go, wash in the pool of Siloam" (Jn 9:7). The man obeyed and his sight was restored.

His neighbors asked him how the miracle happened, and he told them of his cure.

The cured man was questioned by the Pharisees. They tried to trap him in his statements but were unable to do so. They questioned his parents, who testified that he had been blind from birth. The grateful man himself said, "If this man were not from God, he could do nothing" (Jn 9:33). He was then ordered out of the synagogue.

Hearing that the Jews had cast the man from the synagogue, Jesus sent for him and said, "Dost thou believe in the Son of God?" (Jn 9:36.)

He questioned, "Who is he, Lord, that I may believe in him?" (Jn 9:36.)

Jesus answered, "Thou hast both seen him, and he it is who speaks with thee" (Jn 9:37).

The man replied, "I believe, Lord" (Jn 9:38). He received spiritual sight from the merciful Savior who had restored his physical sight.

We have in this miracle the fulfillment of the words of the prophet Isaiah concerning Christ, that in His time "the eyes of the blind should be opened" (Is 35:5). Such a miracle could only be done by one approved by God; hence the anger of the unbelieving Pharisees when they could not disprove the cure of the man who had been born blind.

The Cure of the Ten Lepers

On another occasion, Jesus was met by ten lepers who stood at a great distance from Him and called out, "Jesus, master, have pity on us" (Lk 17:13).

Our Lord replied, "Go, show yourselves to the priests" (Lk 17:14). As they went they were made clean.

Only one of the ten cured proved himself grateful. Jesus noticed this and asked "Were not ten made clean? But where are the nine?" (Lk 17:17.) Jesus said to the grateful man, "Arise, go thy way, for thy faith has saved thee" (Lk 17:19).

The reaction of Jesus shows us the value that God sets upon gratitude. Let us never fail to thank Him for favors received.

Leprosy might be considered an image of the state of a soul in mortal sin. The soul is again made whole through the life-giving sacrament of Reconciliation. We should often thank God for having instituted this wonderful sacrament.

FOR ME TO REVIEW

Questions and Exercises

Part 1: Match column I with column II

Column I	Column II
1. Jesus Calms the Sea	A. Received spiritual sight from Jesus.
2. The Sick Man at the Pool of Bethsaida	B. "Lord, I am not worthy that thou shouldst come under my roof."
3. The Ten Lepers	C. "Girl, I say to thee, arise!"
4. The Deaf and Dumb Man	D. Jesus raised her son from the dead.
5. The Lunatic Child	E. Was cured in the synagogue on the Sabbath.
6. The Man Born Blind	F. "Rise, take up thy pallet, and walk."
7. The Daughter of Jairus	G. This miracle is a type of God's care for His Church.
8. The Man with the Withered Hand	H. "Ephphetha."
9. Centurion	I. This miracle taught the Apostles the necessity of faith.
10. Widow of Nain	J. One returned to thank Christ.

Part 2: Answer yes or no

1. Christ, ever present, never fails to calm the tempest.
2. The Centurion brought his servant to Jesus.
3. The Pharisees wanted to put Christ to death.
4. The cure of the ten lepers shows the value of gratitude.
5. The Apostles could drive the evil spirit out of the demon-possessed child.
6. Jesus cured the deaf and dumb man at Decapolis.

7. Christ prophesied that pagans and Gentiles, because of their faith, would taste the joys of heaven.

8. The Pharisees could always answer Christ's questions.

9. Jesus said, "Ephphetha!" when He cured the man born blind.

10. The Pharisees were severe about enforcing the Sabbath.

11. The Jews blamed Jesus for curing a man on the Sabbath.

12. Jesus proved to the Pharisees that it is lawful to do a good deed on the Sabbath day.

13. The raising of the widow's son symbolizes redemption.

Part 3: Questions to Check Your Reading

1. What incorrect ideas did the Pharisees have about the Sabbath?

2. What incident made the enemies of Christ think of other ways to harm Him?

3. How did the centurion prove his firm faith and his deep humility?

4. Which of the miracles mentioned in this chapter is symbolic of our future resurrection?

5. What lesson does Christ teach in the cure of the ten lepers?

6. Can you name some storms which threaten the Church today?

7. Is Christ's watchful care over His Church clearly evidenced today even as it was when He calmed the sea in the early days of His public life? Explain.

FOR ME TO DO

Have a discussion of how the miracles of Christ reveal His divine power, love, mercy, compassion, wisdom, avoidance of vain-glory, and many other virtues.

CHAPTER 25
Jesus Works More Miracles and Makes Profound Promises

During His Public Life Christ made some profound promises, and two of them are particularly important. He promised the Holy Eucharist, and He promised to found a Church with St. Peter as its head. He also appeared to three Apostles in the Transfiguration, and worked more miracles to strengthen belief in Him.

The Promise of the Eucharist

Christ knew that the people would find it very difficult to accept the mystery of the Eucharist. It would be hard for them to believe that God should enter into the soul of man. Accordingly, our Lord was very careful to teach men that they would share in His own Life of grace by partaking of the Food that He was about to promise them. Before He spoke of the great mystery, He worked two great miracles: the multiplication of the loaves, which proved His power over the bread; and the walking on the water, which proved His power over His own body.

The First Multiplication of Loaves and Fishes

When the Apostles returned from their missionary labors and told Jesus of their journey, He took them into a desert place so that they might rest a while. Many people saw them depart by boat and followed them. Jesus was moved with compassion for the crowd and forgot His own weariness. He taught the people many things, spoke to them of the kingdom of God, and healed the sick who had been brought to Him.

When the evening approached Jesus worked a miracle to help prepare men's minds and hearts for the Holy Eucharist.

The Apostles advised Him to send the people away that they might buy food in a nearby village. Jesus said to them, "You yourselves give them some food" (Mt 14:16).

Philip replied, "Two hundred denarii worth of bread is not enough for them, that each one may receive a little" (Jn 6:7).

Jesus then said, "How many loaves have you?" (Mk 6:38.)

TERMS TO KNOW

- denarii
- primacy
- transfigured

351

Andrew answered, "There is a young boy here who has
five barley loaves and two fishes; but what are these among so
many?" (Jn 6:9.) Jesus told them to have the people sit down.
There were in all five thousand men, besides women and
children.

Jesus took the five loaves and two fishes, looked up to
heaven, blessed, broke, and gave them to His disciples to distribute to the multitude. As they ate some of them may have remembered the prophecy, "Thou gavest them bread from heaven
prepared without labor" (Wis 16:20). All had as much as they
desired, and the fragments which remained filled twelve baskets.

Jesus sought by means of this miracle to prepare the minds
and hearts of His followers for the wonderful mystery of His love,
the institution of the Holy Eucharist. This miracle is the most
striking prefigurement of the Eucharistic Bread which Christ
multiplies in the hands of His priests, and which is fed to millions
daily for the nourishment of their souls.

Seeing the miracles which Jesus worked, the people said,
"This is indeed the Prophet who is to come into the world" (Jn
6:14). Jesus feared that they would try to make Him their king, so
He went into the mountain alone to pray. He told His disciples to
sail to the western shore.

Jesus Walks on the Water

Following His request, the Apostles set out for the other side of
the Lake of Tiberias. After it grew dark, and the ship was well out
at sea, a sudden storm arose. For many hours the Apostles were
unable to make any headway against the wind and the waves.
The darkness increased their fears. Suddenly they saw the form
of a man walking upon the waters. Believing it to be an apparition, they cried out in terror. Jesus, knowing their fright called, "It
is I, do not be afraid" (Jn 6:20).

Peter, recognizing the voice of Jesus, pleaded, "Lord, if it is thou, bid me come to thee over the water" (Mt 14:28).

Jesus answered, "Come" (Mt 14:29).

Peter with great confidence stepped out of the boat and began to walk upon the waves. He then became afraid and at once started to sink. He called aloud, "Lord, save me!" (Mt 14:30.)

Jesus took hold of Peter and chided him, "O thou of little faith, why didst thou doubt?" (Mt 14:31.) As Jesus and Peter entered the boat, the sea became calm, and the vessel came safely to shore.

Jesus had stilled the sea for a second time. The first time He was with the Apostles asleep in the boat. The second time He came to them upon the waters. Should we not conclude that whether in the open or hidden, asleep or awake, He watches over His Church and comes to her assistance when trouble assails her, even as He watched over His Apostles in the boat and delivered them from grave peril. Why should we ever fear?

The Second Multiplication of Loaves and Fishes

At Decapolis Christ for the second time fed a vast multitude with a few loaves and fishes. The food supplies which the people had brought with them were gone, but He did not wish to send them to their homes without food. He told the people to sit down on the ground, and, taking seven loaves and fishes which remained, He gave thanks and blessed them and commanded His disciples to give the food to the people. The crowd numbered four thousand men without counting women and children. After all had eaten, seven baskets of food remained (Mt 15:32–38).

Jesus dismissed the people and walked down to the shore, intending to cross the lake. He was met by a group of Pharisees and Sadducees, who asked Him for a sign from heaven to convince them that He was the Christ, the Messiah. Jesus gave them to understand that they needed no miracle to make them believe in Him. He scolded them for their blindness, and told them that they were able to forecast the weather by noting the heavens, but they neglected to notice the signs which so clearly pointed Him out to be the Promised Messiah. What were some of the signs? What did Jesus say earlier to the disciples of John the Baptist?

The Unbelief of the Jews

Jesus reminded the Jews of certain things about the great mystery of the Eucharist which had been prefigured and foretold in the Old Law. "I am the bread of life" (Jn 6:35), Jesus said. Then He continued, "Your fathers ate the manna in the desert, and have died. This is the bread that comes down from heaven, so that if anyone eat of it he will not die . . . and the bread that I will give is my flesh for the life of the world" (Jn 6:49–52).

Disturbed by our Lord's statement the Jews asked among themselves, "Is this not Jesus, the son of Joseph, whose father and mother we know? . . . How can this man give us his flesh to eat?" (Jn. 6:42, 53.) They understood Christ's words literally, that is, they realized that He meant to give them His body. They refused to believe that He was God to whom all things are possible.

An argument arose between those who believed in Jesus and those who refused to believe that He was God. Some of them said, "This is a hard saying. Who can listen to it?" (Jn. 6:61.)

Christ answered their question kindly. "This is why I have said to you, 'No one can come to me unless he is enabled to do so by my Father'" (Jn 6:66). Our Lord explained that faith is a gift that comes from God, a great gift to be prayed for and valued. After these words many parted from Jesus and no longer went about with Him. Many of His disciples turned away too, and Jesus stood and watched them go. When only the Twelve remained He asked them, "Do you also wish to go away?" (Jn 6:68.)

Peter exclaimed, "Lord, to whom shall we go? Thou hast the words of everlasting life, and we have come to believe and to know that thou art the Christ, the Son of God" (Jn 6:64–70).

St. Peter Head of the Church

One day, several months after the miracle of the loaves, as Jesus and His Apostles were in the pagan territory north of Galilee, near the city of Caesarea Philippi, our Lord asked the Apostles the question, "Who do men say the Son of Man is?" (Mt 16:13.)

"Some say, John the Baptist; and others, Elijah; and others, Jeremiah, or one of the prophets," answered the Twelve, wondering a little at this question. But Jesus asked them: "But who do you say that I am?"

Peter answered for all the others, "Thou art the Christ, the Son of the living God" (Mt 16:14–16).

"Blessed art thou, Simon Bar-Jona," our Lord replied, "for flesh and blood has not revealed this to thee, but my Father in heaven. And I say to thee, thou art Peter, and upon this rock I will build my Church, and the gates of

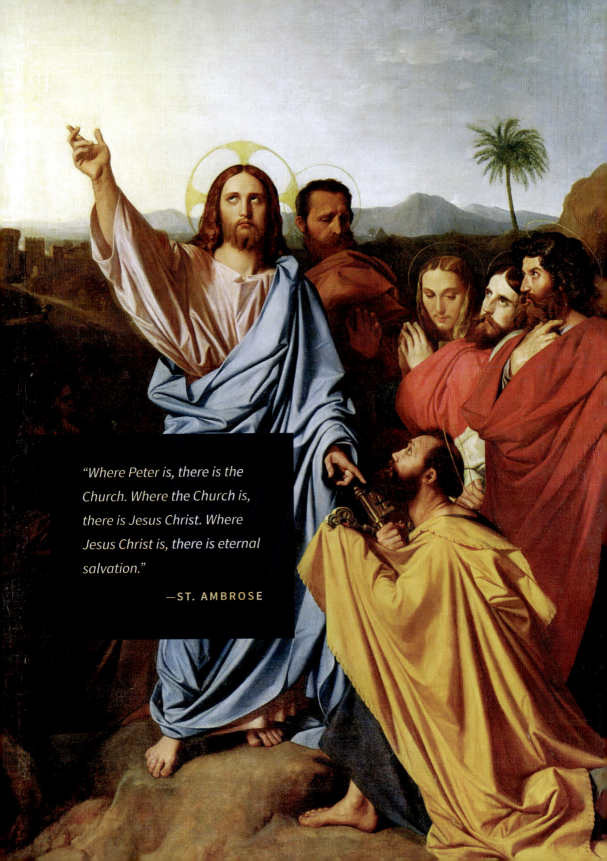

"Where Peter is, there is the Church. Where the Church is, there is Jesus Christ. Where Jesus Christ is, there is eternal salvation."

—ST. AMBROSE

Hell shall not prevail against it. And I will give thee the keys of the kingdom of heaven; and whatever thou shalt bind on earth shall be bound in heaven, and whatever thou shalt loose on earth shall be loosed in heaven" (Mt 16:17–19). What did Christ mean when He told Peter that He would give him the keys of the kingdom? What position in the Church was promised to St. Peter? In what words did Christ say that His Church would last forever? Can you name some enemies who have opposed the Church? Who is Peter's successor today?

Jesus Foretells His Passion and Death

Jesus then said to the disciples, "The Son of Man must suffer many things, and be rejected by the elders and Chief Priests and Scribes, and be put to death, and on the third day rise again" (Lk 9:22).

Peter also refused to believe that Jesus would suffer and die. He said, "Far be it from thee, O Lord, this will never happen to thee" (Mt 16:22). The mind of Peter was filled with dreams of the glory of the Messiah, and he could not fit the picture of suffering, rejection, and death into his dreams.

Jesus said to Peter, "Get behind me, Satan, thou art a scandal to me; for thou dost not mind the things of God, but those of men" (Mt 16:23).

Jesus then told them that all men must follow Him in suffering in order to be saved. He said, "If anyone wishes to come after me, let him deny himself, and take up his cross, and follow me" (Mk 8:34). He also pointed out that earthly glories are as nothing when compared with the salvation of one's soul. He taught them this lesson in the following words, "For what does it profit a man, if he gain the whole world, but suffer the loss of his own soul?" (Mk 8:36.)

Peter and the disciples could not understand the words which Jesus spoke, but they remained with Him.

Christ Is Transfigured

While they were in the district around Mount Tabor, not far from Nazareth, Jesus took Peter, James, and John and went to the top of the mountain to pray. Christ was suddenly surrounded by a brilliant light. His face became as radiant as the sun and His garments were white as snow. The three Apostles were amazed at the dazzling splendor of their Master. Suddenly they noticed that He was not alone. Two men appeared and began to talk with Him of His death in Jerusalem. One was Moses and the other Elijah.

Peter became excited and cried out, "Lord, it is good for us to be here. If thou wilt, let us set up three tents here, one for thee, one for Moses, and one for Elijah" (Mt 17:4).

While Peter was speaking a cloud overshadowed Jesus and His two companions. A voice out of the cloud said, "This is my beloved Son, in whom I am well pleased; hear him" (Mt 17:5).

Frightened by this, Peter, James, and John fell to the ground and covered their faces. Sometime later, they felt a gentle touch and heard the words, "Arise, and do not be afraid" (Mt 17:7). It was Jesus bending over them. Moses and Elijah had disappeared, and the vision was gone. They followed our Lord down the side of the mountain and He said to them, "Tell the vision to no one, till the Son of Man has risen from the dead" (Mt 17:9). Christ revealed His glory to these three Apostles because He wished to strengthen their faith in Him.

In the Transfiguration, Moses represented the Mosaic Law and Elijah stood for the prophets. The purpose of the law and the prophets was to point the way to Christ and to prepare the world for His coming. These two leaders of the Old Testament were present to acknowledge Christ as the promised One and the founder of the New Law. The work of the Old was finished and the New would now fulfill its promises and hopes, and bring forth all that was foreshadowed and prophesied.

The Cure of the Blind Bartimeus

As Jesus was leaving Jericho, He was met by the blind Bartimeus. Jesus, filled with pity, stopped and asked that the blind man be brought to Him. Those who hurried to bring Bartimeus urged him saying, "Take courage. Get up, he is calling thee" (Mk 10:49). The blind man obeyed and hurried to Jesus, who, to reward his faith, restored his sight.

The Resurrection of Lazarus

Jesus was often a guest at the home of a man named Lazarus and his sisters, Mary and Martha. They lived in Bethany, near Jerusalem. One day when Jesus was in Perea, beyond the Jordan, Lazarus was taken sick. His sisters called for Jesus. He did not go at once, but sent word that the sickness was not unto death but for the glory of God. Two days later Jesus informed His disciples, "Lazarus, our friend, sleeps. But I go that I may wake him from sleep" (Jn 11:11). When Jesus arrived, Lazarus had been in the grave four days.

Martha met our Lord and said, "Lord, if thou hadst been here my brother would not have died" (Jn 11:21).

Only three people are spoken of in the Scripture as having been raised from the dead by the Savior. One, the daughter of Jairus, who had just died; the son of the widow of Nain who was carried out for burial, and the third, Lazarus, as we have just seen, who had been in the tomb for some time.

Jesus answered, "Thy brother shall rise" (Jn 11:23).

Martha replied, "I know that he will rise at the resurrection, on the last day" (Jn 11:24).

Jesus responded, "I am the resurrection and the life; he who believes in me, even if he die, shall live; and whoever lives and believes in me, shall never die. Dost thou believe this?" (Jn 11:25–26.)

She replied, "Yes, Lord, I believe that thou art the Christ, the Son of God, who hast come into the world" (Jn 11:27).

Martha called her sister Mary who came to Jesus. He consoled His friends and asked where they had laid Lazarus. As Jesus went to the sepulcher, He was followed by a large crowd. He told them to take away the stone. Then, He cried with a loud voice, "Lazarus, come forth!" (Jn 11:43.) At once Lazarus came forth from the tomb and stood in their midst. Thus was wrought the greatest miracle, save that of His own resurrection, that Christ ever performed. Many of the Jews who were present now believed in Jesus, but others went out and told the Pharisees what had happened.

FOR ME TO REVIEW

Questions and Exercises

Part 1: Match column I with column II

Column I	Column II
SET A	
1. Philip	A. represented the Mosaic Law in the Transfiguration.
2. Andrew	B. said, "Thou art Christ, the Son of the living God."
3. Peter	C. was brought back to life by Jesus.
4. Elijah	D. was cured by Jesus.
5. Lazarus	E. stood for the prophet at Transfiguration
6. Moses	F. said, "There is a boy here who has five barley loaves and two fishes."
7. Bartimeus	G. said, "Two hundred denarii of bread is not enough for them . . ."

SET B	
1. Decapolis	A. Jesus met Bartimeus as he was leaving
2. Mount Tabor	B. where Jesus heard of Lazarus' sickness
3. Jericho	C. Christ worked the second multiplication of loaves and fishes at
4. Perea	D. place where Christ was transfigured

SET C	
1. Manna	A. feeds God's People in the New Testament
2. denarius	B. first in rank
3. Transfiguration	C. fed the Chosen People in the Old Testament
4. primacy	D. a coin
5. Holy Eucharist	E. supernatural change in Jesus' appearance

Part 2: Questions to Check Your Reading

1. How does the bread of the New Law differ from the Manna?

2. What miracles did Christ work to prepare men's minds for the Holy Eucharist?

3. What words of Christ were so difficult for the Jews to believe?

4. Did Christ explain His doctrine when He saw the unbelief of the people?

5. After many of the disciples left Jesus, how did Peter comfort our Lord?

6. Did the Jews accept Christ as the promised Messiah?

7. In what words did Peter make a profession of his faith?

8. How did Jesus reward Peter for his faith?

9. What is meant by the primacy of Peter among the Apostles?

10. Which of the Apostles saw Jesus transfigured?

11. What was the meaning of the appearance of Moses with Christ?

12. Why was Elijah there?

13. Why did Jesus make known His glory to these three Apostles?

✔ FOR ME TO DO

1. Give a short presentation on some examples of how the powers of hell have attacked the Church of Christ.

2. Memorize some important quotations taken from the speeches of our Lord, as, for example: His words to St. Peter making him head of the Church, or His promise to give us the Holy Eucharist, or any others.

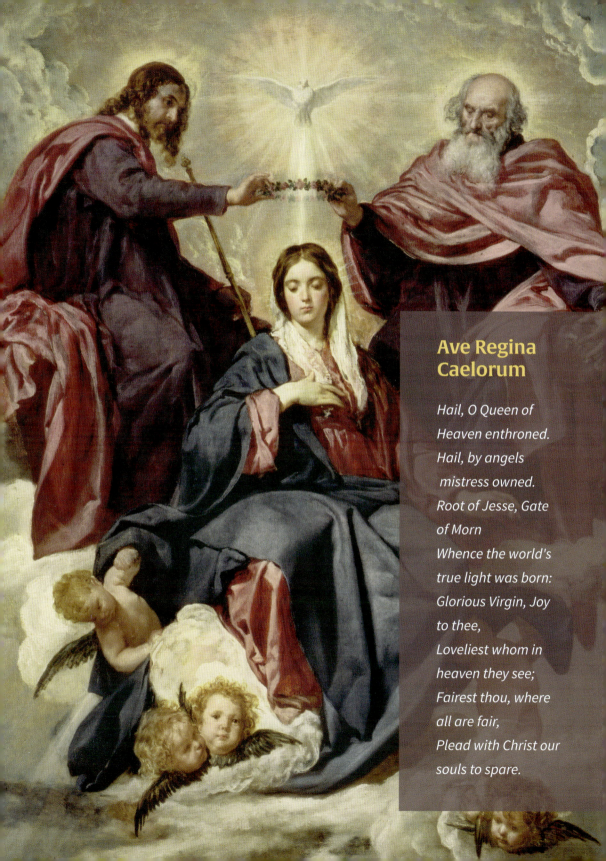

Ave Regina Caelorum

Hail, O Queen of Heaven enthroned.
Hail, by angels mistress owned.
Root of Jesse, Gate of Morn
Whence the world's true light was born:
Glorious Virgin, Joy to thee,
Loveliest whom in heaven they see;
Fairest thou, where all are fair,
Plead with Christ our souls to spare.

CHAPTER 26

Jesus Establishes a Priesthood and a Sacrifice

After the cure of Bartimeus, Jesus and His Apostles continued their journey toward Jerusalem. Because the next day was the Sabbath, and the Jews were forbidden to travel more than a mile on that day, the little company stopped at Bethany. Lazarus and his two sisters, Martha and Mary, welcomed Jesus and the Apostles in their home.

Mary Anoints Jesus

On the Sabbath day a man named Simon gave a banquet for Jesus and His followers. Mary, the sister of Lazarus, took a vase of costly ointment and anointed the head and feet of Jesus. The house was filled with the fragrance of the ointment. The Apostles complained about the waste, and Judas said that the ointment could have been sold and the money given to the poor. Judas had charge of any money that was given to the group, and at times he used some of it for his own benefit. Jesus defended the woman's actions by telling those at the banquet, "For you always have the poor with you, but you will not always have me. By pouring this ointment on my body she has prepared me for burial" (Mt 26:11–12).

Many people in Jerusalem heard that Jesus was in Bethany. They were curious to see Him and Lazarus, whom He had raised from the dead. The leaders of the Jews were angry because some of the people believed in Jesus and wished to follow Him. The leaders planned how they might put Jesus to death. They also sought to do away with Lazarus because many people believed in Jesus because of him.

The Last Journey to Jerusalem

On the first day of the week Jesus and His Apostles started for Jerusalem. When they reached Bethphage Jesus sent two of the group into the village to get a colt. He told them that they should tell the owner that the Lord needed it. The disciples returned with the animal. Jesus mounted the beast.

Jerusalem was crowded at this time with the people who had come to celebrate the Passover. The miracles of Jesus had been

TERMS TO KNOW

- Bethany
- Bethphage
- Gethsemane
- Cedron
- oblation

discussed by the crowds who were eagerly awaiting the Master's coming. As soon as the Lord's little company entered Jerusalem, throngs of people came out to greet them. Palm branches were cut from the trees and garments were spread across the pathway. Their joyous cry of welcome was the age-old "hosanna" which means, "Save, I pray thee."

When Jesus beheld the city of Jerusalem He wept. Because He was God, He could foresee His rejection by the leaders of His own people. He would suffer and die at the hands of these wicked men. In a short time, a great punishment would come to the unhappy city. At this time, Christ prophesied, saying,

> "If thou hadst known, in this thy day, even thou, the things that are for thy peace! But now they are hidden from thy eyes. For days will come upon thee when thy enemies will throw up a rampart about thee, and surround thee and shut thee in on every side, and will dash thee to the ground and thy children within thee, and will not leave in thee one stone upon another, because thou hast not known the time of thy visitation" (Lk 19:42–44).

About thirty-seven years later this prophecy was fulfilled. A Roman army under Titus destroyed the city so completely that historians tell us that not a stone was left upon another stone. Does this serve as a warning to the Chosen People of the New Testament?

The Great Passover Begins

Jesus came with His disciples to the Holy City for the celebration of the Passover.

On Monday before the feast of the Pasch, Jesus went to the Temple, passed through the Court of the Israelites, and entered the Priests' Court. The presence of Jesus caused a stir among the priests who had been angered by His miracles and teachings. The judges of the Sanhedrin, under the leadership of Caiaphas, were searching for a cause to put Him to death.

The next day the Master returned to the Temple to heal and to teach. He denounced the scribes and Pharisees, scattered the money-changers and overturned their tables. When He had finished His teachings, Jesus said openly to His disciples, "You know that after two days the Passover will be here and the Son of Man will be delivered up to be crucified" (Mt 26:2).

Caiaphas and the elders feared to capture Jesus publicly; however, they tried to trap Him by many questions. Christ turned the question on them by saying, "What do you think of the Christ? Whose son is he?" They answered, "David's." But Jesus said, "How then does David in the Spirit call him Lord, saying, 'The Lord said to my Lord: Sit thou at my right hand, till I make thy enemies thy footstool'? If David, therefore, calls him 'Lord,' how is he his son?" (Mt 22: 42–45.) This silenced the Pharisees and convinced the people even more that Christ was a great prophet.

The Traitor

Judas was torn by worldly ambitions. He went to the Sanhedrin and bargained with them to betray his Master into their hands. They agreed to give him thirty pieces of silver, if he would help them arrest Jesus quietly. Judas closed the bargain. Perhaps he tried to ease his guilty conscience by the thought that Jesus could escape from the Jews as He had done when pursued in the Temple.

Few look upon the sin of covetousness as being as serious as it really is, yet here we see it to be the occasion of a great sin— selling the God-Man for a little silver.

The Last Supper

PREPARATION

On Thursday at sundown the Passover began. That afternoon, according to the law of Moses, the Paschal Lamb was to be sacrificed and then eaten in the evening. The disciples said to Jesus, "Where dost thou want us to prepare for thee to eat the Passover?" (Mt 26:17.) In response Jesus told Peter and John they would find a man carrying a vessel of water near the city gate. They were to follow him and tell his master that their Master wished to eat the Passover supper in his house.

Peter and John went on their errand. They entered the city by the southern gate where they saw the man carrying the water pitcher.

Peter and John followed him into the courtyard, giving his master the message our Lord had told them. The owner of the house was honored and took them to the upper room which was prepared for the guests. The two Apostles, having seen that all was ready in the room, went to buy the lamb, the bread, bitter herbs, and wine. They carried the lamb to the temple to be slain and then to the courtyard to be roasted.

THE MEANING OF THE PASSOVER

This Jewish Passover was the most solemn ceremony of the Old Testament. It was a lasting remembrance of the deliverance of the people from the slavery of Egypt and of the angel of death who passed over the doorposts marked with the blood of the Paschal Lamb. Let us review some of its details and their deeper meaning. Everything in the Paschal supper was prophetical.

With the sprinkling of Christ's blood on our souls, we are protected from the angel of death. The bones of the lamb were not to be broken. It was to be without blemish to express the perfect sanctity of Jesus, the Immaculate Lamb of God. The Paschal Lamb was to be sacrificed and eaten because Christ was to suffer and die for us and become the Victim and Food for the people of the New Testament. In every house a whole lamb was eaten, so Christ at communion is received whole and entire.

From the manner in which the Paschal Lamb was to be eaten we learn the condition with which we ought to come to the Christian Passover. The lamb was roasted with fire to express that fire of charity with which we are to come to Christ in the holy mysteries. It was eaten with unleavened bread to teach us not to feast with the old leaven but with the unleavened bread of sincerity and truth. The bitter herbs eaten with the Paschal Lamb signify the contrition for sin with which we are to come to the Lamb of God. To have our loins girt and feet shod, denotes the firm control we are to have over our passions. The staff carried in the hand shows that we are pilgrims who have no lasting home here. We are to leave the land of slavery and go out into the desert with God, and finally reach our true country, heaven.

THE PASCHAL MEAL IS EATEN

In the evening, Jesus and the Apostles reclined at the table and ate the Paschal supper according to the Mosaic Law. This night was to be the sealing of the bond of union between them. Jesus told them so in these words: "I have greatly desired to eat this Passover with you before I suffer; for I say to you that I will eat of it no more until it has been fulfilled in the kingdom of God" (Lk 22:15–16). Here, Jesus is referring to the institution of the Holy Eucharist.

Jesus took the first cup of wine of the Paschal ritual, tasted it, and blessed it saying, "Take this and share it among you; for I say to you that I will not drink of the fruit of the vine until the kingdom of God comes" (Lk 22:18). The Apostles, certain that Christ meant that the kingdom would soon be theirs, began to argue about the place each would hold in this kingdom. Jesus listened patiently and finally quieted them by saying, "Let him who is greatest among you become as the youngest, and him who is the chief as the servant. For which is the greater, he who reclines at table, or he who serves? Is it not he who reclines? But I am in your midst as he who serves. But you are they who have continued with me in my trials. And I appoint to you a kingdom, even as my Father has appointed to me, that you may eat and drink at my table in my kingdom, and you shall sit upon thrones, judging the twelve tribes of Israel" (Lk 22:26–30).

THE WASHING OF THE FEET—A SYMBOL OF PENANCE

As an example to those who wished to be disciples in His kingdom, the Master stood up early during the Paschal supper, laid aside His garments, and poured water into a basin. He took a towel, put it around Himself, and began to wash and wipe the feet of His Apostles. Remembering that Jesus was the Son of God, Peter in a spirit of unworthiness cried out, "Thou shalt never wash my feet!" (Jn. 13:8.)

But the Master replied, "If I do not wash thee, thou shalt have no part with me" (Jn 13:8).

He had touched a deep fear in Peter's heart, the thought of separation, and Peter cried out, "Lord, not my feet only, but also my hands and my head!" (Jn 13:9.)

After He had washed their feet, He said to them, "Amen, I say to you, one of you will betray me" (Mt 26:21).

The disciples were uncertain of whom he was speaking. Peter said to John, "Who is it of whom he speaks?" (Jn 13:24.)

Jesus answered, "It is he for whom I shall dip the bread, and give it to him" (Jn 13:26).

He then dipped the bread and gave it to Judas. Jesus said to him, "What thou dost, do quickly" (Jn 13:27). Judas left immediately.

Christ Institutes the Holy Eucharist and Holy Orders

INTRODUCTION

Our Lord, because of His love for us, would not leave us orphans; therefore, before His death He gave us the greatest gift that the God-Man could bestow—His own self. His sacred body and blood in the Holy Eucharist were to remain with us always as food for our souls. He also ordained priests through whom this holy sacrament could be continued in the Sacrifice of the Mass. They would renew on our altars His sacrifice on Calvary as a daily holocaust to our eternal Father. Thus were fulfilled the words of Malachi, "In every place there is sacrifice, and there is offered in my name a clean oblation" (Mal 1:11). The Old Testament has given place to the New because of the sacrifice of Christ, our Redeemer.

"We must always have courage, and if some spiritual languor comes upon us, let us run to the feet of Jesus in the Blessed Sacrament, and let us place ourselves in the midst of the heavenly perfumes, and we will undoubtedly regain our strength."

—ST. PADRE PIO

THE HOLY EUCHARIST

Jesus looked upon the group of Apostles around Him at the table, and His heart poured out words of love and consolation: "Little children, yet a little while I am with you. You will seek me . . . but where I go you cannot come" (Jn. 13:33). Knowing that this message would make them grieve, He tried to bring them closer to each other by giving them this counsel: "A new commandment I give you, that you love one another; that as I have loved you, you also love one another" (Jn 13:34). Before the evening was over the Master explained what He meant. The Apostles remembered Christ's parting words. The bond that united them to each other in their labors for His Church was so great that the world exclaimed, "See how these Christians love one another." Christ was preparing them for the pledge of His love, the Holy Eucharist, the symbol and the means of His union with them. He wished to end the Last Supper with this divine Sacrament to impress upon these future priests the miracle and mystery of so great a gift.

During the Paschal Supper, probably before the Paschal Lamb was eaten, Jesus, His eyes raised to heaven, took in His hands the unleavened bread, blessed it, broke it, and gave it to these loving Apostles, saying; "Take and eat; this is my body" (Mt 26:26).

Toward the end of the meal Christ took another cup of wine, blessed it, and drank of it. Then He gave it to them saying, "All of you drink of this; for this is my blood of the new covenant, which is being shed for many unto the forgiveness of sins" (Mt 26:27–28).

After the Apostles had received the Sacred Body and Blood, they realized that their Lord lived in them, for His love burned in them as grace began to act within them. The Old Law had passed away and with that sacrifice the New began and was to continue in the Catholic Church. The mystery of this Holy Sacrifice was not a thing of time, it was, like Christ Himself, "yesterday, today, and the same forever." Jesus had just performed for all mankind His outstanding act as a High Priest.

The Master had given them a New Law of Love, sealed by His blood, but He did not stop there. In order to make certain that His sacrament would be continued for all mankind, Christ was about to give His Apostles the power to offer the Holy Sacrifice of His Body and Blood.

THE SACRAMENT OF HOLY ORDERS

Jesus prepared His Apostles for the ministry. He had made Peter their head, the Rock on which His future Church should be built. He had given them the power of miracles, but now He gave them the most miraculous power. Jesus wanted men of all times and places to share in the banquet of His Body and Blood. Thus He conceived of a way whereby He would become a Victim at the words of His Apostles and their successors. His own words would spring from their lips. By the simple phrase, "Do this in remembrance of me" (Lk 22:19) He instituted the sacrament of Holy Orders. He made His Apostles priests and applied to them the Psalmist's words, "The Lord hath sworn, and he will not repent, 'Thou art a priest forever according to the order of Melchizedek'" (Ps 109:2–4).

At that moment these fishermen were given the power of the priesthood of Jesus Christ. Through them and their successors the sacrifice of Christ was to be offered daily to God in adoration and in remembrance of our divine Redeemer.

Christ Speaks to His Apostles After the Last Supper

A NEW COMMANDMENT OF LOVE

After instituting the Holy Eucharist and the priesthood, Jesus spoke some final words to His Apostles. His last wish was to impress upon the Apostles the commandment of loving one another as He loved them. His heart grew sad as He looked around Him at the table. He warned them: "You will all be scandalized this night because of me; for it is written,

'I will smite the shepherd,

and the sheep of the flock will be scattered.'

But after I have risen, I will go before you into Galilee" (Mt 26:31–32).

Their divine Master added that He would stay with them a little while, but where He was going they could not come yet.

Peter declared, "Even though all shall be scandalized because of thee, I will never be scandalized."

"Amen, I say to thee," replied Jesus, "this very night, before a cock crows, thou wilt deny me three times" (Mt 26:33–34).

Peter said, "Even if I should have to die with thee, I will not deny thee" (Mt 26:35).

Jesus turned to the others and warned them of the coming danger referred to in the prophecy of Zechariah, "Strike the shepherd and the sheep shall be scattered" (Ze 13:6–7). The Apostles were afraid and they did not understand the hidden meaning of His words. Jesus tried to strengthen their faith by saying, "Let not your heart be troubled. You believe in God, believe also in me" (Jn 14:1).

To comfort them even more, Christ continued, "In my Father's house there are many mansions. Were it not so, I should have told you, because I go to prepare a place for you. . . . Where I go, you know, and the way you know" (Jn 14:2, 4).

Thomas said, "Lord, we do not know where thou art going, and how can we know the way?" (Jn 14:5.) It was in reply to this question that Christ called Himself "the Way, and the Truth, and the Life" (Jn 14:6). By knowing and loving Jesus, the Apostles—and all of us—are able to reach the Father.

To help them realize it, He said, "If you had known me, you would also have known my Father" (Jn 14:7).

Philip said, "Lord, show us the Father and it is enough for us" (Jn 14:8).

Jesus replied, "Have I been so long a time with you, and you have not known me? Philip, he who sees me, sees also the Father. Do you not believe that I am in the Father and the Father in me. Amen, amen, I say to you, he who believes in me, the works that I do, he also shall do, and greater than these he shall do, because I go to the Father. And whatever you ask in my name, that I will do, in order that the Father may be glorified in the Son" (Jn 14:9–13). Christ spoke of the greatness of the visible miracles and told His Apostles that, after His Ascension, they would do greater miracles than those which He had shown the world.

Then He comforted them, saying, "I will not leave you orphans; I will come to you. Yet a little while and the world no longer sees me. But you see me, for I live and you shall live. In that day you will know that I am in my Father, and you in me, and I in you . . ." (Jn 14:18–20). He continued, "These things I have spoken to you while yet dwelling with you. But the Advocate, the Holy Spirit, whom the Father will send in my name, He will teach you all things, and bring to your mind whatever I said to you. Peace I leave with you, my peace I give to you; not as the world gives do I give to you. Do not let your hearts be troubled, or be afraid . . ." (Jn 14:25–27). The peace of this world is false and deceitful; Christ's peace is true and permanent.

THE VINE AND THE BRANCHES

The Apostles' hearts were saddened by this last farewell. Jesus said to them, "You have heard me say to you, 'I go away and I am coming to you'" (Jn 14:28). He warned them against a weakening of their faith, lack of charity, and fear of suffering. He asked them to keep close to Him in love. He compared Himself to a vine, His Father to a vine-dresser, and His Apostles to the branches. "I am the vine, and my Father is the vine-dresser. Every branch in me that bears no fruit, he will take away, and every branch that bears fruit, he will cleanse that it may bear more fruit" (Jn 15:1–2).

Jesus, in preparing them for their work, wanted them to see Him in their neighbors; He thus continued to instruct them. "As the Father has loved me, I also have loved you. Abide in my love. If you keep my commandments you will abide in my love, as I also have kept my Father's commandments, and abide in his love. . . . This is my commandment, that you love one another as I have loved you. Greater love than this no one has, that one lay down his life for his friends" (Jn 15:9–13). This was what He was about to do for them.

"No longer do I call you servants," He continued, "because the servant does not know what his master does. But I have called you friends, because all things that I have heard from my Father, I have made known to you" (Jn 15:15). He had done this by laying open to them His plans and by giving them graces which He merited for them.

THE HOLY SPIRIT IS PROMISED

Christ then promised the Holy Spirit whom He would send from the Father, the Spirit of truth who proceeds from the Father. He would give testimony of Christ, and with wonderful power cause His teachings to be received by the world.

"And now," said Christ, "I am going to him who sent me, and no one of you asks me, 'Where art thou going?' But because I have spoken to you these things, sadness has filled your heart" (Jn 16:5–6). With what gentle and tender words Our Savior tried to soothe the grief of His chosen disciples. "But I speak the truth to you," He continued, "it is expedient for you that I depart. For if I do not go, the Advocate will not come to you. . . . And when he has come he will convict the world of sin, and of justice, and of judgment" (Jn 16:7–8).

"Many things yet I have to say to you," He added, "but you cannot bear them now, but when the Spirit of Truth has come, He will teach you all truth. For he will not speak on His own authority but whatever He will hear, He will speak, and the things that are to come He will declare to you" (Jn 16:12–13).

"A little while" continued Christ, "and you shall see Me no

longer; and again a little while and you shall see Me, because I go to the Father" (Jn 16:16).

His disciples then questioned, "What is this 'little while' of which He speaks?" (Jn 16:18.)

"Amen, amen, I say to you," He answered, "that you shall weep and lament, but the world shall rejoice; and you shall be sorrowful, but your sorrow shall be turned into joy. And you therefore have sorrow now, but I will see you again, and your heart shall rejoice, and your joy no one shall take from you" (Jn 16:20–22).

Christ then strengthened the confidence of the Apostles in prayer saying: "If you ask the Father anything in my name, he will give it to you. Hitherto you have not asked anything in my name. Ask, and you shall receive, that your joy may be full" (Jn 16:23–24).

JESUS PRAYS TO THE FATHER

Then began the prayer of Jesus Christ, the God-Man, Priest, and Victim. Lifting His eyes to heaven He spoke a beautiful prayer: "Father the hour is come! Glorify Thy Son, that Thy Son may glorify Thee, even as Thou hast given Him power over all flesh, in order that to all Thou hast given Him He may give everlasting life" (Jn 17: 1–2). After this beginning, the prayer was divided into three parts: First, Jesus prayed for Himself; then He prayed for His Apostles, saying: "I pray for them, not for the world do I pray, but for those whom Thou hast given Me, because they are Thine . . . Holy Father, keep in Thy name those whom Thou hast given Me, that they may be one even as We are" (Jn 17:9–11). Lastly He prayed for the Church, "Yet not for these only do I pray, but for those also who through their word are to believe in Me" (Jn 17:20).

When Jesus had finished, they all rose from the table, sang the final Psalm of the Paschal ritual, and then followed Him out of the city, down the hill and over the Brook Cedron, which lies between Jerusalem and Mt. Olivet. On the lower slopes of the mount was the Garden of Olives.

FOR ME TO REVIEW

Questions and Exercises

Part 1: Tell who

1. Accompanied Jesus to Bethany?
2. Was a friend whom Jesus had raised from the dead?
3. Were the sisters who lived with their brother in Bethany?
4. Complained because Mary anointed Jesus?
5. Invited Jesus and the Apostles to a banquet?
6. Were angry because the people came to see and hear Jesus?
7. Rode on a colt to Jerusalem?
8. Did not want Jesus to wash his feet?
9. Offered to betray Jesus to the Chief Priests?
10. Was the true Paschal Lamb of the New Testament?

Part 2: Tell where

1. Jesus journeyed for the last time to celebrate the feast of the Passover.
2. Jesus made an overnight stop on the Sabbath.
3. People would suffer terribly because they would put Jesus to death.
4. The Jewish Nation celebrated the first Passover.
5. The disciples took the Paschal Lamb to be slain.
6. Jesus and the Apostles ate the Pasch.
7. Jesus went with the Apostles after they ate the Pasch.
8. Jesus and the Apostles crossed to enter the garden.

Part 3: Match part A with part B

Part A

1. "By this will all men know that you are my disciples . . . . . ."
2. "If I do not wash thee . . . . . ."
3. "Take and eat . . . . . ."
4. "The cock will not crow . . . . . ."
5. "I am the Vine . . . . . ."
6. "Yet not for these only do I pray . . . . . ."
7. "Thou art a priest forever . . . . . ."
8. "I have many things to say to you . . . . . ."
9. "Whatever you ask the Father in my name . . . ."
10. "Where I go . . . . . ."

Part B

a) according to the order of Melchizedek.
b) before you deny me three times.
c) you shall have no part with me.
d) that I will do.
e) but for these also who through their word are to believe in me.
f) but you cannot bear them now.
g) you cannot come yet.
h) if you have love one for another.
i) you are the branches.
j) for this is my Body.

Part 4: Questions to Check Your Reading

1. What incident occurred while Jesus was in Bethany?
2. How was Jesus greeted on His way to Jerusalem?
3. Why did Jesus weep at the sight of Jerusalem?

4. How did the answers which Jesus gave to the questions of the Pharisees prove that He was God?

5. Why did Judas betray Jesus?

6. Why was the feast of the Passover of great importance to the Jews?

7. Of whom is the Paschal Lamb a symbol?

8. Where did the Apostles prepare the Pasch?

9. What example of humility did Christ give the Apostles?

10. With what words did Christ change bread and wine into His Body and Blood?

11. Why did Christ establish the Priesthood?

12. What new commandment did Jesus give to the Apostles?

✓ FOR ME TO DO

1. Write out a quotation from our Lord's prayer to His Father in John chapter 16.

2. Make a list of questions which you would have asked our Lord if you were present at the Last Supper.

3. Notice if the symbol of the vine and the branches and the Paschal Lamb are used in the decoration of your parish.

4. Overcome feelings of jealousy toward your companions by being kind to them.

5. Admit your guilt when you have done something wrong, and ask our Lord for pardon.

6. Show your gratitude to our Lord for instituting the sacrament of the Holy Eucharist by receiving Him into your heart often.

CHAPTER 27
The Passion and Death of Christ

"Greater love than this no one has, that one lay down his life for his friends" (Jn 15:13). We realize how true these words are when we read the story of our Savior's passion and death. Every moment of His agony in the garden tells us of His love. Each false statement made against Him and every insult proves it. The scourging and crowning are more than any friend could endure, but Christ did more, He gave up His life for us. The last drop of blood, the last bodily pain, the last act of His divine will, everything was given to save His friends. How great should be our return of love when we realize the love our Redeemer has for us.

Our Lord Offers His Agony

At the entrance of the garden of Gethsemane, the Master said to eight of His disciples, "Sit down here while I go over yonder and pray" (Mt 26:36). But He took three along with Him, Peter, James and John, because they had been with Him when He was glorified on Mount Tabor. He knew they would better understand the change that was to come over Him. As He walked with them to His usual place of prayer, He said, "My soul is sorrowful, even unto death" (Mt 26:38). He fell to His knees, and cried out, "Father, if it is possible, let this cup pass away from me; yet, not as I will, but as thou wiliest" (Mt 26:39). The weight of the sins of the world was upon Him, a tormenting and crushing burden.

At the sight of man's grievous sins and ingratitude, Christ fell into an agony until His body was covered with a bloody sweat. His Father sent an angel to comfort Him. But He could not be

consoled, for He knew that even His death would not stop the sins of evil men. Even today men look on Him whom they have crucified and yet continue to sin. Let us pray with the Apostles to be strengthened against our own weaknesses.

Twice the Master walked over to His sleeping Apostles and said to Peter, "Could you not, then, watch one hour with me? Watch and pray, that you may not enter into temptation. The spirit indeed is willing, but the flesh is weak" (Mt 26:40–41). He knew their faith would be tried; therefore, He wanted them to be strengthened by prayer.

TERMS TO KNOW

- Malchus
- Joseph of Arimathea
- Dismas
- Nicodemus
- Caiaphas
- centurion
- Simon of Cyrene

Why is it called "the Passion" of Jesus Christ?

When we hear the word "passion" today, we think of something we are passionate about, meaning something we care deeply about and have strong emotions for. But we also know Jesus's sacrificial death, and the suffering he experienced, both spiritual and physical, in the days leading up to his death is called "The Passion of Christ." This is because the English word "passion" has its roots in the Latin *passio*, which simply means "suffering."

The Betrayal of Judas

The Master, knowing Judas was approaching, rose and went to His weary Apostles, saying, "Sleep on now, and take your rest! Behold the hour is at hand when the Son of Man will be betrayed into the hands of sinners. Rise, let us go. Behold, he who betrays me is at hand" (Mt 26:45–46).

Jesus still hoped to change the traitor's heart. "Friend," He said, "for what purpose hast thou come?" (Mt 26:50.) "Judas, dost thou betray the Son of Man with a kiss?" (Lk 22:48.) Judas resisted the last grace offered him and would not repent. As God once turned the crime of Joseph's brothers to good account, so did He suffer the wickedness of Judas and of the unbelieving Jews to enter into the plan of Redemption. He allowed their sin, the cause of His death, to bring salvation to the world.

Turning to the soldiers Jesus asked, "Whom do you seek?"

They answered, "Jesus of Nazareth." Christ said, "I am he." As though struck by a great force, they fell back in fear. Jesus said, "If, therefore, you seek me, let these go their way" (Jn 18:4–8).

Peter, on seeing his Master in danger, drew his sword and cut off the ear of the soldier Malchus. Stepping forward Jesus said, "Put back thy sword into its place, for all who take the sword will perish by the sword. Or dost thou suppose that I cannot entreat my Father, and he will even now furnish me with more than twelve legions of angels? How then are the Scriptures to be fulfilled?" (Mt 26:52–54). Then, to show His Apostles that He meant what He said about love of enemies, He touched the ear of Malchus and healed it.

The Soldiers Arrest Jesus

Jesus turned to the crowd and asked them why they did not arrest Him while He daily taught in the Temple. He pitied their hardness of heart and said, "This is your hour and the power of darkness" (Lk 22:53). Fearing that Jesus would escape, they surrounded Him while the soldiers dragged Him to the house of Annas, father-in-law of Caiaphas, the high priest. Meanwhile the Apostles fled.

Jesus Is Taken to Caiaphas

Having no authority over Jesus, Annas sent Him to Caiaphas and the Sanhedrin, who had false witnesses ready to accuse Him. They accused Him of claiming to be a king, of saying that God was His Father, of curing on the Sabbath. At last, one witness testified: "This man said, 'I am able to destroy the temple of God, and to rebuild it after three days'" (Mt 26:61). But none of the accusations could stand as real reasons for condemnation to death.

Trying to entrap Him, the chief priests asked, "Art thou the Son of God?" (Lk 22:70).

Jesus answered, "Thou hast said it. Nevertheless, I say to you, hereafter you shall see the Son of Man sitting at the right hand of the Power and coming upon the clouds of heaven" (Mt 26:64).

At these words Caiaphas tore his garments saying, "What further need have we of witnesses? . . . You have heard the blasphemy. What do you think?" (Mt 26:65–66.) And they all condemned Him to death.

They spat on Him, struck Him and shouted, "Prophesy, . . . who is it that struck thee" (Mt 26:68).

Peter's Denial

During the questioning, Peter and John followed the mob to the courtyard. Many people standing around recognized Peter as a follower of Christ. Three times Peter denied such claims saying, "I do not know the man!" (Mt 26:72.) At that same moment he heard the cock crow. Peter's eyes met his Master's gaze. The glance pierced his soul, and he fled in bitter grief. He should have left the courtyard after the first accusation, but he trusted his strength, and sinned from weakness and fear. He forgot to pray as his Master had warned him. God, in His divine wisdom, had permitted His future shepherd to fall, so that all men might learn the power of His grace and the depth of His mercy.

Judas became uneasy about his crime. He hurried to the chief priests, threw the money at them and cried, "I have sinned in betraying innocent blood" (Mt 27:4).

They taunted him, saying, "What is that to us? See to it thyself" (Mt 27:5). Having cast away the blood money, Judas, because of his horrible sin, lost hope in God's mercy and hanged himself with a halter. This was the bitter end of a worldly minded ambitious follower who abused the graces that his Master offered him.

Jesus Suffers at the Hands of His Enemies

The Sanhedrin did not have the power to impose a death sentence on Jesus. The next morning, therefore, they took Him to Pontius Pilate, the Roman governor of Judea. Pilate was told that Jesus claimed to be King and also that He refused to pay taxes to Caesar. A Roman would be greatly concerned by either accusation. Pilate asked Jesus, "Art thou the king of the Jews?" (Mt 27:11.)

Jesus answered, "Thou sayest it" (Mt 27:12). Pilate told the mob that he found no guilt in the Man. They, however, continued their false accusations, saying that He tried to turn the Jews against the Roman government in Galilee and Jerusalem. Christ's silence impressed Pilate.

The Ridicule of Herod

To avoid the responsibility of sentencing Him to death, Pilate, when he heard that Christ was a Galilean, sent Him to Herod who was in Jerusalem. To all of Herod's questions the Divine Prisoner answered not a word. Angered by this, Herod ordered Him to be dressed as a fool in a white robe and sent back to Pilate. How true were the words of Isaiah that He would be led as a sheep to the slaughter and be dumb as a lamb before His shearer, and that He would not open His mouth.

The rulers and Chief Priests were unknowingly carrying out the will of God. Prophecy after prophecy was being fulfilled. Only those who were blinded by sin could fail to see that He was the promised Redeemer.

Jesus Is Bruised for Our Sins

Pilate knew that the Jews had no just cause against the Prisoner. Still anxious to free Christ, he offered to liberate Him or the murderer Barabbas. The angry mob shouted, "Away with this man and release to us Barabbas!" (Lk 23:18).

Pilate had been warned by his wife, Claudia Procula, to have nothing to do with the death of Jesus. Therefore, he tried again to satisfy the blood-thirsty crowd by having Christ scourged. Our Lord was tied to a pillar and His sacred body beaten with bone-tipped leather rods until "from the sole of the foot unto the top of the head there was no soundness therein; wounds and bruises and swelling sores" (Is 1:6). Not satisfied with this torture, the soldiers made a crown of thorns and placed it on His sacred head, so that they might mock Him as a king. His precious blood dried into the cloak that clung to His wounded body. Having put a reed into His hand, they mockingly sneered, "Hail, king of the Jews!"

Pilate had hoped that the Chief Priests would be satisfied and so was shocked when he heard their repeated cries, "Crucify him!" Pilate then washed his hands before the mob and said, "I am innocent of the blood of this just man; see to it yourselves" (Mt 27:24).

The crowd set their own doom by shouting, "His blood be upon us and upon our children" (Mt 27:25).

Jesus Carries the Heavy Weight of Our Sins

The Savior was then turned over to the frenzied mob. He, the Paschal Lamb, was about to be sacrificed for us. The soldiers stripped Jesus of the white robe and clothed Him in His own seamless garment. The heavy beam was thrown on the ground at His bruised feet. It was to be His altar on which, as Priest and victim, He was to offer the sacrifice which would atone for all of our sins. A soldier placed the heavy beam upon His shoulder.

The Way of the Cross

In the midst of a hostile mob, Jesus began His sorrowful journey through the narrow streets. Bleeding and parched, He was pulled and pushed along until He stumbled and fell.

Fearful that Christ would die before they reached the top of Calvary, the soldiers ordered Simon, a Jew from Cyrene, to

help Him. At first he refused, feeling that it was a disgrace to aid a criminal. On the way, Simon's heart must have been moved by grace, for later he and his two sons became Christians.

As He trudged along, Christ fell again. A group of holy women, weeping and sorrowful, tried to console Him, but He told them to weep for themselves and for their children. He knew that many of them would see the destruction of Jerusalem. The Jews would then remember the curse they brought upon themselves and their descendants.

Finally Christ reached the top of Calvary. Our Priest and Victim, bowing to the will of His heavenly Father, had carried the wood of the cross for His own sacrifice, as Isaac in the Old Law carried the wood, and in obedience to Abraham offered himself as the victim.

The crowd circled around to see the rough soldiers nail the body of our Savior to the cross. He stretched His sacred arms on the altar of Redemption; and, as the executioners with a heavy hammer drove the spikes through His sacred hands and feet, Jesus prayed: "Father, forgive them, for they do not know what they are doing" (Lk 23:34). Here another prophecy was completed, "They have dug my hands and feet; they have numbered all my bones" (Ps 21:17). They then raised the cross. Christ Himself had predicted, "As Moses lifted up the serpent in the desert, so must the Son of Man be lifted up" (Jn 3:14). Above His head was nailed the inscription which Pilate had ordered. It read, "Jesus of Nazareth, the king of the Jews" (Jn 19:19).

Christ longed to draw all things to Himself. He thirsted for men to love Him. He had said, "And I, if I be lifted up from the earth, will draw all things to myself." His Church, His Mystical Body, is keeping that promise by preaching Christ crucified to all nations and bringing to all men the graces He merited.

The Good Thief

Two thieves were crucified with Christ. One said to Jesus, "If thou art the Christ, save thyself and us!" (Lk 23:39.)

The other, Dismas, the repentant sinner, replied, "This man has done nothing wrong." And he begged Christ: "Lord, remember me when thou comest into thy kingdom" (Lk 23:41–42).

Jesus, always ready to forgive, answered: "Amen, I say to thee, this day thou shalt be with me in paradise" (Lk 23:43). What an awful contrast between a man dying in despair and one dying in hope of God's mercy!

Beneath the cross the soldiers were casting lots for the seamless robe that Mary had made for her Son. As He looked down, He repeated the prophet's words, "They have parted my garments amongst them, and upon my vesture they have cast lots" (Ps 21:19).

Mary, Our Mother

At the foot of the cross, when Jesus spoke to John, his beloved apostle, and gave Mary to him, it was a sign and symbol of him giving Mary to all of us. With the words, "Behold thy mother," Jesus gives his mother to all of us. Some Church fathers and theologians have pointed to Mary's suffering at the foot of the cross as her "childbearing pain" in becoming the mother of humanity.

The Pharisees, not interested in such trifles, turned away to scoff at our dying Savior. They cried out, "Thou who destroyest the temple, and in three days buildest it up again, save thyself! If thou art the Son of God, come down from the cross!" (Mt 27:40.)

Mary Our Mother

Jesus was concerned about the little group at the foot of the cross. Touched by the sorrow of His Mother, He would not leave her alone. Looking tenderly at her He said, "Woman, behold thy son." Trustingly He turned to John and added, "Behold thy mother" (Jn 19:27). Thus the Mother of the Head of the Mystical Body is also the Mother of its members.

The Death of Jesus

Christ knew that His work was finished; He had done His Father's will. He cried out: "It is consummated" [It is finished] (Jn 19:30) and then, "Father into thy hands I commend my spirit" (Lk 23:46). After He had spoken these words, Jesus bowed His head and died. At that moment the veil of the Temple tore from top to bottom; the earth shook; the rocks split; and the bodies of some saints rose from the graves which were carved in the rocky hillside of Jerusalem. The centurion, seeing the wonders which accompanied the death of our Lord, was seized with terror and said, "Truly this man was the Son of God" (Mk 15:39).

Jesus Is Buried

Joseph of Arimathea, a wealthy and God-fearing Jew, received permission from Pilate to bury the body of his Master. In the meantime, the soldiers came to break the legs of the crucified. When they found that Jesus was dead, they did not break His legs, but instead drove a lance through His sacred heart.

The body of Jesus was wrapped in linens and placed in the arms of His Blessed Mother. The last sword of sorrow pierced her heart as she remembered the words of Simeon, "Behold, this child is set for the fall and for the rise of many in Israel, and for a sign which shall be contradicted. And thy own soul a sword shall pierce, that the thoughts of many hearts may be revealed" (Lk 2:34). Joseph and Nicodemus, together with Mary, John, and the others hurriedly anointed the Body with precious ointments and carried it to Joseph's garden and laid it in his tomb. John then led the Blessed Virgin back to Jerusalem.

Remembering that Jesus had predicted His Resurrection, the Pharisees asked for guards to watch the tomb. Pilate permitted soldiers to seal and guard it.

FOR ME TO REVIEW

Questions and Exercises

Part 1: Complete the following

1. The Apostles who witnessed our Lord's agony were
   _____.

2. Judas betrayed Jesus by a _____.

3. The mob first brought Jesus to the house of _____.

4. The high priest was _____.

5. The Roman governor was _____.

6. _____ was forced to help Jesus carry the cross.

7. _____ told Pilate not to condemn Jesus.

8. _____ asked Jesus to remember him.

9. _____ asked Pilate for permission to bury the body of
   Jesus.

10. _____ accused Peter of knowing Christ.

Part 2: Who said

1. "Woman, I do not know him."

2. "Mother, behold thy Son."

3. "I have sinned in betraying innocent blood."

4. "Lord, remember me when thou comest into thy kingdom."

5. "Father, into thy hands I commend my spirit."

6. "Watch and pray that you may not enter into temptation."

7. "Hail Rabbi."

8. "What further need have we of witnesses?"

9. "This man has done no wrong."

10. "What is that to us? See to it thyself."

Part 3: Questions to Check Your Reading

1. What caused the bloody sweat of our Lord in the garden?

2. How did Jesus treat Judas?

3. Why was Jesus taken to Pilate?

4. Why did Pilate send Jesus to Herod?

5. What attempts did Pilate make to save Jesus?

6. Who helped Jesus to carry His cross?

7. Tell some incidents that happened on the way to Calvary.

8. What did our Lord promise the good thief?

9. How did Jesus give us His Blessed Mother?

10. What wonders accompanied the death of our Lord?

11. Who took charge of the burial of our Lord?

12. Why did the Pharisees ask for guards to watch the tomb?

✔ FOR ME TO DO

1. Compare the characters of St. Peter and St. John.

2. Compose a prayer for the fourth and thirteenth Stations of the Cross.

3. Write a conversation between Pilate and his wife Claudia about Christ's trial.

CHAPTER 28
Christ's Victory

Christ's Resurrection is the foundation stone of the Christian religion and the greatest proof of Christ's divinity. It is a key to the prophecies in the Old Testament concerning the Messiah. It was almost impossible for the Jewish mind to realize that the Messiah was not to deliver their nation from the Romans. The Apostles were not fully convinced, even as they walked to the Mount of Olives to be witnesses of His Ascension. They asked our Lord at that time about His temporal kingdom. The Apostles had to await the coming of the Holy Spirit to see how all things fit into the pattern of God.

The Resurrection

Sometime after midnight, our Lord's body and soul were reunited. He left the tomb without breaking the seals that secured the stone to the opening. The Gospels do not mention to whom He showed Himself first.

The guards about the tomb were struck with terror. When they recovered from their fright some went into the city and told the chief priests all that they had seen. The priests, after consulting the leaders, bribed the soldiers to say that the disciples came and stole the body of Jesus while they were asleep. The chief priests promised to save the soldiers from Pilate's anger and punishment in case the story reached him.

Holy Women at the Tomb

It was dawn when Mary Magdalen and the other pious women set out for the sepulcher to anoint the body of Christ. As they walked along, they must have questioned each other as to what they would do about rolling back the stone from the entrance to the tomb. On reaching the burial place they were surprised to find the sepulcher open and two angels sitting where the body of Jesus had been laid (Jn 20:12). They spoke to the women.

Mary Magdalen ran back to the city to tell the Apostles all that the angels had said. Peter and John set out immediately after receiving the startling news. As they neared the place they began to run. John, younger and more swift-footed, arrived first and, stooping down, looked in and saw the linen cloths lying by themselves, but he did not enter. When Peter reached the scene he went into the sepulcher followed by John. Peter noticed that the napkin that had been wrapped about Christ's head had been folded and was lying in a corner. Not understanding the Scripture, "That he must rise again from the dead," the two bewildered Apostles returned to the Upper Room.

Jesus Appears to Mary Magdalen

Mary Magdalen did not return to the city with the Apostles but remained at the tomb weeping. Stooping down and looking into the sepulcher, she saw two angels sitting where the body of Jesus had rested. They asked her why she wept. She answered, "Because they have taken away my Lord, and I do not know where they have laid him" (Jn 20:13).

She then turned around and saw a Man standing before her who said, "Woman, why art thou weeping?" He added, "Whom dost thou seek?" (Jn 20:15.)

Mary, thinking she was speaking to the gardener, said, "Sir, if thou hast removed him, tell me where thou hast laid him and I will take him away" (Jn 20:15).

Jesus said to her, "Mary!" (Jn 20:15.)

Instantly she recognized Him and exclaimed, "Rabboni!" and fell at our Lord's feet.

Jesus, who understood so well the heart of Mary Magdalen, asked her to go into the city and say to His disciples, "I ascend to my Father and your Father, to my God and your God" (Jn 20:17). Mary left at once and announced that she had seen the Risen Christ.

"The Lord's triumph, on the day of the Resurrection, is final. Where are the soldiers the rulers posted there? Where are the seals that were fixed to the stone of the tomb? Where are those who condemned the Master? Where are those who crucified Jesus? He is victorious, and faced with his victory those poor wretches have all taken flight. Be filled with hope: Jesus Christ is always victorious."

—ST. JOSEMARIA ESCRIVA

Jesus Appears to the Two Disciples on Their Way to Emmaus

That same day two of the disciples decided to go to Emmaus, a town situated several hours' journey to the northwest of Jerusalem. As they walked along, they spoke of what had taken place in Jerusalem during the last few days. While they were talking, Jesus, whom they mistook for a traveler, came up and joined them. He asked them what they had been speaking about, and the disciples were astonished that He did not know what had taken place in the city. Since this Man was evidently a stranger, they told Him what had occurred.

Then Jesus said, "O foolish ones, and slow of heart to believe in all that the prophets have spoken. Did not Christ have to suffer these things before entering into his glory?" (Lk 24:25–26). He began to explain to them the different passages from Scripture that Moses and the Prophets had written concerning the Savior.

When they reached Emmaus He seemed about to continue His journey, but they urged Him to stay with them. Jesus accepted their invitation. While He sat at the table with them, He took bread, blessed and broke it, and gave it to them. By this action their eyes were opened; however, as soon as they recognized who He was, He vanished from their sight. The disciples, filled with wonder, said to each other: "Was not our heart burning within us while he was speaking on the road and explaining to us the Scriptures?" (Lk 24:32). The disciples rose and hastened back to Jerusalem. After learning that our Lord had appeared to Simon Peter they told the others what had occurred on the journey.

Jesus Appears to His Apostles

Late that same day the Apostles were together behind closed doors because of their fear of the Jews. Jesus suddenly appeared in their midst and greeted them with the words, "Peace be with you!" (Jn 20:21). Then He breathed upon them and said, "Receive the Holy Spirit; whose sins you shall forgive, they are forgiven them; and whose sins you shall retain, they are retained" (Jn 20:22–23).

Jesus Appears to Thomas

One of the Apostles, Thomas, was not with them at this time. When he was told

Seeing the Mass in the Road to Emmaus

The story of Jesus appearing to His disciples on the road to Emmaus has a strong connection to the Holy Sacrifice of the Mass. Note that at first the disciples did not know it was Jesus, but their hearts burned as He spoke to them about the Scriptures and the words of the prophets. Then, when they invited Him to stay and dine with them, "their eyes were opened" when He blessed and broke the bread; they suddenly realized it was Him. Similarly, the Mass begins with the Liturgy of the Word, when we read from the Sacred Scriptures, and then, during the Liturgy of the Eucharist, our eyes our opened and we see Jesus in the Eucharist.

by the others that they had seen the Lord, he refused to believe them. "Unless I see in his hands the print of the nails," he said, "and put my finger into the place of the nails, and put my hand into his side, I will not believe" (Jn 20:25).

Eight days later the Apostles were again assembled together, and this time Thomas was with them. The doors were shut as before, when Jesus suddenly appeared in their midst, and repeated the same greeting: "Peace be with you!" Then turning to Thomas He said, "Bring here thy finger, and see my hands; and bring here thy hand, and put it into my side; and be not unbelieving, but believing" (Jn 20:27).

Thomas not only expressed his belief in the Resurrection, but made an act of faith in Christ's divinity, saying, "My Lord and my God!" (Jn 20:28).

Then Jesus said to him, "Because thou hast seen me, thou hast believed. Blessed are they who have not seen, and yet have believed" (Jn 20:29).

"For the healing of the doubting hearts," says St. Augustine, "the marks of the wounds were still preserved." They will remain for all eternity in Christ's glorified body.

Peter, the Head of the Church

When the Feast of the Passover was ended, the disciples returned to Galilee, there to wait the fulfillment of the promise. "Behold, he goes before you into Galilee: there you shall see him" (Mk 16:7).

One evening after their arrival the Apostles went fishing. They spent the night at work and had caught nothing. Returning in the morning, they saw Jesus standing on the shore, but they did not recognize Him. He called to them, asking if they had any food. They answered that they had none.

Then Jesus told them to cast their net on the right side of the ship. They obeyed, and so great was the number of fishes that the boat was almost sinking. With this, John recognized the stranger and called to Peter, "It is the Lord." In his desire to see Jesus, Peter plunged into the sea and swam ashore. The other Apostles brought the ship to land. As soon as they came to shore, they saw a fire prepared with a fish on its hot embers, and a quantity of bread. Jesus then invited them to come and eat.

When the meal was finished Jesus turned to Peter and asked him: "Simon, son of John, dost thou love me more than these do?"

"Yes, Lord," Peter answered, "Thou knowest that I love thee."

Jesus said to him: "Feed my Lambs."

A second time He asked: "Simon, son of John, dost thou love me?"

"Yes, Lord," came the reply. "Thou knowest that I love thee."

Jesus said to him: "Feed my lambs" (Jn 21:15–16).

Again for the third time Jesus repeated the question. Remembering his threefold denial of the Master, Peter replied humbly and with great emotion: "Lord, thou knowest all things, thou knowest that I love thee" (Jn 21:17).

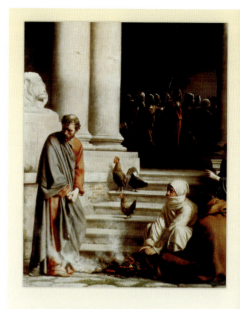

The Reversal of Peter's Denial

In this story of Jesus asking Peter if he loves Him, the Church teaches us that Jesus was inviting Peter to undo his denial of Him on the night of his passion. Just as Peter denied Jesus three times, so he would here confirm his love for Christ three times.

Jesus said to him: "Feed my sheep." Then Jesus foretold by what manner of death Peter would glorify God. At length Jesus said, "Follow me" (Jn 21:19).

In this commission to St. Peter to feed the lambs and sheep of His flock, Christ gave Peter the duty to guide, rule, and govern His Church. Thus He fulfilled the promise of making him the head of His whole Church when He said, "And I say to thee, thou art Peter, and upon this rock I will build my Church, and the gates of Hell shall not prevail against it. And to thee I will give the keys to the kingdom of heaven, and whatsoever thou shalt bind on earth shall be bound in heaven, and whatsoever thou shalt loose on earth shall be loosed in heaven" (Mt 16:17).

By this commission to feed the lambs and sheep of the flock, St. Peter and his successors were made Vicars of Christ on earth and the visible shepherds and rulers of the Catholic Church.

Jesus Appears to the Eleven

Jesus again appeared to the Apostles in Galilee where He had told them to go. They fell down in worship at His feet but some still were in doubt concerning Him. Jesus spoke saying: "All power in heaven and earth has been given to me. Go, therefore, and make disciples of all nations, baptizing them in the name of the Father, and of the Son, and of the Holy Spirit, teaching them to observe all that I have commanded you, and behold I am with you all days, even to the consummation of the world" (Mt 28:19–20).

The Ascension

Jesus appeared to the Apostles on the fortieth day after His Resurrection while they were assembled in Jerusalem. He gave them their final instructions and told them that they must wait there for the fulfillment of the promise of the coming of the Holy Spirit. He then led them forth to the Mount of Olives. There, with hands uplifted, He gave them His parting blessing; and as He blessed them, He raised Himself up before their eyes from the earth toward Heaven. As He ascended, a cloud took Him out of their sight.

The Apostles stood gazing upward after Him, until two angels stood by them and said, "Men of Galilee, why do you stand looking up toward heaven? This Jesus, who has been taken up from you into heaven, will come in the same way as you saw him go into heaven" (Acts 1:11). Then the Apostles fell on their knees and adored Him, after which they returned to Jerusalem full of joy and praising God. There they stayed as Christ had commanded, to await the coming of the Holy Spirit.

The Election of Matthias

After our Lord's Ascension, about one hundred twenty disciples were gathered in Jerusalem. Peter, who had been appointed chief of the Apostles, invited them to fill the place which had become vacant by the fall of Judas. Two at first were selected, Barsabbas and Matthias. After they had prayed for divine guidance, the lot fell upon Matthias. He was now numbered with the other Apostles, thereby fulfilling the prophecy written in the book of Psalms "His ministry [Judas'] let another take" (Ps 108:8).

The Descent of the Holy Spirit

On the fiftieth day after the Passover, the Jewish people celebrated the great Feast of Pentecost, also called the Feast of Weeks, and of Harvest. This festival brought Jews from all nations into the city to commemorate the giving of the Law on Mt. Sinai.

The Apostles and the holy women were assembled in the Upper Room as usual when suddenly there came a sound from heaven as of a mighty wind, which filled the whole house. Then there appeared above them a beautiful fiery red mass, which separated into tongues of fire and rested upon each of the disciples. Immediately all were filled with the Holy Spirit, and they began to speak in different languages according as the Holy Spirit inspired them to speak.

Beyond this outward sign the divine Spirit infused into them the grace of strength and courage to profess the religion they had learned from their Master. They fearlessly went forth to preach Christ crucified. Many curious people gathered about the Apostles and were astonished to hear them speak the languages of the different countries. Some of the Jews mocked the Apostles and said that they were filled with new wine. When Peter heard this he came forward and spoke to the people. He spoke to them about the prophecies concerning Jesus whom they had cruci-fied. St. Peter's words touched the hearts of those assembled, and all who received his word and believed in the truth which he preached were baptized. On this first Pentecost three thousand were converted. The Church had started to grow.

 ### FOR ME TO REVIEW

Questions and Exercises

Part 1: Complete the following

1. Who went to our Lords sepulcher early Sunday morning?

2. The Ascension took place _____ days after the Resurrection.

3. The two Apostles who went to the sepulcher after the Resur-rection were _____ and _____ .

4. Our Lord greeted the frightened disciples with the words _____ .

5. The Upper Room was called the _____ .

6. The greatest proof of Christ's divinity is the _____ .

Part 2: Match column I with column II

Column I	Column II
1. St. Thomas	A. Cloven tongues of fire
2. The Holy Spirit	B. Converted over 3000 on Pentecost
3. St. Peter	C. "My Lord and my God"
4. "Rabboni"	D. 50 days after the Passover
5. Pentecost	E. Chosen in place of Judas
6. Matthias	F. Master

Part 3: Questions to Check Your Reading

1. When did the Resurrection of Christ take place?

2. What did the holy women find at the tomb?

3. Why were Peter and John bewildered when they did not find Jesus in the tomb?

4. How was Mary Magdalen rewarded for her love of Jesus?

5. When did the two disciples on the way to Emmaus recognize Jesus?

6. What power did the Apostles receive from Jesus the first time He appeared to them? What were His words?

7. What duty did Christ give Peter and his successors when He said, "Feed my lambs. Feed my sheep"?

8. What command did Christ give the Apostles just before He ascended into heaven?

9. When did Christ ascend into heaven?

10. What important event took place fifty days after the Resurrection of our Lord?

11. How did the coming of the Holy Spirit change the Apostles?

12. What did Christ say in: Jn 20:22? Mt 16:17? Jn 21:15–19?

 FOR ME TO DO

1. Pretend that you are a television news reporter living at the time of these events. Describe events to the class while groups dramatize the various scenes.

2. Imagine you were in Jerusalem at this time. Write a letter to a friend who lived in Nazareth and tell him all that has taken place.

UNIT

3

Christ In His Church

Unit 3 Introduction

We have learned in our study of the Old Testament that those who lived before the birth of Christ were saved by belief in His coming and by obedience to the Law revealed through Moses. Then Christ came. He lived to show us how to live. He died and gave us His Church, the Church of prophecy fulfilled, in which He lives in His members. Christ established His Church to help us gain supernatural happiness with God. By faith in Christ and by obedience to Him and His Church we can surely come to this eternal life.

Christ founded His Church by choosing and appointing His Apostles as bishops over His people. He made Peter the supreme head. "Thou art Peter, and upon this rock I will build my Church" (Mt 16:18). The Law of Christ was set down for the new kingdom, which is universal and is to last until the end of time. It includes all the faithful everywhere. Who are they? They number all those who, baptized in the Holy Trinity, profess the same faith in union with Christ's vicar on earth, the pope. The Church also includes, though imperfectly, any Christians who are not in full union with the Catholic Church:

> "The Church knows that she is enjoined to the baptized who are honored by the name of Christian, but do not profess the Catholic faith in its entirety or have not

preserved unity or communion under the successor of Peter. Those who believe in Christ and have been properly baptized are put in a certain, although imperfect, communion with the Catholic Church" (CCC 838).

The Catholic Church is a supernatural organization founded by Christ to help all men win eternal life. It is a visible society of all the faithful. Christ is its head, we the faithful are the members, the Holy Spirit is its unifying and sanctifying soul. The Church is doing Christ's work on earth, and Church History is the record of how it is accomplishing this. As the Mystical Body of Christ, the Church is Christ prolonged in time and operative in history through His members.

The First Christians

On Pentecost, immediately after the descent of the Holy Spirit, St. Peter and the other Apostles began to preach the gospel in Jerusalem, converting three thousand Jews with their first sermon. Gradually the number of believers increased as the Church spread through Judea, Samaria, Galilee and into the surrounding countries.

One day while Peter and John were praying in the Temple, a lame man called out to ask them for alms. Peter turned to him and said, "Silver and gold I have none; but what I have I give thee. In the name of Jesus Christ of Nazareth, arise and walk" (Acts 3:6). The man was cured at once. Peter was thrown into prison because of his preaching, but soon he was freed by an angel.

The preaching and miracles of the Apostles caused many to embrace the faith of Christ, and the example of the early Christians brought others into the Church. We are told that the early Christians had but "one heart and one soul," and that, because of their great charity, no one lacked the essentials of life (Acts 9:22). A pagan, later converted to the Church, could find no better way to describe them than to say, "See how they love one another."

As the number of Christians increased, the Apostles found it difficult to distribute the goods held in common and at the same time to preach. Accordingly, they appointed seven deacons to help them gather the gifts and distribute them to the poor.

St. Stephen, the First Martyr

Stephen and Philip were two of the deacons appointed by the Apostles. Philip preached to the people of Samaria, baptizing

those who were led to believe in Christ through his words. Peter and John came from Jerusalem to confirm Philip's converts.

Stephen, a man full of faith and the Holy Spirit, preached in the synagogues. He was so successful that he aroused the anger of the Jews. He was arrested and brought before the Sanhedrin and accused of blasphemy. Stephen defended himself in a speech in which he proved from Scripture that Christ is the Messiah. But the Pharisees condemned him to death.

As they led him outside the city to stone him, Stephen raised his heart to God and prayed, "Lord, do not lay this sin against them" (Acts 7:60). Just before he died he said, "Lord Jesus, receive my spirit" (Acts 7:59). In this inspiring manner, Stephen became the first martyr for Christ.

A young man named Saul stood by during the martyrdom of Stephen. Those who stoned the first martyr placed their garments at Saul's feet. He thus aided in this terrible deed. Yet it was this Saul who later became the great St. Paul.

Paul, the Persecutor, Becomes a Zealous Apostle

Saul was a Pharisee, but this fervent Jew was also a Roman citizen. As one of the persecutors of the Church he hunted the Christians, putting them into prison. Hearing that there were many Christians in Damascus, he planned to go there and bring them back to Jerusalem in chains.

On his way to Damascus, Paul was miraculously changed from the bitterest of Christ's persecutors to one of His most zealous followers. When he came near to the city, a light shone around him and he fell to the ground. He heard a voice saying, "Saul, Saul, why dost thou persecute me?"

Saul said, "Who art thou, Lord?"

The voice replied, "I am Jesus whom thou art persecuting."

Saul asked, "Lord, what wilt thou have me do?"

Jesus told him, "Arise, and go into the city, and it will be told thee what thou must do." Saul had been struck blind. His companions had to lead him into Damascus (Acts 9:1–8). In the city Saul met Ananias, who cured his blindness and baptized him. Paul at once began to work for Christ.

St. Paul was not one of the original twelve Apostles. Because of his miraculous vocation, marvelous preaching, and great suffering for the spread of the Church, he is numbered among them as a true Apostle of the early Church.

Paul made three great missionary journeys in a day when travel was truly difficult. He covered thousands of miles to preach the gospel, establishing the Church in a number of important cities. During this time Paul endured many sufferings; he was scourged, imprisoned, and even shipwrecked.

Because he worked chiefly among those who were not Jews, St.

Paul is called the "Apostle of the Gentiles." The Epistles, or letters, which he wrote to his converts are a storehouse of Catholic teaching. Toward the end of Nero's reign, St. Paul was beheaded at Rome. He had served Christ well; he gave witness to Him in his blood.

St. Peter Is Martyred for the Faith

St. Peter as head of the Church played a leading part in preaching the gospel, in working miracles, and in confirming. He converted Cornelius, the first Gentile, to the faith of Christ, and by so doing showed that the way to Christ's Church was open for all peoples and nations.

After an Assembly or Council of the Apostles in Jerusalem about the year 50, where one of the most important matters discussed was the reception of Gentile converts, Peter traveled widely, visiting the churches, baptizing, confirming, and instructing. For a while, Antioch was the center or seat (see) of his activities, but eventually Peter established himself at Rome, where, with Paul, he suffered death for Christ. Peter was crucified head downward. He asked to be crucified in this way because he did not feel worthy to die in the same way as his Lord before him.

The Blood of the Martyrs

Great-souled men and women have belonged to the Church since its very beginning. Through them the Church has been able to give glory to God and to sanctify men. Countless Christians in the early days of the Church were victims of severe persecutions, which the Roman emperors hoped would destroy the Church. There were approximately ten great persecutions, lasting on the whole for about two hundred and fifty years. The three worst and bloodiest were the first under Nero, the seventh under Decius, and the last under Diocletian.

The First Persecution—Under Nero

A terrible fire broke out in the city of Rome during the reign of Nero. It lasted for several days and destroyed a good part of the city. Many citizens thought that the Emperor Nero himself had started it because in his pride he wished to build a more beautiful city.

"The blood of the martyrs is the seed of the Church."

—Tertullian

When Nero learned that he was being accused of this horrible deed, he blamed the Christians for it. He ordered them to be persecuted, claiming that they were enemies of the Roman gods and of the State. Nero deprived them of their property, denied them freedom of worship, cast them into prison, and inflicted on them all sorts of cruel tortures. Some were drowned; others were crucified; many were thrown to the wild animals in the Colosseum; others were covered with pitch and set on fire to light the city.

Persecutions Under Other Rulers

The second persecution lasted about two years. During this persecution, St. John, the beloved disciple, or a disciple of his, also called John, was sent into exile on the island of Patmos, where he had the vision which he described in the book of Revelation.

It was during the third persecution that St. Ignatius of Antioch was cast to the lions. In a letter which he wrote to the Romans he said, "I am the wheat of God, and I shall be ground by the teeth of the wild beasts, that I may be found pure bread of Christ." St. Clement, the fourth pope, was also martyred during this same persecution.

In the fourth persecution, St. Polycarp, a disciple of St. John, suffered martyrdom at the stake, at the age of eighty-six. When asked to deny Christ he said: "I have served Christ for six and eighty years, and never has He done me evil. How, then, can I blaspheme my King and Savior?"

Saints Perpetua and Felicitas were martyred during the fifth persecution. Perpetua's father, a pagan and a Roman senator, begged her on his knees to deny Christ for the sake of his gray hair and of her own small child, but the noble lady refused. She was led with St. Felicitas into the arena where both suffered martyrdom.

The terrible tenth great persecution, under Diocletian at the beginning of the fourth century, surpassed all others in violence and cruelty; it numbered more victims than any of the others. At this time St. Sebastian, tribune of the imperial guard, died a lingering death, shot through with arrows. Young St. Tarcisius gave his life in defense of the Blessed Sacrament. Through his care of and love for the Holy Eucharist, which he was carrying to imprisoned Christians, Tarcisius bore witness to the Faith, which is Christ's great gift to us.

St. Lucy and St. Agnes won the double crown of virginity and martyrdom. The Church has kept alive their memories and those of five other martyrs of the early persecutions by inserting their names into the Canon of the Mass. The others are Felicitas, Perpetua, Agatha, Cecilia, and Anastasia. With other saintly men and women, they gave their lives to Christ.

The Roman Emperors tried to put an end to the Christian religion. They all failed. Indeed, Julian the Apostate confessed: "Galilean, thou hast conquered." Despite persecution, the Church grew; we can truly say, the blood of martyrs is the seed of Christians.

The Catacombs

During the persecutions the Christians sought refuge in underground rooms and cemeteries in and about Rome. These were called "catacombs." The Christians also used them as meeting places. They even made chapels in them where Mass could be offered. The catacombs, being cemeteries, were sanctuaries protected by law. On their walls the Christians painted scenes taken from both the Old and New Testaments. They also wrote prayers and petitions. These may be seen today in the catacombs in Rome. Evidence dug up by archaeologists shows that St. Peter and St. Paul were in Rome.

Constantine and the Edict of Milan

A glimpse of the sufferings to which the Church was subjected in the first three centuries proves to us that the triumph of

Christianity was neither quick nor easy. It proves also that the courage of those who serve Christ overcomes all opposition.

Diocletian's successor, Galerius, continued the persecution of the Church. However, he gradually came to realize that he could not crush the Church, and in 311 A.D. he issued a Decree giving the Christians limited toleration. His son Constantine, who had been impressed by the vitality of an institution which two centuries and more of oppression had failed to destroy, reportedly saw a sign in the sky prior to the battle of Milvian Bridge. This was the sign of the cross, with the words, "In this sign thou shall conquer." His subsequent victory and his realization that the Church was here to stay led him to issue the Edict of Milan in 313 A.D. By his decree Christians and all others were granted freedom to practice their religion. The great persecutions of that time were ended.

FOR ME TO REVIEW

Questions and Exercises

Part 1: Match column I with column II

Column I	Column II
1. Ananias	A. Issued the Edict of Milan
2. Philip	B. Preached to the people of Samaria
3. St. John	C. The first Christian martyr
4. Constantine	D. Cured Paul of his blindness
5. Nero	E. A tribune of the imperial guard
6. Stephen	F. Won the double crown of virginity and martyrdom
7. St. Sebastian	G. Made three missionary journeys
8. Cornelius	H. Rome was partly destroyed by fire during the reign of
9. Saints Lucy and Agnes	I. Only Apostle to die a natural death
10. St. Paul	J. First gentile convert

Part 2: Questions to Check Your Reading

1. How and when did the Church begin her divine mission?

2. Give a good reason for the rapid spread of Christianity.

3. What duties were performed by the deacons in the early Church?

4. Name two of the deacons.

5. What group of people was instructed by Philip?

6. Who was the first Christian martyr? Be able to describe the circumstances of his death.

7. What people were confirmed by Peter and John?

8. Who showed that the way to Christ's Church was open for all people?

9. Which persecutions were the most severe?

10. How long did the persecutions last?

11. What were the catacombs? Why were they used?

12. Why did Roman emperors persecute the Church?

13. How did Constantine help to bring about the triumph of Christianity?

✅ FOR ME TO DO

1. Try to find a detailed account of the story of St. Ignatius and his martyrdom.

2. Find the prayer in the Canon of the Mass in which the names of seven women martyrs are mentioned.

3. Give a report on St. Agnes, early Christian martyr, and on St. Maria Goretti, who is known as the "St. Agnes of modern times."

4. Look up some information on some of the other martyrs who were mentioned in this chapter.

5. Give a report on the catacombs. An excellent description can be found in the book *Fabiola* by Cardinal Wiseman.

6. Write a news story on some phase of the persecution under Nero.

7. Discuss ways in which some of the martyrs spoken of in this chapter resemble Old Testament characters.

CHAPTER 30

The Church Draws Good from Heresy

The Church has never been wholly free from attacks, sometimes from those outside the Church, and at other times from within. A Catholic who attempts to change or denies any dogma of the Faith is called a "heretic", and the false doctrine he proposes is called a "heresy." Never was there a fiercer struggle against heresy than during the first six centuries of the Church.

Christ presented His teachings very simply. He knew, however, that arguments would arise over the meaning of the truths He taught. Thus, one of the rights He entrusted to His Church was the faithful preservation and interpretation of His teachings. He entrusted His Church to the Holy Spirit, the Spirit of Wisdom and Knowledge, and under the direction of the Holy Spirit the Church infallibly teaches and explains the content of revelation.

Heresies often arise because men frequently fail to follow the leadership of the Church in their attempts to find answers for the questions they ask about the meaning of Christ's words. Yet God knows how to draw good from evil; for instance, because of heresies the true teachings of Christ have become more clearly defined and thus better understood. Although many heresies were advanced in the early days of the Church, only a few of them will be discussed here.

The Fathers of the Church Defend Her Teaching

ARIANISM

One of the early and widespread heresies was that of Arianism, which gravely endangered the Church during the fourth century. Popularized by a priest of Alexandria named Arius, it spread quickly and won over many persons of influence, especially in the government. Its central teaching was that Christ, the Son of God, is a creature, not eternal nor of the same substance as the Father. Eventually it was necessary to call a general council, or meeting of the bishops, to combat it.

At this general council the bishops defined the true doctrine concerning the Son of God and His relation to the Father. The Council, which met in the city of Nicaea in 325, is known as the Council of Nicaea. In it, Arianism was condemned and a solemn profession of faith was written. It was called the Nicene Creed. This Creed was made even more explicit by later additions, particularly at the Council of Constantinople in 381. The combined Creed, known as the Nicene-Constantinople Creed, is a part of our Mass today. When Arius obstinately continued to deny that Christ is God, the Church declared him anathema and cut him off from the Mystical Body.

TERMS TO KNOW

- heresy
- commentaries
- manuscript
- patriarchs
- council
- heretics
- doctrine
- revision
- exile

423

ST. ATHANASIUS

The staunchest defender of the Faith at this time was the deacon Athanasius. He was a man of unusual talent, and had a great love of God.

After the Council of Nicaea, the Arians split up into various groups and continued to spread their errors far and wide. One of the biggest factors explaining the growth of this heresy was the fact that many emperors were either Arians themselves or sympathetic to Arianism.

By courageously defending the true doctrine of the Church, Athanasius aroused the hatred of the Arian party. They had him banished several times from Alexandria. In the end, Athanasius returned and spent the remaining years of his life laboring to restore unity to the Church.

ST. JOHN CHRYSOSTOM

After the teaching of Arius had died down, the Church was at peace for forty years. During this time St. John Chrysostom strengthened the faith of the people by his powerful sermons. He preached so well that his fame spread far and wide and he was called "Chrysostom" (the "golden-mouthed"). Because of his great talent and his labors in correcting abuses, he was named Patriarch of Constantinople. A patriarch is a bishop of an important city who rules several provinces.

The Arian bishop of Alexandria brought false charges against St. John. He was sent into exile, which he suffered patiently. During his exile John wrote many letters to his friends, giving instructions as to how to direct their missionary labors. He died in exile. His final prayer was, "May God be glorified for everything."

ST. CYRIL OF ALEXANDRIA

Another great supporter of the Church who arose at this time was St. Cyril of Alexandria. He defended the true doctrines of the Church against the false teachings of Nestorius. The Church teaches that there is but one person in Christ—a divine person. Nestorius claimed that there were two persons in Christ, a human person and a divine person. Nestorius taught that Mary is the mother only of the human person, and therefore not the Mother of God. To stop the heresy and explain the teaching of the Church, Pope Celestine called the General Council of Ephesus in 431, sending St. Cyril to it as his representative. In it the doctrine of Nestorius was condemned, and Mary was declared to be truly the "Mother of God." The faithful rejoiced.

The Great Fathers of the Western Church

ST. AMBROSE

The title "Doctor" is conferred on certain saints who have taught Christian truths in all their purity. (The meaning of the Latin word *doctor* is "one who teaches.") St. Ambrose is a great Doctor of the Western or Latin Church. He had received an education in law at Rome, and later became governor in northern Italy. At the death of the Arian bishop of Milan, the people gathered together to elect a successor. It is said that a little child cried out, "Ambrose, Bishop." At once the people took up the cry and proclaimed him bishop against his will; he was still a catechumen, that is, one preparing for Baptism. Ambrose was baptized, received Holy Orders and consecrated Bishop.

Ambrose devoted himself to the task of explaining the truths of the Faith to his people. He is called a patron of Catholic Action—a Christopher of his day—because he insisted that his flock make Christ the center of their daily lives and their activities. He was most courageous in defending the cause of the Church against Arianism.

When the emperor Theodosius unjustly ordered a massacre, Ambrose rebuked him to his face and refused to permit him to enter the church until he had done public penance for his crime. The emperor obeyed, publicly atoning for his sin. This softened the anger of the people toward Theodosius. Later on, Ambrose received help from Theodosius. Together they succeeded in winning the pagans of the area to the flock of Christ.

Saint Jerome and Saint Ambrose

The people of Milan loved and respected Ambrose, especially the poor and needy, for whom he provided out of his own personal inheritance. He was a great bishop, a scholar and preacher, a father to his flock, and, like Paul the Apostle, a strong and fearless leader. Christ's Church was able to do much through him. Among his converts to the Faith was St. Augustine, who also did much to further Christ's work on earth.

ST. AUGUSTINE

The mother of St. Augustine, St. Monica, prayed fervently that her son, who was leading a sinful life, would repent and live as a Christian should. After St. Augustine had listened to the sermons of St. Ambrose, he began to read the life of St. Anthony the Hermit, and to study the Epistles of St. Paul. After many years, Monica's prayers were answered; her son was finally convinced of the truth and—eventually, by a special grace—repented of his past sins and lived upright. To his mother's great joy, he was baptized by St. Ambrose.

Augustine formed the Order of Hermits of St. Augustine and became a promoter of religious communities. While he was visiting the city of Hippo in Africa, he was ordained a priest and shortly afterward was consecrated Bishop of Hippo in what is today Algeria.

Augustine is best remembered for his *Confessions*, wherein he praises God for His great goodness, and for his *City of God*, which is the greatest defense of Christianity ever written.

ST. JEROME

At the request of the pope, Jerome undertook the great work of revising the text of the Bible from the oldest manuscripts and of translating it into Latin. His completed work is known as the Vulgate. This has been the official Latin text of the Scripture in the Church since the sixth century. St. Jerome wrote many letters and commentaries on the Old Testament. He is often entitled Doctor of Sacred Scripture.

Jerome also fought against the heretics of his day. He condemned those who accused the Church of being too mild toward sinners who repented; he attacked those who denied the virginity of the Blessed Virgin Mary; he battled against those who condemned as idolators all persons who honored the relics of the saints. In his writings he opposed Pelagius, who denied the necessity of grace for salvation. This was a dangerous heresy. Many today still act as if they believe grace is not necessary to gain eternal life.

Conclusion

The Church has triumphed, and will continue to triumph, over all heresies, preserving whole and entire the revealed truths entrusted to her by Christ. One, holy, catholic (universal), and apostolic, the Church is for all men of all times. She is the guardian of all God's truth. From the time of Peter, the first pope, to today, the Church has fearlessly and ceaselessly proclaimed all that God has revealed as necessary for salvation. Founded on the rock—Peter—and guided by the Holy Spirit, Christ's Church will continue to preach those truths "from the housetops," until the Son of God comes in glory to judge the world. Our Lord told His Apostles and, through them, told us: "I am with you all days even to the end of the world." This divine promise should be guarantee enough to keep the weakest Christian united to the True Vine.

FOR ME TO REVIEW

Questions and Exercises

Part 1: Choose the correct words in the following statements

1. A Catholic who changes or denies a doctrine of our faith is called a: patriarch, apostate, heretic, hermit

2. The heretics who denied the Divinity of Christ were: Nestorians, Manicheans, Arians, Laterans

3. Arianism was condemned at the Council of: Ephesus, Jerusalem, Milan, Nicaea

4. Bishops who were in authority over many provinces were called: Cardinals, Patriarchs, Hermits, Confessors

5. Three great Fathers of the Church were: Theodosius, Ambrose, Pelagius, Augustine, Jerome

6. The revision of the Bible called the Latin Vulgate was the chief work of: St. Basil, St. Augustine, St. Jerome, St. Ambrose

7. The chief opponent to the Pelagian heresy, which claimed that grace was not necessary for salvation, was: Ambrose, Jerome, Valens, Augustine

8. The heresy that stated that Mary was not the Mother of God was started by: Arians, Nestorians, Macedonians, Vigilantes

9. Because of his eloquence, the title "Golden-mouthed" orator was given to: St. Basil, St. Gregory, St. Ambrose, St. John Chrysostom

10. When the Emperor Theodosius had ordered a cruel massacre he was condemned to do public penance by the bishop: Ambrose, Gregory, Augustine, Cyril

Part 2: Questions to Check Your Reading

1. What false doctrine did Arius teach?

2. At what general Council were the errors of Arianism condemned?

3. The articles of faith prepared at this time are found in what creed?

4. What great saint defended the divinity of Christ against the errors of Arianism?

5. What saint was called "golden-mouthed," and why?

6. Why were some bishops called patriarchs?

7. Explain the heresy of Nestorius.

8. Who could well be called the "Christopher" of his day?

9. What great saint was a convert of St. Ambrose? How did he serve Christ's Church?

10. What saint prayed many years for her son's conversion?

11. Who translated the Bible into Latin?

12. What did Pelagius teach?

13. What do we mean when we say that the Church has triumphed over all heresies?

 **FOR ME TO DO**

1. Give a report on the Council of Nicaea telling:
   a) Why it was held
   b) Who took active part
   c) What were the results

2. Write a conversation between St. Ambrose and the Emperor Theodosius.

3. Write a short article on the Mystical Body of Christ.

4. Debate the question: "More good came to the Church from heresies than from persecutions."

CHAPTER 31

The Church Overcomes the Barbarians With Charity

Despite the attacks by her enemies, Christ's Church continued to grow and become strong. When heresies occurred, God raised up great saints to defend the truth, and led the Church to define more clearly the teachings of Christ, so that they would be better known and understood. But now another danger threatened the early Church—the invasion of barbarian tribes. When the nations of northern and eastern Europe swept south and west, there was some danger that the Church would be destroyed along with the old Roman Empire. The Church, however, stood firm even after the Empire was destroyed by the barbarians.

The Barbarian Invasions

Within the boundaries of the Roman Empire there were already a number of barbarian tribes—the Goths, Franks, Vandals, and other powerful Teutonic tribes. They roamed the land north and east of the Rhine and Danube Rivers. Beyond these tribes dwelt the Huns, a people probably of Mongolian origin, who had been driven out of China. They, too, began pushing toward the West, driving the others before them. Even though these people, in comparison with the more cultured Romans, were called barbarians, they had a sturdy civilization of their own.

The Roman Empire had become vast and wealthy. Slavery was the lot of most who lived in her cities; the others became careless and sinful because of soft and luxurious living. The Roman army at this time was made up largely of men paid to fight. As a consequence, Rome became invitingly weak.

The barbarian nations had been longing to occupy certain Roman provinces. Finally, under the pressure of the Huns, the tribes closer to the Roman provinces began to invade her borders. Pitched battles took place throughout Europe.

Pope Leo I

Under the leadership of Attila, the Huns crossed the Alps and marched on Rome. They laid waste to the countryside as they moved along, and prepared to sack the capital, so as to add its treasures to their spoils.

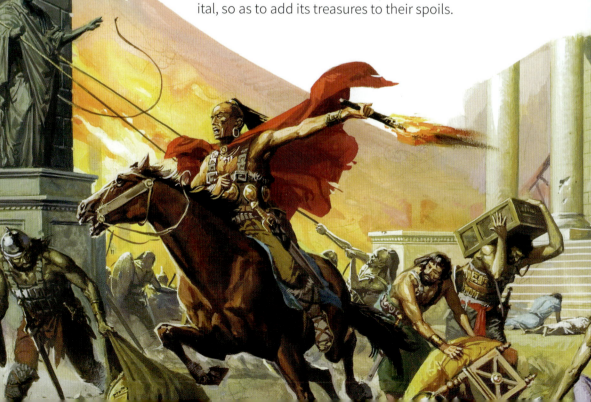

As they approached the city, they were met by Pope Leo I. This courageous Pontiff, imitating the True Shepherd in the care of his flock, went out unarmed to ask Attila to spare the city because it had been made sacred by the Apostles Peter and Paul. Attila admired the courage of the pope and respected his authority. As if by miracle, Attila promised to spare Rome and to leave its people unharmed.

Three years later the Vandals in their turn descended upon Rome. Again, St. Leo defended his people from the invaders. He went to the gates of the city and there met the leader of this horde. Although he failed to prevent them from entering and plundering the city, he did stop them from burning it and from massacring its inhabitants.

Fall of the Empire

A very large part of Europe was now overrun by barbarian people. The Kingdom of the Visigoths was established in Spain, while the Ostrogoths settled in Italy. Frankish tribes expanded into what is now northern and western France, while the Burgundians made their home in the valley of the Rhine River, and the Lombards in Africa.

Rome never regained her ancient splendor after the attack of the Vandals. In 476 the last Western Emperor was dethroned, and Odoacer ruled Italy. The mighty Roman Empire, once the proud mistress of the world, had become weak and corrupt. Her overthrow was but a matter of time. The seat of Christendom, where martyrs had shed their blood, was reduced to ruins by the invading barbarians.

The Catholic Church, however, did not disappear along with the Empire. Founded by and on Christ, and guided by the Holy Spirit, the Church was not dependent upon worldly power or conquests. She was *in* the world but not *of* it, and she proved that she could go on without ancient Rome. Upon the ruins of Rome

God built the earthly home of the Roman Pontiffs, and it became the Eternal City. Because of her mission, the Church turned to the barbarians and offered them the "good news" of salvation: they accepted it. By so doing, they laid the foundation for a new Europe.

The Conversion of the Nations

Among the first to accept Christianity was a group of tribes known as the Franks, who poured into the Empire and lived in the country west of the Rhine and south of the Loire. Clovis, one of the warrior kings, chose Clotilda, a lovely Christian maiden, for his queen. She was a Burgundian princess who later was canonized a saint. Through her influence and prayer Clovis became interested in the Church.

The Baptism of Clovis

During an important battle Clovis saw that his men were about to go down in defeat. He also noticed that they were no longer fighting with spirit and courage. He thereupon decided to follow the advice of Clotilda; he prayed to her God for help in this hour of sore need. The tide of the battle changed before his very eyes and his men emerged victoriously. Clovis promised to be baptized, and many of his subjects followed his example. This began the conversion of the whole Frankish nation.

St. Patrick, the Shamrock, and the Trinity

Few people in Ireland at the time Patrick lived were Christian, or well educated, and so it was difficult for him to explain his faith and all the Catholic teaching he had received himself. One famous story tells how he used the clover (or shamrock) to help explain how God is one God, but exists as three distinct Persons: Father, Son, and Holy Spirit. Many clover species are trifoliate, meaning they have leaves in sets of three, and so one plant is made up of three distinct leaves. Each leaf is fully of the plant, but each is also its own separate leaf. Likewise, Jesus is fully God, as are the other persons in the Trinity. Three persons, one God. The use of explanations like this must have helped since many people converted to Christianity through St. Patrick's witness. This story explains why St. Patrick is often depicted with an image of a clover, or shamrock, in religious art.

The Conversion of Ireland

Ireland honors St. Patrick as her great Apostle. He had been taken to Ireland as a captive when a boy of seventeen. While there he learned the language, customs, and religion of her people. Then he returned to the continent and prepared himself for his great task, the conversion of the Irish. His success in Ireland was very great. In about thirty years he won practically all the people over to Christianity.

St. Patrick built monasteries, convents, and schools. Because of him the Irish people chose as their emblem the shamrock, whose three-leaf stem he used to teach the mystery of the Blessed Trinity.

The Conversion of Scotland

St. Columba was born in Ireland, and at the age of forty went to Scotland to bring Christianity to its people. He took with him a number of Irish monks as helpers. For many years they worked together in northern Scotland. They converted the King of the Picts and won many of his people to the Faith of Christ. St. Columba also built churches and monasteries. With the aid of his companions, he built the famous monastery of Iona, where the work of conversion was continued long after his death. Because of his labors in this land he is known as the "Apostle of Scotland."

The Conversion of England

Christianity had existed among native Britons before the barbarian inroads. But England was invaded by the Angles, Saxons, and Jutes, who drove out the priests and bishops and destroyed all the churches. For over a century the Anglo-Saxons practiced their pagan religion where Christianity had flourished. Through Pope Gregory the Great and his missionaries, Christianity was again brought to that land.

St. Gregory became interested in the Anglo-Saxons even before he was made pope. It is said that one day he noticed a group of young men in a Roman slave market. Gregory was drawn to them by the beauty of their faces and the dignity of their appearance. When he was told they were English (Angles) he burst out, "These are not Angles, but angels." Gregory determined to do all in his power to win these people for Christ.

After Gregory became pope, he sent missionaries to England. These were led by a monk called Augustine, who later became the bishop of Canterbury. He is not to be confused with St. Augustine of Hippo, whom we have already met.

Augustine arriving in England

Augustine and his band landed on the coast of England and sent word to King Ethelbert of their arrival. This king was married to Ethelberta, a Frankish princess, who is said to have been the great-granddaughter of St. Clotilda and Clovis. The queen won over the king to grant favors to the missionaries. As a result, they were permitted to preach the Faith to the people of England. The king himself became a convert and was baptized. Several thousand of his people followed his example.

The Conversion of Germany

Winfred was a Benedictine monk who desired greatly to convert the people of Germany. To realize his desire, he had an audience with the pope, who changed his name to Boniface and appointed him Missionary Apostolic to whatever people the Holy Spirit might direct him. Boniface went directly to the heart of Germany to do his work. He planned to convert the pagans and, through them, win others to Christ. His first efforts were not successful.

St. Boniface pointed out the errors of the nature worship which the German people practiced. They held a great oak "Tree of Thor" as sacred. Acting with courage like that of Gideon in the Old Testament when he overthrew the altar of Baal, Boniface destroyed the tree. When he was not punished the people were convinced that their god, Thor, was powerless. Many of them asked to be baptized.

A few years later the pope sent for Boniface, to learn more about his missionary work. He then made him an archbishop and sent him back to his work of conversion. For more than thirty years Boniface labored to spread Christianity among the pagan people of Germany and the surrounding country. On the way to confirm some newly baptized people he met a group of pagans. One of them struck him with a sword and killed him instantly. They also killed some of his companions. Thus, St. Boniface crowned his life as missionary with martyrdom.

Scandinavia

The great-souled men of these centuries were aflame with the spirit of the Apostles. They wanted to convert the entire world. In their zeal they turned to the north. Men of these parts were called "Norsemen," a fierce and war-loving people. Their conversion to Christianity was important to the peace and civilization of Europe. St. Ansgar carried the Faith to the people of Denmark. He is, therefore, called the "Apostle of the North." In Denmark he drew people to the true Faith by working to free captives from slavery and to better the conditions of the poor. He then went to Sweden and established the Church there. Christianity was finally adopted by the people of Norway through the efforts of two of their Christian kings.

The Slavs

Most of the people of within Slavic nations were pagans until the ninth century. They occupied the whole of eastern Europe. Two brothers, the Greek monks Cyril and Methodius, preached the Gospel to these people. They are called the "Apostles of the Slavs."

They translated the Gospels as well as the liturgy of the Mass into the Slavic language. Objections were raised about using the language of the people in celebrating Mass. These complaints were relayed to the pope, who immediately sent for Cyril and Methodius. When the Supreme Pontiff heard their story, he approved of their work and sanctioned the Slavonic Liturgy.

Both brothers were consecrated bishops. St. Cyril died in Rome. Methodius, however, continued his missionary work until he had spread the Faith among the Bohemians and the Poles in Northern Moravia.

FOR ME TO REVIEW

Questions and Exercises

Part 1: Match column I with column II

Column I	Column II
1. Huns	A. Apostle of Germany
2. Columba	B. sent Augustine to convert England
3. Attila	C. attacks on the Church from within
4. Ansgar	D. succeeded in converting the people of the Slav nation
5. Boniface	E. pagan god of the German people
6. Patrick	F. monastery of Iona was built by
7. St. Gregory	G. barbarian people
8. Cyril and Methodius	H. Apostle of the North
9. heresies	I. wife of Clovis
10. Pope Leo I	J. Apostle of Ireland
11. Thor	K. met Attila and defended his people
12. Clotilda	L. leader of the Huns

Part 2: Questions to Check Your Reading

1. What rivers formed the boundaries of the Roman Empire?

2. Give two reasons why the power of Rome was weakened?

3. How did Pope Leo protect the people of Rome?

4. Describe the fall of the Roman Empire.

5. How did the Church react to the barbarian invasion?

6. What incident in the life of King Clovis brought about his conversion?

7. Who labored for the conversion of Scotland?

8. Who carried the light of Faith to England?

9. In what way did Queen Ethelberta help the missionaries of England?

10. How did St. Boniface win the respect of the people of Germany?

11. Who were the missionaries who worked among the Slavic people?

12. What lessons do the lives of these great missionaries teach us?

✓ FOR ME TO DO

1. Write a report on one of the following topics:
   a) Missionaries to the Slavs
   b) Barbarians invade Europe
   c) Church saved Europe from barbarism
   d) The Franks are converted
   e) The work of St. Boniface

2. Name five requirements for a boy or girl who would be a real Christian leader.

3. Write a good descriptive paragraph on one of the following incidents:
   a) Baptism of King Clovis
   b) Queen Ethelberta persuades the king to help missionaries
   c) St. Boniface destroys the Sacred Oak

4. Choose a saint whose feast is celebrated this month. Tell what he did to increase the love of God in the hearts of others.

5. Find out what opportunities exist for the members of your parish to do missionary work.

CHAPTER 32

Islam and the Greek Schism

Persecution, heresies, and barbarian invasions all posed serious threats to the Church during its formative years. Yet the Church, guided by the Holy Spirit, weathered these storms and not only survived but grew stronger. In this chapter we shall see two further threats to the Church which imperiled it from the sixth to the tenth centuries. One of these was an external threat, a religion springing from a man named Mohammed; the other was internal, issuing from disputes between the East and West.

Islam

THE ORIGIN OF ISLAM

Although most of the lands around the Mediterranean were part of the Roman Empire and were at least partly Christianized, Arabia remained almost entirely pagan.

About the end of the sixth century Mohammed was born in the city of Mecca, in Arabia. As a youth he became a camel driver and traveled with the caravans which in those days served the same purposes as freight carriers today. His work and travels brought him into contact with both Christians and Jews, from whom he learned much about their religious beliefs. Later in life he claimed that the Angel Gabriel appeared to him in a vision, commanding him to "arise and preach."

ISLAM

The religion Mohammed set out to preach was a mixture of his own ideas and those he borrowed from both Christians and Jews. He taught that there is only one God—Allah—and that he, Mohammed—was his prophet. To give his teachings definite form and to provide his followers with a handbook of their faith, Mohammed composed a book called the Quran. His religion he called Islam, from the Arabic word meaning "to submit," i.e., to submit to the will of Allah. The adherents of this faith are also known as Muslims as well as Mohammedans or Moors.

THE FLIGHT OF MOHAMMED

The people of Mecca did not accept Mohammed's teaching. Their hostility, in fact, compelled the prophet of this new faith to flee to Medina. This flight from Mecca to Medina is known as the Hegira, and it is from this date that Muslims reckon the beginning of their era, as we reckon our era from the birth of Christ. Later, after he had united the nomadic tribes of Arabia, Mohammed took the city of Mecca by force, making it the headquarters of his religion. Even today, followers of Mohammed are urged to make at least one pilgrimage to Mecca during their lifetime.

TERMS TO KNOW

- Constantinople
- patriarch
- Mecca
- Cerularius
- Iconoclasm
- Islam
- Photius
- excommunicated
- Muslims
- Orthodox
- Mohammed
- Charles Martel

THE RAPID SPREAD OF ISLAM

One factor in the rapid spread of the new faith was its simplicity. The moral code which Mohammed required of his followers was not too exacting, since a simple code of external rites such as prayers at stated intervals during the day were claimed to justify the believer and keep him holy.

Another factor was the zealous enthusiasm that Mohammed stirred in his followers. For the faithful Muslim, there was a sacred obligation to propagate his belief—by war if necessary—and in this new faith the chieftains of the desert tribes found a superb means of uniting against the armies of the Emperor. Since Mohammed's followers believed that death in battle against the infidels insured an eternity of pleasure, the enthusiasm which Mohammed and his successors could whip up among the desert tribesmen was immense.

After Mohammed's death his successors, who found in Omar a military genius of first-rate ability, not only united all of Arabia but became masters of the Persian Empire, of Egypt, of Palestine, and of Syria as well. By the end of the seventh century they also controlled all of northern Africa and were able to push into Europe, crossing the Straits of Gibraltar in 711 and conquering Spain, even advancing into portions of southern France. In addition, all the islands of the Mediterranean Sea, except Corsica, were under the sway of the Prophet's followers.

THE PROGRESS OF ISLAM IS CHECKED

By this time all of Europe—both West and East—was in danger of falling completely to the Muslims.

Two important battles, however, turned the tide. In the East, the Islamic forces besieging Constantinople were defeated by the Emperor Leo III, and in the West the Frankish forces under Charles Martel won a great victory at Poitiers (Tours) in 732. These two decisive battles stemmed the advancing Muslims, but they retained control of parts of southern France, Spain, and the

Mediterranean islands for a long time afterward. In fact, it was not until the time of Christopher Columbus that the Moors, as the Muslims in Spain were called, were finally defeated.

After the barbarian invasions the Church in Europe flourished because the barbarians were converted. However, the lands where the Muslim's maintained control were lost to the Christian world, primarily the Middle East and northern Africa.

The Great East-West Schism

SEPARATION FROM THE CHURCH—SCHISM

A schism is a division or separation from the Catholic Church which is brought about by failure to submit to the authority of the pope. Such a break from the authority of the Church in Rome occurred in the eleventh century, but its causes began several centuries earlier. This disturbance centered at Constantinople and caused a division in the Church, known as the Great Schism, which has continued to our own day.

Pope fell into disfavor on several occasions because he warned the East to put an end to certain heresies which were spreading there.

ICONOCLASM

In most Catholic homes, we can find a crucifix or a picture or statue of the Blessed Virgin or some saint. We do not adore or worship these representations. We revere them because of what they represent. They help to awaken our devotion. In the East, such pious objects caused a great disturbance among Christians. A heresy called Iconoclasm, which means "image-breaking," broke out in the Eastern Church. The Iconoclasts opposed the use and veneration of holy pictures and statues; in fact, they even destroyed them. The emperor in the East issued an order against the use of images and ordered their removal from the churches. He even commanded the Pope to obey his order. As head of the Church both in the East and the West, the Pope explained to the emperor that the use of images was lawful, and forbade the emperor to disturb the Church.

As a result of this heresy many valuable works of art, whole libraries, and certain monasteries were destroyed. Finally, a General Council, held at Nicaea in 787, set forth the Church's teaching on the veneration of images. The relations, however, between the East and the West remained unfriendly, and the question of iconoclasm was to return on many occasions in the coming centuries.

PATRIARCHS OF CONSTANTINOPLE OPPOSE AUTHORITY OF POPE

A great distance separated the Holy See in Rome from the Church in the East. Communication between them was slow. As a result, it was difficult for Rome to settle disputes that arose. For this reason, the bishops in the Eastern Empire looked to the Patriarchs of Constantinople for leadership. Things went so far that certain patriarchs of Constantinople tried to make themselves powerful and to become a kind of pope in the East. Hostile feelings multiplied, until relations between the Church in the East and the Church in the West became severely strained.

PHOTIUS PREPARES THE WAY FOR THE GREAT SCHISM

The first break between the Greeks and the Latin Church took place in the middle of the ninth century, when Ignatius was the patriarch of Constantinople. He refused to give Holy Communion to the uncle of the Emperor, because this man led an immoral life and would not do penance for the public scandal he caused. Ignatius was exiled for doing his duty, and Photius, who was not a priest at the time, was named his successor.

Ignatius appealed to the Pope. The Pope studied the matter and declared that Ignatius was the rightful patriarch. Photius refused to submit to the Pope's decision. He accused the Pope, and with him the Catholic Church in the West, of heresy. Photius went so far as to list as errors certain doctrines and practices of the Latins such as the distribution of Communion under the species of bread alone, the primacy of Peter, and the insertion of the words "from the Son" in the Creed. This last doctrinal matter is known as the "Filioque Controversy."

Photius had many followers, but, when a new emperor came into power, he was forced to relinquish his unlawfully attained post. Under this new emperor, Ignatius was again named patriarch. Ignatius died ten years later. Photius again asked to be named patriarch. The Pope granted his request, but only after Photius asked pardon for his past offenses. No sooner was he in office, however, than he began to oppose the Pope's authority and to object to some doctrinal teachings and liturgical practices observed by the Latin Church.

Ultimately the emperor removed Photius from office, but the motive behind the emperor's action does not seem to have been a desire to uphold the Faith of Rome. Rather, it seems that he wanted to install his brother as patriarch. Photius himself died in communion with Rome.

THE GREAT SCHISM

For nearly two hundred years after the death of Photius there was at least outward peace between the Greeks and Rome. Underneath, however, dissension smoldered. It burst into flame again when Michael Cerularius was made patriarch of Constantinople.

Michael was particularly opposed to the use of unleavened bread in the Sacrifice of the Mass and to the Latin insistence on an unmarried clergy. He was also irritated by the attempt of Rome to impose on the Greeks certain liturgical and ritual reforms. Like Photius, he also claimed that the Roman Church was heretical in changing the Creed to say, "I believe in the Holy Spirit, the Lord, the giver of life, who proceeds from the Father *and the Son*." The "and the Son" is referred to as the "filioque." The Greek version just says "who proceeds from the Father." Finally, Michael issued a decree which demanded that all Latin churches in Constantinople be closed. He ordered the priests to adopt the Greek Rite, that is, the language, ceremonies, vestments, and practices of the Eastern Church. When they refused, Cerularius declared them excommunicated.

The Pope sent his legates to Constantinople to try to patch up the difficulty. Their efforts were without success, and to a large extent the fact that the legates did not know the historical facts was a cause of their failure. For example, they maintained that the words "and from the Son" were a part of the original Nicene-Constantinople Creed and that the Greeks had deliberately taken these words out, whereas the Greeks were right in insisting that these words did not appear in the original Creed. Ultimately, the papal legates excommunicated the patriarch, Michael Cerularius. The Pope, whose legates they were, had died in the meantime. The breach, thus started, widened into definite schism as the years passed.

RESULTS OF THE SCHISM

Gradually, other Eastern patriarchs joined the schism, and the Church lost many countries. Deprived of the authority of the pope, the schismatics soon broke into various groups and placed themselves under the authority of the emperor.

The effects of the Great Schism have lasted even until our own day. However, attempts at reconciliation have been partially successful, particularly with the efforts of the Second Vatican Council (1962–1965). Both Pope Paul VI and the Ecumenical Patriarch Athenagoras I of Constantinople lifted their excommunications towards one another, and mutually recognized their shared apostolic priesthood and valid sacraments.

During his papacy, Pope St. John Paul II asked that the Church of the East and West might breathe with "both lungs," through mutual respect and a willingness to learn from the richness of each respective tradition. In 2011, Pope Benedict XVI echoed John Paul II when he called the Church of Rome to pray "that the Eastern Catholic Churches and their venerable traditions may be known and esteemed as a spiritual treasure for the whole Church." Many within the Eastern Church have come under the authority of the Pope all the while maintaining their traditions and liturgical rites, such examples include Byzantine Catholics. The traditions of the East are a great source of grace and beauty, all Catholics would do well to learn from them.

FOR ME TO REVIEW

Questions and Exercises

Part 1: Match part A with part B

A

1. Mohammed quickly won followers because . . .
2. The Muslims did not succeed in taking western Europe because . . .
3. We know that the Catholic Church is the true Church because . . .
4. Islam made rapid conquests because . . . . . .
5. The Orthodox church is not in full union with the Church because . . .
6. We know that the Catholic Church was established for all the people because . . .
7. The discord between the Greek and Latin Church increased because . . .
8. Photius planned to separate from the Apostolic See because . . .
9. The Church cannot make mistakes in matters of faith because . . .
10. It was not difficult for Cerularius to bring about the Great Schism because . . .

B

A. Christ said, "I am with you . . . , even to the consummation of the world."
B. He was determined to remain the patriarch of Constantinople.
C. Charles Martel defeated them in the Battle of Poitiers.
D. It broke away from the authority of the Pope.
E. Minor differences in liturgy and ritual were magnified because of the argument over the Filioque.
F. Christ said, "Thou art Peter; and upon this rock I will build my Church."

G. It united the tribes of Arabia, firing them with enthusiasm.

H. The harm which was done by the temporary schism of Photius was never completely repaired.

I. Christ said: "Go, teach all nations."

J. He offered them a religion whose creed was simple and whose moral code was relatively easy to fulfill.

Part 2: Complete the following

1. Mohammed began to spread his religion at the beginning of the _____ century.

2. The religion founded by Mohammed is called _____ .

3. Mohammed claimed that the greatest prophet that ever lived was _____ .

4. Islam began in the country of _____ .

5. The progress of the Muslims into western Europe was checked in the Battle of _____ .

6. The Frankish leader opposing the Muslims was _____ .

7. Mohammed wrote his teachings in a book called the _____ .

8. The emperors began to interfere with the Eastern Church when the capital of the Empire was transferred to _____ .

9. The language of the Eastern Church was _____ .

10. A heresy rejecting the veneration of images was called _____ .

11. Those people in the Eastern Empire who always remained faithful to the true Church or those who fell away and later returned are known as the _____ .

12. Those who no longer acknowledge the authority of the pope are usually referred to as _____ .or . . . . . .

Part 3: Questions to Check Your Reading

1. What are some of the teachings of Mohammed?

2. Why were the Muslims able to make such rapid conquests?

3. What were the religious beliefs of the Muslims?

4. Where was the advance of the Muslims in western Europe checked? How?

5. What were the results of the Islamic conquest?

6. Do dishonest leaders and people do much harm to Christ's Church?

7. What were some of the things that led to the Great Schism?

8. What effect did the moving of the capital of the Empire to Constantinople have upon the unity of the Church?

9. How did Photius pave the way for the Great Schism?

10. How did the final break between the Church in the East and the West take place?

11. What were the results of the Great Schism?

12. What is the difference between Byzantine Catholics and the Greek Orthodox?

✅ FOR ME TO DO

1. Make posters which illustrate the unity and universality of the Catholic Church.

2. Make a list of the marks and attributes of the Catholic Church. Include from the Bible our Lord's words which prove

that it is the Catholic Church which has these marks and attributes.

3. With the help of your dictionary give a correct and clear explanation of the following words which you are often apt to meet in connection with religions: Catholic, Christian, heretic, schismatic, Orthodox.

4. Find out if there is a Byzantine Catholic community in your diocese; on any particular Sunday, consider attending their Divine Liturgy.

5. If you do not already have one hanging up in your room, seek to acquire a traditional Eastern Icon of your favorite saint.

6. Let these questions help you make a resolution for today:

   - Do I pray for the conversion of those nations that have been drawn away from the true religion?

   - Do my words and behavior in public leave others with a favorable attitude toward the Catholic Church?

   - Do I thank God for having allowed me to be born in the Holy Catholic Church? How?

   - Does the kind of life I lead have an influence on the welfare of the Church?

CHAPTER 33
In Calmer Waters—
The Middle Ages

While still suffering from the invasion of Islam, the Church now entered into a period much calmer than the previous ones. This period is known as the Middle Ages. It had its slow beginnings in the seventh century; it ended with the close of the fourteenth century.

During these years, which are often called the Ages of Faith, the flame of Christianity burned low for a while—the so-called Dark Ages—but then sprang up brightly and led to wonderful achievements. The Church triumphed after many trials. Universities were founded. The arts flourished. This growth was not limited to one country but was experienced throughout Europe. A great civilization was created by a people united by the bonds of Christian faith and charity.

The Reign of Charlemagne

THE FRANKS PROTECT THE POPE

After the capital of the Roman Empire was moved from Rome to Constantinople, the emperors neglected Italy, so that the burden of protecting Rome from the barbarians had to be taken up by the popes. The barbarian Lombards, who had settled in the north of Italy, constantly threatened Rome. When peaceful methods failed to move them and when the Eastern Emperors neglected to help in their removal, the Pope asked Pepin, the king of the Franks, for military aid.

Because of the work of St. Remigius the Franks had become Catholics and were closely united to the Holy See. Moreover, of all the barbarian nations who had been evangelized, the Franks

alone were not Arians. Pepin crossed into Italy with his army and forced the Lombards to return to the Church the stolen territories.

CHARLEMAGNE BECOMES KING OF THE FRANKS

Pepin's son, Charlemagne, also known as Charles the Great, succeeded him as ruler of the Franks.

The Teutonic tribes (the Saxons, Goths, Franks, Vandals, etc.) were at this time separate nations. When Charlemagne became king of the Franks he united them into one people. He recognized the wisdom of allowing these various tribes to observe their own customs, but he also thought that the most secure means for winning their lasting allegiance was to impose upon them the Christian faith. Although he did much for European culture by establishing monasteries throughout his realms and by fostering the spread of the Gospel, yet the sometimes harsh methods he used in achieving this goal show the excesses to which even well-intentioned men may go.

The Lombards began anew to cause the Pope trouble by invading the papal lands. The Pope appealed to Charlemagne for help.

TERMS TO KNOW

- Romanesque
- crosier
- serf
- Gothic
- lay investiture
- apprentice
- feudalism
- concordat
- journeyman
- vassals
- mendicant
- fief

457

Charlemagne crossed the Alps and defeated the Lombards, hurrying off the Lombard king to exile in a monastery and taking for himself the title "King of the Lombards."

CHARLEMAGNE IS CROWNED EMPEROR OF THE WEST

The emperor in Constantinople, far from events in the West, was little interested in what happened to the Pope in Rome or in maintaining peace and order in the West. The Pope, feeling that there should be some one with temporal authority to maintain public peace and order, ultimately decided to crown this powerful Frankish monarch the Emperor of the West. Accordingly, on Christmas day of 800, while Charlemagne was attending Mass at St. Peter's, Pope Leo III crowned him Roman Emperor.

This revival of the Roman Empire in the West was of tremendous importance. It emphasized the jurisdiction of the Pope by contrasting his position as spiritual head of the people with the emperor's role as temporal head. For centuries there was fairly good cooperation between Pope and Emperor. However, there was the constant danger that the Emperor would try to take over the authority of the Pope. Charlemagne himself tended in this direction, and it was probably due to the fact that the popes of his day were strong-minded men that he did not meddle more seriously in the affairs of the Church.

CHARLEMAGNE ESTABLISHES SCHOOLS

Charlemagne was a patron of learning, gathering about himself the best teachers and scholars of Europe. To one of the most noted, Alcuin, he gave the charge of establishing schools and libraries and of fostering a love for learning.

Feudalism

THE RISE OF FEUDALISM

Charlemagne ruled his empire for nearly fifty years. After his death the Frankish Kingdom gradually broke apart. A period of trouble followed. His whole empire was divided among his three grandsons. As a consequence, a strong central government was lacking. Europe became defenseless against the Vikings who now began to pour in from the North, and against the Saracens who invaded the South.

Without protection from such forces, the people themselves banded together, building castles and fortresses for themselves. In times of danger the people fled to them for refuge. For still greater protection people grouped themselves around a lord or ruler, and this ruler in turn had the right to call on them when invasion threatened. During this period most people made their living by tilling the soil. Soon it became a custom for rulers to assign certain lands to their warlords or favorites as a price for their services. This entire system of landholding became known as feudalism. The followers of the lord, who had received land from his hands, were known as vassals. They promised to help their lord in time of battle and to perform other services for him. The vassal's land was called a fief.

The ordinary laborer in the feudal system was called a serf. The serf was not a slave, because his lord could not sell or transfer him to another lord. On the other hand, the serf was not free, as we understand freedom, for he was bound to the land. If the land, that is the fief, changed hands, the serf continued to live on the same land under the new master.

FEUDALISM AND THE CHURCH

Many times, the feudal lords interfered in the affairs of the Church. Sometimes the clergy became vassals and were obliged to perform military tasks and court duties. These obligations led to great abuses. Many of the nobles quarreled among themselves so that a constant state of war existed in some places. This unrest caused the Church much hardship.

The Church tried by every means in her power to remedy the abuses of feudalism. The "Peace of God" was instituted to protect women, children, and others who were not of the military. The "Truce of God" insured a certain amount of peace each year. This truce forbade fighting during Lent and Advent, and from Wednesday night until the following Monday morning each week during the rest of the year. Those who were warned three times for breaking the truce, but persisted, were excommunicated.

LAY INVESTITURE

Differences often sprang up between Church authorities and laymen. One difference was the abuse known as lay investiture. This practice meant that a temporal ruler, a layman such as king or lord, bestowed a fief, to which was connected a bishopric or abbey on a candidate of his own choice. In other words, the layman took it upon himself to appoint a man to a spiritual office as well as to a fief and to transfer to his candidate the ring and crosier, the symbols of spiritual authority. As a result, unworthy men were appointed as bishops and abbots, and found their way into other positions. By 1073 the problem of lay investiture had become acute. As long as lay lords appointed bishops and abbots the needed reforms in Christian life could not be carried out. Finally, in 1073, a monk named Hildebrand became Pope Gregory VII. Strong of character, Gregory realized that the Papacy alone could save the Church. He did away with the right of lay investiture, declaring that anyone who had received a spiritual office from a layman was deposed from that office. This order caused great dismay throughout Europe. For the removal from office was intended not only for those who had received the office, but also for those who had conferred it upon others.

The Emperor of Germany, Henry IV, had practiced lay investiture. He refused to obey Gregory's order. The Pope then ordered Henry to proceed to Rome. When Henry refused, Gregory excommunicated him and decreed that his subjects were no longer required to obey him. As a result, his subjects deserted him, and the princes of his empire stated that he would have to stand trial before the Pope. He was to live in retirement until the trial.

Henry could do nothing save submit. He journeyed to Italy to make his peace with the Pope. He did penance and was released from the sentence of excommunication after he had solemnly promised not to practice lay investiture. Henry did not keep his word, and he was again punished.

The dispute over lay investiture continued for some years. The abuse was finally corrected by a concordat, that is, an agreement between Church and State. This concordat was important because by it the rulers agreed not to invest bishops and abbots with ring and staff. The Pope in turn agreed to appoint as bishops and abbots men who would be acceptable to the secular rulers. The important point, however, was that the Pope could see that worthy and properly qualified candidates were selected as bishops and abbots.

Following fearlessly the example given by His Divine Master, Pope Gregory drove the buyers and sellers of spiritual things out of the Temple of Christ. He compelled the world to respect the spiritual authority of Christ's Church.

The Crusades

THE CAUSE OF THE CRUSADES

In the eleventh century a Turkish tribe living in the East was converted to Islam. The Turks overran Palestine, gaining control of the Holy Land. The places made sacred by our Lord have always been dear to the heart of every Catholic. Over the centuries many Christians made pilgrimages or visits to the Holy Land. When the Muslims conquered Palestine, they imposed hardships on the Christians living there or on those making pilgrimages to the Holy Places. When they returned home, the pilgrims told of what they had suffered, seen, and heard.

The Eastern Emperor appealed to the Pope to help him save his kingdom from the Turks. Heeding the plea, the Pope went to France, where a great Council of the Church was to be held in the

city of Clermont. There he met bishops, knights by the thousands, and a great multitude of people. Peter the Hermit, who had been a pilgrim to the Holy Land, spoke to the Council on the subject of a holy war. He was followed by the Pope, who gave a stirring challenge to the crowd standing in the square. The Pope said, "Christian warriors, you seek without end for vain pretexts for war. Rejoice, for today you have found true ones! Go and fight against the infidels (Turks). Go and fight for the deliverance of the Holy Places. If you triumph, the kingdoms of the East will be yours. If you are conquered, you will have the glory of dying in the very same place as Jesus Christ; and God will not forget that He found you in His holy ranks."

At the end of the Pope's talk, the whole assembly cried out, "God wills it; God wills it!"

Great excitement spread throughout Europe. Not only the nobility responded to the call of the Pope, but also the common people.

The first crusade began. It is sometimes called the Knights' Crusade. When it reached the Holy Land, it met with stubborn resistance. The Crusaders, however, finally succeeded in taking Jerusalem. Godfrey of Bouillon was named the first king of Jerusalem. When the ceremony of coronation took place, he refused to wear the crown. He said that he would never consent to wear a golden crown where his Savior had worn a crown of thorns.

Other crusades were led by the kings of England, France, and Germany. The motives behind them were not always unmixed. Some of them were partially successful; others were failures. St. Louis, king of France, led the last crusade. While on the crusade he was taken sick with a fever and died in Egypt.

The crusades ended by the thirteenth century. Gradually the Christians retreated from the East. The Turks recaptured Jerusalem, after it had been in the power of the Christians for about eighty years. The Turks remained in possession of the holy places until an English army, operating in Palestine during World War I, seized Jerusalem.

RESULTS OF THE CRUSADES

Although the crusades failed in their chief aim, the recovery and liberation of the Holy Lands, they did produce great benefits for both Christianity and civilization. Some of these were:

1. They prompted a spirit of unity among the nations of Europe. They did this by bringing together their rulers in a common cause.

2. They renewed Christian faith and charity.

3. They strengthened the influence of the Church.

4. They fostered the religious spirit among Christian knights.

5. They gave European princes objectives other than quarreling among themselves or with their rulers.

6. They broadened knowledge, increased commerce, and improved the art of navigation.

7. They encouraged intellectual development, art, science, and literature.

8. They temporarily prevented the Turks from moving farther into Europe.

MILITARY ORDERS

The crusades prompted chivalry. Chivalry refers to following the rules and ideals of knighthood, which had begun to develop earlier but reached a peak during the Holy Wars. The knight was sworn to lead a pure and honorable life, to protect the weak, and defend the faith. He was considered to be a real Christian gentleman of his times.

There were three important orders of knights. *The Knights Templar*, so called because they once had their headquarters on the site of the Temple of Solomon. They were outstanding fighters and were distinguished by their white cloaks and red crosses. *The Knights of St. John*, who built hospitals in the Holy Land and took care of the sick and wounded, wore a black cloak upon which was sewed a white cross. *The Teutonic Knights*, in white cloaks adorned with black crusader's crosses, were German nobles. Like the Knights of St. John, they too, built hospitals and cared for the sick.

MENDICANT ORDERS

Some religious orders, known as Mendicant Orders, were founded at this time. The word *mendicant* means "beggar." Members of these orders went out among the people and asked for alms. They were living models of the Gospel they preached. Their aim was to serve as a haven of holiness among the ever growing number of townsmen. The monks of older communities, who were attached to a given monastery and who lived in rural areas, could not, by the very nature of their religious life, do much for the urban peoples.

THE FRANCISCANS

In such disturbed times, Francis of Assisi was born. He was the son of wealthy parents, but as a young man he decided to give away all that he had and to live a life of poverty. Some of his friends joined him. They went about preaching and helping the poor. His little band soon blossomed into an order, and the Pope granted them permission to carry on the work of preaching by word and example. Today this great order of Franciscans, divided into many branches, carries on the work of its founder.

With the help of St. Clare, St. Francis founded another order called the Poor Clares for women who wished to live a life of penance. They practiced great poverty and consecrated their lives to God by prayer and fasting.

St. Francis did not forget about the men and women who lived in the world. He knew that they too were destined for eternal life. To help them he founded a Third Order, whose rules were such that people living in the world could observe them without too great hardship. Through the centuries many kings, queens, nobles, and ordinary laymen have joined the Third Order. Many are numbered among the Church's greatest saints.

"Men lose all the material things they leave behind them in this world, but they carry with them the reward of their charity and the alms they give. For these, they will receive from the Lord the reward and recompense they deserve."

—ST. FRANCIS OF ASSISI

The Rosary: The Sword of the Dominicans

St. Dominic is known as the saint that helped spread the practice of the praying of the Rosary. The order he founded, the Dominicans, today wear a long rosary on their hips. This is meant to symbolize how a knight wore his sword on his hip, teaching us that the rosary is a powerful weapon in spiritual warfare.

THE DOMINICANS

At about the same time St. Dominic, a Spanish nobleman, founded the Dominicans. He was ordained a priest at the end of brilliant university studies. Shortly after this, the Pope ordered him to go to southern France and there to preach against certain heretics. Dominic, together with a few companions, labored for a number of years among these heretics. One of the weapons that he used to bring about their return to the Faith was the Rosary.

Dominic later decided to organize his preachers into an order that would fight heresy throughout the world. St. Dominic also founded an order for women who had as their aim the education of girls and women who had been converted from heresy. He also established a Dominican Third Order, to help in the sanctification of laymen.

The Church Encourages the Arts and Sciences

ARTS IN THE SERVICE OF RELIGION

The eleventh century saw a great era of building begin. With it a new style of architecture, called Romanesque, developed in northern Italy, France, and Germany. It is recognized by its rounded arches and by its thick walls.

Gothic architecture also can be found in practically every country of Europe.

Many Gothic cathedrals were begun in the first quarter of the twelfth century. The main features of the Gothic style are: thinner and higher walls, and large windows topped by pointed arches instead of round ones.

These cathedrals, which were raised all over Europe, were not the work of a few men. Whole cities, and people from all walks of life, worked on them. As a consequence, they may be considered as monuments to the faith and craftsmanship of the people of the Middle Ages.

Religion entered into the whole life of the Middle Ages. That is why the most important buildings of the time are religious buildings. Nourished by the liturgy of the Church, the people of those days were determined that the place where the redeeming sacrifice was offered should far surpass a baron's castle or a prince's palace both in beauty and greatness.

SCHOLASTICISM

Theologians, that is, those devoted to the scientific study of God's revealed truths, developed a method of teaching which was called the Scholastic method or Scholasticism. The scholastics, or schoolmen, had the rich intellectual heritage of the Fathers and Doctors of the Church to draw from. They were, moreover, faced with interpreting and evaluating the ancient wisdom of Greece, whose thought flowed into western Europe at this time through the medium of Islamic culture. The story told by faith and that told by the Greeks differed on many counts. The work of relating the two and of meeting the problems posed by the discovery of Greek thought was taken up by the schoolmen, chief of whom was St. Thomas Aquinas. The patron of Catholic learning, Thomas infused new life into theology and drew together the most splendid features of past thought, both pagan and Christian, into an original and magnificent whole. His writings are used in every Catholic university and seminary. The "*O Salutaris*" and "*Tantum Ergo*," sung at Benediction of the Blessed

Sacrament, were written by St. Thomas, revealing him as a poet as well as a theologian.

The Church also gave the world the great Christian poet Dante. He wrote the *Divine Comedy*, one of the greatest religious poems of all times. The poem tells the story of a soul who makes a journey through hell, purgatory, and heaven. To some extent it enshrined St. Thomas in magnificent poetry, as the cathedrals enshrined the Catholic faith in stone and glass.

THE GUILDS

During these centuries merchants and craftsmen who were engaged in the same business or occupation banded together into groups called "guilds." The aim of the guilds was to promote both the spiritual and temporal welfare of the merchants and workers. When a young man wished to become a member of a guild, he began as an apprentice. This was his training period. As a journeyman, he practiced his trade or craft. After a few years as a journeyman, he could become a master guildsman. Men who turned out careless work were expelled from the guilds.

The Church encouraged the guilds and bestowed upon them spiritual benefits. Each guild had its own patron saint, sometimes its own chapel. At certain times during the year the members of a guild would attend Mass and receive Holy Communion in a group. They were lavish in their gifts to religion. On great festivals of the Church each guild marched in procession, carrying its own banner. These organizations, guided by the Church in justice and charity, afforded protection to the workers and helped to promote their spiritual and social life. They made possible a condition of stability and justice in society.

FOR ME TO REVIEW

Questions and Exercises

Part 1: Complete the sentence

1. A system of landholding during the Middle Ages was known as _____.

2. Under the feudal system, a person who was assigned a grant of land in exchange for a promise of military service was called a _____.

3. The estate which such a person held was called a _____.

4. The problem of lay investiture was finally settled by an agreement or _____.

5. In 800 A.D. _____ was crowned Emperor by the Pope.

6. The _____ forbade fighting during Lent and Advent and, during the remaining part of the year, from Wednesday night until the following Monday morning.

7. Two of the mendicant orders in the Church were the _____ and the _____.

8. Workingmen's organizations during the Middle Ages were called _____.

9. _____ referred to the rules and ideals of knighthood.

10. Two types of architecture which developed at this time were the _____ and _____

Part 2: Match column I with column II

Column I

1. Pope Gregory
2. Charlemagne
3. Concordat
4. St. Francis
5. St. Dominic
6. Lay investiture
7. Crusades
8. Feudalism
9. Guilds
10. Truce of God

Column II

A. Protected the merchants and workers

B. A system of landholding

C. Founded the Franciscan Order

D. The appointment of bishops and abbots by temporal rulers

E. Emperor of the Roman Empire in the West

F. Fought against the evil of lay investiture

G. Forbade fighting at certain times of the year

H. Preached against some heretics in southern France

I. Agreement between Church and State

J. Aimed to get the Holy Places back from the Turks

Part 3: Questions to Check Your Reading

1. How did Charlemagne help the Church's efforts in education?

2. How did the universities come into existence?

3. What was the work of the vassal in the feudal system?

4. Explain the practice of lay investiture.

5. Name some benefits derived from the Crusades.

6. Why were the Military Orders important during these centuries?

7. Why were the religious orders founded at this time called mendicant?

8. What was the purpose of the Third Order of St. Francis?

9. Describe the Romanesque type of architecture.

10. What were the main features of the Gothic style?

11. How did the Church enter into the spirit of the guilds?

12. What did the guilds do for the worker?

13. What did St. Thomas Aquinas do? Dante?

 FOR ME TO DO

1. Draw a Romanesque and a Gothic arch.

2. Write a story of a boy who is apprenticed to a craftsman. Tell of his labors as an apprentice, his adventures as a journeyman, his skill as a craftsman. Stress the part religion played in his life as a member of the guild.

3. Read about the life of St. Francis, St. Clare, and St. Dominic.

4. Read the book *King Arthur and the Knights of the Round Table.*

CHAPTER 34

The Church and the Renaissance

During the fourteenth and fifteenth centuries vast changes swept across Europe. These affected the political, cultural, and religious outlook of Europe and marked the transition from the medieval to the modern world. As with most changes in human history, good and bad elements intermingled, and all had their repercussions on the Church.

These centuries saw an intense study of the classics of pagan Greece and Rome, the invention of the printing press and the consequent diffusion of knowledge on a wider scale, the discovery of distant lands and the subsequent scurry by European princes to establish far-flung empires, and a growing desire on the part of expanding urban populations for more direct participation in government.

By the end of the fifteenth century the old Empire of the West was merely a symbol of past greatness; new nation states had come into existence, with political authority vested in national princes and with a rising middle class seeking ways to curb and limit that authority. The period of creative genius among the Scholastics had passed, their successors being at times more concerned with victory in argument than with truth. In the process the popes, who had almost singlehanded preserved the unity of the old Roman Empire, lost much of their prestige and political power, and strong secular princes were only too ready to fill and intensify the vacuum created by this decline in papal authority and respect.

The Renaissance was a fast-moving era in European history. Here we shall merely try to trace some of the more striking aspects of this period in so far as they affected the life of Christ's Mystical Body, the Church.

The Political and Religious Scene

TERMS TO KNOW

- Renaissance
- Savonarola
- Papal Humanism
- classics
- Black Plague
- nepotism

THE TRIAL AT ANAGNI

By the end of the thirteenth century France towered above Germany as the leading nation of the world; but she needed money to carry on her wars and to make her progress permanent. Therefore King Philip, the Fair, grandson of St. Louis IX, levied heavy taxes on his people, and he did not spare the Church. When the clergy protested to Rome, Pope Boniface VIII insisted that taxes could not be levied on the Church without the Church's consent. Philip retaliated by holding back the papal taxes due from France. Eventually Boniface issued a bull in which he claimed that salvation depends on obedience to the Pope. Philip, enraged, sent troops to Italy to arrest the Pope. The Pope was imprisoned in his palace at Anagni, a town in central Italy. Boniface stood firm, however, and refused to repeal his decrees on the supremacy of the spiritual over the temporal. Philip's agents were perplexed, for they feared to kill the Pope and they realized that the people would never allow them to carry him captive to France.

Finally, the people of Anagni freed the Pope and carried him back to Rome, where he died soon afterward.

THE POPE SPEAKS

Benedict XI, the successor of Boniface, tried to make peace with Philip, but would not bow to his demands. The Pope did, however, appoint many French cardinals who attained great influence in the Church. Benedict issued a decree in which he stated that the Lord's anointed may not be outraged.

Benedict died suddenly, in 1304, after a nine-month reign. Philip seized this opportunity to have a Frenchman elected Pope in the person of Clement V.

THE BABYLONIAN EXILE (1309–1377)

At the pressing invitation of Philip, Pope Clement V transferred the Papal court to a Papal City, Avignon ('a-vin-yon), in south-eastern France. This began a period lasting seventy years during which seven popes, all Frenchmen, reigned at Avignon. The Italians called it the Babylonian Captivity, in memory of the Jews of the Old Testament who had been in exile in Babylon for a comparable period. Other nations resented the control that the French kings thus exercised over the Church.

Although Clement moved the Papal court to Avignon he did not yield to Philip's demands that he condemn his predecessor Boniface and repudiate his decrees. But Clement did yield to one of Philip's demands for the suppression of the Knights Templar, whose property Philip coveted.

Clement's reign is notable for the numerous examples of piety which nourished the Faith in various countries. In France, there were holy women like St. Delphine and St. Roselind, and men like St. Roch who, while nursing those stricken by the plague, was himself afflicted with the dread disease.

The Papal Palace in Avignon, France

Clement's successor, John XXII, was elected after the chair of Peter had been vacant for two years. His reign saw Germany the scene of a prolonged battle between Lewis of Bavaria and Frederick of Austria for sole command and for the title, by now hereditary for the German kings, of "Holy Roman Emperor." Lewis eventually won out, but John refused to recognize him as Emperor. Lewis found allies and eventually Lewis even declared Pope John deposed and installed a rival "pope," known as Nicholas V.

Trouble with the German princes continued to plague John's successors, Benedict XII and Clement VI. During the latter's reign (1342–1352) more trouble for Europe arose, this time in the form of disease—The Black Plague.

This was brought from China and India by Italian trading ships. About two thirds of the people of Europe died of the Black Death. When Clement heard that the Jews were being accused of poisoning wells, and were being put to death, he forbade this injustice, under pain of excommunication.

It is hard to exaggerate the effects of this horrible plague which killed some forty million people in less than two years. It left the people dispirited, listless, although Clement sought to revitalize Christian life by proclaiming a jubilee year in 1350.

A TRUE APOSTLE

Clement was followed by Innocent VI, who enacted wise rules and initiated reforms. To soothe the princes, Innocent modified somewhat the proclamations of his predecessors regarding the rights of temporal rulers, but he chose cardinals of tried skill and political genius to send to Italy. If he could rescue the Papal States, he planned to return to Rome with his court. "Church dignities," said Innocent, "should be the reward of virtue, not of birth." Innocent died before he could carry out plans to return to Rome.

THE PROPHECY OF ST. BRIDGET

Pope Urban V announced to the cardinals and princes of Europe that he would follow Innocent's plan. True to his word, in 1376 he left Avignon with a fleet of twenty-three ships. Hailed in Italy with great joy, he went directly to the tomb of the Apostles, and then took possession of the Vatican. The peace he was supposed to bring unfortunately lasted but a short while. The Italian princes again seized the Papal States and fought savagely to hold them.

Urban had an audience with the Swedish princess Bridget, who asked permission to found an Order, with God's help, under his direction. The Pope recognized her great fervor and learned of her penances. Bridget, in turn, having heard of Urban's plan to return to France, foretold that he would die suddenly.

After landing at Avignon, the Pope was struck with a fatal disease. In a short time he died. St. Bridget's virtues were recognized by the Church in later years, and she was canonized.

THE END OF THE EXILE

Pope Gregory XI settled the Roman question once and for all, despite the special pleading of the French cardinals. He left Avignon, and returned to Rome. The "Babylonian Exile" of the popes was, fortunately, ended.

Gregory's return of the Papacy to Rome was due in large measure to the prayers and courageous leadership of St. Catherine of Siena, truly one of the greatest saints of the fourteenth century.

The Papacy was "home" again, but the return proved to be a martyrdom. To add to the Pope's worries, news came that a detestable heresy was being preached in England by John Wycliffe. This heretic declared that God had abandoned the world to evil, and that there was no need of either pope or clergy. Sorely oppressed by these terrible calamities in the Christian world. Gregory died one year later.

THE GREAT WESTERN SCHISM

Immediately after Gregory's death in 1378 the cardinals, amid great unrest, elected an Italian Pope, Urban VI. They crowned him at St. Peter's and paid him homage. Three months later the French cardinals returned to Avignon, where six other cardinals had remained. They proceeded to "elect" a Frenchman, who called himself Clement VII, after charging that Urban's election had been swayed by Italian mobs. Thus began the great Western Schism with two men claiming to be pope. Matters were even more confused later on, when a third "pope," called Alexander V, was "elected" by some of the cardinals in Pisa.

During this period the people were greatly confused. Even saints were divided in their opinions. Though Christendom was sorely put, the Divine Shepherd did not desert His true Vicar Urban VI and his legitimate successors. It was difficult, however, for many people to know surely who was actually the true Vicar of Christ.

CATHERINE SPEAKS

St. Catherine lent her support to Urban. "Can it be true," she wrote to the cardinals, "that you who should be the bucklers of faith, the defenders of the Church, the pastors of the flock, have become hirelings and ungrateful children! For you know the truth, you know you have repeatedly proclaimed that Urban is the rightful Pope, . . . instead of shining as lights set upon a mountain you have become followers of the angel of darkness."

The dispute over who was the true pope lasted for forty years, 1378–1418. During all this there were four who falsely claimed to be the pope, two antipopes at Avignon, and two at Pisa.

THE COUNCIL AT CONSTANCE

Gregory XII, successor of the true Pope, Urban VI, secretly urged Emperor Sigismund to call a General Council to put on end to this schism. Churchmen and nobles went. The antipope, John XXIII (of Pisa) was deposed. Gregory resigned his rightful title, and finally the antipope Benedict XIII (of Avignon) was forced to resign.

Success of the council was no doubt partly due to the prayers of great saints living at that time, such as St. Vincent Ferrer and St. Bridget.

THE END OF THE SCHISM

After the Chair of Peter had been vacant for two years, the council called the Papal electors from France, Italy, Spain, England, Germany, and other smaller countries. They elected Martin V to the Papal throne in 1417.

Martin appointed only a few but fervent Cardinals to help him reform the abuses that had crept into the Church. One of Martin's chief troubles was trying to make peace between England and France. These countries had quarreled over crowns and about lands for about a hundred years. Each had asked the help of the Pope. A frail girl was the means which God used to put an end to the turmoil.

THE MAID OF ORLEANS

In Domremy, France, a virtuous peasant girl, Joan of Arc (1413–1431), was granted visions, and favored with heavenly voices who revealed themselves as St. Michael, St. Catherine, and St. Margaret. These voices told her to go to the aid of the king of France. He put her in charge of his army. She armed herself with a sword and held in her hand a white standard, spangled with golden lilies and bearing as a pledge of victory the names of Jesus and Mary. Under her leadership the French troops won a victory at Orleans and continued to drive the English back into the English Channel.

Through her victories Joan succeeded in having the king crowned Charles VII of France, at Rheims (rēmz). In a decisive battle, the French army was victorious, although in a counttercharge Joan was captured by the English.

She was betrayed by a group of traitorous Frenchmen, tried for heresy and witchcraft, and condemned to death. The maid of Orleans, calling on the name of Jesus, was burned at the stake in the market place.

A few years after her death her case was reopened. Then, it was publicly declared that she had died a martyr for her faith, for her king, and for her country. The Church, in 1920, proclaimed that her virtues and miracles merited for her the title "St. Joan of Arc."

"If I said that God did not send me, I should condemn myself; truly God did send me."

—St. Joan of Arc

SPAIN UNITES

At this time Spain finally became a truly unified country. The Moors, who had gradually been pushed back, still held on to the kingdom of Granada. The other leading kingdoms were those of Aragon and Castile, and they were united in the marriage of Ferdinand of Aragon to Isabella of Castile. Ferdinand and Isabella defeated the Moors in the famous battle of Granada in 1492, and thus Moslem rule in Spain came to an end.

In the same year Columbus left Spain to discover a new route to the Far East. His voyages would not have been possible without the generous aid and personal interest of Queen Isabella. Through Spain's efforts, Christianity was first brought to the new world. The importance of Columbus' discoveries and those that followed cannot be appreciated rightly unless we study the Church and her triumphs in America.

True, the worldly spirit behind the development of great nations in Europe had turned the minds of men away from spiritual truths. This spirit of worldliness had crept into the lives of men, causing them to lose their sense of spiritual values. Because of the new learning and new developments, Christian ideals exerted less influence over men. The Church could not be but greatly affected by those changes, as we shall now see.

The Cultural and Religious Scene

HUMANISTS

A revival of the pagan classical writers of Greece and Rome at the beginning of the century spread far and wide. Some made use of these classics to teach Christian ideals. Others promoted the pagan ideas and ideals.

The Church tried to direct the study of the classics through Christian leaders. Following the trend of the times, popes became patrons of the arts and letters. They invited to the Papal Court hosts of writers, artists, and scientists. They aimed to make

Italy the center of this great revival. Unfortunately, they were sometimes led astray by the magnificence and worldly splendor of their surroundings.

CONDITIONS OF THE TIMES

The popes were often forced to protect the Papal States from greedy kings. To do this they raised armies, collected taxes, and appointed officers who would be loyal to the Church. Sometimes they gave important positions to their own relatives, a practice called "nepotism." Many of these were priests or ordained noblemen who used their power for selfish purposes.

A PATRON OF HUMANISM

Pope Nicholas reigned when the Turks captured Constantinople, the capital of the Greek Church (1453). To him, and to the Roman Church as well, this was a calamity. All had hoped and prayed that the Greeks would unite under the Pope. Many Greeks fled to Italy. They brought with them numerous classics. These were added to the thousands of manuscripts already in the Vatican Library, which had just been completed. They gave an added impetus to humanism.

LIBERATORS OF ITALY

Many French nobles ruled large kingdoms in Italy, including church property. Pope Julius raised an army and drove them out. His fearlessness in saving the Papal States won for him the title "Savior of the Church."

The Pope planned to build a new St. Peter's Cathedral. He invited Michelangelo to decorate the ceiling of the Sistine Chapel in the Vatican. He sought to make Rome, the Holy Land of Europe, as beautiful as the Jerusalem of old.

LAST OF THE RENAISSANCE POPES

Leo X continued to support many scholars at the Papal residence. He encouraged the circulation of books, which he was able to do because the printing press had just been invented. Students in all the schools and universities were interested not only in reading the classics, but also in reading books of devotion, and especially the Bible, which was printed in many languages. Some popes of this period were very worldly and used their power for unworthy purposes.

SAVONAROLA

One courageous Dominican, Savonarola preached violently against the evils practiced in his native city of Florence and urged reform for the clergy. Eventually Savonarola's zeal for reform carried him to excess. He refused to obey the Pope and was eventually excommunicated. Charges of heresy were brought against him. He was imprisoned along with some of his followers, and was finally burned at the stake. Later it was proved that he had not been guilty of false teachings.

RENAISSANCE ARTISTS

In the fine arts the Humanists produced much that has gained world-wide acclaim. Most of the paintings and sculpture dealt with religious subjects but with a humanistic style. This humanistic style focused on the greatness of man, often turning the attention of the viewer to earth. Such a focus differs from the medievalists, whose works pointed heavenward.

Fra Angelico, a saintly Dominican, was perhaps the greatest painter of religious subjects. His masterpiece the "Annunciation" expressed best the spirituality of his art.

One of the greatest pioneers in science and invention was Leonardo da Vinci. He also excelled in sculpture, music, philosophy, experimental science (he designed an airplane), and architecture. His painting the "Last Supper" is renowned for its portrayal of the emotions of the twelve Apostles at the moment when Christ announced His betrayal.

Raphael is considered one of the greatest painters of all times. His "Sistine Madonna" is a religious masterpiece which has never been surpassed.

Another great genius of the period was Michelangelo, whose famous statue of "David" showed his ability to transform cold stone into energetic lifelike statues. His paintings on the ceiling of the Sistine Chapel proved that he was outstanding in this field of endeavor, too. He designed the dome of St. Peter's, since called one of the wonders of the world.

All of this artistic beauty would have been lost to the world had the Church not been true to her title "Patron of Arts and Letters." The examples of art in our churches today are evidence of the interior spiritual beauty which Christian artists tried to express. Our great universities and libraries are a heritage of scholars of past centuries, and they are also so many torches to light the way for the children of today and tomorrow.

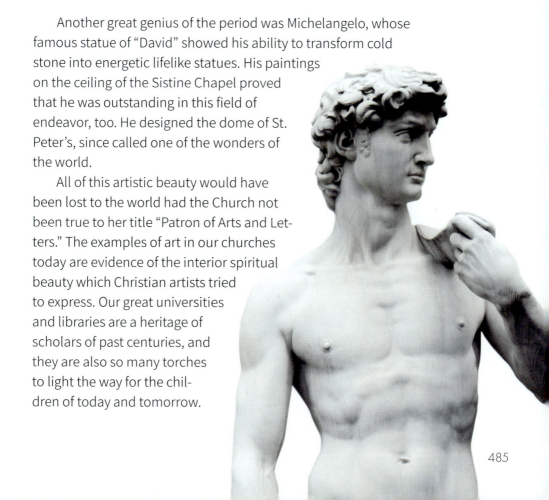

FOR ME TO REVIEW

Questions and Exercises

Part 1: Complete the following statements

1. Renaissance is a French word which means _____.
2. The struggle between France and England lasted for a long period of about _____.
3. The great Spanish rulers at this time were _____ and _____
4. The Queen of Spain encouraged and helped the explorer _____.
5. The saint who pleaded with the Pope to return to Rome was _____.
6. A Dominican friar who was excommunicated for his disobedience _____.
7. The movement which had for one of its purposes the study of the classics was called _____.

Part 2: Match column I with column II

Column I	Column II
1. Joan of Arc	A. "The Annunciation"
2. Fra Angelico	B. Statue of Moses
3. Michelangelo	C. Sistine Madonna
4. Leonardo da Vinci	D. urged Pope Gregory to return to Rome
5. Pope Boniface VIII	E. foretold that Pope Urban V would die suddenly
6. Pope John XXIII	F. "Maid of Orleans"
7. Raphael	G. "The Last Supper"
8. Philip the Fair	H. antipope of Pisa who was deposed
9. St. Catherine of Siena	I. disagreed with Pope Boniface VIII
10. St. Bridget	J. was imprisoned in his palace at Anagni

Part 3: Questions to Check Your Reading

1. Give some important points about the Babylonian Exile.

2. Tell how the Great Western Schism came about.

3. What was the effect of the Great Western Schism on the Church?

4. Tell some interesting facts about St. Joan of Arc.

5. What was one of the purposes of Humanism?

6. In this period what was the meaning of the word Classics?

7. What was the practice of nepotism?

8. What was the effect of the Renaissance on Christianity?

☑ FOR ME TO DO

1. Research some famous pictures painted by the great artists of the Renaissance. Discuss them in class. Notice the use of religious subjects.

2. Make a class scrapbook containing exterior and interior views of St. Peter's Basilica. Write short explanations of the artist and his art work depicted in the pictures.

3. Write a scene from the life of St. Joan of Arc. Present it to the class.

4. Read a more detailed account of King Ferdinand and Queen Isabella and their battles against the Moors.

CHAPTER 35

The Revolt Against the Authority of Christ's Church

During the Middle Ages the people of Europe, despite the differences that divided them, were united in the Catholic faith and were one in calling the pope, Peter's successor, Christ's Vicar on earth. During the sixteenth century this unity of faith was shattered, and soon whole nations broke from Rome.

The Protestant Reformation

ITS MEANING

The movement which drew nations away from the true Church is often called the Protestant Reformation: "Protestant," because the leaders protested against the teaching and practices of the Church; "Reformation," because they claimed that they were reforming the Church. This movement was also called the Protestant Revolt, because it was a rebellion against the authority of Christ's Church. As a result of this revolt most of the countries of northern Europe broke away from the Catholic Church.

ITS CAUSES

The Church is Christ's Mystical Body and has been entrusted by Our Lord to the guidance of the Holy Spirit. But the Church is also a visible society, and her members on earth are men of flesh and blood who are not yet confirmed in grace. Although the Church, enlightened by the Holy Spirit, infallibly and ceaselessly preaches the whole of Christ's message, her members are not all saints, and this has been true, at times, of popes and bishops and priests as well as of religious and laymen. Thus, there is constant need for

true Christians to dedicate themselves anew to the example of Christ. During the period prior to the Protestant Reformation, many abuses had crept into the lives of Christians. Frequently, high posts in the Church were given to unqualified, unworthy men. Moreover, the pagan trends of the Renaissance, and the prolonged absence of the popes from Rome during "The Babylonian Captivity," coupled with the Great Western Schism, and many other events disturbed the faithful. Discontent found its way into the hearts of many. A genuine revitalization of Christian life was needed. This was to come with the Council of Trent (1545–1563), but not before the seamless garment of Christ had been torn by heresy and great numbers were lost to the Church.

TERMS TO KNOW

- Reformation
- indulgences
- Protestant
- Lutheranism
- revolt
- Council

THE REFORMATION IN GERMANY

The Preaching of Indulgences

The Pope, Leo X, wanted to raise money for the rebuilding of St. Peter's in Rome. To encourage people to donate to this worthy cause, he offered a plenary indulgence, the remission of all the temporal punishment due for sins already remitted, to all who would contribute. The indulgence was to be granted, of course, on the usual conditions of confession, Communion, a complete detachment from sin, even venial sin, and a prayer for the intentions of the Holy Father.

John Tetzel, a Dominican, was appointed by the Pope to preach this indulgence in Germany, and to collect the alms of the people. However, we must not disregard the view that Tetzel's preaching appeared less like a call for "alms" (i.e., freely given gifts, usually for the aid of the poor) and more like a fraudulent and spiritually corrupt scheme that put monetary gain before the genuine spiritual good of Christ's flock. Tetzel, though himself not ignorant of the correct doctrine regarding indulgences, unduly emphasized the giving of money itself as sufficient for obtaining the indulgence; as a result, it appeared as if the Church was "selling" indulgences. Specifically, it is known that some of Tetzel's public speeches inclined people to believe that as soon as they handed over their money, the souls of their deceased loved ones, who—as Tetzel vividly reminded them—were suffering in purgatory, would be immediately released into heaven. Though indulgences may be directed at aiding those in purgatory, this was certainly an irresponsible, false, and manipulative presentation of indulgences and their proper role. In time, the Church took this problem seriously, for at the Council of Trent the selling of indulgences was categorically prohibited.

Martin Luther, an Augustinian monk and learned professor of theology, used this indulgence controversy to call attention to his own views. He summarized the differences between his interpretation of the Gospel and that traditionally held by the Church in ninety-five propositions, which he nailed to the church door of Wittenberg.

Luther's Teaching

In his personal life, Luther had always been very fearful about salvation. He had become a monk, but he still was tormented, for he wanted positive assurance that he would be saved. Ultimately,

Luther concluded that original sin had so damaged human nature that it was impossible to be good. Because the penance which he performed in the monastery did not put an end to his fears and did not bring him peace, perhaps we can see why Luther was inclined to think that good works were not necessary for salvation. At any rate, Luther drew heavily from Scripture and the early Church Fathers to defend the charges he made against the Church of his time. He thought that the offense of sin was too grave to be wholly blotted out, and that good works were useless for our justification before God. Hence, along with his public attack on indulgences, Luther began to preach the key Lutheran doctrine that faith alone—without works—is sufficient for salvation. But the Catholic Church teaches that faith alone is not sufficient; good works must accompany it. Hear these words from the letter of James: "What good is it, my brothers and sisters, if you say you have faith but do not have works? Can faith save you? If a brother or sister is naked and lacks daily food, and one of you says to them, 'Go in peace; keep warm and eat your fill,' and yet you do not supply their bodily needs, what is the good of that? So faith by itself, if it has no works, is dead" (James 2:14–17).

Now, Luther also taught that each person was able to interpret the Bible for himself; that is, in rejecting the existence and need of the Catholic Church as the final authority on biblical interpretation, he was left to assert the doctrine of private interpretation. Because of this doctrine, the Protestants came to have serious differences concerning their own teachings, which in turn, led to animosity and further schism. As is very evident today, the Protestant churches became more and more divided, until many different denominations and sects arose.

In addition, Luther denied the authority of the Pope. He also maintained that there were only two sacraments founded by Christ, Baptism and the Holy Eucharist, although he did recognize the usefulness of the other five.

News of Luther's errors reached the Pope. At the Diet of Worms (1521), an official assembly called on behalf of the Church, Luther would not recant his teaching, which by then had been spread throughout Germany. As a result, Luther was excommunicated and charged as a heretic. Had Luther not been rescued afterwards by his sympathizers, it is very likely that the Church would have publicly executed him, as was the fate of Jan Huss, who was burned at the stake in 1415 on charges of heresy.

Rapid Spread of Lutheranism

During the lifetime of Luther about half of the people of Germany left the Church and became Lutherans. His doctrines also found acceptance in the Scandinavian countries and in parts of France. However, the basic principle of Lutheranism, namely, that the individual believer was free to interpret Scripture, justified in advance opposing interpretations of Christ's revelation. Soon, therefore, others arose who offered men different forms of Protestantism.

In Switzerland, Huldrych Zwingli, a major leader of the Protestant revolt, did away with the Mass, with vestments, altars, and pictures. He also denied the Real Presence in the Blessed Sacrament. Protestantism was brought from Switzerland into France by John Calvin. According to Catholic teaching, God is the principal cause of our salvation. Grace is a gift, freely given, and God knows those who will persevere in this gift and gain eternal life. According to Catholic teaching, man is also a free being and is responsible for his actions and for his cooperation with God's grace. Calvin lost sight of this second teaching and overemphasized the first. For him, man is so weak because of original sin that he can do nothing to gain heaven. According to Calvin, God has ordained that some be saved while others be damned, despite what they do.

In Scotland, the leader of the Protestants was John Knox who preached the doctrines of Calvin. For both, Baptism and the Holy Eucharist are the only two genuine sacraments, and both denied Christ's real presence in the Eucharist.

THE REBELLION IN ENGLAND

Henry VIII

When Martin Luther denied the authority of the Church and spread his false teachings in Germany, Henry VIII, King of England, defended the Pope and opposed Luther. He wrote an excellent book on the seven sacraments. Because of this defense, the Pope gave Henry the title of "Defender of the Faith." Yet Henry soon revolted against the Church himself and became its bitter enemy.

The separation of England from the Church followed a different pattern from that of the revolt of other countries. Henry VIII had been married to Catherine of Aragon. After many years of marriage, he asked the Pope to declare the marriage invalid. The Pope, however, declared that the marriage was valid. Finally, Henry declared himself the head of the Church of England, put away Catherine, his lawful wife, and quickly married Anne Boleyn. He soon tired of her, and within a short time, married four others.

The Church of England

Henry VIII ordered all his subjects to take an oath against the authority of the Pope. In its stead, they were told to accept the king as their spiritual leader. Thousands of Catholics remained true to their faith, and refused to take the oath against the Pope. Many of these were martyred and others were put into prison.

St. John Fisher, Bishop of Rochester, refused to take the oath with the words, "I dare not tear the seamless robe of Christ." He was beheaded with others who were brave enough to oppose the king. St. Thomas More, a famous scholar, chancellor, and a favorite at the royal court, also surrendered his life rather than deny his faith.

Because of his many extravagances, Henry VIII was on the verge of bankruptcy. He stole land from monasteries and convents, and ordered all church money to be given to him. As a result, the charitable organizations, such as orphanages and poor houses of the Church, were unable to carry on, and poor people were deprived of the relief which the Church had formerly given. But during Henry's time Mass was still offered and there was little change in the doctrines proposed by those churchmen who weakly yielded to Henry's demands that they regard him as head of the Church in England.

The Successors of Henry VIII

Henry was succeeded by his son, Edward, a nine-year-old boy, who reigned for only six years. It was at this time that vast changes of doctrine worked their way into the Church of England. Many of Edward's advisers were taken by the ideas of the European reformers, and they cleverly reworked the liturgy and ritual to give it a Protestant meaning. The Mass was abolished and church laws were passed against "Romanists." Mary Tudor, the daughter of Henry and Catherine of Aragon, was crowned queen after the death of Edward. She ruled for five years and sought to re-establish the Catholic Church. She returned some property that had been stolen from the Church, and acknowledged the Pope as the supreme head of the Church. Mary, unfortunately, was harsh in re-establishing the faith, even ordering four Protestant bishops and certain of their followers to be burned at the stake. As a result, she has been called "Bloody Mary" by her enemies.

Elizabeth, the daughter of Henry VIII and Anne Boleyn, was crowned queen when Mary died. She professed to be a Catholic during Mary's reign, but as soon as she was crowned she declared that she was a Protestant. With great harshness, she re-enacted the laws of Edward VI against the Catholic Church. She required all her subjects to take the oath which declared her to be the head of the Church. She was finally excommunicated by the Pope.

Various tests and laws penalizing both Catholics and Protestants who disagreed with the policies of the Anglican Church were in effect in England until the nineteenth century.

EFFECTS OF THE REFORMATION

Bad Effects

The Protestant Reformation did much damage to the Church. The unity of faith was weakened, if not destroyed, in certain countries. People of the same race and nation professed different beliefs. Several religious wars brought misery and death to once happy nations. The denial of the Pope's authority led many to doubt, if not to lose, their faith. Gradually the way was prepared for the secularism and naturalism of the nineteenth and twentieth centuries.

Good Effects

Because it divided the Mystical Body of Christ (the Church), the Protestant Reformation as such was evil. Yet God allows evil only to draw from it a greater good. His Church needed genuine reforms to correct abuses that had crept into the life of its members. The reformers, who went to extremes in their reaction to some existing evils within the Church, dramatically called attention to the need for a re-examination of the Catholic faith and a rededication on the part of the faithful, both clergy and lay, to Christ their Lord.

The Council of Trent

Paul III, who became Pope in 1534, determined to call a General Council. Although many obstacles kept Paul from realizing this goal for several years, the Council finally met in the city of Trent in 1545 and lasted, off and on, for eighteen years. Because of wars and other emergencies, the bishops who attended sometimes had to return home until the trouble was over.

The content of our faith is the same as that of the Apostles. Thus, nothing new is taught when the Church meets in a General Council. The bishops who meet in Council under the direction of the Pope simply make these points explicit, especially those which have been the occasion of confusion or which have been denied by heretics.

During the Protestant Reformation, false teachings had been spread through Germany and other countries. Many of these teachings touched on dogmas which had not, at that time, been clearly defined by the Church. The Council took up all of these teachings, studied them carefully, showed why they were wrong, and then stated explicitly the true belief of the Catholic Church on each point.

In addition to defending and explaining the teachings of the Church, rules were made to regulate the instruction of the people, and the duties of priests and bishops. These rules were intended to help Catholics to lead a better life, and to bring about a closer union of the people with the pope, the bishops, and the priests.

St. Charles Borromeo

St. Charles Borromeo is sometimes called the "Saint of the Council of Trent." He worked very hard when the Council was in session. When it was over he took the main points of Catholic teaching which were settled by the Council, and with the help of a committee worked them into a Catechism. This book is called the *Catechism of the Council of Trent*. In it, Christian doctrine is explained most clearly. Charles Borromeo was later created Archbishop of Milan. There he worked long to correct abuses and to show his flock why the Protestant interpretation of God's revelation was erroneous.

Popes of the Reform

During this period the Church was blessed with worthy popes. The holiness of their lives served as a model for bishops, priests, and people. These popes appointed worthy cardinals, and approved new religious orders to carry out the reforms which the Council of Trent had begun.

NEW RELIGIOUS ORDERS IN THE CHURCH

The Society of Jesus

God, in His mercy, did not abandon His Church during the Reformation. New religious orders, well suited to meet the problems of the time, were founded in great numbers. Perhaps at no other

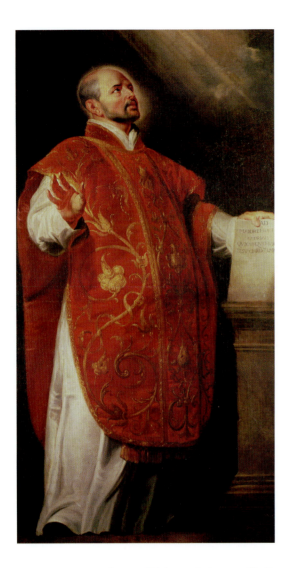

time has the Church had more glorious saints than during this period. One of these was St. Ignatius Loyola, who founded the Jesuits or the Society of Jesus.

Ignatius was a soldier in the Spanish army. During a battle he was seriously wounded. While recovering, he read the *Life of Christ* and the *Lives of the Saints*. These two books impressed him greatly, and as a result he decided to devote his life to the service of God.

Ignatius started his order with six companions, who were also inflamed with love for Christ and their fellow men. His society fought bravely to bring back those whom the Protestant Reformation had torn away from the Church. His purpose was to defend the faith at home, and to spread it abroad. His motto was, "For the greater glory of God."

One of the first six members of this society was St. Francis Xavier, a Spanish nobleman. Ignatius met him while they were studying in Paris. When he told Ignatius about his plans for the future, Ignatius said to him, "Francis, 'what does it profit a man if he gain the whole world, but suffers the loss of his soul?'" Ignatius later sent Francis Xavier as a missionary to the Far East. He is called the "Apostle of India and Japan" because of the great sacrifices he made to bring the Gospel to the people of Asia.

Other Congregations

Many other congregations were founded at this time. Some were designed to instruct priests and people, others were destined for missionary work, still others for the education of youth, and several for the care of the sick and the poor. Each congregation strove to give glory to God and the Church. It is impossible to name all of them, so we shall speak briefly of only a few.

The Capuchins, a branch of the Franciscan Order, were established in Italy. They spent their lives caring for the spiritual needs of the common people. The Visitation and Ursuline nuns devoted themselves principally to the care and education of young girls. St. Philip Neri loved the poor. Many people came to him for help. The Congregation of the Oratory was founded by him in the city of Rome. St. Philip is sometimes called the "Apostle of Rome."

The Sisters of Charity owe their origin to St. Vincent de Paul. They served the sick, the poor, orphans, prisoners, and the wounded on the battlefield. Many of them have died martyrs to duty. Their numbers increased, and today they are found not only in Europe but in America and throughout the world.

FOR ME TO REVIEW

Questions and Exercises

Part 1: Match column I with column II

Column I	Column II
1. Charles Borromeo	A. Was called "The Apostle of Rome"
2. Martin Luther	B. Renewed the laws of Henry VIII
3. Mary Tudor	C. Was given the title of "Defender of the Faith"
4. Thomas More	D. A book which clearly explains Catholic doctrine
5. Society of Jesus	E. Tried to re-establish the Catholic Church in England
6. St. Philip Neri	F. A bishop who refused to take the oath denying the authority of the Pope
7. Francis Xavier	G. A branch of the Franciscan Order
8. John Tetzel	H. Was called the "Saint of the Council of Trent"
9. Capuchins	I. Was Chancellor of England under Henry VIII
10. Sisters of Charity	J. The people of this country took an oath denying the authority of the Pope
11. Germany	K. Preached the indulgence in Germany
12. England	L. Was founded by St. Ignatius Loyola
13. Henry VIII	M. Denied the doctrine of indulgences
14. Elizabeth	N. The country in which the Protestant Revolt was started
15. John Fisher	O. Was called the Apostle of India and Japan
16. Catechism of the Council of Trent	P. Owe their origin to St. Vincent de Paul

Part 2: Questions to Check Your Reading

1. What is the Protestant Reformation?
2. What is meant by "Faith without good works"?

3. Why was Henry VIII given the title "Defender of the Faith"?

4. How did Henry VIII take to himself the power of the Church?

5. Did Bishop Fisher oppose Henry's action?

6. Why did Henry VIII close monasteries and convents?

7. What did Mary Tudor do for the Catholic Church in England?

8. Tell some things that happened to the Catholic Church during the reign of Queen Elizabeth.

9. Why was it necessary to hold a General Council at this time?

10. Did the Council of Trent teach new doctrines of Faith?

11. Why was Charles Borromeo called the "Saint of the Council of Trent"?

12. How did the popes of this time help to overcome heresies?

13. Name some religious orders established at this time.

14. Who was the "Apostle of Rome"?

✓ FOR ME TO DO

1. Give a short oral report on one of the following topics:
   a) The Beginning of Protestantism
   b) The Influence of Martin Luther
   c) Queen Elizabeth and the Catholic Church
   d) Religious Orders and Congregations

2. Write a letter in which you explain the errors of Lutheranism to an imaginary friend.

3. Create a quiz using the names of people and events mentioned in this chapter.

4. Write an article on one of the following:
   St. Ignatius of Loyola, Martin Luther, St. Francis Xavier, Henry VIII, St. Charles Borromeo, or Queen Elizabeth.

5. Choose one faithful man of this period and show how he helped spread the kingdom of God.

CHAPTER 36
The Enlightenment's Conflict With Revealed Religion

The Protestant Reformation led to the idea that each person was free to interpret the Bible in his own way, apart from any higher and final authority. We shall see how this false doctrine led to other evils which also drew people away from God.

Rulers began to interfere with and curb the rights of the Church. The kings of France, in particular, sought to separate the Church from Rome. Eventually, the Church in France was nearly destroyed by the French Revolution.

Despite the violent attacks and local losses, the Church remained firm. She continued to grow and to spread just like the mustard seed in the parable.

God Does Not Abandon Man

ST. MARGARET MARY ALACOQUE

As God in His divine mercy had repeatedly aided His Chosen People in the Old Testament, so in the New Testament He still sends individuals to lead people back to Christ. This they do by their holy lives and by good example.

At a time when indifference was increasing, the Sacred Heart appeared to St. Margaret Mary Alacoque in Paray-le-Monial and revealed His great love for mankind. Through her, and her confessor, He spread the devotion to His Sacred Heart. This devotion helps man to practice his faith and to awaken love and repentance in his heart.

ST. VINCENT DE PAUL

In the latter part of the sixteenth century, St. Vincent de Paul was born of a poor family in France. This family loved God above all things. Vincent was always touched by the poor and thought nothing of depriving himself to help them. In the course of time he was sent to school, and finally became a priest.

On one of his journeys as a priest something happened which persuaded him to devote his life to helping the poor and destitute. He was captured by Turkish pirates and sold as a slave in Tunis. Vincent succeeded in converting one of his masters, and together they returned to Europe. From then on, he strove only to free men from the slavery of sin and the devil. His works of charity took him to the slums, where the poorest and most debased human beings lived. He worked among galley slaves, prisoners, the insane, and the sick. St. Vincent's love of neighbor was a powerful instrument in God's hands for the salvation of men.

TERMS TO KNOW

- Enlightenment
- Secularism
- Freemasonry
- Rationalism
- indifferentism

Gradually the charity of Vincent de Paul attracted other men who wished to share his work. He accepted them and with them founded the community of St. Lazarus, popularly known as the Lazarists. This community is engaged chiefly in missionary work.

JOHN BAPTIST DE LA SALLE

John Baptist de La Salle, on the contrary, was born of well-to-do parents, in the middle of the seventeenth century. After ordination to the priesthood, he became interested in teaching, especially poor boys, many of whom he had rounded up in the street.

Later he formed the school masters who joined him in his project into a religious community, the Brothers of the Christian Schools. The order grew despite many struggles and poverty. He himself was treated with contempt, but he relied on God and went about his work.

God chose St. John Baptist as His instrument to save the poorest and the most abandoned children. Cooperating with God's grace, he threw himself into teaching. He introduced so many new ideas that he is considered a pioneer in modern education. John Baptist founded the first school for the training of teachers. He was the first to organize the elementary schools into grades. Realizing, moreover, that most of the poor boys would necessarily leave school at an early age, he provided training to prepare them to earn a decent living. He also left us excellent rules for the guidance of children.

Threats to the Church

RATIONALISM

Religious debate and even religious wars shook Europe for many years, leading some men to reject the notion of supernatural religion. They rejected faith and divine revelation and claimed that man should accept as true only what he could reason for himself. Thus, all doctrines, such as the Trinity and the Incarnation, were rejected by such Rationalists, as they were called.

THE ENLIGHTENMENT

The movement which embraced rationalist principles is known to history as the Enlightenment. We can think of it as being a series of ideas, writings, and teachings of various individuals and groups, all directed to this idea: Man should believe only what he can understand by thinking things through for himself; for many, this meant discarding the faith and the guidance of the Church. This movement was called the Enlightenment, because its leaders claimed that by it they were freeing the people from the ignorance and the darkness in which they believed the Church kept them. While the scientists and philosophers were mistaken in their view of the Church's relationship to reason, it remains true that at times the Church did not always eagerly accept their new scientific discoveries. The most famous instance was that of the astronomer Galileo Galilei. Galileo presented the Copernican system of "heliocentrism" to the Church, which challenged the pre-existing notion of "geocentrism." Geocentrism was important to the Church in that it fit with many scriptural descriptions of the earth's central relationship to the solar system, and therefore it's unique place within God's cosmos. While the Church till this day praises discoveries in the sciences and encourages the use of reason, many members of the Church were and continue to be imperfect. Additionally, many rightly feared the repercussions of giving science alone full rein over the minds of the people. "Faith and reason are like two wings on which the human spirit rises to the contemplation of truth" (Pope St. John Paul II, *Fides et Ratio*). But when reason abandons faith, as was common practice during the Enlightenment, men are left in the dark of their own fallen self. Many in the Enlightenment denied original sin and the consequent darkening of man's reason. They forgot that God bestows the grace of faith to enlighten man. In fact, some of them went so far as to deny the existence of God.

INDIFFERENTISM

Though the Enlightenment undeniably led to progress in the natural sciences and other arts, it brought along many assumptions that did a great deal of harm to religion. A spirit of indifferentism began to appear. Indifferentism as a doctrine teaches that one religion is as good as another. It maintains that it does not really matter what a person believes, so long as he observes the "golden rule" and is a good citizen. Although it is important to observe the "golden rule," it is even more important to accept God's word and to know the love of Christ (who taught us the Golden Rule). This, the men of the "enlightenment" forgot.

FREEMASONRY

During this era Freemasonry, a secret society, came into being. Because it was secret and because it worked against the Church it was condemned repeatedly by the Church, and Catholics were forbidden to become Freemasons under pain of excommunication. Freemasonry nonetheless grew and attained great influence, especially in Western Europe.

VOLTAIRE AND ROUSSEAU

In France two very convincing but misguided leaders promoted the liberalism of the Enlightenment. Voltaire had great animosity for Christianity and the Church, and—among other things—he became famous for ridiculing the Church and Christian belief.

Jean-Jacques Rousseau taught that no restrictions of any kind should be placed on liberty. He denied the natural connection between rights and responsibility. He denied original sin and its effects. Consequently, he taught that all education should be controlled by the desires of human nature and should not be supervised by authority. He claimed that the right to govern comes from the people, though he left God out of the picture.

In terms of morality, Rousseau often mistook license (i.e., uncontrolled liberty) for true freedom. Politically, Rousseau's writings paved the way for the French Revolution. This was, in many ways, a revolution against the authority of both the State and the Church at that time. His ideas were condemned by the Archbishop of Paris and many others as contrary to what Christ taught. Many false educational ideas of today can be traced to him.

The Church and the French Revolution

THE FRENCH REVOLUTION

Like many major historical events, the French Revolution (1789) had mixed causes and mixed outcomes, both good and bad. On the one hand, the enactors of the French Revolution were fighting for many of the ideas and principles which undergird the genuine political freedoms enjoyed in today's modern democracies; on the other hand, some of the ideals, and many of the events of French Revolution, are emblematic of the dangerous modern tendency to divorce ourselves from tradition and from the structures that give order, value, and protection to man and his soul. As such, the Church's relationship to the French Revolution is also mixed. From the beginning of Church history, the Church has always struggled to be *in* the world but not *of* the world.

When we consider that the King of France, just before the time of the Revolution, was the authority responsible for selecting the Bishops of the Church, we get but one glimpse of how the Church was too much *in* the world. But it also must not be forgotten that the Church and its people were violently persecuted during and after the French Revolution. The heads of the people were turned by the ideas of men like Rousseau, whose writings inclined them against the truths of the Catholicism. Many desired uncontrolled liberty and hoped to gain it by a revolution. Since the Church in France had been closely linked with the State, many evils that were then current were blamed on the Church. But those of the clergy, then known as the Third Estate, were also guilty of evil

The Taking of the Bastille, July 14, 1789

against others and the common good. In addition many of the newly rich middle class opposed both Church and State and sought power for themselves. The poor also felt oppressed. Led by Voltaire's party, which had attained great power, these elements worked for the destruction of Church and State.

During the last ten years of the eighteenth century a horrible, bloody revolution raged in France. The monarchy was overthrown. Churches, monasteries, and convents were torn down or burned and great numbers of priests, religious and faithful Catholics, as well as members of the nobility, were beheaded or exiled.

The Church Spreads to Many Lands

THE CHURCH CONTINUES TO GROW

During the turmoil caused by the various godless movements in Europe, missionaries were carrying the word of God to distant countries. The persecutions themselves forced many priests and religious into exile. This served to spread the knowledge of the kingdom of God, as the exile of the Israelites had done when they were held captive in Babylon. Missionaries found their way to China, India, and Japan in the East, and many came to America. The prophecy of Isaiah that the kingdom of God would spread throughout the entire world was literally being fulfilled.

GROWTH OF THE CHURCH IN AMERICA

Missionaries, among them Franciscans, Jesuits, and Dominicans, closely followed the explorers into all parts of the New World. The missionaries were faithful to the work with which God had entrusted them. They were men of great courage and possessed a deep love of God and man. They underwent every kind of suffering and hardship. Some were martyred, as was St. Isaac Jogues.

ST. ISAAC JOGUES

In the seventeenth century, while America was still being explored, a young Jesuit came from France to bring the Faith to the Indians. The first six years Father Jogues spent working among the Hurons around the Great Lakes. He suffered much. The superstitious Indians blamed all ill fortune on the "Black-robes," as the Jesuits were called. His life was constantly in danger.

Father Jogues, together with his companions, was captured by the Iroquois tribe, enemies of the Hurons. They were subjected to indescribable tortures. The Indians chewed off one of Father Jogues' fingers and cut off his left thumb. The captives were allowed to live, but only as slaves of the Iroquois.

Some kindly Dutch traders managed to obtain freedom for Father Jogues. He returned to France. However, no sooner had he regained his health than he expressed his wish to return to his missionary work among the Indians. This time he was sent to the Mohawks in New York. By a special permission from the Pope, he was permitted to celebrate Mass even though his hands were so badly mangled.

Father Jogues did not long have the joy of teaching about Christ to the Mohawks. His presence caused suspicion, and he was again tortured. All his life he wished to be a martyr. His wish was granted. On entering a hut where he had been invited for a meal, a hostile Indian struck him with a tomahawk and killed him. The feast of St. Isaac Jogues and other Jesuit Martyrs of America is celebrated on October 19 in the ordinary form and September 26 in the extraordinary form.

THE CHURCH IN THE UNITED STATES

Gradually, as more Catholics came from Europe to America, permanent parishes were formed. The first one was in St. Augustine, Florida. In 1789 Father John Carroll was appointed and consecrated the first bishop of the United States of America. His diocese of Baltimore embraced the entire United States. When he was first named bishop there were only thirty priests in the country, and all had come from other lands.

A number of the priests were exiles from France. Others came from the Catholic French settlements in Canada. Bishop Carroll immediately established St. Mary's Seminary in Baltimore so that American boys could be trained for the priesthood. Soon four more dioceses were established, and Baltimore became an archdiocese. The United States was considered a missionary country until the beginning of the twentieth century.

Secularism Reaches the United States

SECULARISM

Secularism, which really is a part of Rationalism, did not have much influence in the United States until after the Constitution was adopted. Secularists do not deny the existence of God, they simply show Him indifference. They act as if God does not concern Himself with us, and as if we His creatures have no obligation toward Him. They teach that man should be guided in everything he does by earthly values. They forget that life here upon earth is not the end.

SECULARISM IN THE UNITED STATES

In the beginning, American education was basically religious. Religion was taught in all the schools up to the middle of the nineteenth century. Gradually, over the years, the religious ideas upon which our Constitution rests were misinterpreted by the secularists. The Church strongly opposed their interpretations. Nevertheless, people resigned themselves to them. Religion, the very heart of early American education, ceased to be important to many outside the Church. Gradually it was dropped from our public schools and as a consequence secularism spread.

CHRIST'S CHURCH SHALL CONQUER

Although at times it appears as if the Church were fighting a losing battle, we must remember that Christ has foretold that hardships would be the lot of all who are loyal to Him. The hatred of Christ's enemies will never die out, but in the end, as God has foreordained, the Church will emerge victorious. We have Christ's promise for that, and His promises have already been fulfilled many times in the course of history.

In the United States at present, well-intentioned people are beginning to realize that taking religion out of education was not a good idea. By depriving children of the knowledge of God and His commandments, it has done much harm to the moral life of youth. This is clearly evident in the increasing amount of misconduct and crime among youth. Happily, we are witnessing a growing demand that religion again become a part of every child's education.

As Catholic boys and girls who have had the opportunity of learning about God and our many important responsibilities, we must live according to our Catholic Faith. By practicing it we will promote the plans of God among those with whom we come in contact. Living good Christian lives is the best way of combating the enemies of the Church.

FOR ME TO REVIEW

Questions and Exercises

Part 1: Match column I with column II

Column I   Column II

                                        A

1. Enlightenment   A. Teaches that man should be guided in everything by earthly values

2. French Revolution   B. Teaches that even if God exists, his existence doesn't matter

3. Rationalism   C. A secret society that seeks to destroy the Church

4. Secularism   D. Truths we know from God Himself

5. Freemasons   E. Set out to overthrow the Church as well as the State

6. Indifferentism   F. Movement which ushered forth new discoveries in science and reason but with disdain for Divine Revelation

7. Divine Revelation   G. Claimed that all truth can be known by reason alone

                          B

1. Margaret Mary Alacoque   A. First Bishop of the United States

2. John Carroll   B. Missionary among the Indians

3. John Baptist de La Salle C. Spread the devotion to the Sacred Heart

4. Isaac Jogues   D. Established the first schools for the training of teachers

5. Vincent de Paul   E. Apostle of the poor

Part 2: Complete the following statements

1. The Rationalists denied all _____ truths.

2. Those who do not believe in Divine Revelation soon deny _____ .

3. We as Catholics believe not only what we can prove by reasoning, but also what we believe by _____ .

4. Catholics should not be surprised when they are persecuted

because _____ .

5. The false idea that all education should be based on the desires of human nature was introduced into schools by _____ .

6. During the time when the Church was being persecuted in Europe, it was _____ in other lands.

7. Those who wish to take the teaching of religion out of schools forget that man not only has a material body but also a _____ .

8. Rationalism spread because its false ideas were taught in _____ .

9. Even during the worst attacks on the Church, God gave signs of His _____.

Part 3: Questions to Check Your Reading

1. Name some of the faulty teachings of the rationalists.

2. What is meant by indifferentism?

3. Why does the Church forbid Catholics to join the Freemasons?

4. What evils result when the State is completely separated from God and religion?

5. List some saints of this period and tell how, by cooperating with Christ and His Church, they accomplished much good.

6. What errors did Rousseau teach?

7. What qualities did the American missionaries show?

8. What were some of the hardships Father Isaac Jogues had to endure in his missionary labors?

9. Where was the first parish in the United States formed? The first diocese? When? Who was its first bishop?

10. How was the faith of the American Catholics tried?

11. What results did secularism have upon the people of the United States?

12. Why should Catholics not become discouraged when hardships befall them and the Church?

13. What can a Catholic boy or girl do to help the Church?

✓ FOR ME TO DO

1. Read about Father Junipero Serra and the California Missions. Then make a bulletin board display illustrating the more important missions. You might give a few interesting historical notes about them.

2. Find what charitable Catholic institutions have been established in your diocese. Report on the work of any one of them.

3. Give examples from the Old Testament and from modern history that prove there has been neither peace nor happiness in those countries from which God was exiled.

4. Read and report on the history and progress of the Catholic Church in the diocese in which you live.

5. Read *Mangled Hands* by Neil Boynton, S.J.

6. Do not throw away any Catholic literature when you finish reading it. Pass it on to those who do not know Christ as you do. Be mission-minded.

7. Try to perform at least one corporal or spiritual work of mercy each day.

8. The "Salve Regina" was the favorite prayer of St. Vincent de Paul. Say it often.

9. If possible, receive your education only in Catholic schools, in order to safeguard your faith.

CHAPTER 37
God's Church Today

The Church passed through many trials in the nineteenth and twentieth centuries. Certain governments had fallen into the hands of the enemies of the Church. In our own day false teachings or "isms" have attacked every element of our social living: education, business; politics, and religion. Christ warned that the Church would suffer, but He also gave the assurance, ". . . the gates of hell shall not prevail against it" (Mt 16:18). As a lighthouse sends forth its beacon to guide ships, so that Church beams forth the light of Christ, showing us the path we must follow if we would enjoy the peace that only Christ can give.

Europe Desires to Control the Church

NAPOLEON SEIZES THE PAPAL STATES

Following the French Revolution, Napoleon gained control of the French government. Because he saw no other way of restoring peace save through the Church, Napoleon made a concordat with Pope Pius VII. This agreement promised freedom to the Church. Shortly after it went into force, however, Napoleon seized the Papal States and for a time held the Pope a prisoner in France. Peaceful days followed for the Church only when Napoleon was dethroned and exiled to Elba.

EUROPEAN RULERS OPPOSE CHURCH

As we have learned in the previous chapter, the denial of God and His authority was not restricted to France; it spread to other countries. The legitimate demand of the people for a more direct

voice in their government was exploited by some individuals, who lured the people on with promises of national greatness and visions of national destinies. Nations became greedy for wealth and sought political power. One European country after another interfered with the spiritual power of the Church.

The Church was persecuted in Switzerland, as also in the Scandinavian countries. The Catholics of England and Ireland were deprived of many basic rights. In Germany, Spain, and Portugal civil wars broke out. Christians suffered, and the authority of the Church was weakened.

ITALY SEIZES THE PAPAL STATES

Many of the movements against the Church took place during the reign of Pope Pius IX. He tried his best to bring peace, but the wars and revolutions continued to rage. The crisis came in 1870, when King Victor Emmanuel of Italy seized the Papal States and made Rome the capital of the newly united kingdom. The Pope spent the last seven years of his life as a voluntary prisoner in the Vatican Palace. He refused to become the subject of the King of Italy. His successors continued the policy until the tiny state of Vatican City was established in 1929.

TWO IMPORTANT DOGMAS

Though these events occupied his attention, the Pope did not neglect the spiritual needs of the people. In 1854, in answer to

TERMS TO KNOW

- dogma
- materialism
- liturgy
- modernism
- dictator
- infallibility
- laity
- Fascist
- encyclical
- communion
- nuncio
- Nazi
- Novus Ordo

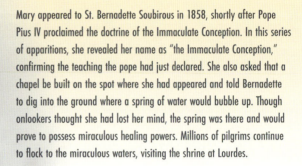

the earnest petitions of the bishops and faithful all over the world Pope Pius IX proclaimed the doctrine of the Immaculate Conception as a dogma of faith.

In 1869 he also convened the Vatican Council. During this Council the infallibility of the pope in matters of faith and morals was proclaimed and defined. You recall that when the pope speaks infallibly he cannot err in matters of faith and morals.

Mary appeared to St. Bernadette Soubirous in 1858, shortly after Pope Pius IV proclaimed the doctrine of the Immaculate Conception. In this series of apparitions, she revealed her name as "the Immaculate Conception," confirming the teaching the pope had just declared. She also asked that a chapel be built on the spot where she had appeared and told Bernadette to dig into the ground where a spring of water would bubble up. Though onlookers thought she had lost her mind, the spring was there and would prove to possess miraculous healing powers. Millions of pilgrims continue to flock to the miraculous waters, visiting the shrine at Lourdes.

POPE PLUS IX

Pope Pius IX reigned for thirty-two years. He was an outstanding pope, loved and respected by all. Because of the invention of the steamboat, the railroad, and the telegraph, communication was easier. The world became smaller. Contact between the individual churches and Rome became closer. Many more of the faithful were able to make pilgrimages to the Eternal City.

Clergy and Laymen Promote the Work of Christ

THE CURÉ OF ARS

During the terrible days of the French Revolution, John Baptist Vianney was born. His earliest memories were those of the persecution of the Church in France. Because the churches were closed and no catechism was taught in schools, few children knew much about their religion. John liked to teach them their prayers and catechism which he himself had learned from his father.

John wanted to become a priest, although he found studies difficult. In his final examinations he became so frightened that he failed. But one of the examiners was convinced of John's vocation. He helped him eventually to be ordained.

Shortly after his ordination, Father Vianney was appointed to a poor village named Ars. The people there no longer practiced their religion. Father Vianney found the church empty Sunday after Sunday. It was disheartening to preach to a practically empty church. So he began to visit the people in their homes, blessed their children, and spoke to them of God. The people of Ars, awakened by his love, began to attend services at the church, and even hardened sinners repented. The church became too small to hold all who wished to attend. Thousands from all parts of the globe streamed into Ars to hear him preach and to go to confession to him. Father Vianney was enlightened by God so that he knew even the secret thoughts of his penitents and could tell what they needed before they asked.

The evil spirits were jealous of the saint's success, and sought to discourage him by causing him many hardships and annoying him constantly. Father Vianney was not afraid of the devil, nor was he afraid of hard work. He heard so many confessions daily that he scarcely found time to rest. Often when he was cold and numb from sitting in the confessional, he would say, "I have to search for my poor feet." He is known as the "Martyr of the Confessional."

Despite ill health, John Baptist spent forty years as parish priest of Ars. He worked so hard and prayed so fervently that he was able to help thousands on their way to heaven. He himself became a great saint through such heroic efforts.

LEADERS AMONG THE LAITY AND CLERGY

The popes were not alone in their efforts to preserve the true faith of Christ. They were aided by great men not only among the clergy but also among the laity. These gave themselves to Christ and His Church as willing instruments. Daniel O'Connell, as a member of the English Parliament, obtained the repeal of certain unfair laws against the Catholics in Ireland. Francois Chateaubriand took up his pen for the Church of France. A student in a university in France, Frederick Ozanam organized the Society of St. Vincent de Paul. Its members strove for personal holiness through prayer, good example, and through the care of the poor and suffering. In England Doctor Wiseman's scholarly lectures made a deep impression on highly educated non-Catholics. Renowned converts, such as Henry Cardinal Manning and St. John Cardinal Newman, strove untiringly to spread the Catholic faith. In Germany, Bishop von Ketteler opposed the evils caused by the revolution. By his preaching and writing he defended the Church against the interference of the State.

"Whatever you do, think of the glory of God as your main goal."

—St. John Bosco

ST. JOHN BOSCO

A young priest in Turin, Italy, John Bosco, chose to spend his life helping neglected boys. He gathered them from the streets and slums of the city, and provided a home for them. In his vocational schools he taught them an honest trade, directed their play, and instructed them in the truths of their religion. Later he organized the men who volunteered to help him into the Salesian society. They were so called after St. Francis de Sales whom they chose as their patron. The Salesian fathers are training youths in all parts of the world today.

The Workingman's Friend—Pope Leo XIII

THE POPE OF THE WORKINGMAN

The pope is the supreme visible head of the Catholic Church. The faithful from all corners of the earth look to him for guidance in matters of belief and practice. They are also accustomed to look to the Church for guidance when they suffer from evils which afflict them.

The invention of machinery resulted in the factory system. Workingmen were often forced to submit to unjust and wretched conditions. They had no way of protecting themselves.

Pope Leo XIII, the successor of Pius IX, wrote an encyclical, that is, a learned letter to the people, in which he explained the rights and duties of the workingman and the obligations and rights of the employers. This great encyclical has merited for Pope Leo XIII the title of "Friend of the Workingman."

Pope Leo was a scholar and showed a great interest in education. To encourage study he opened the Vatican archives so that students of the whole world could use the valuable documents to be found there.

The Pope also worked energetically to restore all men to the Mystical Body of Christ. He promoted mission societies, and encouraged religious communities to enter into or to increase their missionary work.

AMERICAN SAINT

After Francesca Cabrini founded a missionary order in Italy, she visited the Supreme Pontiff, Leo XIII. "Shall I go to China or the United States?" she asked.

"Go to the United States," he told her.

So, Mother Cabrini sailed for the United States with six of her missionary Sisters. They began their work among the neglected Italian immigrants, especially those who had settled in New York and Chicago. Mother Cabrini, however, wished to serve the entire world. As a consequence she opened orphanages, schools, and hospitals in all parts of the United States. Then she sent Sisters to South America and to Europe.

Mother Cabrini was the first American citizen to be canonized a saint. During the ceremonies of her canonization, American planes flew over St. Peter's Basilica and dipped their wings in salute.

Pope of the Eucharist—Pius X

THE HERESY OF MODERNISM

At the very beginning of his reign, Pope St. Pius X had to combat the heresy of modernism, a combination of modern errors. This heresy made bold to say that everything should be "emancipated" from ecclesiastical authority. It demanded that the Church should become more "democratic." By that its disciples meant that the Church should adapt and alter the teaching of Christ and the regulations of the Church to fit the desires of so-called modern minds.

To stop the spread of these false ideas, which he condemned in an encyclical, Pope St. Pius X advocated frequent reception of Holy Communion. He first urged and then commanded pastors to allow children to receive First Holy Communion as soon as they had reached the age of reason. He wanted children to go to Christ so that they could get from Him the strength to stay pure and the courage to live as Christians. The saintly Pope once wrote, "Holy Communion is the shortest and surest way to heaven."

Pope St. Pius X was a holy man. He always kept on his desk a statue of the Curé of Ars, because he wanted to be the kind of

priest the Curé had been. He loved the poor and helped them all he could.

St. Pius X was also responsible for bringing together the Code of Canon Law, for quickening an interest in the liturgy, for reforms in Church music; in all, he was a genuine apostle who wanted to use every means to make the faithful realize their heritage and participate actively in the life of the Church.

The saintly Pope was also a great promoter of peace. When World War I threatened, he instructed his nuncios that is, the representatives of the Holy See in the various European countries, to do everything in their power to prevent war from breaking out. It is said that the Austrian ambassador at the beginning of the war begged Pius X to bless the armies of the Central Powers. The Pope replied, "I bless peace, not war."

A few days after the war broke out, the Pope died suddenly. He was canonized a saint by Pope Pius XII in 1954.

World War I—Pope Benedict XV

The next pope chose the name of Benedict. He began his apostolic labors by asking all to pray that God would move the civil rulers to work for peace and stop war. In an encyclical the Pope, as had the prophets of the Old Testament, spoke of the evils which war caused and listed means by which peace could be restored to the world. The warring nations refused to listen to the proposals. The war was carried on, and during it violence, hatred, and prejudice increased.

Deeply disappointed, the Pope did not lose heart. Throughout the war Pope Benedict XV, like Christ whose vicar he was, gave proof of his abundant charity. He made no distinction as to faith, race, or nationality. His concern extended to all who suffered. He died knowing that the countries which had rejected God and ruled out charity and justice in the peace treaty would soon engage in another, a still greater war; for Christ has said, "Without me you can do nothing."

Promoter of Peace and Catholic Action—Pope Pius XI

POPE OF PEACE

For almost a century zealous popes had occupied the throne of St. Peter. Pope Pius XI was a worthy successor of the Apostles. He had been a librarian, a scholar, nuncio, and prelate. He could speak French, German, and Polish well. He had contact with great scholars and had visited many lands.

Pope Pius XI took for his motto, "The Peace of Christ in the Kingdom of Christ." After his election, the Pope devoted all his energy to promoting peace. He began by giving his blessing from the outer balcony of St. Peter's, instead of from within the basilica as had been customary since the Papal State had been seized. He did this to show that the blessing was for the whole Church and the whole world.

CATHOLIC ACTION

Pius XI issued an encyclical on Catholic Action. By it the Pope hoped to lead people to cooperate with the hierarchy as apostles. The command of Christ "Go teach all nations" was meant not only for the Apostles and clergy but for everyone, laymen as well. From the very beginning of Christianity the laity worked along with the bishops and the priests in spreading among the pagans the knowledge of the Church which Christ founded. In our age, when the world was forsaking God and His Church and choosing materialism instead, the laity were badly needed to help the bishops to spread the Kingdom of God upon earth. This cooperation of the laity with the bishops in the apostolate of the Church Pope Pius XI called "Catholic Action."

In the same encyclical, the Pope established the Feast of Christ the King; it was to be celebrated on the last Sunday of October. This feast brings us to the realization that the Kingdom of Christ includes all nations and Christ is its King.

Pope Pius XI wrote many other encyclicals. Among them are those on "Christian Marriage," "Christian Education of Youth," and "Forty Years After," pertaining to the social order and labor.

LATERAN TREATY

The most momentous act during the pontificate of Pope Pius XI was the Lateran Treaty in 1929, between the Church and the government of Italy. This treaty freed the Pope from all political bondage. The Vatican City was made a tiny independent state and the Pope was its sole ruler. Italy also agreed to pay a small sum of money to the Church for the Papal States taken during the reign of Pope Pius IX.

RISE OF THE "ISMS"

As Pope Benedict XV foresaw, World War I did not bring peace but discord. Dictators arose. They made capital of the sorry conditions which lack of charity and justice produced, and succeeded in getting people to follow them. The dictators encouraged nationalism, that is, an undue love of country, and promised the people freedom, prosperity, and happiness. The poorer class of people were only too willing to believe these promises because they suffered so much. In Italy the Fascist party gained power. The Nazi or National Socialistic Party seized control of affairs in Germany. Even prior to that, before World War I ended, a revolution had resulted in atheistic Communism usurping power in Russia. All three dictatorships deprived man of God-given rights, and proclaimed that there was no higher authority than that of the State. Pope Pius XI was distressed by these evils and denounced them publicly.

The false teachings of the dictators began to spread during the closing years of the reign of Pope Pius XI. Despite his illness, he kept on working and offered his own sufferings for peace. Pope Pius XI died shortly before World War II broke out.

The Church in the Latin Countries

PERSECUTIONS

Although Latin America is largely Catholic the Church has often been at a disadvantage in the Latin American countries, and even persecuted. One of the worst persecutions occurred in Mexico in 1924. Catholic churches and schools were closed, teaching orders were driven out, priests and sisters were killed or exiled, and the teaching of religion in schools was strictly forbidden.

Father Miguel Pro, a Mexican Jesuit, was one of the martyrs of this persecution. He died repeating the words, "¡Viva Cristo Rey!" That is, "Long live Christ the King!"

THE CHURCH IN THE AMERICAS

Communism also has made headway in Central and South America, being helped by the conditions that exist there. A few are very rich. The majority of the people are very poor and unable to read. Cities are scattered, travel is difficult, and a great shortage of priests and sisters exists. In many sections of these countries a large part of the population is unable to attend church or to receive the sacraments because they are without priests. Catholic education often labors under difficulties and restrictions. The people have no way of knowing their religion. The United States and other countries, especially Spain, are sending as many missionaries as they can spare to these countries, but many more are needed. Protestant missionaries are very active in Latin America.

PERSECUTIONS IN SPAIN

In 1936 the government of Spain fell into the hands of the Communists. Civil war followed. The Church underwent a violent persecution. Thousands of priests, religious and Catholic people were martyred. The war lasted for three years before peace could be restored.

SPIRITUAL DIFFICULTIES

Perhaps you have realized that the history of the Church is an account of the battles waged between the Church and her enemies. At times the Church is victorious; but when her children become selfish, worldly, and lax in their faith, she is defeated. Was not this also true of the Chosen People from the beginning of their history? The Church will continue, however, until the end of time and will never be destroyed. The sooner we turn wholeheartedly to God and live as Christ teaches us to live through His Church, just so much the sooner will there be true peace and happiness among men and nations.

Growth of the Church in the United States

THE CHURCH IN THE UNITED STATES

The United States has up to the present escaped violent religious revolutions. However, as was mentioned in the history of the Church, American Catholics have suffered. Organizations such as the Know-Nothing Party, and later the Ku-Klux-Klan once stirred up ill-will toward Catholics. But opposition to the Church in our country has been sporadic. From colonial days, when the Protestants of Rhode Island and Pennsylvania offered Catholics refuge, the American public, by and large, has been at least tolerant of the Church.

Since religion cannot be taught in the public schools, the education of Catholic boys and girls in the United States has been a cause of great concern to Catholic parents and church officials. A Plenary Council of the bishops of the United States, presided over by Cardinal Gibbons, met in Baltimore in the 1880s. Education was one of the main problems discussed. During it the bishops decided that an elementary school should be built in every parish and should be supported by the parishioners. Fortunately, the rapid spread of teaching orders made it possible to staff the schools with religious nuns and priests. Much of the growth and strength of the Church in the United States can be credited to the Catholic school system and its dedicated teachers.

In recent years, however, the growth of religious orders has not been able to keep pace with the growth of parochial schools. Recently the Church has been depending on more and more Catholic lay teachers to staff its schools.

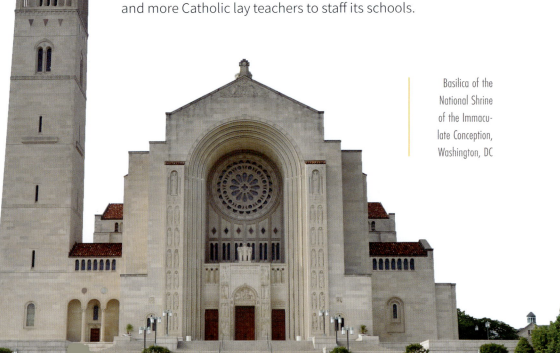

Basilica of the National Shrine of the Immaculate Conception, Washington, DC

DANGERS TO THE CHURCH IN THE UNITED STATES

The increase of Catholics in the United States has been steady. Nevertheless, there are grave dangers to be met. One danger is secularism, which takes God out of education, business, and politics. Another danger is materialism—attachment to the goods of this world and earthly comforts and possessions. Materialism can even manifest in an undue dependence on the government—expecting the government to solve the problem of sin and evil through political means. These things threaten faith as they slowly convince the human heart that it has no need of God.

The Church in Asia and Africa

While the Church was gaining strength and prestige in Europe and America, it was also beginning to grow in Asia and Africa. The Philippines is the only Christian nation in the East, but the Church grew in China, India, and all the countries and islands of the East. In Africa, also, great gains have been made among the African natives.

A Great Pope—Pius XII

For over two thousand years the successors of St. Peter have fed the sheep of Christ with the life-giving sacraments and the teaching of the Catholic Church. In 1939, Pope Pius XII took over this great task in very difficult times. Scarcely six months after his election, World War II broke out.

In His Divine Providence, God prepared Pope Pius XII for his difficult labors. While the Papal Envoy and Secretary of State, he had seen the rise of the dictators. Through his work he learned to speak many languages and knew almost all the leading statesmen personally. His information on world problems was up to date. He had even visited the United States before he was elected Pope. Most important, however, he loved God and the men of all nations, races, and religions. His desire was to lead his entire great flock to God.

No one opposed war and injustice more than he did. He used every means at his disposal to bring about peace. He pointed out the dangers of war policies and showed which road would lead to peace. He organized agencies for providing relief and for tracing prisoners. He was able to furnish information about thousands of them.

THE JUBILEE YEAR

Several million pilgrims from all over the world visited the center of Catholic unity in Rome during the Jubilee Year of 1950. The occasion of greatest rejoicing was the solemn definition of the dogma of the Assumption of the Blessed Virgin into heaven.

Numerous canonizations took place during the Jubilee Year. Among these was the canonization of Maria Goretti, the young Italian girl who preferred death to sin.

COMMUNISM

The greatest modern opponent of the Church is atheistic communism. It denies there is a God, makes the State more important than the individual, makes the State owner of all property, and persecutes the Church. Communism says that it is trying to regenerate the human race. It teaches that everything that helps communism is good, even lies, oppression, enslavement, murder. Where it has gained control, freedom, democracy, and justice have disappeared; and fear, death, and slavery have been the lot of its victims. It can be conquered only by Christian sanctity, charity, and justice. It can be prevented only by resisting it from the start.

CHANGES IN CHURCH LITURGY

To help the faithful participate more fully in the liturgy, Pope Pius XII eased the fast before Communion. He revised the rites of Holy Week to allow people to take a greater part in them, and made provisions for evening Masses so that no one would miss Mass. He was also interested in the liturgical movement which has as its objective the closer participation of the faithful in the Mass and other services of the Church. The Catholic liturgy would receive extreme changes during the Second Vatican Council with the introduction of the Novus Ordo.

Pope John XXIII—Pastor of the World

Pope Pius XII was succeeded by Pope St. John XXIII, who had served for twenty-seven years as a Vatican diplomat. He was Apostolic visitor to Bulgaria, Apostolic delegate to Turkey and Greece, Nuncio to France, and Patriarch of Venice.

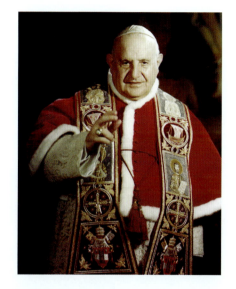

Pope John XXIII, the son of an Italian sharecropper, has always been above all else a pastor, a shepherd of souls. He has always held the poor most dear, and he has become well known for his charitable works. In 1961, Pope John issued his important encyclical on man's social and economic life, *Mater et Magistra*. He is perhaps most famously known for issuing the Second Vatican Council, which lasted from 1962–1965. In 2014, Pope John XXIII was canonized by Pope Francis.

Pope St. John XXIII was succeeded by Pope St. Paul VI, most known for his promulgation of the Novus Ordo and the closing out of Vatican II. His prophetic encyclical *Humanae Vitae—On Human Life*—also received great attention as it boldly proclaimed the Church's teachings on life related issues. Here, Pope Paul VI condemned the use of contraceptives and warned the modern age that such artificial preventions of life would issue in a new and destructive evil in our times--women would be treated as objects, the relationship between men and women would be greatly jeopardized, the sacredness of marriage would be made a mockery, abortions would increase, and the sanctity of human life would be disrespected. These predictions, as we can observe today, have come true. The Church continues to be attacked for her seeming rigidity regarding the sacredness of marriage and the sanctity of human life. However, the Church has remained strong against these attacks, and continues to provide her faithful with a moral compass during these dark times.

Between Pope Paul VI and Pope John Paul II, Pope John Paul I remained in office for only 33 days. In his honor, Pope John Paull II took his name, becoming one of the youngest popes in history and the first Polish Pope. Pope John Paul II canonized more saints than any other pope, he established the first World

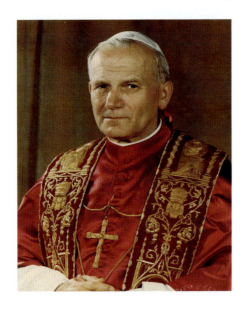

Youth Day, provided the Church with some unprecedented theological development known as "Theology of the Body," helped defeat communism in Poland and Europe, and spread devotion to Our Lady of Fatima. His life is worth pondering and studying, especially as a model of holiness in the modern era. He was canonized in 2014 along with John XXIII by Pope Francis.

After his death in 2005, Pope St. John Paul II was succeeded by Pope Benedict XVI, a man of letters and great academic achievement. He brought many Anglicans into the Church by introducing the Anglican Ordinariate. As Cardinal Ratzinger, he authored many theological works, including *The Spirit of the Liturgy* and *Introduction to Christianity*. As Pope, he continued to contribute to the development of the Church's mind through his series entitled *Jesus of Nazareth*. In 2013, he resigned from his office, being the first to do so since Celestine V in 1294. He was succeeded by Pope Francis.

The Catholic Church Upheld by Divine Power

The Church has encountered and overcome obstacles and dangers of every sort in every age. At present, when the world situation threatens the Church, we need not lose hope. The Church will survive the dangers of the twentieth century as it has those of previous centuries. The Holy Spirit, whom Christ sent to guide, watch over and console the Church, will remain with her till the end of time.

The Catholic Church, the Mystical Body of Christ, shall never fail. She may meet defeat when her members fail, but like the Ark of Noah, she will ride the floods of time till the end of the world. May we all resolve ever more to help her and never to harm her in her work for Christ and the salvation of the human race. "Such as we are, such are the times," St. Augustine once said. Let us strive through virtue and penance to sanctify our age.

FOR ME TO REVIEW

Questions and Exercises

Part 1: Match column I with column II

Column I	Column II
	A
1. Ozanam	A. Held Pope Pius VII prisoner in France
2. Napoleon	B. English convert who became a Cardinal
3. Victor Emmanuel	C. Cardinal in the United States
4. Von Ketteler	D. Organized the St. Vincent de Paul Society
5. O'Connell	E. Bishop who defended Church rights in Germany
6. Newman	F. Won certain rights for Catholics in Ireland
7. Gibbons	G. King of Italy who seized Papal States
	B
1. Pius IX	A. Lateran Treaty
2. Leo XIII	B. Encyclical on the Conditions of the Workingman
3. John XXIII	C. World War I Pope
4. Pius X	D. Changes in Liturgy of the Church
5. Benedict XV	E. Encouraged frequent Holy Communion
6. Pius XI	F. Italy seized Papal States
7. Pius XII	G. Succeeded Pope Pius XII
	C
1. John Bosco	A. A martyr of the confessional
2. Francesca Cabrini	B. Cared for neglected boys of Italy
3. Father Pro	C. Young girl who preferred death to sin
4. Maria Goretti	D. Martyr in the Mexican persecution
5. John Vianney	E. Worked among Italian immigrants

Part 2: Complete the following statements

1. Doing the work of the Church under the direction of the bishop

2. Recommending changing the teachings of the Church to please the modern mind

3. Taking God out of education, industry, and politics

4. A letter from the Pope to the people

5. A solemn proclamation of a doctrine of faith

6. The Pope's representative in a foreign country

7. The treaty which again made the Pope an independent ruler

Part 3: Write the words DOGMA or ENCYCLICAL after each title

1. Immaculate Conception

2. Christian Education of Youth

3. Christian Marriage

4. Infallibility of the Pope

5. Assumption of the Blessed Virgin Mary

6. Condition of the Workingman

7. *Humanae Vitae*

Part 4: Questions to Check Your Reading

1. Why did the European rulers wish to control the Church?

2. Why did Pope Pius IX consider himself a prisoner?

3. List some of the accomplishments of Pope Pius IX.

4. Name some saints and Catholic leaders of this period and tell for what each is noted.

5. In what fields did Pope Leo XIII show great interest?

6. What did the heresy of modernism teach?

7. How did Pope Pius X combat modernism?

8. Why did Pope Benedict XV think that the peace after World War I would not last?

9. What important encyclicals did Pope Pius XI write?

10. Why was the Lateran Treaty of great importance to the Church?

11. Why were the teachings of the modern dictators wrong?

12. Why is it possible for Communism to spread in the Latin American countries?

13. When does God allow His enemies to gain victories over the Church?

14. Why were parochial schools established in the United States?

15. What changes in the liturgy of the Church did Pope Pius XII make?

16. Why has Pope John XXIII often been called "a traveler of God"?

17. What were some of the predictions made by Pope Paul VI in *Humanae Vitae*?

18. Who was the next pope to resign from office after Celestine V in 1294?

19. Why can we be sure that the Catholic Church will never fail?

20. What must we do to insure the welfare of the Church in the United States and in our world?

 **FOR ME TO DO**

1. Other saints of this period are: Bernadette Soubirous, Thérèse of the Child Jesus, and Dominic Savio. Give a report on one of them.

2. Read about the work of Father Damien in Molokai.

3. On an outline map of the world indicate places where American missionaries are laboring.

4. Post on the bulletin board pictures and clippings of the Holy Father, St. Peters Basilica, and scenes of Vatican City.

5. Interview a member of the Knights of Columbus to learn how the organization takes part in the work of the Church.

6. Learn the names of the Cardinals of the United States. Tell about some of their activities.

7. Read about Father John de Smet and his work among the Indians west of the Rocky Mountains.

8. Two religious communities that were founded for missionary work are the Josephite Fathers and the Sisters of the Blessed Sacrament. Try to find out how these communities began and in what countries they work.

9. Volunteer to spend some time with the poor and homeless at nearby shelters.

10. Find out how to partake in Pro-Life ministries at your parish church.

11. Pray to the Holy Spirit that He may guide the rulers of Church and State.

12. Do not believe anything which contradicts the teachings of the Church.

Prayers

The Sign of the Cross
In the name of the Father, and of the Son, and of the Holy Spirit. Amen.

The Lord's Prayer
Our Father who art in heaven, hallowed be Thy name; Thy kingdom come; Thy will be done on earth as it is in heaven. Give us this day our daily bread; and forgive us our trespasses as we forgive those who trespass against us; and lead us not into temptation, but deliver us from evil. Amen.

The Hail Mary
Hail Mary, full of grace, the Lord is with thee; blessed art thou among women, and blessed is the fruit of thy womb, Jesus. Holy Mary, Mother of God, pray for us sinners, now and at the hour of our death. Amen.

Glory Be to the Father
Glory be to the Father, and to the Son, and to the Holy Spirit. As it was in the beginning, is now, and ever shall be, world without end. Amen.

The Apostles' Creed
I believe in God, the Father Almighty, Creator of heaven and earth; and in Jesus Christ, His only Son, Our Lord; who was conceived by the Holy Spirit, born of the Virgin Mary, suffered under Pontius Pilate, was crucified, died, and was buried. He descended into hell; the third day He arose again from the dead; He ascended into heaven, and sits at the right hand of God, the Father Almighty; from thence He shall come to judge the living and the dead. I believe in the Holy Spirit, the Holy Catholic Church, the communion of saints, the forgiveness of sins, the resurrection of the body, and life everlasting. Amen.

The Confiteor

Ordinary Form

I confess to almighty God
and to you, my brothers and sisters,
that I have greatly sinned
in my thoughts and in my words,
in what I have done,
and in what I have failed to do;
through my fault, through my fault,
through my most grievous fault;
therefore I ask blessed Mary ever-Virgin,
all the Angels and Saints,
and you, my brothers and sisters,
to pray for me to the Lord our God. Amen

Extraordinary Form

I confess to Almighty God,
to blessed Mary ever Virgin,
blessed Michael the Archangel,
blessed John the Baptist,
the holy Apostles Peter and Paul,
and to all the saints
that I have sinned exceedingly
in thought, word, and deed,
through my fault,
through my fault,
through my most grievous fault.
Therefore, I beseech blessed Mary ever Virgin,
blessed Michael the Archangel,
blessed John the Baptist,
the holy Apostles Peter and Paul,
and all the saints,
to pray for me to the Lord our God. Amen.

Morning Offering

O Jesus, through the Immaculate Heart of Mary, I offer Thee my prayers, works, joys and sufferings of this day for all the intentions of Thy Sacred Heart, in union with the Holy Sacrifice of the Mass throughout the world, in reparation for my sins, for the intentions of all our relatives and friends, and in particular for the intentions of the Hold Father. Amen.

The Angelus

V. The angel of the Lord declared unto Mary.
R. And she conceived of the Holy Spirit.

Hail Mary, full of grace! the Lord is with thee; blessed art thou among women, and blessed is the fruit of thy womb, Jesus. Holy Mary, Mother of God, pray for us sinners, now and at the hour of our death. Amen.

V. Behold the handmaid of the Lord.
R. Be it done unto me according to thy word.

Hail Mary, etc.

V. And the Word was made flesh.
R. And dwelt among us.

Hail Mary, etc.

V. Pray for us, O holy Mother of God.
R. That we may be made worthy of the promises of Christ.

Let Us Pray
Pour forth, we beseech Thee, O Lord, Thy grace into our hearts, that we to whom the Incarnation of Christ, Thy Son, was made known by the message of an angel, may by His passion and cross be brought to the glory of His resurrection, through the same Christ Our Lord. Amen.

Regina Coeli

(Said during Eastertide, instead of the Angelus)

Queen of heaven, rejoice, Alleluia.

For He whom thou didst deserve to bear, Alleluia.

Hath risen as He said, Alleluia.

Pray for us to God, Alleluia.

V. Rejoice and be glad, O Virgin Mary! Alleluia.

R. Because Our Lord is truly risen, Alleluia.

Let Us Pray

O God, who by the resurrection of Thy Son, Our Lord Jesus Christ, have vouchsafed to make glad the whole world, grant, we beseech Thee, that, through the intercession of the Virgin Mary, His Mother, we may attain the joys of eternal life. Through the same Christ Our Lord. Amen.

Hail, Holy Queen

Hail, Holy Queen, Mother of Mercy; hail, our life, our sweetness, and our hope! To thee do we cry, poor banished children of Eve; to thee we do send up our sighs, mourning and weeping in this vale of tears. Turn, then, most gracious advocate, thine eyes of mercy toward us; and after this our exile, show unto us the blessed fruit of thy womb, Jesus. O clement, O loving, O sweet Virgin Mary!

An Act of Faith

O my God, I firmly believe that Thou art one God in three Divine Persons, Father, Son, and Holy Spirit; I believe that Thy Divine Son became man, and died for our sins, and that He will come to judge the living and the dead. I believe these and all the truths which the Holy Catholic Church teaches, because Thou hast revealed them, who canst neither deceive nor be deceived.

An Act of Hope

O my God, relying on Thy almighty power and infinite mercy and promises, I hope to obtain pardon of my sins, the help of Thy grace, and life everlasting, through the merits of Jesus Christ, my Lord and Redeemer.

An Act of Love

O my God, I love Thee above all things, with my whole heart and soul, because Thou art all-good and worthy of all love. I love my neighbor as myself for the love of Thee. I forgive all who have injured me, and ask pardon of all whom I have injured.

An Act of Contrition

O my God, I am heartily sorry for having offended Thee, and I detest all my sins, because of Thy just punishments, but most of all because they offend Thee, my God, who art all-good and deserving of all my love. I firmly resolve, with the help of Thy grace, to sin no more and to avoid the near occasions of sin.

The Blessing Before Meals

Bless us, O Lord, and these Thy gifts, which we are about to receive from Thy bounty, through Christ Our Lord. Amen.

Grace After Meals

We give Thee thanks for all Thy benefits, O Almighty God, who livest and reignest forever; and may the souls of the faithful departed, through the mercy of God, rest in peace. Amen.

The Mysteries of the Rosary

The Five Joyful Mysteries

1. The Annunciation
2. The Visitation
3. The Birth of Our Lord
4. The Presentation of Our Lord in the Temple
5. The Finding of Our Lord in the Temple

The Five Luminous Mysteries

1. The Baptism of Our Lord in the Jordan
2. The Wedding Feast at Cana
3. Our Lord's Proclamation of the Kingdom of God
4. The Transfiguration of Our Lord
5. The Institution of the Eucharist

The Five Sorrowful Mysteries

1. The Agony of Our Lord in the Garden
2. The Scourging at the Pillar
3. The Crowning With Thorns
4. The Carrying of the Cross
5. The Crucifixion and Death of Our Lord

The Five Glorious Mysteries

1. The Resurrection of Our Lord
2. The Ascension of Our Lord into Heaven
3. The Descent of the Holy Spirit Upon the Apostles
4. The Assumption of Our Blessed Mother into Heaven
5. The Coronation of Our Blessed Mother in Heaven

The Immaculate Conception with the Fifteen Mysteries
of the Rosary

Answer Key

Chapter 1

Part 1

1. Pentateuch
2. Ancestors
3. Genesis 1-11
4. Moses
5. Literary form
6. Hebrews
7. Tradition

Part 2

1. Yes
2. No
3. Yes
4. Yes
5. Yes
6. Yes
7. Yes

Chapter 2

Part 1

1. E
2. F
3. B
4. C
5. D
6. A

Part 2

1. Sanctifying grace
2. Angels (or the entire world)

3. Genesis
4. Religious truths
5. Garden of Eden

Part 3

1. Yes
2. Yes
3. No
4. Yes
5. Yes
6. Yes
7. No
8. Yes
9. Yes

Chapter 3

Part 1

1. Covenant
2. Flood
3. Ark
4. Babylon (Babel)
5. Sem, Ham, Japheth
6. Ham
7. Sem
8. Babel
9. Mts. of Ararat
10. Rainbow

Part 2

1. God sent the deluge to cleanse the world of its wicked inhabitants.
2. Yes, God was very pleased with Noah's act of sacrifice.
3. As the Ark rested on the Mountain of Ararat, so the Church built upon Christ will last until the end of time and the gates of hell shall not prevail against it.

4. They decided to make themselves famous by building a tall tower.
5. The sons of Noah were Sem, Ham, and Japheth.
6. The story teaches: (1) pride displeases God; (2) God wants no nation to conquer the world; (3) He wants all nations to be free.
7. God promised Noah that He would never again destroy the world or man by flood.
8. The flood is considered a symbol of Baptism because in this sacrament the faithful pass over into a new life, but their sins like enemies are washed away.
9. The flood served as a warning to men in the future because it taught them that at any time God might punish the evil and reward the good in a similar manner.
10. By the story of Noah and the Deluge, God wished to teach that the Deluge was not only a punishment for sin but also a warning to sinful men in the future. He also intended to turn men's minds to the Ark of the New Covenant, the Catholic Church, which was to save men from the deluge of sin by the word of Christ's cross.
11. Answers will vary.

Chapter 4

Part 1
2-5-4-6-1-3-7

Part 2
1. Sara was Abraham's wife.
2. Lot was Abraham's nephew.
3. Thare was Abraham's father.
4. Melchizedek is not related to him, he was the Priest-King of Salem. Melchizedek offered bread and wine and blessed Abraham when he met him.

Part 3

1. Sodom
2. Sodom and Gomorrah
3. The Lord (God)
4. Palestine (the Promised Land)
5. Types (figures)

Part 4

1. To preserve the knowledge and worship of the one true God.
2. a) To make Abraham's descendants into a great nation.
   b) The Messiah would descend from Abraham.
3. c) A son, through whom a blessing would come to all people.
4. a) His herds increased.
   b) Abraham became rich.
   c) God promised the land of Canaan to the descendants of Abraham.
5. a) Obedience - At the Lord's command Abraham left home and relatives to settle in an unknown country among strange people.
   b) Faith - Abraham believed God's word unreservedly, even though it would have been quite natural to doubt; for example, how a great nation could spring from him when at an old age he had no children.
   c) Gratitude - He offered sacrifice to God in thanksgiving for favors received.
   d) Love of peace - He would not quarrel with Lot.
   e) Self-sacrifice - He gave Lot first choice of land.
   f) Love of neighbor -
      1) He hastened to help the captured Lot
      2) He interceded for the cities of Sodom and Gomorrah.
   g) Hope - He trusted that God would fulfill His promise.
   h) Humility - He served the three strangers himself.
6. Melchizedek was both a king and a priest. He offered bread and wine. Christ also is a King and a priest who offered

Himself to His Eternal Father at the Last Supper, under the form of bread and wine. He continues to do so in the Mass today.

7. The one of the promised Redeemer.

8. His omnipotence.

9. Lot was saved from destruction because Abraham prayed for him.

10. The story of Lot and his wife teaches us that obedience is pleasing to God and rewarded generously while disobedience is displeasing to Him and brings destruction.

11. The story of Sodom and Gomorrah teaches us the evil of sin and its consequences.

Chapter 5

Part 1

A.

1. D
2. H
3. G
4. E
5. F
6. A
7. C
8. B

B.

1. E
2. D
3. A
4. C
5. F
6. B

Part 2

1. God's promise to Abraham is important because a great race would be descended from him. This race would be called the "Chosen People" because God would give it His special aid and from it choose the mother of His Son.

2. The race descended from Abraham was called the "Chosen People."

3. When God promised a son to Abraham, who was quite old, he believed, even though God did not fulfill that promise for a long time. (Answers may vary).

4. Abraham took Isaac and prepared to sacrifice him to the Lord.

5. Isaac is a type of Christ in that both carried the wood for the sacrifice to the place that God appointed. Both were to be offered as victims to God. Both were to be offered as victims to God.

6. For his obedience, God promised Abraham descendants as numerous as the sands of the seashore.

7. Isaac's sons were named Essu and Jacob.

8. The right of the first-born meant that he acquired a double portion of his father's wealth and became head of the family at his father's death.

9. Mortal sin is like the selling of the birthright, because the sinner sells his birthright to Heaven for a short sinful pleasure.

10. Jacob saw in a vision a ladder standing upon the earth, the top touching heaven. Angels were moving up and down the ladder, and God was at the top of it.

11. Bethel means the House of God.

12. We call the Catholic Church the "Gate of Heaven" because it is through our membership in the Church that we are able to enter heaven.

13. a) Jacob is a figure of Christ, and his sons prefigure the twelve apostles.

b) In allowing Jacob to obtain the birthright God showed how Christ and His spiritual sons and daughters would supplant the Chosen People of the Old Testament.

Chapter 6

Part 1

a) 10.

b) 2.

c) 1.

d) 7.

e) 3.

f) 4.

g) 11.

h) 12.

i) 13.

j) 9.

k) 8

l) 5

m) 6

Part 2

1.   B

2.   A

3.   D

4.   C

Matched and in chronological order

1.   3-D

2.   1-B

3.   4-C

4.   2-A

Part 3

1. Joseph's father and mother were Jacob and Rachel.
2. The brothers were jealous of Joseph because:
   Jacob preferred him to his brothers.
   a) Jacob gave him a long tunic.
   b) His reports of his dreams of his future greatness irritated his brothers.
3. Ruben did not want Joseph killed. He suggested they put him into an empty well from which he hoped later to deliver him.
4. They sold him to some Egyptian merchants as a slave.
5. They told their father that Joseph had been killed by wild beasts and showed him the tunic after they had dipped it in blood.
6. Potiphar was a courtier of Pharaoh.
7. Joseph was put into prison because he was falsely accused by Potiphar's wife.
8. Joseph interpreted the dreams as follows:
   a) To the butler he said that in three days he would be restored to his office.
   b) The baker was told that he would be hanged on a gibbet and the birds would eat his flesh.
9. Joseph told Pharaoh that there would be seven years of great abundance in Egypt followed by seven years of severe famine.
10. Pharaoh respected Joseph's wisdom and made him governor.
11. Joseph married the daughter of an Egyptian prince.
12. Joseph stored the grain harvested during the years of plenty.
13. Joseph returned good for evil by saving his people from starvation.
14. Joseph knew his brothers but they did not know him, so he decided to try them and demanded the presence of

Benjamin. After the boy arrived Joseph entertained them, and had his silver cup put into Benjamin's sack. When the bags were searched, the cup was found and Benjamin was not permitted to return. However, Ruben, speaking for his brothers, asked to stay in place of Benjamin because of the grief that the father would suffer.

15. Joseph and his brothers were given possession of the land of Gesen.

16. Yes, he welcomed his father.

17. Joseph was innocent and hated by his brothers and sold into slavery by them, even as Christ was by us. Joseph fed his brothers, forgave his persecutors, and saved God's Chosen People of the Old Laws, thus foreshadowing Christ who would save His Church from the slavery of sin and Satan.

18. Simeon.

19. Juda.

Chapter 7

Part 1

1. Paschal Lamb
2. Pillar of Fire
3. Yahweh
4. Plagues
5. Moses
6. Amalecites
7. Aaron
8. Manna
9. Promised Land
10. Mara

Part 2

1. Moses' mother put him into a basket near the water's edge and the daughter of Pharaoh took him and treated him as her own son.

2. God told Moses that he should go to Pharaoh and tell him that God had appointed Moses to lead the Israelites out of Egypt.

3. God sent the plagues because the Pharaoh would not grant the request that Moses made.

4. Pharaoh oppressed the Israelites by making them slaves.

5. To protect the Israelites, God went before them by day in a Pillar of Cloud, and by night in a Pillar of fire.

6. a) The Pillar of Cloud kept the Egyptians from coming close to the Israelites

   b) The cross of the Red (Reed) Sea.

   c) The miracle at the Fountain of Mara

   d) The manna and the quail.

   e) The waters of Horeb.

7. To provide for the needs of His Chosen People.

Chapter 8

Part 1

A.

1. D
2. E
3. B
4. A
5. C

B.

1. G
2. D
3. E
4. F
5. H
6. A
7. B
8. C

Part 2
1. Holy of Holies
2. Tent Temple
3. Images
4. Day of Atonement
5. Moses
6. Jacob
7. Prophet
8. The Catholic Church

Part 3
1. God gave the Ten Commandments to Moses on Mt. Sinai.
2. The Israelites were compelled to wander in the desert for forty years because they murmured against God.
3. The Israelites lacked faith, trust, and obedience.
4. The struggle of the Israelites to enter the Promised Land corresponds to our struggle in that we must keep the laws of God.
5. A thick cloud enfolded Mt. Sinai, lightning flashed, and thunder peeled forth.
6. The temple was a tent supported by wood frames. A curtain hung behind the columns at the entrance. The tent itself was divided by a curtain into two parts, the Sanctuary and the Holy of Holies.

Chapter 9

Part 1
1-3
2-5
3-1
4-2
5-4

Part 2

1. Silo
2. Jacob
3. Jericho
4. Prayed and offered sacrifice to God
5. Juda
6. Christ, who leads us to heaven

Part 3

1. The difficulties were:

   a) The crossing of the Jordan River.

   b) Overcoming fierce tribes.

   c) Conquering the cities of Canaan.

2. Joshua showed trust in God when he:

   a) Obeyed all God commanded in spite of evident impossibil-ities.

   b) Gave orders to cross the waters of the Jordan.

   c) Followed God's directions faithfully in the attack of the various cities.

   d) Prayed for guidance when in doubt or need.

3. The siege of Jericho:

   a) For six days the priests, followed by an army, carried the Ark around the city.

   b) Encircled the city once more on the seventh day

   c) Sounded seven trumpets

   d) All the Israelites raised a mighty shout

   e) Walls of Jericho fell apart, making capture easy.

Chapter 10
God Calls Gideon to Guide the Israelites

Part 1

1. (3)
2. (3)
3. (1)

4. (2)
5. (2)

Part 2

1. Esdraelon
2. Jerobbaal
3. a sign
4. a lamb
5. fortitude and faith

Part 3

1. The Canaanites, a source of evil:
    a) They were a bad example to the Israelites.
    b) The Israelites intermarried with the pagans and thus endangered and often lost their faith.
2. The Israelites were opposed by hostile tribes:
    a) As a punishment for sin.
    b) To bring the Israelites to repentance.
    c) To lead us to see the unhappy result of sin.
3. God's forgiveness was shown when:
    a) He sent them good leaders.
    b) He helped them to conquer their enemy.
4. Signs Gideon received:
    a) At the angel's touch, the sacrifice was set on fire.
    b) The dew fell on the fleece but not on the ground.
    c) The following night, the dew fell on the ground but not on the fleece.
5. God proved that the strength of Israel lay in Him when He ordered Gideon to decrease the Israelite army before attacking the huge forces of the enemy.
6. Gideon overcame the enemy by:
    a) His trust in God.
    b) Surprise attack.
    c) Confusing the enemy by blowing trumpets and flashing

light.

d) In confusion the Madianites killed one another.

e) The escaping soldiers were met and conquered by the tribes of Ephraim.

7. Gideon's humility:

a) He did not feel capable of leading Israel to victory over the Madianites.

b) He refused to be a king.

8. Yes. There are many lessons we can learn from the story and how God will treat us:

a) Wars and other troubles may be a punishment for sin.

b) God forgives us when we are repentant.

c) By associating with bad companions, we may lose our faith.

d) If we have confidence in God, He will give us the special help we need to follow our vocation.

e) With God's help we can accomplish much.

Samson Portrays the Strength of the Son of God and the Weakness of Man

Part 1

1. No
2. Yes
3. No
4. Yes
5. Yes
6. No
7. Yes
8. Yes
9. No
10. Yes

Part 2

1. Canaan became known as Palestine when the Philistines invaded the country.
2. The news announced to Manoe and his wife was:
   a) A son would be born to them.
   b) He would save the Israelites from the Philistines.
   c) He was to be a Nazirite
3. Samson proved his strength:
   a) Tore a lion apart.
   b) Alone, slew thirty men.
   c) Broke heavy cords binding him.
   d) With the jawbone of a donkey slew a thousand men.
   e) Raided cities of the Philistines and escaped unharmed.
4. Led to Samson's defeat:
   a) Marriage to a Philistine woman against God's wish.
   b) Association with the pagan Philistines.
   c) Not observing the vow of the Nazirite.
   d) Forsaking God's Laws.
5. Samson fulfilled work assigned by God by:
   a) Holding the Philistines in check.
   b) sacrificing his own life to kill many Philistines and thus weakening their power.
6. Samson leads our minds to Christ:
   a) In his strength he points to Christ who is the Strong One of God.
   b) Samson gave his life to save his people; Christ gave His life to redeem the world.

God Speaks to Samuel

Questions to Check your Reading

1. Samuel went to live with the high priest because his mother made a vow that, if God would give her a son, she would give him to the service of God.

2. Eli was guilty because he knew of the wickedness of his sons, but he did not correct them.

3. Samuel receives messages from God.
   a) God called Samuel three times.
   b) At the advice of Eli, Samuel asked God what He wished.
   c) God told him to inform Eli of the punishment that awaited him for his negligence in reprimanding his wicked sons.

4. Samuel was considered a Prophet because God gave him messages for the people.

5. The Ark was brought to the battle:
   a) To inspire the Israelite army to fight better.
   b) To gain help from God.

6. Results of the battle with the Philistines:
   a) The Israelites suffered a great defeat.
   b) Thousands of Israelites were killed together with the sons of Eli.
   c) The Ark of the Covenant was captured by the Philistines.
   d) At the news of the captured Ark, Eli fell, broke his neck, and died.

7. The sons of Jechonia were struck dead when they locked into the Ark - God demanded great reverence to be shown for the Ark, where God dwelt in a special manner.

8. The Israelites would conquer the enemy by:
   a) Placing their confidence in God.
   b) Worshiping the one true God.
   c) Improving their sinful lives.

9. God helped the Israelite because:
   a) The Israelites had faith in Samuel's power with God.
   b) God rewarded with a victory the prayer and sacrifice of Samuel.

10. Samuel's responsibility:
    a) To be faithful to God himself.
    b) To encourage and demand faithfulness to God among all the tribes of Israel.

Ruth

Part 1
1. Eli
2. Judges
3. Philistines
4. Israelites
5. Rama
6. Old Testament (or Mosaic Law)
7. Samuel
8. Boaz
9. New Testament (Law of Christ)
10. Silo

Part 2
1. Samuel
2. Anna
3. Eli
4. Samuel
5. Ruth

Chapter 11
The Israelites under Saul

Part 1
1. Samuel
2. Ammonites and Amalecites
3. Philistines
4. victorious
5. the kingship
6. Benjamin
7. Jonathan
8. Goliath
9. Obedience
10. Samuel

Part 2

1. Three reasons why the Israelites wanted a king are:
   a) they wanted a leader
   b) they wanted to win battles
   c) they wanted to be a mighty nation

2. Samuel knew that Saul was to be the King of Israel because when he first saw Saul, God spoke to him saying, "Behold the man of whom I spoke to you. This man shall reign over my people" (1 Sm 9:17).

3. When Samuel anointed Saul as king, he prophesied that Saul would deliver god's people from the enemies that surrounded them as a sign that God had anointed him as king.

4. Once Saul was anointed, he was humble and probably a little timid. For example, when he returned home, Saul did not tell his father about his anointing and he stayed away from the people. The crowds had to come find him in order to celebrate his anointing.

5. We are anointed by God's priests in two of the sacraments of initiation and the Anointing of the Sick:
   a) First at Baptism when we are anointed as Christ was anointed priest, prophet, and king.
   b) We are also anointed at the sacrament of Confirmation, in which we affirm our faith and receive more fully the gifts of the Holy Spirit.
   c) It is possible to obtain the sacrament of the Anointing of the Sick, when a sick person's head and hands are anointed with chrism in blessing.

6. Saul gave renewed courage to the Israelites by uniting them to fight against the Ammonites and winning the battle.

7. God punished Saul for offering the sacrifice in Samuel's place by refusing to allow Saul's reign to continue.

8. Saul disobeyed God in the war against the Amalecites by refusing to kill the king and his people and refusing to

destroy all their possessions. Instead, Saul let the king live and took all the best possessions for himself.

9. Saul made David his armor-bearer because David's music was extremely pleasing to Saul.

10. David escaped from Saul's wicked plans ultimately by trusting in God and depending on Him. Saul, in his sinfulness, attempted to kill David many times but always failed.

The Israelites under David

Part 1

1. Handsome, fearless, humble, kind, pious, etc.
2. a) Because David was the best known of the Psalmists
   b) Because his influence pervades a large portion of the Psalter
3. a) Victory over Isobeth proved God wanted David to be king
   b) Victory over Philistines, etc.

Part 2

A
1. F
2. E
3. H
4. I
5. B
6. D
7. C
8. J
9. A
10. G

B
1. E
2. C

3. G

4. F

5. A

6. D

7. B

Part 3

1. The taking of Jerusalem was important because it helped to unite the tribes of Israel.

2. David showed respect for the Ark of the Covenant:

   a) Selected choirs to sing before the Ark

   b) Formed the priest and the people into a great procession to lead the Ark

   c) David himself led the entire procession

   d) Offered sacrifice during the procession

   e) He joined in the religious dancing before the Ark

   f) Desired to build a beautiful temple for the Ark

3. David was successful in war because God helped him.

4. The punishment of David's wife was that she never had children.

5. No, David was told through the prophet Nathan that he was not to build the temple.

6. The three important things God promised David through the prophet Nathan are:

   a) The kingship over the Chosen People would remain forever in his family line

   b) God also promised posterity so that David's line would continue after his death

   c) Most importantly, God promised that the Messiah would come from his line of descendants.

7. Yes, David was extremely grateful to God for His blessings. After hearing of God's promises, David went to the Ark of the Covenant to give thanks and praise to God for His abundant gifts.

8. David showed kindness to Saul's family by seeking out people from the house of Saul who may still be alive. Jonathan's lame son was the only one who remained. David took him into the palace, promising Jonathan's son that he would restore the lands of Saul and that he would always be taken care of.

9. When the gravity of David's sin was revealed to him, through Nathan, David acknowledged his sin and was truly sorry.

10. Absalom brought sorrow unto David by revolting against his father. Absalom succeeded in deceiving/convincing many people to join his side against his father; including some of David's friends.

11. Absalom died while trying to escape when he rode into a tree branch and became unconscious. Joab then threw three lances into him, his soldiers took him down, and he was buried in the forest.

12. Yes. David was very sorry about the victory. At no point in the battles did David want any harm to come to Absalom. When he heard of Absalom's death, his grief was immeasurable.

13. The message David gave to his son Solomon was the message he had heard from God. God had told David that his son Solomon was to build His temple. David then gathered all the materials Solomon would need and told him how to build the temple.

14. David foreshadows what Christ would be and do because;
a) he was extremely kind and showed mercy to his people; Jesus is known for the love and mercy He maintained for all peoples
b) when he was betrayed by Absalom, he showed mercy and forgiveness; Jesus showed mercy to those who crucified him
c) he did his best to follow God's will and trust in Him; even before His passion and death, Jesus trusted God and followed His will

The Reign of Solomon

Part 1
1. C
2. E
3. B
4. D
5. F
6. A
7. H
8. G

Part 2
1. Solomon
2. Samuel
3. Solomon
4. Jonathan
5. Holy of Holies
6. Wisdom
7. Proverbs
8. Psalms
9. Goliath
10. Nathan

Part 3
1. Solomon used his wisdom to rule his people in many ways, including writing the proverbs. The proverbs, or rules of life, were instructions on how Solomon's people could do good and avoid evil.
2. God showed His pleasure/gratitude for Solomon's prayer for wisdom by granting his prayer and riches and honors.
3. The Queen of Saba visited Solomon because she heard rumors of his great wisdom and she wanted to see for herself if the rumors were true. After visiting with Solomon and asking him many questions, she gave him the gifts of gold and

precious stones she had brought and left satisfied that he was as indeed very wise.

4. Solomon married wives from other nations in order to have these nations allied to him. Solomon ultimately misused his gift of wisdom, became proud, and drew away from God.

5. Solomon got the wood needed for the Temple by asking Hiram, the King of Tyre, for trees from the Lebanon Mountains. Hiram gave Solomon both cedars and fir trees.

6. The main parts of the temple:
   a) The outer and inner walls surrounding the entire area of the Temple.
   b) The courtyard.
   c) The Holy Place containing the Altar of Incense, the Table with Showbread, and the Seven branched candlestick.
   d) The Holy of Holies containing the Ark of the Covenant.

7. Answers will vary.

8. The Holy of Holies was in the shape of a cube of thirty feet. The Interior was concealed by a violet, purple, and scarlet veil richly embroidered with Cherubim.

9. Dedication of the Temple:
   a) Took place on the Feast of Tabernacles.
   b) People were gathered for the event.
   c) Priests and Levites brought the Ark into the Holy of Holies.
   d) Many sacrifices were offered.
   e) It was a day of happiness for all the tribes of Israel.

10. Solomon did not remain true to God. He married pagan women, built temples to pagan gods, and even worshiped these gods himself. He also became inordinately fond of pleasure and taxed his people unjustly.

11. Consequences of Solomon's sins:
   a) was a bad example to his people
   b) destroyed the religious unity of the Jews
   c) was responsible for the division of the kingdom

Chapter 12
The Division of the Kingdom

Part 1

1. Rehoboam
2. Jeroboam
3. Jeroboam
4. Rehoboam
5. (Kingdom of) Juda

Part 2

1. Rehoboam succeeded his father Solomon.
2. Causes of division of the kingdom:
   a) Punishment for the wicked life of Solomon
   b) Rehoboam's mean treatment of the people
3. The rulers:
   a) Jeroboam ruled Israel the northern kingdom of ten tribes
   b) Rehoboam ruled Juda, the southern kingdom composed of the tribes of Juda and Benjamin
4. Jeroboam had two temples built, one in Bethel and another in the city of Dan. Here pagan gods were installed and priests not of the tribe of Levi were hired to offer the unworthy sacrifice. Thus, people were kept from going to the Temple in Jerusalem.
5. The people of Juda, while worshiping the true God, also worshiped false gods.
6. God's displeasure was evident:
   a) The king of Egypt was allowed to gain control over Rehoboam
   b) There was no peace in Juda
   c) War waged between Juda and Israel
7. Eventually both kingdoms would be destroyed.

Elijah the Prophet

Part 1

1. C
2. D
3. G
4. E
5. F
6. A
7. B
8. H

Part 2

1. King Ahab's offense:
    a) Committed many crimes
    b) Forced people to worship false gods
    c) Worshiped false gods himself
    d) Built a temple to the false god Melkart
    e) Killed the true priests of God
2. Resulting punishments:
    a) No rain for three years
    b) Crops failed
    c) Terrible famine
3. To prove who was the true God, first the false prophets called, but in vain, upon their gods to light their sacrifice. Then Eli prayed to God. Soon fire fell from heaven and burned the prepared sacrifice.
4. Eli foreshadows Christ:
    a) Eli was miraculously fed with bread: Christ's Church feeds her children with the Miraculous Bread of Life, the Eucharist.
    b) Eli was taken alive into heaven; Christ's glorified body ascended into heaven.
5. God's Providence towards Eli:
    a) God directed Eli to the Jordan Valley where a raven

brought him bread daily.

b) When no water was available, God told Eli to go to Sarepta where he received food and drink from a window.

c) A fire from heaven destroyed the soldiers who came to seize him.

6. Ahab's unlawful desires led to:

a) Calumny - Naboth was falsely accused of blasphemy

b) Murder - Naboth was stoned to death

c) Stealing - The King took Naboth's vineyard

7. When Ahab was sorry and did penance, God forgave him some of his temporal punishment.

8. Miracles Eli performed:

a) The widow's meal and oil were never exhausted.

b) He brought the widow's son back to life.

c) His prayers brought fire from heaven to light the sacrifice.

9. By using a little salt and blessing a spring, Elisha purified the water.

10. Prophets were sent to people to:

a) Bring messages from God

b) Teach and explain the Old Law

c) Lead the people back to God

d) Acquaint the people with the coming Messiah

e) Prepare the way for the kingdom which the Redeemer was to establish on earth

11. The King of Assyria came with a great army, took the capital city, Samaria, and led most of the people into captivity to Assyria. The kingdom of Israel was ended.

Chapter 13
The Prophet Isaiah

Part 1

1. Cyrus
2. Hezekiah

3. Holy, Holy, Holy, etc.
4. Babylonians
5. Juda
6. Isaiah
7. Sennacherib

Part 2

1. While Isaiah was praying in the temple God sent him a vision.
2. The warning was that God was about to destroy their country.
3. Ahaz practiced in many ways the religion of the pagans.
4. Hezekiah did the following:
   a) Destroyed all the altars where idols were worshipped
   b) Restored the services of the Temple
   c) Commanded the priests and Levites to cleanse the Temple
   d) In atonement had the Passover celebrated.
5. God gave him the strength and courage to rebel against the Assyrians and gain a victory over the Philistines.
6. Isaiah warned Hezekiah so that he would place all his trust in God.
7. The country of Juda was happy under Hezekiah because the people had returned to the worship of God.
8. Isaiah, chapter 29 (conversation of the Gentiles),
   Isaiah, chapter 45 (Cyrus as a figure of Christ the great deliverer of God's people) Isaiah, chapter 49 (Christ shall bring the Gentiles to salvation)
   Isaiah, chapter 53 (Prophecy of the Passion of Christ)
   Isaiah, Chapter 7, 14 (The Virgin Birth)

Jerimiah, a Tender Prophet

Part 1

1. Egypt
2. Nabuchodonosor
3. Baruch

4. Jeremiah
5. Sedecia
6. Babylonians
7. Nebuchadnezzar
8. Josiah

Part 2

1. With the exception of Hezekiah and Josiah all the kings of Juda were wicked.
2. Josiah taught the people to love and serve God.
3. Jeremiah foretold the destruction of Jerusalem.
4. Jeremiah at first refused God's call because he was afraid, he was not gifted in speaking. An angel touched his mouth and at the same time he had a vision in which he saw the message he was to carry to the nations.
5. The king of Babylon, Nebuchadnezzar, destroyed Jerusalem and carried the people into captivity.
6. God abandoned the Jews because they again practiced idolatry.
7. Yes, they were preserved.
8. The Church reads the Lamentations during Holy Week.
9. He prophesied that the Babylonians would take Egypt.
10. Jeremiah with the help of Baruch, his servant, wrote all the messages God sent to the Chosen People. Jeremiah died in Egypt.
11. The Ark of the Covenant contained the Tablets of the Law and a measure of manna. It was kept in the Holy of Holies.
12. Yes, the Babylonian captivity was a warning to the Chosen People of the New Testament.

The Prophet Ezekiel

Part 1

1. Yes
2. No

3. Yes
4. No
5. Yes
6. No
7. Yes

Part 2

1. Because the Jews were living among pagan people.
2. God sent His prophet Ezekiel to guide His Chosen People.
3. He spoke of the trouble and punishment that was to come.
4. He reminded them that God would take care of Israel and defend His People against hostile nations.
5. Because he repeated to them the promise that they would return from exile.
6. No, he did not live to see the restoration.
7. Because his writings were similar to those of Isaiah.

Chapter 14
Haggai and Zechariah

Part 1

1. Yes
2. Yes
3. No
4. Yes
5. No
6. Yes
7. Yes
8. Yes
9. Yes

Part 2

1. A
2. D
3. E

4. C

5. B

Part 3

1. Cyrus, the King of Persia, permitted the Jews to return to Juda.

2. Zorobabel was the leader and governor; Joshua was the high priest.

3. Haggai and Zechariah urged the people to continue rebuilding the Temple and to have regular services in honor of God.

4. God permitted the Chosen People to suffer to keep them faithful to Him.

5. The prophets told the Jews to continue to rebuild the Temple. God was displeased because they built their own homes first and allowed the Temple to remain in ruins.

6. Darius gave the Jews large sums of money and great herds of cattle.

7. Haggai promised the people a greater Temple and predicted the Church which Christ would establish.

8. The following are the things that Zachariah foretold about the Messiah:

   a) Christ's entry into Jerusalem seated upon a colt

   b) the price that was to be paid to his betrayer

   c) that the enemies would strike the shepherds and scatter the sheep

Malachi

Part 1

1. Babylon

2. Nehemiah

3. Sabbath

4. St. John the Baptist

5. Old Law

The Rule of Antiochus

Part 1

1. D
2. E
3. G
4. I
5. A
6. C
7. H
8. J
9. B
10. F

Part 2

1. The Jews were permitted to practice their religion as long as they paid taxes and adhered to the foreign policy of the overlord.

2. The lesson we learn is that we, too, must suffer courageously for our faith.

3. Mathathia and his sons were national heroes because they attacked many towns and drove out the forces of the king. They were religious heroes because they punished the Jews who disobeyed God.

4. Judas Maccabeus cleansed the Temple and restored the divine worship.

5. Two of Daniel's prophecies are:
   a) Daniel was able to prophesy the rise and fall of many nations.
   b) Daniel also saw that God's Church on earth would never be destroyed

6. Daniel was saved from death in the den of lions as proof that the God of the Israelites was the true God.

7. Several people mentioned in the chapter who were to be

closely connected with the Savior are: Anna and Joachim, the parts of Mary; Zachary and Elizabeth, the parents of John the Baptist; Joseph, the spouse of Mary; Mary, who was to become the Mother of Jesus, and others.

Chapter 15
The Story of Job

Questions to check your reading

1. Job's outstanding virtue was patience. He proved it by accepting all of his trials with patient resignation.
2. God rewarded Job for his patience in suffering by blessing him more abundantly than before his trials.
3. Answers will vary
4. The story of Job teaches us that suffering is not always a punishment for sin. God allows trials to come upon the just man, to enrich him with His graces.

The Story of Jonah

Questions to check your reading

1. The story of Jonah teaches us that we cannot flee from God. His omnipotence and justice reach to the farthest ends of the earth.
2. A sinful nation or people can still obtain mercy from God by showing repentance.
3. Jonah was commanded by God to do missionary work in Nineveh. Today missionaries are called to pagan lands to preach the Gospel. Boys and girls of today do sometimes try to avoid God's call to serve Him.
4. School children can help the missions by prayer and sacrifice.
5. Christ came to save all nations.

Tobit

Questions to check your reading
1. The works of charity Tobit performed are:
   a) he comforted his fellow captives
   b) he relieved the miseries of others
   c) he buried the dead
2. Tobit proved his loyalty to God by:
   a) continuing to perform the works of mercy despite the danger involved and his wife's disapproval
   b) bearing his blindness patiently
   c) refusing to complain when poverty overtook him
   d) teaching his son to be faithful to God
3. The young Tobit was protected on his journey by the Archangel Raphael who accompanied him.
4. Parts of the story that prove young Tobit loved his parents:
   a) promised to follow his father's advice to lead a good life
   b) set out to collect a debt to please his father
   c) looked for a guide because his father wished it
   d) desired to return home quickly to prevent his parents from worrying
5. God sometimes allows the faithful to be visited by misfortune in order to test their virtue and loyalty to him.
6. Through the book of Tobit, God is trying to teach us that we have duties towards the dead, the lesson of giving alms, respect for family life, and a regard for the sacredness of marriage.

Esther

Questions to check your reading
1. Haman hated Mordecai because he discovered Haman's plot to kill the king.
2. To save her people Esther fasted and prayed and then risked her life by presenting herself to the king without being

summoned.

3. The king offered Esther anything she wished, even half of the kingdom.

4. The elevation of Mordecai and Esther, and the deliverance which resulted, reminds us of the history of Joseph because he was persecuted, then exalted for the salvation of his people.

5. God protected the children of Israel because they were His Chosen People and from them the Redeemer was to come.

6. The story of Esther points out how surely God disposes of all things. He brings about His designs either for the punishment of the wicked, or for the protection of the good.

Judith

Part 1

1. Jonah
2. Younger Tobit
3. Job
4. King of Persia
5. Older Tobit
6. Esther
7. Older Tobit
8. King of Persia

Part 2

1. G
2. E
3. J
4. M
5. H
6. C
7. L
8. K
9. D

10. I
11. A
12. B
13. N
14. F

Part 3

1. Holofernes threatened the city of Bethulia by digging a trench around the city of Bethulia and thereby cutting off the water supply.
2. Judith was disappointed with the inhabitants of Bethulia because they showed lack of trust in God by setting a limit of time for help to arrive.
3. Judith asked the people to pray and fast that God might strengthen her in her undertaking and keep her from sin.
4. Judith had great trust in God because after praying for help she was not afraid to undertake the difficult task of saving her people. She knew that God would deliver His people from the enemy.

Chapter 16

Part 1

1. Son
2. Malachi
3. Holy Place
4. God
5. Dumb
6. Benedictus
7. Relatives
8. Prepare the way for Christ
9. Penance and prayer

Part 2

1. God tested the perseverance in prayer of Zechariah and Elizabeth by not granting their prayer until they were well advanced in age.

2. The things the angel revealed to Zechariah:

    a) a son would be born

    b) his name would be John

    c) his son would prepare the way for the Redeemer

    d) that Zachary would be dumb until the event would take place

3. The connection between John the Baptist and the coming Redeemer is that John was to be the Precursor of the Redeemer.

4. Zechariah and Elizabeth insisted on the name John because it was the name revealed by the angel.

5. Some lessons we can apply to our own lives from the story of Zechariah and Elizabeth are:

    a) Perseverance in prayer

    b) Obedience to the Will of God

    c) Trust in God

6. The fact that the son was born in the old age of his parents was proof to the neighbors that John was destined for great things.

7. Zechariah, in his prayers, is grateful for the following favors:

    a) the redemption of the people

    b) salvation from enemies

    c) a knowledge of salvation through forgiveness of sin

    d) "And thou, child, shalt be called a prophet of the Most High, for thou shalt go before the face of the Lord to prepare His ways," (Lk 1:76).

8. John the Baptist prepared for his mission by leading a life of prayer and penance in a nearby desert.

Chapter 17

Part 1

1. C
2. B
3. B
4. A
5. C
6. C
7. B
8. A
9. C
10. A
11. B
12. B
13. A
14. B

Part 2

1. Mary was a maiden of the family of David who lived in Nazareth.
2. The angel Gabriel came to Mary to tell her that she would become the Mother of the Savior.
3. The angel's greeting was confusing to Mary because she wondered why the angel should praise her so highly.
4. The angel revealed to Mary that:
   a) she would become the Mother of the Redeemer
   b) his name would be Jesus
   c) he would be great - Son of the Most High - given the throne of David His father - His Kingdom would have no end.
   d) Elizabeth would have a son
5. One of the prophecies Mary fulfilled was, "Behold a maiden shall conceive, and bear a son, and his name shall be called Emmanuel" (Is 7:14).

6. Mary shares in the work of the redemption by the fact that she consented to become the Mother of the Savior.

7. Mary made the journey to help Elizabeth and to rejoice with her over the favors and blessings God had sent them.

8. The part of the Hail Mary that is composed of Elizabeth's words is, "Blessed art thou among women."

9. In the Magnificat, Mary gave praise and glory to God in thanksgiving for the gifts He bestowed on her and all the world through the fulfillment of His promise of a Messiah.

10. An angel revealed the privilege to him.

11. Mary and Joseph went to Bethlehem to be enrolled according to the Emperor's command.

12. They had to go to Bethlehem, the city in which the Redeemer was to be born.

13. Practices from the life of Mary and Joseph that we can apply to our own lives are:
a) obedience to the Will of God; obedience to lawful superiors.
b) humility
c) gratitude to God for His mercies
d) purity
e) kindness to others

Chapter 18

Part 1

A.

1. D
2. J
3. H
4. G
5. F
6. B
7. C

8. I
9. E
10. A

B.
1. B, D
2. A, E, G
3. C, F, H

C.
1. F
2. D
3. E
4. B
5. C
6. A

Part 2

1. Joseph and Mary sought shelter in a stable because they were unable to find lodging in the crowded city of Bethlehem.
2. Christ, the Son of God, was born that night in Bethlehem.
3. The shepherds learned of the birth of the Savior because a brilliant light changed the dark sky and the angel gave the message about the Savior.
4. The name Jesus was given to the Infant eight days after the birth.
5. Mary and Joseph obeyed the law which obliged parents to bring their first-born to the Temple to offer him to the Lord.
6. Simeon spoke of the salvation that had come to Israel, of a light of revelation to the Gentiles and the glory of Israel.
7. The people in Jerusalem heard of the birth of the Messiah because Anna spread the news to the people of Jerusalem.
8. The Magi came to adore the "King of the Jews" because they

cooperated with the grace of God when they saw the star.

9. Herod's plan was unsuccessful because an angel warned the Magi to return home by another road.

10. The Holy Family's flight into Egypt should help us to remember that those who are with Christ will suffer many hardships because of the hatred of the enemies of God. We also learn to promptly obey the will of God.

11. We call these years Christ's hidden life because the Evangelists do not say anything about these years except that He "advanced in wisdom and age and grace before God and men" (Lk2:5).

12. The one incident recorded in the Gospels from Christ's hidden life is the pilgrimage to the Temple.

13. The Holy Family was happy because there was an abundance of love, unity, and peace in their humble little home.

14. Some of the important prophecies that were fulfilled in the birth and early life of the Savior are:
    a) Prophecy of Isaiah: "Behold a maiden shall conceive, and bear a son, and his name shall be called Emmanuel" (Is 7:14).
    b) Prophecy of Isaiah: "And the Gentiles shall walk in the light, and Kings in the brightness of thy rising" (Is 60:3). etc.

Chapter 19

Part 1
1. B and E
2. D
3. C, F, and I
4. A, G, and H

Part 2
1. Penance
2. change - sinful
3. Repentance
4. members of the Sanhedrin

5. Charity - duties of state
6. leaders
7. Jordan River
8. Herod Antipas
9. Christ (Jesus)
10. John the Baptist

Part 3

1. John the Baptist prepared the people to receive the Redeemer by urging the people to change their sinful lives and do penance.
2. John's mission is similar to the priests of today because he warned the people of his time to repent and to do penance.
3. John baptized as a symbol of repentance, but it was not a sacrament.
4. The Sacrament of Baptism puts upon us the obligation to follow the teachings of Christ and, if necessary, to be ready to face martyrdom.
5. The Sanhedrin took a keen interest in John the Baptist because he attracted such large crowds, and they alone claimed the authority to grant permission to preach.
6. The Sanhedrin was composed of seventy-two members chosen from the chief priests, scribes, and elders presided over by the high priest. The Sanhedrin had authority in matters pertaining to government and religious practice. In regard to the death sentence, the permission of the Roman procurator had to be obtained.
7. The Pharisees believed very strongly in tradition and the Sadducees disregarded it completely.
8. The Scribes were men specialized in the study of the Law of Moses.
9. John spoke more severely to the leaders because he knew they were evil with no intention of improving.
10. Examples:

a) John humbly admitted to the leaders that he was only "the voice of one crying in the desert" and not Elijah nor the Messiah (Jn 1:23).

b) John preached under opposition from the leaders, and because of his faithfulness to duty, suffered imprisonment and death.

c) He spoke severely to the leaders of the people. He also denounced Herod for his wickedness.

d) John lived a penitential life of prayer and fasting.

11. John was martyred because he defended the sanctity of marriage.

12. John set an example for us by following his vocation and doing all that God required of him.

Chapter 20

Part 1

1. God the Father to Jesus
2. Christ to Satan
3. John the Baptist to his disciples
4. Nathaniel to Philip
5. Mary to Jesus
6. Christ to Philip (or Andrew)
7. Christ to Priests and Pharisees
8. Christ to His Blessed Mother
9. Christ to Satan
10. Mary to the servants

Part 2

1. 4
2. 2
3. 3
4. 5
5. 1
6. 6

Part 3

1. Philip
2. Simon (Peter)
3. Nathaniel
4. Andrew
5. John

Part 4

1. Before Christ began His public teaching He was baptized by John, and He fasted in the desert for forty days.
2. During the baptism of Jesus, St. John saw the Holy Spirit, the Third Person of the Blessed Trinity, in the form of a dove appeared over the head of Christ, the Second Person of the Blessed Trinity, and he heard the words of the Father, the First Person of the Blessed Trinity.
3. Christ allowed the devil to tempt Him that we might learn how we ought to prepare for important events in our life.
4. The devil tempted Christ first to the sin of gluttony, second to the sin of pride, and third to the sin of greed and ambition.
5. To the first temptation He said, "not in bread alone does man live…" To the second temptation He said, "Thou shalt not tempt the Lord thy God." to the third temptation, "Be gone, Satan, the Lord thy God…:
6. John pointed Christ out to his disciples with the words, "Behold the Lamb of God who takes away the sins of the world."
7. The first disciples of Christ were: Peter, Andrew, John, Philip, and Nathanael.
8. John and Andrew followed Christ because St. John pointed Him out. Andrew told Peter and brought him to Jesus. First met Philp and said, "Follow me," which Philip did. Philip in turn introduced Nathanael to Christ.
9. Christ attended the Marriage Feast of Cana because the couple were related to His Mother, and to sanctify the marriage

bond.

10. At the Wedding Feast of Cana Christ performed His first miracle at Mary's request.
11. The miracle at Cana strengthened the faith of Christ's disciples.
12. Christ was angered at the buying and selling of animals and the money-changing that was going on within the court of the Gentiles before the Holy Place.
13. Christ showed His authority by making a whip of little cords and driving out the merchants and overturning the tables of the money-changers.
14. The Scribes and Pharisees were angered because they thought that Jesus was usurping their authority.
15. When Christ spoke of the temple, He was referring to Himself.

Chapter 21

1. H
2. D
3. I
4. J
5. A
6. B
7. G
8. C
9. F
10. E

Chapter 22

Part 1

1. Parable
2. Simon's
3. James and John
4. Nathanael

5. Fulfill
6. Beatitudes - blessing - reward
7. The Scribes - Pharisees
8. Love of God and love of neighbor
9. Matthew
10. Wise man

Part 2.

1. The Savior's great mission was to establish a Kingdom in order to give back to man the grace that had been lost through Adam, and by means of this Kingdom which is His Church to unite all men with His Father into one family.
2. James and John were the sons of Zebedee. They became Apostles.
3. Before our Lord chose His Apostles He spent the whole night in prayer.
4. Matthew was a publican who became an Apostle.
5. Jesus instructed the Apostles to preach the Gospel after His own example by action more than by word, by doing good more than by preaching.
6. The word "apostle" means sent.
7. The eight rules for happiness are called the Beatitudes.
8. The New law was a law of love - while the Old Law was one of fear.
9. Our Lord called His Apostles "light of the world" because just as a light expels darkness, so the Apostles by the light of the truth they preached and their own good example would drive out the darkness of ignorance and wrong ideas from the minds of men and show the way to heaven.
10. The New Law is a fulfillment and perfection of the Old Law.
11. Answers will vary.
12. Answers will vary.

Chapter 23

Part 1

1. The Mustard Seed
2. The Leaven
3. The Wheat and the Cockle or the Net
4. The Sower
5. The Treasure or the Pearl of Great Price
6. The Sower or the Wheat and the Cockle
7. The Net
8. The Pearl of Great Price or the Treasure
9. The Sower
10. The Wheat and the Cockle or the Net

Part 2

1. Jesus foretold the growth of His Church in the parable of the mustard seed.
2. In the parable about the net which the fishermen cast into the sea and drew out filled with fish of every kind, Christ points out how the good and bad are together in His Church on earth.
3. In the parable of the leaven, Jesus taught that the Kingdom of God is life which grows from within. It permeates ma, changes his sinful life to one of virtue, and makes him acceptable to God.
4. Answers will vary.
5. Our Savior compares Faith to a gift.
6. Rich people are poor in spirit when they use their wealthy wisely and share it unselfishly with those who need it.

Chapter 24

Part 1

1. G
2. F

3. J
4. H
5. I
6. A
7. C
8. E
9. B
10. D

Part 2

1. Yes
2. No
3. Yes
4. Yes
5. No
6. Yes
7. Yes
8. No
9. No
10. Yes
11. Yes
12. Yes
13. Yes

Part 3

1. They made so many regulations about keeping holy the Sabbath that people became confused. Christ tried to teach them that the Sabbath was made for man and not man for the Sabbath.
2. The cure on the Sabbath of the man with the withered hand made the Pharisees think of other ways to harm Him.
3. The centurion showed that he had faith and humility when he said, "Lord, I am not worthy that you should come under my roof…"

4.   a) The Son of the Widow of Naim; b) The Daughter of Jairus.
5.   It teaches the lesson of gratitude.
6.   The storms of error and persecution.
7.   Answers will vary.

Chapter 25

Part 1

A.
1.   G
2.   F
3.   B
4.   E
5.   C
6.   A
7.   D

B.
1.   C
2.   D
3.   B
4.   A

C.
1.   C
2.   D
3.   E
4.   B
5.   A

Part 2

1.   The Bread of the New Law differs from the Manna in that those who eat of this Bread will not die.
2.   Christ worked the First and Second Multiplication of the Loaves and Fishes to prepare men's minds of the Holy

Eucharist.

3. The Jews found the word, "I am the bread of life...if anyone eat of it he will not die... and the bread that I will give is my flesh for the life of the world," hard to believe.

4. Christ did not explain His doctrine when He saw the disbelief of the people.

5. Peter comforted Christ by his great faith when he said, "we have come to believe and to know that thou art Christ, the Son of God."

6. No, the Jews as a people did not accept Christ as the promised Messiah.

7. Peter made his profession of Faith in these words, "Thou art the Christ, the Son of the Living God."

8. Jesus rewarded Peter by making him the head of His Church and giving him the highest authority and power on earth.

9. By the primacy of Peter among the Apostles is meant that he is the first among them. Jesus made Peter the pope.

10. Peter, James, and John saw Jesus transfigured.

11. In the transfiguration, Moses represented the ancient Mosaic Law.

12. Eli stood for the prophets.

13. Jesus made His glory known to the three Apostles because He wished to strengthen their faith in Him.

Chapter 26

Part 1

1. His Apostles
2. Lazarus
3. Mary and Martha
4. Judas
5. Simon
6. Jewish leaders (Pharisees)
7. Jesus

8. Peter
9. Judas
10. Christ

Part 2

1. Jerusalem
2. Bethany
3. Jerusalem
4. Egypt
5. Temple
6. Jerusalem
7. Garden of Olives
8. Brook of Cedron

Part 3

1. H
2. C
3. J
4. B
5. I
6. E
7. A
8. F
9. D
10. G

Part 4

1. While Jesus was in Bethany Mary anointed Him, and the Jewish leaders planned to put Him to death.
2. Throngs of people greeted Jesus with palm branches and welcomed Him with Hosanna, an age-old saying which means "Save, I pray thee."
3. Jesus wept over Jerusalem because He could foresee His rejection by His own people.
4. They were unable to answer Him and were convinced that He

was a great prophet.

5. Judas was filled with worldly ambitions.
6. The Passover was a remembrance of the deliverance of the people from the slavery of Egypt.
7. The Paschal Lamb is a symbol of Christ.
8. The Apostles prepared the Pasch in the house of an unknown man in Jerusalem.
9. Christ washed the feet of the Apostles.
10. "Take and earth; this is my Body." "Take this and drink; this is my Blood."
11. Christ established the priesthood to make certain that His sacrament would be continued for all mankind.
12. Christ gave His Apostles a new commandment of love. "This is my commandment that you love one another as I have loved you."

Chapter 27

Part 1
1. Peter, James, and John
2. Kiss
3. Annas
4. Caiaphas
5. Pilate
6. Simon of Cyrene
7. Claudia
8. Dismas
9. Joseph of Arimathea or disciples
10. Maidservant

Part 2
1. Peter
2. Christ
3. Judas
4. Dismas

5. Christ
6. Christ
7. Judas
8. The Jews
9. Pilate
10. The Jews

Part 3

1. The weight of the sins of the world caused the bloody sweat of our Lord.
2. Jesus treated Judas kindly and hoped to change his heart.
3. The Sanhedrin did not have power to impose a death sentence so they sent Jesus to Pilate.
4. To avoid the responsibility of giving the death sentence Pilate sent Christ to Herod.
5. Pilate tried to save Jesus by offering to liberate Him or Barabbas, by having Christ scourged and appealing to the sympathy of the people.
6. Simon of Cyrene.
7. Answers will vary.
8. Jesus promised forgiveness and heaven to the good thief.
9. Christ, though St. John, gave us His Blessed Mother to be our heavenly mother.
10. The veil of the Temple tore from top to bottom; the earth shook; the rocks split; and on Easter the bodies of some saints rose from the graves.
11. John, Joseph, and Nicodemus together with Mary took charge of our Lord's burial.
12. The Pharisees remembered that Jesus had predicted His Resurrection.

Chapter 28

Part 1

1. Mary Magdalen (or holy women)

2.   40
3.   Peter and John
4.   "Peace be to you"
5.   Cenacle
6.   Resurrection

Part 2

1.   C
2.   A
3.   B
4.   F
5.   D
6.   E

Part 3

1.   The resurrection took place sometime after midnight on Easter Sunday.
2.   The women found the sepulcher open and two angels sitting where the body of Jesus had been laid.
3.   The Apostles did not understand what Scripture meant by "That He must rise again from the dead."
4.   Mary Magdalene was rewarded by an apparition of Christ.
5.   The Apostles recognized Christ when He sat at the table with them, took bread, blessed it, and broke it and gave it to them.
6.   They received the power to forgive sins when Christ breathed upon them and said, "Received the Holy Spirit; whose sins you shall forgive, they are forgiven them; and whose sins you shall retain; they are retained."
7.   By these words Christ made Peter head of His Church.
8.   Just before His Ascension Christ commissioned the Apostles to make disciples of all nations and to baptize them in the name of the Father, and of the Son and of the Holy Spirit.
9.   On the 40th day after His Resurrection.

10. Fifty days after the Resurrection the Holy Spirit descended upon the Apostles and infused into them grace and strength. On this first Pentecost 3000 were converted.

11. The Apostles became fearless, spoke languages of different countries and were able to touch the hearts of those who listened to them preach.

12. Look up these quotations.

Chapter 29

Part 1

1. D
2. B
3. I
4. A
5. H
6. C
7. E
8. J
9. F
10. G

Part 2

1. The church began her divine mission on Pentecost day, when the Apostles preached the gospel in Jerusalem and converted many Jews.

2. The example of the holy lives of the earthly Christians brought thousands into the Church.

3. The deacons cared for the poor and helped the Apostles with the preaching.

4. The two outstanding deacons were Philip and Stephen.

5. Philip preached to the people of Samaria.

6. The first Christians martyr was Stephen, the deacon. He was stoned to death: while dying he prayed for his persecutors.

7. Peter and John came from Jerusalem to confirm the many

Samaritans whom Philip had baptized.

8.   St. Peter converted the first Gentile and thus opened the way to Christ's Church to all peoples and nations.

9.   The first, seventh, and tenth persecutions were the most severe.

10. The persecutions lasted for a period of about two hundred fifty years.

11. The catacombs were underground places and passageways in and about Rome. They were used as burial places, chapels where Mass could be offered for the faithful, and for places of refuge for those who were fleeing from persecutors.

12. Roman emperors persecuted the Church in an attempt to destroy it.

13. Constantine granted freedom in the exercise of religion in his decree, the Edict of Milan.

Chapter 30

Part 1

1.   Heretic
2.   Arians
3.   Nicea
4.   Patriarchs
5.   St. Jerome, Ambrose, Augustine
6.   St. Jerome
7.   St. Augustine
8.   Nestorians
9.   St. John Chrysostom
10. St. Ambrose

Part 2

1.   Arius denied that Christ is God.
2.   The errors of Arianism were condemned at the Council of Nicaea.
3.   The articles of faith prepared at the Council of Nicaea are

found in the Nicene Creed.

4. St. Athanasius defended the divinity of Christ against the errors of Arianism.

5. St. John Chrysostom was called "golden-mouthed" because of his powerful sermons.

6. Some bishops in the East were called Patriarchs because they ruled many provinces.

7. Nestorius taught there were two persons in Christ, and Mary was not the mother of God.

8. St. Ambrose could well be called the "Christopher" of his day.

9. St. Augustine was a convert of St. Ambrose. He formed the order of Hermits of St. Augustine.

10. St. Monica prayed for many years for her son's conversion.

11. St. Jerome translated the Bible into Latin.

12. Pelagius denied the necessity of grace of salvation.

13. When we say that the Church has triumphed over all heresies, we mean that heresies have never been able to deprive it of any of the truths deposited with it.

Chapter 31

Part 1

1. G
2. F
3. L
4. H
5. A
6. J
7. B
8. D
9. C
10. K
11. E
12. I

Part 2

1. The Rhine and Danube Rivers.
2. The people of Rome had become wealthy and so lived easy, careless lives. They paid men to fight in their armies.
3. Pope Leo I went unarmed to ask Attila to spare Rome, and his request was granted.
4. The mighty Roman Empire fell in 476 when Odoacer conquered Italy and took over the rule himself. A large part of Europe was overrun with barbarian people.
5. The Church maintained her own existence and turned to the Barbarians and offered them her good tidings of salvation.
6. It was during an important battle that Clovis saw his men losing ground and becoming weak and discouraged. He decided to follow the advice of his queen, Clotilda, and pray to her God for help. The scene of battle changed and his men were victorious. Clovis gave his promise to be baptized.
7. St. Columba took with him a number of Irish monks and for many years they worked in Scotland, converting the King of the Picts and many of his people to the Faith.
8. St. Augustine with forty Benedictine monks went to England to convert the people.
9. The Queen influenced King of Ethelbert in favor of the missionaries, and they were given permission to preach the Faith to the people.
10. St. Boniface destroyed a great oak "Tree of Thor" which the people held sacred. When nothing unusual happened the people believed that their god, Thor, was powerless and asked to be baptized.
11. Two Greek monks who were brothers, Cyril and Methodius worked among the Slavic people.
12. Answers will vary.

Chapter 32

Part 1

1. J
2. C
3. F
4. G
5. D
6. I
7. H
8. B
9. A
10. E

Part 2

1. Seventh
2. Islamism or Mohammedanism
3. Mohammed
4. Arabia
5. Tours
6. Charles Martel
7. Koran
8. Constantinople
9. Greek
10. Iconoclasm
11. Orthodox - Dissidents (schismatics)

Part 3

1. Teachings of Mohammed:

   a) There is only one god, Allah.

   b) Mohammed is the greatest prophet that ever lived.

   c) Christ is only another prophet.

   d) A Moslem who was killed in battle against the unbelievers would be highly rewarded in heaven.

2. Reasons why the Muslims made rapid conquests:

a) Religion spread by force.

b) The Eastern Empire was too weak to resist.

c) Misunderstandings between Eastern and Western Church.

d) Islam - an easy to follow religion.

e) Love of plunder encouraged.

f) the Muslims conquered and destroyed Christianity in Palestine, Syria, and Egypt, then pushed into Europe taking Sicily and Spain.

3. Religious beliefs of the Muslims:

a) prayers at stated intervals would keep them holy.

b) Death in battle against infidels insured an eternity of pleasure.

4. The Muslims were checked by the arm of the Franks under Charles Martel near the city of Tours.

5. Results of the Muslim conquest:

a) Did more damage to the East than the Barbarians did to the West.

b) Damage was lasting.

c) Destroying all signs of Christianity in conquered countries.

6. Possible answer: No, though at times it may seem that much damage is done to the Church. The enemies of the Church can do no more harm than God will allow. Often God confounds the enemies of the Church by changing the evil deeds into blessings for the Church by changing the evil deeds into blessings for the Church. Recall how the captivity of the Chosen People in the Old Testament spread the knowledge of the Redeemer. The persecutions brought more converts into the Church and sent missionaries into other lands.

7. Led to Greek Schism.

a) Heresies, especially Iconoclasm, breaking out in the East.

b) The transfer of the capital of the Roman Empire to Constantinople.

c) Interference of the emperors with the Church in the East.

d) Decline of reverence and respect for the Pope.

e) Distance separating the East from the West.

f) Slow communication.

g) Feeling of superiority of the East over the Barbarian-flooded West.

8. Residing in Constantinople, a great distance from the Pope in Rome, the emperor was in a position to meddle with the affairs of the Eastern Church. Since many of the emperors were Arians, they felt it was their right to control the Church.

9. Manner in which Photius paved the way for Greek Schism:

a) Disobeyed decisions of the Pope.

b) Accused the Pope and the Latin Church of heresy.

c) Convinced the people in the East that the West was in error.

10. Led to the final break between the Church in the East and West:

a) Patriarch of Constantinople, Cerularius, desired a separation.

b) Compiled a list of grievances against the Latin Church.

c) Aroused the people in the East to a hatred of the Church of Rome.

11. Results of the Greek Schism:

a) Many countries lost to the Church.

b) Only a few groups of people returned to the Church.

c) Greek Schism still exists.

12. The Byzantine Catholics remained faithful to the true Church or returned to the Church. They acknowledged the Pope as the visible head of the Church. The Greek Orthodox do not acknowledge the authority of the Pope.

Chapter 33

Part 1

1. Feudalism

2. Vassal

3. Fief

4. Concordat

5. Charlemagne
6. Truce of God
7. Franciscans and Dominicans
8. Guilds
9. Chivalry
10. Romanesque and Gothic

Part 2

1. F
2. E
3. I
4. C
5. H
6. D
7. J
8. B
9. A
10. G

Part 3

1. Charlemagne established schools and libraries and made education available to the people.
2. Groups of students gathered together and hired a professor or professors to teach them. This usually took place in the city rather than in a secluded monastery.
3. The vassal helped the lord in time of battle and was required to render other services.
4. A layman took it upon himself to appoint a high Church officer and transfer to him the ring and crosier, a symbol of his authority.
5. (Any five from the list under topic Results of Crusades.)
6. The Military Orders were important at this time because they aided in the Crusades by fighting, and by caring for the wounded and sick.

7. Religious orders founded at this time were often called mendicant because their monks did not live like the monks of the time, instead they went about begging.

8. The purpose of the Third Order of St. Francis was to aid people living in the world to save their souls.

9. The Romanesque style of architecture had rounded arches and thick heavy walls.

10. The gothic style of architecture was characterized by thin high walls, with windows rather high and topped by pointed arches.

11. The Church enriched the guilds with many spiritual benefits.

12. The guilds promoted the temporal and spiritual welfare of the members.

13. St. Thomas infused new life into theology and drew together the most splendid features of past thoughts, both pagan and Christian, into a magnificent whole. Dante wrote the Divine comedy, one of the greatest religious poems of all times.

Chapter 34

Part 1

1. Revival or rebirth
2. Century
3. Ferdinand and Isabella
4. Christopher Columbus
5. St. Catherine of Siena
6. Savonarola
7. Humanism

Part 2

1. F
2. A
3. B
4. G
5. J

6. H
7. C
8. I
9. D
10. E

Part 3

1. Through the influence of the French King the papal residence was moved from Rome to Avignon. Severn popes lived at Avignon over a period of nearly seventy years. St. Catherine of Siena urged the Pope to return to Rome.

2. The Great Western Schism grew out of the rivalry between the French and Italian interest regarding the papal throne. Difficulty settled at the Council at Constance.

3. The authority of the Church was weakened by the Great Western Schism.

4. St. Joan of Arc was born in Domremy, France. Voices urged her to go to the aid of the uncrowned King of France. She succeeded in having the King crowned, in winning many victories for the French, and in driving back the English. She was finally captured, suffered an unfair trial, and was buried in the marketplace of the city of Roun.

5. One of the purposes of the Humanities was a study of the classics.

6. The word "classics" means the books written by the Greek and Latin authors.

7. Nepotism was the practice of appointing one's own relatives to high positions to secure loyalty and favors.

8. Answers may vary. One possible answer, Christianity was able to express many of its beauties through art and architecture which elevates the mind and brings us closer to God.

Chapter 35

Part 1

1. H
2. M
3. E
4. I
5. L
6. A
7. O
8. K
9. G
10. P
11. N
12. J
13. C
14. B
15. F
16. D

Part 2

1. The Protestant Revolt is sometimes called the Reformation because the heretical leaders claimed they reformed the Church.
2. Luther taught that faith in the promises of Christ was the only thing necessary.
3. The title "Defender of the Faith" was given to Henry VIII for his writings against Lutheranism.
4. Henry VIII broke away from the Church and established a new Church. He forced his subjects to take an oath denying the authority of the Pope and making the king the supreme head of the Church in England.
5. St. John Fisher, the Bishop of Rochester, refused to take the oath, and he was beheaded with others who were brave

enough to oppose the King.

6. Henry VIII closed monasteries and convents and robbed them of their land and Church revenues because he was in need of money.

7. Mary Tudor solemnly declared the Pope the Supreme head of the Church, and she did as much as she could to restore stolen Church property.

8. Elizabeth enforced the law of Henry VIII and punished those who refused to take the oath denying the authority of the Pope. She declared it an act of treason for anyone to say or hear Mass or in any way practice the Catholic religion.

9. Because of the grave results of the Protestant Revolt, it was necessary to hold a General Council.

10. It was not the purpose of the council to teach anything new. It clearly explained the doctrines of the Church denied by Protestants.

11. St. Charles Borromeo is called the "Saint of the Council of Trent" because of his untiring zeal to correct the abuses which had been brought about by Protestantism. He took the main points that were settled in the Council and worked them into a catechism.

12. The popes of this time worked hard to carry out the reform so necessary to guard the faithful against the heresies that were so prevalent. They appointed worthy cardinals, approved new religious orders, carried out the reforms of the Council of Trent, and issued an Index of Forbidden Books.

13. Some religious orders established at this time: the Ursulines, Order of the Visitation, Sisters of Charity, the Society of Jesus, and many others.

14. St. Philip Neri was called the "Apostle of Rome."

Chapter 36

Part 1

A.
1. F
2. E
3. G
4. A
5. C
6. B
7. D

B.
1. C
2. A
3. D
4. B
5. E

Part 2

1. Revealed
2. God
3. Divine Revelation
4. Christ foretold it
5. Rousseau
6. Spreading
7. Spiritual soul
8. Schools
9. Divine Providence

Part 3

1. Rationalist taught:
   a) Nothing is true unless it can be proved by reasoning.
   b) God did not reveal any truths to man.
   c) There is no original sin.

d) man does not need the grace of God.

e) There is no God.

2. Indifferentism teaches that one religion is as good as any other.

3. Catholics are not allowed to join the Freemasons because:

a) Secretly it works against the Catholic Church.

b) It advocates complete "separation of the Church and State."

c) It attempts to control the government of a country.

4. Evils resulting from separation of State and Church:

a) State is cut off from God's grace.

b) Justice and charity disappear.

c) Men become evil.

5. Saints of this period:

a) Margaret Mary Alacoque - spread the devotion to the sacred Heart.

b) St. Vincent de Paul - devoted life to help the poorest and lowest people: founded the Lazarists.

c) John Baptist de La Salle - taught uncared-for boys from the streets; organized a religious community; founded first school for the training of teachers; organized the elementary schools into a graded system; formed excellent rules for the guidance and education of children; introduced manual training into schools.

6. Rousseau thought that no restrictions of any kind should be placed on liberty; the right to govern comes from citizens, not God.

7. Qualities of American missionaries:

a) Great courage.

b) Heroic endurance.

c) Faithfulness to work.

d) Love of God and man.

8. Hardships of Father Jogues:

a) Suffered blame for misfortune of the Native Americans.

b) Live always in danger.

c) Was cruelly tortured.

d) Was held captive and slave of the Indians.

e) His fingers were mangled and his thumb cut off.

9. The first parish was founded in St. Augustine, Florida, and the first diocese was that of Baltimore, established in 1789. Its first bishop was John Carroll.

10. Faith of American Catholics tried:

a) Suffered great disadvantages.

b) Persecuted openly at times.

c) Deprived of privileges granted to others.

11. Results of Secularism in the United States:

a) The Constitution misinterpreted at times.

b) religion dropped out of public schools.

12. Catholic should not become discouraged because:

a) Christ foretold that misfortunes would befall them.

b) Christ promised that the Church would be victorious in the end.

13. We can help fight the enemies by being good practical Catholics and so give a good example in our contact with others.

Chapter 37

Part 1

A

1. D

2. A

3. G

4. E

5. F

6. B

7. C

B
1. F
2. B
3. G
4. E
5. C
6. A
7. D

C
1. B
2. E
3. D
4. C
5. A

Part 2

1. Catholic Action
2. Modernism
3. Secularism
4. Encyclical
5. Dogma
6. Nuncio
7. Lateran

Part 3

1. Dogma
2. Encyclical
3. Encyclical
4. Dogma
5. Dogma
6. Encyclical
7. Encyclical

Part 4

1. States wished to control the Church because they:
   a) Denied that authority came from God.
   b) Claimed all authority belonged to the people.
   c) Became greedy for material riches and political power.

2. Pope Pius IX considered himself a prisoner because:
   a) Italy seized the Church property.
   b) Pope did not wish to be subject to the State.

3. Accomplishments of Pope Pius IX:
   a) Proclaimed two dogmas.
   b) Encouraged greater unity between the individual churches and Rome.
   c) Encouraged art, literature, science.
   d) Gave the United States her first Cardinal.

4. Saints and Catholic leaders of the nineteenth century:
   a) Father John Vianney - converted many people in France.
   b) Daniel O'Connell - had certain unfair laws against Catholics in Ireland repealed.
   c) Frederick Ozanam - organized the Society of St. Vincent de Paul.
   d) Dr. Wiseman - influenced non-Catholics.
   e) Cardinal Manning and Cardinal Newman - spread Catholic truths in England.
   f) John Bosco - helped neglected boys to become good Catholics.
   g) Mother Cabrini - missionary work.

5. Interests of Pope Leo XIII:
   a) Workingman - wrote encyclical to help the workingman.
   b) Education - opened Archives of Vatican to students.
   c) Missions - promoted missionary societies, encouraged missionary work.

6. Modernism claims:
   a) The Church should be subject to State.

    b) The Church should change the teachings of Christ and the regulations of the Church to please the modern minds.

7.   Manner in which Pope Pius X fought Modernism:

    a) Encouraged frequent reception of Holy Communion.

    b) Allowed children to receive Communion as soon as they reached the age of reason.

8.   Peace could not last because:

    a) God, charity, and justice were left out of the treaty.

    b) Christ said, "Without me you can do nothing."

9.   Importance encyclicals of Pope Pius XI:

    a) Catholic Action.

    b) Christian Marriage.

    c) Christian Education of Youth.

    d) On Social Order and Labor.

10. Importance of the Lateran Treaty:

    a) Made the Pope free of any political power.

    b) Vatican City became an independent state.

11. Dictators are wrong because they:

    a) Deny God.

    b) Deprive man of all his God-given rights.

    c) Recognize no higher authority than the State.

12. Communism spread in Latin America because of existing conditions:

    a) People poor and unable to read.

    b) distances are great.

    c) Transportation difficulties.

    d) Shortage of priests and Sisters.

    e) People unable to attend church or receive sacraments.

    f) People do not know their religion well.

13. God allows enemies to win victories over the Church when people become selfish, worldly, and weak in their faith.

14. Parochial schools established in the United States:

    a) catholic religion not allowed to be taught in public schools.

b) Third general Council decided that parochial schools taught by Sisters would take care of religious instructions.

15. Changes in Liturgy by Pope Pius XII:
    a) Eased Communion fast.
    b) Revised rites of Holy Week.
    c) Allowed evening Masses.

16. Pope John XXIII has often been called "a traveler of God" because he has served for many years as a Vatican diplomat in many different countries.

17. *Humanae Vitae* predicted:
    a) that contraceptives would issue in new evils
    b) Women would be treated as objects
    c) the relationship between men and women would be jeopardized
    d) marriage would be made a mockery
    e) abortion would increase
    f) human life would be disrespected

18. Pope Benedict XVI resigned

19. The Church can never fail:
    a) We have Christ's word for it.
    b) The Holy Spirit sustains and guides the Church.

20. To ensure the welfare of the Church in the United States and in our world we must resolve ever to help the Church and never to harm her in her work for Christ and the salvation of the human race.

Image Credits

Cover: Resurrection (oil on panel), Garbo, Raffaellino del (c.1466-1524) / Italian, Photo © Nicolò Orsi Battaglini / Bridgeman Images

p xii-1 Israelites passing through the Wilderness, West, William (1801-61) / English, © Bristol Museums, Galleries & Archives / Purchased, with the assistance of the Victoria & Albert Museum Purchase Grant Fund, 1974. / Bridgeman Images

p 2–3, 12–13, 34–35, 42–43, 50–51, 68–69, 82–83, 96–97, 116–117, 124–125, 144–145, 176–177, 192–193, 218–219, 236–237, 258–259, 264–265, 274–275, 286–287, 294–295, 306–307, 312–313, 320–321, 338–339, 350–351, 364–365, 382–383, 396–397, 412–413, 422–423, 432–433, 442–443, 456–457, 474–475, 488–489, 502–503, 516–517, 538–539: Christ and Saint John the Baptist in Hagia Sophia (mosaic), Tarker / Bridgeman Images

p 3 The Great Isaiah Scroll, columns 28-30, Qumram Cave I, c.100 BC (parchment), © Israel Museum, Jerusalem / Shrine of the Book / Bridgeman Images

p 4 The Resurrection, right hand predella panel from the Altarpiece of St. Zeno of Verona, 1456-60 (oil on panel), Mantegna, Andrea (1431-1506) / Italian, Bridgeman Images

p 6 God creating the sun, the moon and the stars in the Firmament, c.1650 (oil on copper), Brueghel, Jan the Younger (1601-78) / Flemish, Photo © Christie's Images / Bridgeman Images

p 7 Moses by Ignazio Jacometti on the base of the Colonna dell'Immacolata, Rome Italy, by Only Fabrizio/Shutterstock

p 8–9 Creation of the World and Expulsion from Paradise, by Giovanni di Paolo, 1445, Renaissance painting, by Everett Collection/Shutterstock

p 10 Creation of the World and Expulsion from Paradise, by Giovanni di Paolo, 1445, Renaissance painting, by Everett Collection/Shutterstock

p 13 Chaos (The Creation), 1841 (oil on canvas), Aivazovsky, Ivan Konstantinovich (1817-1900) / Russian, Bridgeman Images

p 14–15 The Creation of Heaven, Earth and Water (oil on copper), Herp, Willem van the Elder (1614-77) / Flemish, Johnny Van Haeften Ltd., London / Bridgeman Images

p 17 The Creation of the Birds and Fishes (oil on copper), Oosten, Isaak van (1613-61) / Dutch, Johnny Van Haeften Ltd., London / Bridgeman Images

p 18–19 Beautiful mountain isolated on white background, 3d landscape illustration by Dotted Yeti/Shutterstock

p 20 Inside a Catholic Church by photomatz/Shutterstock

p 21 Reaching hands from The Creation of Adam of Michelangelo illustration reproduction by Freeda Michaux/Shutterstock

p 22 The Creation of Adam, modelled by J Physick (engraving), English School, (19th century) / English, Look and Learn / Illustrated Papers Collection / Bridgeman Images

p 24 The Creation (coloured engraving), German School, (19th century) / German, © Look and Learn / Bridgeman Images

p 25 A vintage angel illustration (circa 1890) by Victorian Traditions/Shutterstock

p 27 Madonna and Child, detail from the Sant'Emidio polyptych, 1473 (tempera on panel), Crivelli, Carlo (c.1430/35-1495) / Italian, Photo © Nicolò Orsi Battaglini / Bridgeman Images

p 29 The murder of Abel. 1) Le Sainte Bible: Traduction nouvelle selon la Vulgate par Mm. J.-J. Bourasse et P. Janvier. Tours: Alfred Mame et Fils. 2) 1866 3) France 4) Gustave Doré, by ruskpp/Shutterstock

p 30 Cain and Abel (colour litho), Illustration from Katholische Familienbibel (Catholic Family Bible) (Verlag Koesel-Pustet, Munich, 1940), © Look and Learn / Bridgeman Images

p 33 The Creation of the World (oil on canvas), Le Sueur, Eustache (1617-55) / French, Bridgeman Images

p 36 Noah's Ark, illustration from 'Brevis Narratio...', published by Theodore de Bry, 1591 (coloured engraving), Bry, Th. (1528-98), after Le Moyne, J.(de Morgues) (1533-88) / Flemish, Bridgeman Images

p 36–37 Noah's ark, 3D illustration by Fer Gregory/Shutterstock

p 39 The Tower of Babel, Dudley, Robert Ambrose (1867-1951) / British, © Look and Learn / Bridgeman Images

p 43 Abraham, Sara and an Angel, c.1520 (oil on panel), Provost, Jan II (1465-1529) / Dutch, Bridgeman Images

p 44 Abraham and Lot dividing the land (colour litho), English School, (19th century) / English, © Look and Learn / Bridgeman Images

p 45 Melchisedech offers Bread at the Altar, detail of the lunette on the South wall depicting the offerings of Abel and Melchisedech (mosaic), Byzantine School, (6th century), Bridgeman Images

p 51 The Dismissal of Hagar, 1660s (oil on canvas), Fabritius, Barent (1624-73) / Dutch, © Ferens Art Gallery / Bridgeman Images

p 53 Abraham tooking Isaac to Mount Moriah, illustration from a catechism 'L'Histoire Sainte', published by Charles Delagrave, Paris (colour litho), French School, (19th century) / French, Bridgeman Images

p 54 Abraham about to sacrifice Isaac, German School, (19th century) / German, © Look and Learn / Bridgeman Images

p 57 Esau selling his birthright, English School, (19th century) / English, © Look and Learn / Bridgeman Images

p 58 Voice of Jacob, Hands of Esau, Flinck, Govaert (1615-60) (after) / Dutch, © Look and Learn / Bridgeman Images

p 60 Jacob's dream, Illustration for The Beautiful Story by J W Buel (Historical Publishing, 1890), © Look and Learn / Bridgeman Images

p 62 Jacob meeting his brother Esau, Original artwork for illustration in The Bible Story or Look and Learn (issue yet to be identified). Lent for scanning by The Gallery of Illustration, © Look and Learn / Bridgeman Images

p 64 Jacob blessing his Twelve Sons (engraving), Illustration for Cassell's Illustrated Family Bible Superior Edition (Cassell, Petter and Galpin, c 1880). Old Testament, © Look and Learn / Bridgeman Images

p 69 Joseph sold by his brethren, Illustration from The Children's Pictorial Bible (Ward Lock, c 1860), © Look and Learn / Bridgeman Images p 75 Joseph recognised by his brothers in Egypt (colour litho), French School, (19th century) / French, © Look and Learn / Bridgeman Images

p 84 Moses in the bullrushes, Illustration from unidentified nineteenth century book on boys in the Bible, © Look and Learn / Bridgeman Images

p 85 'Fear grew in Moses' heart', illustration from 'Through the Bible', Venture Publishing, 1928 (colour litho), Brock, Charles Edmund (1870-1938) / English, Bridgeman Images

p 86 Egypt: Moses and the Burning Bush. A Byzantine mosaic at St Catherine's Monastery, Sinai, Pictures from History / Bridgeman Images

p 87 The Egyptian locust, Anacridium aegyptium, by Danut Vieru/Shutterstock

p 87 Fly by Nataliia K/Shutterstock

p 88 Agnus Dei, 1850, Universal History Archive/UIG / Bridgeman Images

p 90–91 Parting of the Red Sea, English School, (20th century) / English, Original artwork for The Bible Story (issue as yet to be identified), © Look and Learn / Bridgeman Images

p 92 Golden monstrance by MARI TERE/Shutterstock

p 97 Moses and the Ten Commandments (1963), Uptton, Clive (1911-2006) / English, © Look and Learn / Bridgeman Images

p 99 Moses receiving the Ten Commandments from God on Mount Sinai (colour litho), Illustration from Katholische Familienbibel (Catholic Family Bible) (Verlag Koesel-Pustet, Munich, 1940), © Look and Learn / Bridgeman Images

p 100 Moses descending from Mount Sinai, Illustration for Brown's Self-Interpreting Family Bible (John G Murdoch, c 1880). Kronheim engraving, © Look and Learn / Bridgeman Images

p 101 Television and video game addiction by Cagkan Sayin/Shutterstock

p 106 Moses naming Joshua as his Successor (chromolitho), Illustration for Altar of the Household (London Printing and Publishing Company, c 1880), © Look and Learn / Bridgeman Images

p 107 Land of the Semites, Illustration from With the World's People by John Clark Ridpath (Clark E Ridpath, 1912), © Look and Learn / Bridgeman Images

p 109 The Brazen Serpent, right hand section (oil on canvas), Vouet, Simon (1590-1649) / French, Bridgeman Images

p 110–111 Balaam and His Ass, Breenbergh, Bartholomeus (1599-1657) / Dutch, Bridgeman Images

p 117 The Seven Trumpets of Jericho (w/c on paper), Tissot, James Jacques Joseph (1836-1902) / French, Bridgeman Images

p 120 Joshua Commanding the Sun to Stand Still Upon Gibeon, c.1840 (oil on canvas)

p 126 Gideon and the Fleece, c.1490 (oil on panel), French School, (15th century) / French, Bridgeman Images

p 132 Verdun Altar: the birth of Samson, 12th century (enamel on gilded copper), Nicholas of Verdun (fl.1181-1205) / Netherlandish, Luisa Ricciarini / Bridgeman Images

p 241 Jonah and the Whale, c.1305 (fresco), Giotto (Giotto di Bondone) (c.1266-1337) / Italian, Bridgeman Images

p 244 Raphael and Tobias, 1507-8 (oil on panel), Titian, Tiziano Vecelli (c.1488-1576) (follower) / Italian, Bridgeman Images

p 247 Esther crowned by King Ahasuerus, Lawson, John (19th century) / English, © Look and Learn / Bridgeman Images

p 251 Judith with the head of Holofernes (chromolitho), Spanish School, (19th century) / Spanish, © Look and Learn / Bridgeman Images

p 255 The Transfiguration, 1594-95 (oil on canvas), Carracci, Ludovico (1555-1619) / Italian, Bridgeman Images

p 256–257 Adoration of the Magi detail, 1423 (tempera on panel), Fabriano, Gentile da (c.1370-1427) / Italian, Photo © Raffaello Bencini / Bridgeman Images

p 260 St. John the Baptist, Boltraffio, Giovanni Antonio (1467-1516) (attr. to) / Italian, National Trust Photographic Library/John Hammond / Bridgeman Images

p 261 The Birth of St John the Baptist (Birth of St John the Baptist) Painting by Sebastiano Conca (1680-1764) 18th century Museo dell'Abbazia di Monte-cassino Italy, Luisa Ricciarini / Bridgeman Images

p 266–267 Italy Tuscany Florence, Uffizi Gallery: The Annunciation, Painting by Leonardo da Vinci (1452-1519), Oil on wood, photo by Jean Bernard, Bridgeman Images

p 268 The Visitation, 1491 (tempera on panel), Ghirlandaio, Domenico (Domenico Bigordi) (1449-94) / Italian, Bridgeman Images

p 273 The Annunciation, 1426 (tempera and gold on panel), Angelico, Fra (Guido di Pietro/Giovanni da Fiesole) (c.1387-1455) / Italian, Bridgeman Images

p 275 The Christmas Story: The Shepherds' Tale (gouache on paper), Watt, John Millar (1895-1975) / British, © Look and Learn / Bridgeman Images

p 276 The Madonna and Child in Glory with Cherubs (oil on canvas), Sassoferrato, Il (1609-85) (Giovanni Salvi) (follower of) / Italian, Photo © Christie's Images / Bridgeman Images

p 278 Gold, frankincense, and myrrh and an old wooden box by marilyn barbone/Shutterstock

p 278 Adoration of the Magi, 1857 (oil on card), Flandrin, Hippolyte (1809-64) / French, Bridgeman Images

p 281 Statue of Saint Joseph by Andrew F. Kazmierski/Shutterstock

p 285 The Madonna and Child, 1855 (oil on canvas), Schnorr von Carolsfeld, Julius (1794-1872) / German, Photo © Christie's Images / Bridgeman Images

p 289 John the Baptist, Copping, Harold (1863-1932) / English, © Look and Learn / Bridgeman Images

p 290 St John the Baptist, St John Chrysostom, St John the Evangelist and St Theodore (oil on canvas), Piombo, Sebastiano del (S. Luciani) (c.1485-1547) (after) / Italian, © Museum of the Order of St. John / Bridgeman Images p 294 The Baptism of Christ (gouache on paper), © Look and Learn / Bridgeman Images

p 296 The Temptation of Christ, 1854 (oil on canvas), Scheffer, Ary (1795-1858) / Dutch, National Gallery of Victoria, Melbourne / Bridgeman Images

p 299 Christ Calling the Apostles James and John, 1869 (oil on canvas), Armitage, Edward (1817-96) / English, © Sheffield Galleries and Museums Trust / Photo © Museums Sheffield / Bridgeman Images

p 300, 301 The Marriage at Cana, 1819 (oil on canvas), Schnorr von Carolsfeld, Julius (1794-1872) / German, Bridgeman Images

p 305 Rosary with brown beads and silver cross by ArtOfPhotos/Shutterstock

p 308–309 Christ with Fishermen (gouache on paper), © Look and Learn / Bridgeman Images

p 314 Sermon on the Mount, Bloch, Carl, Restored Traditions

p 321 The Sower of the Seed (gouache on paper), Uptton, Clive (1911-2006) / English, © Look and Learn / Bridgeman Images

p 325 The Good Samaritan (gouache on paper), © Look and Learn / Bridgeman Images

p 328–329 The Return of the Prodigal son (gouache on paper), © Look and Learn / Bridgeman Images

p 333 Hiding the talent (chromolitho), Scene from the Parable of the Talents (Matthew XXV 14-30). Illustration for Bible Stories and Pictures (Religious Tract Society, c 1890), © Look and Learn / Bridgeman Images

p 342 The Widow of Nain, illustration from 'Women of the Bible', published by The Religious Tract Society, 1927 (colour litho), Copping, Harold (1863-1932) / English, Bridgeman Images

p 343 Christ on the Sea of Galilee (gouache on paper), Hayes, Jack (20th Century) / English, © Look and Learn / Bridgeman Images

p 344 The Healing of the Deaf and Dumb Man (engraving), Illustration for The Child's Life of Christ with Original Illustrations (Cassell, 1882), © Look and Learn / Bridgeman Images

p 347 The Ten Lepers, Uptton, Clive (1911-2006) / English, © Look and Learn / Bridgeman Images

p 351 The Miracle of the Five Loaves and Two Fishes, by Clerck, Hendrick, de (ca. 1560-1630). Oil on canvas, ca 1590, Photo © Fine Art Images / Bridgeman Images

p 353 Lord, save me, English School, (20th century) / English, © Look and Learn / Bridgeman Images

p 356 Jesus Returning the Keys to St. Peter, 1820 (oil on canvas), Ingres, Jean Auguste Dominique (1780-1867) / French, Bridgeman Images

p 358 The Transfiguration (oil on panel), Raphael (Raffaello Sanzio of Urbino) (1483-1520) / Italian, Photo © Stefano Baldini / Bridgeman Images

p 360 'Lazarus, come forth', Copping, Harold (1863-1932) / English, © Look and Learn / Bridgeman Images

p 363 Coronation of the Virgin, c.1641-42 (oil on canvas), Velazquez, Diego Rodriguez de Silva y (1599-1660) / Spanish, Bridgeman Images p 365 The Magdalen washing Christ's Feet in the House of Simon, (oil on canvas), Giordano, Luca (1634-1705) / Italian, Photo © Christie's Images / Bridgeman Images

p 371 The Last Supper (oil on panel), Macip, Vicente Juan (Juan de Juanes) (c.1510-79) / Spanish, Bridgeman Images

p 372 The Eucharist (oil on panel), Kessel, Jan van, the Elder (1626-79) / Flemish, Photo © Rafael Valls Gallery, London, UK / Bridgeman Images

p 383 Christ in the Garden of Gethsemane, from a series of Scenes of the New Testament (fresco), Barna da Siena (fl.1350-55) / Italian, Bridgeman Images

p 384 Christ carrying the Cross (chromolitho), European School, (19th century) / European, Look and Learn / Valerie Jackson Harris Collection / Bridgeman Images

p 385 Christ in the Garden of Gethsemane, Jordaens, Hans III (1595-1643/44) / Flemish, Photo © Bonhams, London, UK / Bridgeman Images

p 388 Jesus is condemned to death, Stations of the Cross, 1747 (oil on canvas), Tiepolo, Giandomenico (Giovanni Domenico) (1727-1804) / Italian, Cameraphoto Arte Venezia / Bridgeman Images

p 390 Jesus carrying his cross (carrying the cross or path of the cross), c.1651 (oil on canvas), Le Sueur, Eustache (1617-55) / French, Le Sueur, Eustache (1617-55) / French, Luisa Ricciarini / Bridgeman Images

p 392 Christ on the cross, the Three Marys on mourning by John and the Donor or Patron, 1514, by Pier Francesco Sacchi, called Il Pavese (1485-1528), Tarker / Bridgeman Images

p 397 Mary Magdalene at the Jesus' tomb, Morris, Philip Richard (1838-1902) / English, Lebrecht Authors / Bridgeman Images

p 399 The Resurrection, 15th century (tempera on panel), Master of the Osservanza, (fl.c.1436) / Italian, Founders Society Purchase / Gift of Mr & Mrs Henry Ford II / Bridgeman Images

p 400 The Supper at Emmaus, c.1535 (oil on canvas), Titian (Tiziano Vecellio) (c.1488-1576) / Italian, Bridgeman Images

p 401 Jesus appearing to two disciples on the road to Emmaus, Hole, William Brassey (1846-1917) / English, © Look and Learn / Bridgeman Images

p 403 Peter's Denial (oil on canvas), Bloch, Carl (1834-90) / Danish, Bridgeman Images

p 408–409 Giving of the Keys to St. Peter, from the Sistine Chapel, 1481 (fresco), Perugino, Pietro (c.1445-1523) / Italian, Bridgeman Images

410–411 St. Peter's Square (Vatican City) by Marti Bug Catcher/Shutterstock

413 The death of Saint Stephen: Saint Stephen stoned by the Jews is considered the first Christian martyr. Anonymous engraving from the middle of the 19th century, Stefano Bianchetti / Bridgeman Images

p 415 Disputation with Simon Magus and Crucifixion of Peter, 1482-1491 (fresco), Lippi, Filippino (c.1457-1504) / Italian, © Mondadori Portfolio / Bridgeman Images

p 416 The Christian Martyr's Last Prayer, 1863-83 (oil on canvas), Gerome, Jean Leon (1824-1904) / French, Bridgeman Images

p 490 Portrait of Martin Luther (1483-1546) 1529 (oil on panel), Cranach, Lucas, the Elder (1472-1553) / German, Photo © Raffaello Bencini / Bridgeman Images

p 493 Portrait of Henry VIII aged 49, 1540 (oil on panel), Holbein the Younger, Hans (1497/8-1543) / German, Bridgeman Images

p 496 The First Chapter of the 25th Council of Trent, Venetian School, c.1630, Italian School, (17th century) / Italian, Photo © Bonhams, London, UK / Bridgeman Images

p 498 St. Ignatius of Loyola (1491-1556) Founder of the Jesuits (oil on canvas), Rubens, Peter Paul (1577-1640) / Flemish, Bridgeman Images

p 503 St Vincent de Paul (coloured engraving), Illustration for Le Plutarque Francais by Ed Mennechet (Crapelet, 1837-1841). Digitally cleaned image, © Look and Learn / Bridgeman Images

p 506 Masonic Freemasonry Emblem by In-Finity/Shutterstock

p 508 The Taking of the Bastille, 14 July 1789 (oil on canvas), French School, (18th century) / French, Bridgeman Images

p 510 St Patrick's Cathedral : Front Gate sculpture : St Isaac Jogues, New York's first Catholic priest, New York, United States, Godong / Bridgeman Images

p 518 Statue of Our Lady of Immaculate Conception. Lourdes, France, by J. Borruel/Shutterstock

p 520 Portrait of Saint John Bosco or Don Bosco (Giovanni Melchior Bosco) (1815-1888) 19th century (engraving) in "Les Missions Catholiques au XIX-eme Siecle"" by Louis-Eugene (Louis Eugene) Louvet, Stefano Bianchetti / Bridgeman Images

p 523 Portrait of Pope Pius X (b/w photo), Petit (19th-20th century) / French, Bridgeman Images

p 528 Basilica of the National Shrine of the Immaculate Conception in Washington, DC by Orhan Cam/Shutterstock

p 529 One of the first pictures of Pope Pius XII after his coronation, Rome, 1939 (b/w photo), Bridgeman Images

p 531 Pope John XXIII (Giovanni 23, Angelo Giuseppe Roncalli, 1881-1963), Farabola / Bridgeman Images

p 532 Pope John Paul II in 1978, Farabola / Bridgeman Images

p 544 The Virgin in Prayer, 1640-50 (oil on canvas), Sassoferrato, Il (Giovanni Battista Salvi) (1609-85) / Italian, Bridgeman Images

p 551 The Immaculate Conception with the Fifteen Mysteries of the Rosary (oil on canvas), Cabrera, Miguel (1695-1768) (circle of) / Mexican, Photo © Christie's Images / Bridgeman Images

p 552 Interior of a Scriptorium, School of Segovia (oil on panel), Spanish School, (16th century) / Spanish, Bridgeman Images